## About the editors

*Saskia E. Wieringa* is honorary professor at the University of Amsterdam, holding the chair in Gender and Women's Same-Sex Relations Crossculturally. She has a long experience of activism in both the women's and Third World solidarity movements. Since the late 1970s she has done research on women's movements and same-sex relations in many parts of the world, particularly in Indonesia. Her latest books include: *Female Desires: Same-Sex Relations and Transgender Practices across Cultures*; *Sexual Politics in Indonesia*; *Lubang Buaya*, a novel; *Tommy Boys, Lesbian Men and Ancestral Wives: Women's Same-Sex Experiences in Southern Africa*; *Engendering Human Security* (co-edited with Thanh-Dam Truong and Amrita Chhachhi); *Women's Sexualities and Masculinities in a Globalizing Asia* (co-edited with Evelyn Blackwood and Abha Bhaiya); *Traveling Heritages and the Future of Asian Feminisms* (with Nursyahbani Katjasungkana). She has received various awards for her scholarly work, most recently the 2011 award for Best Paper from the *Journal of Contemporary Asia*.

*Horacio F. Sívori*, PhD, is an Argentinean anthropologist, a post-doctoral fellow at the Institute for Social Medicine, State University of Rio de Janeiro, and the regional coordinator for the Latin American Center on Sexuality and Human Rights. He trained in Argentina, the USA, and Brazil and taught in Argentina, Brazil, Chile, and Peru. He is the author of *Locas, chogos y gays*, as well as journal articles, book chapters, and collective volumes on gay sociability, sexual rights, and AIDS activism. He is co-editor of *Sexualities*, a working paper series by CLAGS/CUNY's International Resource Network, and has acted as co-chair for the Sexuality Studies Section of the Latin American Studies Association. His current research looks at LGBT rights activism in Argentina and Brazil.

# The sexual history of the global South

sexual politics in Africa, Asia, and Latin America

EDITED BY SASKIA WIERINGA AND HORACIO SÍVORI

Zed Books
LONDON | NEW YORK

*The sexual history of the global South: sexual politics in Africa, Asia, and Latin America* was first published in 2013 by Zed Books Ltd, 7 Cynthia Street, London N1 9JF, UK and Room 400, 175 Fifth Avenue, New York, NY 10010, USA

www.zedbooks.co.uk

A catalogue record for this book is available from the British Library
Library of Congress Cataloging in Publication Data available

ISBN 978 1 78032 403 6 hb
ISBN 978 1 78032 402 9 pb

# Contents

# Foreword

This book is the outcome of a long-term program focused on a historically grounded and comparative analysis of sexualities in the South. It was carried out by the Sephis program, the South-South Exchange Programme for Reserach on the History of Development, a research initiative aimed at stimulating the critical study of development in the global South within a comparative framework.

The Sephis program was established in 1994 and financed by the Dutch Ministry of Foreign Affairs. Its main objective is to reinsert a historically grounded perspective into the thinking about the development of the 'global South' (to employ the term developed by recent critiques of colonial geopolitics to depict countries struggling in different ways with problems of colonialism and underdevelopment). It aims at fostering dialog and collaboration between researchers with diverse visions of development and history, to encourage comparative research, and to strengthen research capacity in the South.

In 2007, Sephis received a grant from the Ford Foundation to support a research program on the History of the Sexualities in the South that could take advantage of the experiences of the Sephis program in South-South academic exchange. In addition, it allowed for the training of a new generation of researchers in comparative and historically grounded approaches to practices and ideologies surrounding sexuality in different parts of the global South. The objective of this program was to allow young scholars in the humanities and social sciences to engage in new field research and link it with national and international debates and advocacy for sexual rights.

The ultimate aim was to gain a deeper historical understanding of the complex interplay between cultural genealogies and the politics of gender relations and sexual behavior. Related themes of interest to the program were the legal regulation of and public policies on sexuality, sex- and gender-based claims of identities, sexual expression, and sexual knowledge. These claims are located within wider processes of state formation and global transformations and are often connected to a strengthening of patriarchal relations, heteronormativity, and conservative control in many parts of the world. The program also aimed to stimulate linkages between social science research and advocacy on sexual rights, working from a human and sexual rights perspective.

The program was designed to train a relatively small group of sexuality researchers from different countries of the global South, stimulating them to compare their different experiences and conceptual frameworks. Most of them were pursuing graduate studies and conducted their field research in specific countries within the global South. A related goal was to build an international community of researchers around these issues with the objective of fostering the exchange of information on research and advocacy and of encouraging high-quality research through enhancing the research capacities of all involved.

These cross-cultural and trans-disciplinary conversations took place in the individual projects of the participants and in the virtual contact that is part and parcel of today's academic work. They were especially intensive during a number of academic encounters organized in different parts of the world. An expert meeting was organized at the University of Cape Town, South Africa, in February 2008. The first training workshop for the selected grantees took place in September 2008 at the Latin American Center on Sexuality and Human Rights (CLAM) in Rio de Janeiro, Brazil. The second workshop, for a second batch of grantees, was organized at the Institute of Women's Studies of the University of Dhaka, in Bangladesh, in March 2009. A peer review workshop took place in Cairo and was organized in collaboration with the Institute for Gender and Women's Studies of the American University in Cairo in May 2009. The program ended with an international policy dialog at the Gajah Mada University in Yogyakarta, Indonesia, co-organized with the Kartini Asia Network for Women's/Gender Studies in August 2010.

Many people participated in this project at one stage or another. First of all we wish to thank the Ford Foundation, and especially Barbara Klugman, for its unwavering support for this adventurous project. We hope this book fulfills their expectations, albeit perhaps inevitably in a partial and incomplete way. Shamil Jeppie, co-chair of Sephis in the period 2006–11, and Ulbe Bosma, Sephis coordinator from 1994 to 2007, laid the foundations for this program by writing the grant proposal. Saskia Wieringa and Sanjay Srivastava were involved as lecturers and Horacio Sívori as host at the first training workshop in Rio de Janeiro and continued their involvement in the program in different ways. Imtiaz Saikh was coordinator of the program from April 2008 till April 2010, working closely with the Sephis Secretariat in Amsterdam. Jacqueline Rutte, office manager of Sephis, was involved in every aspect of the organization of the grants, the workshops, and the publication. We are very grateful to each one of them for their contribution to making this program successful.

In the different locations where activities were organized we could count on the support and enthusiasm of many people working in or with the institutions mentioned. We cannot acknowledge them all, but they can rest assured that their support has been duly and gratefully noted and recognized by all participants. Without them, the project's success would not have been possible. Last but not least we would like to thank the editors of this volume, Saskia Wieringa and Horacio Sívori, who both, in their own ways, have contributed tremendously to the success of this program. Without their commitment and dedication to training young scholars from the global South in the study of sexuality, the program would never have been the same, and this book would never have seen the light of day.

*Michiel Baud, co-chair, Sephis*
*Shamil Jeppie, co-chair, Sephis*
*Marina de Regt, coordinator, Sephis*

# 1 | Sexual politics in the global South: framing the discourse

SASKIA WIERINGA AND HORACIO SÍVORI

## Introduction

What does a global South perspective mean to historical studies of sexuality and sexual politics? If, as Weeks (1981), Foucault (1978, 1985, 1988), Halperin (2002), and others have argued, sexuality – as a separate domain of human experience and an object of regulation – is a recent Western invention produced by discourses of modernity about identity, subjectivity, bodies, and population control, what space is there to investigate non-Western historical discourses on sexuality and sexual politics? How to investigate not only the genealogies and figurations of the sexual in different sociocultural contexts, but also the constitution of the gaze that sees 'non-Western' sexuality as fundamentally distinct from the modern? How has sexuality historically been articulated in contexts that cannot be designated as either colonial or post-colonial, such as China and the Arab world? How to do justice to the manifold local contexts that feed into the production of global discourses on sexuality? How to document the often overlooked agency and desires of individuals and collectives whose location at the margins of a Eurocentric, (post-)colonial discourse sets them apart as pre-rational or 'traditional'?

Addressing these questions means investigating a diversity of beliefs, practices, and cultural traditions that shape and challenge sexual meanings and classifications in the context of pre-colonial realities and peripheral modernities (see Andaya 2006; Blackwood 2005; Peletz 2009; and Wieringa 2010). It also means examining the role of the sexual – e.g. of reproduction and the family, of sexual morality, of sexual health, of sexual classifications, and sexual selves – in contemporary societies, in development programs (Pigg and Adams 2005), and in processes of nation-building (Ndjio, Biswas, Kumaramkandath, and Sierra Madero, this volume).

Globalization and transnational flows have had tangible effects on sexual relations, identities, and subjectivities. In the wake of an increasingly globalized world order under waning Western dominance,

1

within ideologies of modernity, civilization, and programs for social improvement, discourses on population control, 'safe sex,' and 'sexual rights' (Petchesky 2000) coexist with moral tales of purity and decay. From a Eurocentric perspective, in a manner analogous to the colonial map of the world, sexuality was conceived in the form of center–periphery relations: the 'normal,' the 'modern' at the centre, the 'deviate' and 'traditional' on the periphery (Bleys 1995; Epprecht 2004). But, as Appadurai (1996) rightly asks, does modernity come only from the places that geopolitical conventions have designated as the West? Does modern thinking exclusively arise in colonial or neocolonial metropolitan centers and then spread to global peripheries? Are eroticism, morality, and the social organization of bodies, pleasure, reproduction, well-being, and disease merely the result of exogenous geopolitical arrangements and struggles?

Dislocating sexuality studies from an exclusively metropolitan perspective means not just looking at those issues from different locations, but primarily asking different questions, addressing the asymmetries of power involved in processes of globalization. Historians and anthropologists have documented the extent to which the racist social order of colonial regimes also produced gendered and sexualized relations between colonizers and colonized peoples (Hyam 1991; Stoler 1995). Third World feminists and feminists of color in North America have interrogated the persistence of gender and racial asymmetries in both neocolonial and metropolitan cultural politics, intellectual traditions, and liberation movements (Mohanty et al. 1991; Basu et al. 2001). Scholars in the humanities and the social sciences, mostly based in Europe and North America, have begun addressing sexuality transnationally by establishing links between feminist, lesbian/gay/queer, and post-colonial theories (Ahmed 2005; Manalansan and Cruz-Malavé 2002; Manalansan 2003; see also Loomba 2005). A number of such authors have produced general studies of sexuality and globalization, mainly from a Northern-centred perspective (Altman 2001; Binnie 2004). Accounts based in the South, by scholars from the South, are still rare.

The global circulation of knowledge has, until recently, drawn a deep divide between the West and the rest, and within first- and second-class citizens both at metropolitan centers and at the global periphery. This is evident in the uneven distribution of access to higher education, the academy, and academic publishing. As a consequence, direct exchange of scientific knowledge and literature between Africa, Asia, and Latin America has not been consistent. Scholarly exchange – when it happens – takes place almost exclusively between those regions and North America and western Europe, rarely among Southern nations. In spite of that, each region of the global South has a burgeoning production (most of it in languages other than English), which is often ignored overseas. Voices from the global South have begun to be heard in the North only as the boundaries between North and South begin to dissolve and the influence of the BRIC countries begins to be felt globally.

For sexuality studies to become truly transnational, a careful trajectory of sexual politics all over the globe is required. From these microgeographies a global perspective can be built that is neither reflective of hegemonic Western concerns nor dispersed into unconnected fragments. This book is meant as a contribution to the growing body of transnational sexuality studies by scholars from the global South trained in their own countries, reflecting on theoretical, political, and empirical interests emerging at the crossroads of local, regional, and global circuits of intellectual exchange. They look at sexual morality (Vasudevan, Biswas, Sierra Madero); sexual identities (Kumaramkandath, Teutle Lopéz, Al-Ghafari); state policy (Ndjio, Sadock); media representations of sexuality (Biswas); culture, sexuality, and subjectivity (Masvawure, Cordeiro); sexuality and social movements (Sempol); and the scientific study of sexuality (Huang). The focus of these studies is often on the agency of individuals and collectives: female dance performers in India (Vasudevan); university students in Zimbabwe (Masvawure); prison inmates in Brazil (Cordeiro); homosexual men in urban Mexico (Teutle López) and southern India (Kumaramkandath); and lesbian and gay activists in Argentina (Sempol). A related concern is the sexual politics in processes of nation-building and social transformation. Authors in this volume address that link in colonial (Biswas, Sadock) and post-colonial (Sierra Madero, Vasudevan, Ndjio, Masvawure) situations; in societies emerging from dictatorship (Sempol); in processes of national refoundation (Huang); in large-scale population policies (Cordeiro); in the policing of national morality (Sierra Madero, Teutle López); and the control of the public visibility and the speakability of female bodies and passions (Al-Ghafari).

Indeed, this list of subjects and issues is somewhat arbitrary too. This volume is the result of an academic research training venture, which largely reflects the current conditions of a field. Although neither this introduction nor the book's chapter composition intends to be representative of 'the state of the art' in sexual politics research, some relevant missing topics should be acknowledged. Those include new perspectives on heterosexuality and reproductive (but also nonreproductive) health and rights. And particularly the radical political and theoretical innovations brought by actors who have more recently emerged into the global sexual rights arena, such as transgender communities and sex workers' movements. Each of those issues and subjects – all rising to public visibility particularly at global South locations – challenge received notions of sexual morality, normativity, the materiality of bodies, language, and sexual relations, and would have been relevant here.

Authors in this volume draw on post-colonial theories, deconstructing the colonial past and the way its tentacles stretch into the present, and address globalization issues, focusing on present-day theories of the influence of Western discourses on the rest of the world. Though approaching sexual politics from different theoretical backgrounds, from the humanities and the social sciences respectively, they converge in critical ways, as Krishnaswamy and Hawley (2008) stress, sharing the geopolitical focus that is relevant for this project. A common theme is the creation of normativities as a biopolitical project, situated in time and space (Ahmed 2005).

In this introductory chapter we address two themes that cut across the empirical contributions in the various chapters: the interrogation of the colonialist gaze that has constituted sexuality and sexual subjects as an object of scientific inquiry, state repression, and bio-political intervention in the global South; and the conception of sexualities as an inherently localized phenomenon.

### Whose sexuality, whose gaze?

If the meanings of sexuality and the production of sexual knowledge are part of a social process, it becomes important to interrogate its cultural and historic conditions, and locate the actors involved in that process. Colonialism, modernization, the Cold War, the surge of neoliberal policies over the past few decades, and the rise of new economic centers of power have a large impact on gender orders, bodily practices, and sexual subjectivities. National political and economic elites, religious leaders, international organizations such as WHO, UNAIDS, UN Women (formerly UNIFEM), and the World Bank, as well as Western and non-Western intellectuals and experts, have played a substantial role not only in shaping sexual subjectivities and regulating sexuality, but also in the classification of 'sexual subcultures' globally. The historical trajectory of studies of sexuality in the global South is also the history of a gaze constituted at the confluence of modern medical science and Western colonial expansion, which catalogued

Southern perspectives on gender and the erotic as exotic innocent curiosities, at best, or degenerations at worst.

Until roughly the 1970s, sexuality in former colonies and 'Third World' nations was an object of interest in the writings of missionaries, travelers, colonial administrators, historians, anthropologists, archeologists, and national intellectuals, under a master narrative in which indigenous beliefs, cultural practices, economy, and social organization were situated at the bottom of a hierarchy headed by modern science and forms of government.[1] 'Non-Western' sexualities acquired meaning strictly within the bounds of indigenous cultures, reinforcing their exterior and inferior status vis-à-vis the uncontested authority of modern Western knowledge. As described and codified by colonial administrators, researchers, and social reformers, sexualities were frozen in the culture, social organization, magic, and religious beliefs of peoples of lesser worth.

Since then, researchers and intellectuals in the global South, along with critical scholars in the North, have started questioning hegemonic narratives, challenging the commonplace assumption of their marginal, subordinate, or 'developing' status (Bhabha 1994; Spivak 1999; Loomba 2005). Critical studies of colonial relations, development rationalities, and the role of class, race, and gender hierarchies within those frameworks have merged with theoretical perspectives on the history of sexuality to analyze the shifting meanings of eroticism, gender orders, and bodily practices in the context of unequal power relations (Brah and Coombes 2000; Manalansan and Cruz-Malavé 2002; Stoler 1995). Instead of an exotic 'other,' Southern researchers have become agents of a double engagement, at once involved in local political and also theoretical debates drawing upon, and challenging, assumptions widely established in global social science research.

This is by no means an easy task. On the one hand, inherited theoretical frameworks may predetermine the way they frame research questions, the concepts and the analytical tools available to them, as well as their findings (Cook and Jackson 1999). On the other hand, in the Northern literature that has set trends in the social sciences and the humanities, the meaning and value of contributions by scholars and activists based in the global South are often recognized merely as 'cases,' or 'native knowledge,' rather than theoretical and political perspectives worth engaging in as part of an intellectual debate. Thus, in a global division of knowledge, countries in the South are considered the realm of 'culture,' whereas analysis, interpretation, and debate take place in a separate public sphere, to which Southern

5

intellectuals can claim access only by means of a Northern education, and where they will remain marked as representatives of that foreign culture. Likewise, in studies of changing sexual discourses in Northern countries, the 'West' often goes unmarked, such as in Richardson's important study on sexuality since the 1960s (Richardson 2000). Perhaps as a result of the unchallenged hegemony of the English language in international academic practices, networks of sexuality scholars have rarely altered the self-referencing conventions of the Anglo-Saxon academic world, or treated the work of Southern activists and researchers as relevant to their understanding of global theoretical concerns.[2] Southern intellectuals find themselves back in footnotes, providing the empirical material upon which Northern academics build their theories.

The field of sexuality studies is itself part of a power/knowledge regime where conventions are generated and contested, ethical standpoints elaborated, and esthetic sensibilities developed. An example is the global use of categories such as 'lesbian,' 'gay,' and 'queer.' As the basic vocabulary of global 'lesbian and gay studies,' they carry social connotations from the white middle-class Western milieu where they were first adopted. In a globalizing world, they constitute an ethnocentric toolkit that scholars and activists from the South have to grapple with.[3] As Povinelli and Chauncey have pointed out, the significance of transnational processes in the production of localized sexual subjectivities is reflected in the 'tension between increasingly powerful global discourses and institutions of homosexuality and heterosexuality, and between local sexual ideologies and subjectivities' (1999: 446). If theory is seen as the sediment of empirical knowledge, one might expect that analyses of localized, Southern experiences would influence the development of global theories as well. Yet global discourses of 'gay/lesbian' and 'queer' remain largely based on Western middle-class values.

Some scholars argue that local terms are preferable to concepts developed in the global North (Wieringa et al. 2007). Indeed, some chapters on same-sex practices, identities, and communities in this volume (Kumaramkandath, Sierra Madero, Teutle López, Cordeiro) analyze the use of specific terms that point to particular, localized subjectivities and behaviors. Yet there is no consensus. Vasudevan and Kumaramkandath argue in this volume that the univocal identification of such concepts with a specific cultural ecology might contribute to exoticizing people with same-sex desires in global South locations. Would it not be better to broaden definitions of same-sex practices and desires, so that they point not only to Western sensibilities, but to non-Western ones as well? Al-Ghafari (this volume) insists on the use of 'lesbian' as a transhistorical category, applicable to the investigation of women's same-sex relations in Arab cultures across centuries.

## Sexual science and political control

Sexuality emerged as a field of knowledge from the end of the nineteenth century onwards in Europe, as a response to the Industrial Revolution, in the wake of eugenics and the belief that the destiny of nations could be controlled by means of manipulating the somatic makeup of its population. It was the context of debates over female suffrage, and of increasing state intervention in the domestic sphere (Weeks 1981). The new science of sexology set itself the task of uncovering the 'laws of nature' to make sexual instincts intelligible. Sexual classifications became a medicalized concern, the object of a naturalistic approach imbricated with the construction of racial and ethnic traits. Medical and psychological theories became immensely influential. The works of Havelock Ellis, Magnus Hirschfeld, and other pioneers attracted wide attention and became popular in many corners of the globe (Bland and Doan 1998; Robinson 1976).

For over one hundred years, criminological and then psychiatric theories presided over the study of and state policy on sexual 'weakness,' degeneration,' and 'vices.' Freud's invention of psychoanalysis as a 'science of desire' in late nineteenth-century Vienna was a main contribution to the popularization of the assumption that humans were born with a sexual nature, and that there was a 'normal' course in the development of sexual subjectivity, in which male dominance and women's receptivity – naturalized as biologically determined – were eroticized (Jeffreys 1985; Wieringa 2002). Ideas about sexual orientation at the time were inextricably embedded in biomedical theories of gender inversion, such as those of Krafft-Ebing (see Weeks 1981). Expanding the influence of the clinical method, modern science set itself the task of making the sexual intelligible in an individualizing regime (Gagnon and Parker 1995; Weeks 1981). The study of the diversity of sexual customs and of the domestication of sexual instincts among 'natives' as a marker of civilization was a fundamental focus of attention for early twentieth-century anthropology (Vance 2007 [1991]).

This essentialist perspective on sexuality also spread to countries beyond Western centres, as policy-makers and intellectuals in New World nations, as well as in African and Asian colonies and empires, were well versed in the latest scientific theories and were as concerned about the design of a healthy, productive population as their metropolitan counterparts (Stepan 1991; Wieringa 2009). Major sexological treatises were quickly translated, for instance into Japanese (Frühstück 2003). The medical and psychiatric establishment has held primacy in the definition and control of sexual desires across the globe. After the Second World War, when the center of power shifted from war-torn Europe to the USA, American sexologists took center stage. Spearheaded by the groundbreaking Kinsey reports that detailed the varieties of sexual behavior among the US population, a second wave in the field of sexology tied experimental research to the clinical treatment of 'sexual dysfunctions,' while Chicago-trained social scientists Simon and Gagnon designed a micro-sociological approach to sexual conduct and the production of sexual difference in North American society (Robinson 1976). On the other side of the Atlantic, Foucault (1978) and Weeks (1981) argued for the thesis that the historical invention of sexuality was a disciplinary device, which had transferred the control of human conduct from the sovereign to the individual and produced a new form of subjectivity. In their narrative, this individualized form of knowledge, sensibility, and care of the self originally developed within the medical field and was later disseminated by psychoanalysis and sexology, taking hold in the public imagination throughout the West. The deployment of sexual knowledge established a regime of authorized knowledge whereby the 'normal sexual response' became the bedrock of public health and morality, naturalizing the social norms that regulated the distinction between licit and illicit desires and acts.

Sexual desire, subjectivity, and identity are intrinsically embodied and gendered experiences. Desires are lived and made intelligible within the regime of knowledge that sets the modern individual apart as a social unit, with a distinct psychology and biological makeup that determines his or her capacities as a member of society (Foucault 1978, 1988). Based on her reading of psychoanalytic theory, Braidotti (2011) maintains that those capacities are pre-discursive. Deeply felt – as persons who challenge heterosexual norms know only too well – the lived experiences of gender identification and sexual orientation are a paramount foundation of individual and collective social commitments. In the intellectual project giving life to this book, we assume neither an essentialist understanding of sexuality as purely determined by biological processes, nor a deterministic approach that understands the social construction of sexuality as disembodied discourse, a mere effect of cultural conventions. The empirical study of sexual politics in locations as varied as republican Cuba, post-communist China, and twenty-first-century

Keralam requires an open-minded exploration of a diversity of historical processes, embodied perspectives, and public claims.

## Bio-politics and heteronormativity

In exploring historical articulations of modernity, sexuality, and the production of sexual knowledge in connection with processes of state formation and nation-building, a central concern in this volume is the notion of 'dangerous desires' (Hollibaugh 2000), whose deployment has not only inflicted suffering upon, and led to the unfair treatment of, sexual dissidents (Al-Ghafari, Kumaramkandath, Cordeiro, Sierra Madero, and Sempol, this volume), but has meant the sexual disciplining of modern nations' citizenry (Ndjio, this volume). Bio-power refers to the numerous and diverse techniques for achieving the subjugation of bodies and the control of populations (Lemke 2001) and is a constitutive component in the government of colonial territories and modern nation-states. In early twentieth-century Latin America, bio-politics peaked with the expansion of eugenics (Stepan 1991), which reverberated in the late twentieth-century development rationalities of population control, public health, reproductive policies, disease prevention, and, lately, the expansion of a human rights framework across the global South (Pigg and Adams 2005). While, to a certain degree, the success of feminist and LGBT movements, together with the expansion of the human rights discourse and a global concern with gender equality, has led to the empowerment of women and sexual minorities, the circulation of notions such as reproductive and sexual health implies the continued medicalization of sexuality.

Heteronormativity is a core element of the workings of bio-power, regulating the moral codification of sexuality. The heterosexual family is a central site for the production of sexuality, of its pleasures, but also for the policing of counter-normative desires, deemed dangerous to the stability of the patriarchal order. More than a reference to a normalized sexual practice, the heterosexual order encompasses the normativity of daily life, institutions, laws, and regulations, as well as the moral imperatives that guide people's personal lives, extending to the deepest layers of their subjectivities and identities (Wieringa 2012).

Heteronormativity creates a liminal area for forbidden, abject desires, which provides unity and consistency to the heterosexual norm. On the other hand, several contributors to this volume show how stepping out of the family sphere may mean entering a site of pleasures. Masvawure (this volume) reports on the sexual adventures of women students in Zimbabwe, who, in the liminal period between the constraints of their home towns and the pressures of heterosexual married life, actively create the conditions for their own sexual pleasures on a university campus. This liminality both enables sexual adventuring and signals its limitations. Beyond its boundaries, heteronormative injunctions prevail. This order entails the public vilification of intimately enjoyed practices, as for masculine-identified women and their same-sex romantic partners in Brazilian prisons (Cordeiro); same-sex female couples accused of witchcraft in Cameroon (Ndjio); and same-sex-desiring Arab women (Al-Ghafari). The same goes for feminine men, masculine women, and same-sex-desiring men and women in republican Cuba (Sierra Madero); men seeking sexual adventures with other men in contemporary Keralam, India (Kumaramkandath); and gender-bending and same-sex-desiring men and women in postcolonial Cameroon (Ndjio). Each of those engagements subverts – as Kumaramkandath would have it – the modern enthroning of the domestic sphere as the legitimate site for private pleasures.

The precariousness of heteronormative institutions is illustrated by both its variability and by the force deemed necessary to stabilize its borders (Wieringa 2012). The authors in this book document the 'passionate aesthetics' (ibid.) of heteronormativity in a variety of contexts in the global South. These range from severe forms of criminalization and public violence (Ndjio, on contemporary Africa) and censorship against sexual dissidents (Al-Ghafari, on Arab cultural and religious traditions), to the emotional work of adapting public norms to the intimacy of relations among women in jail (Cordeiro, on Brazil), and to episodic intercourse among men in public places (Kumaramkandath on southern India). Other chapters document the lust-generating vilification of female desire in early modern Bangla pornography (Biswas) and the negotiations women make to sidestep their subordinate sexual status (Masvawure, Vasudevan). The modern sacralizing of particular gendered, classed, and racialized forms of heterosexuality has served the purposes of national independence projects (Sierra Madero) and of redemocratization (Sempol).

Class stratification, refracted by color, women's subordination, and heteronormativity, are converging phenomena. The differences between colonial, post-colonial, and modern national regimes in sexual politics are more those of degree than of substance: the tropes are similar. If in colonial days 'tradition' was constructed as the site of 'moral decay,' nowadays it is invested with nostalgia and reconfigured as a site of heteronormativity, while the West is seen as the site of perverse desires (Morgan and Wieringa 2005). Paradoxically at present, the West prides itself on its freedom, respect for human rights and tolerance, while its own racist, misogynous, homophobic past and present are conveniently ignored in the interests of defending 'Fortress Europe' (Mepschen et al. 2010).

## The selective memory of sexual pasts

Sexual violence was constitutive to the script of the colonial encounter. Gendered forms of physical violence remained a prevalent expression of colonial domination. Once war and conquest gave way to the 'peaceful' government of colonial populations, the regulation of sexuality operated as a prime marker of social difference. The production of cultural alterity was sexualized, as much as it was racialized and intersected by gender hierarchies. Despite deep contrasts between regions in terms of their political histories and cultural and religious traditions, the persistence of inequality and the centrality of sexual regulation in processes of rapid social change remain a constant throughout the global South. All over Latin America, for instance, Catholic canon law regulated marriage among men and women of Spanish descent as a way of securing the inheritance of land and the rights to a 'legitimate' male offspring, while the 'lower castes' of enslaved and servile indigenous and mixed-blooded populations were considered morally inferior, uncivilized, at the mercy of their instincts.

The social regulation of sexual relations by means of a kinship system is the cultural path to the biological and social reproduction of any given society. The Judeo-Christian heritage that shaped Western family ideologies determined the establishment of a heteronormative regime and the condemnation of same-sex relations as sins. The profound political and economic reconfigurations brought by independence movements seldom meant significant changes in class and gender relations. Moreover, narratives of revolutionary takeovers invariably feature a plethora of male heroes whose conventional masculinity is a powerful symbol of a people's will to self-government. Post-colonial transitions have invariably featured a construction of sexual dissidence as a threat to national integrity, as the negative counterpart to the ideal subject of the nation-state (Sierra Madero on Cuba, Ndjio on Cameroon, both this volume). At times of political instability, national identity politics and heteronormativity have emerged time and again to purge sexual dissidents. Sexual abjection becomes the strategic locus of disease, weakness, degeneration, and sterility.

The scapegoating of sexual dissidence in newly independent nation-states is often propped up by what Wieringa has termed the 'postcolonial amnesia' of contemporary nations grappling with their colonial past (Wieringa 2009; Ndjio, this volume). Vasudevan (this volume) traces the origins of this amnesia back to moral panics generated both before and after Indian independence. Given the centrality of sexual symbolism and sexual politics in processes of independence, the development of a national imagination involves a selective memory of indigenous, pre-colonial, and colonial sexual customs, regimes, and institutions. The motivation for moral panics shifted from the imposition of the hegemony of colonial racialized caste relations in imperial times, to the establishment of an often cosmopolitan national ruling class in post-colonial times. In both cases, the patriarchal family represents the promise of civilized society. The other side of the same coin is the subordination of women (Vasudevan, Sadock, Sierra Madero, Masvawure in this volume), the silence over, and institutionalized violence against, men and women who engage in same-sex practices, and the censorship of sexual expressions and desires outside the patriarchal family (Biswas, Kumaramkandath, Sempol, Al-Ghafari, Sierra Madero, Teutle López, Ndjio, Cordeiro, this volume).

Contemporary moral and sexual panics are fomented by two imbricated, seemingly paradoxical processes. On the one hand, there is the post-colonial amnesia over ancient sexual practices, relations, politics, and expressions, particularly those related to same-sex practices and women's sexual autonomy. This has critical consequences, both for individuals whose lives threaten to destabilize the unstable borders of the heteronormative gender regime on which contemporary forms of domination are based; and for those whose pleasures and longings have been 'normalized' for the sake of the nation. On the other hand, we witness a striking continuity between the sexual politics of post-colonial regimes and their colonial predecessors. Religious leaders join in mobilizing emotions to naturalize the fiction of the 'always-already' patriarchal, heterosexual nation. The sexual is manipulated to appear to be the moral bedrock beneath the social contracts present-day leaders impose on their subjects. As Ndjio argues, 'post-colonial nativist conceptions of sexuality replicated the colonial essentialist construction of African sexuality, [creating] a number of myths about the hyper-virility of African men and the lasciviousness of native women' (this volume).

Arguing about the selectiveness of memory is not to project a nostalgic version of a paradise lost. In pointing to the moral construction of the sexual past as a contested, manipulable territory, we stress that the sexual is as much a moral battlefield as it is a political one in which colonial and post-colonial policies are played out along remarkably similar lines. The post-colonial amnesia over earlier forms of women's sexual agency and same-sex relations among both men and women is a major device of social control.

But local histories differ widely. In the North, historians of sexuality have shown that, until fairly recently, same-sex practices did not constitute the kinds of offenses that they came to represent under the Inquisition and British sodomy regimes. This also holds true for some countries in the global South. In India, for instance, GLT movements have been increasingly vilified over the past two decades. Women and men who engage in same-sex practices do not follow the same trajectory: while homoerotically inclined men and MTF transgender persons often encounter public hostility, women in same-sex relations are more often (kept) invisible and locked in marriages where they are violated and imprisoned.[4] In present-day Latin America, while countries like Argentina, Brazil, Colombia, Mexico, and Uruguay are quickly extending positive legal recognition of LGBT rights (Corrales and Pecheny 2010), in the capital cities of those same countries, 70–80 percent of lesbians, gays, bisexuals, and trans persons interviewed for a survey reported having been harassed, attacked, and discriminated against in multiple public and private settings owing to their sexual identity (Sívori 2011). Although in some African countries certain transgender identities and same-sex practices have been tolerated or accepted in defined spaces and moments (Morgan and Wieringa 2005; Murray and Roscoe 1998), in most modern African countries today persons publicly identified as gay, lesbian, or trans face a state of heightened criminalization, police persecution, public (including media) harassment, and imprisonment (Ndjio, this volume).

In complex ways, in many parts of the South, including in the Middle East, while the exclusion of non-heteronormative sexualities seems to be forged as a universal condition for the formation of contemporary nation-states, tolerance for 'discreet' same-sex sociability and cultures is growing. The urban expansion of a 'pink market' and gay tourism, press and audiovisual media has created a niche of acceptance and respect for LGBT communities, valued as a sign of cosmopolitanism; while in other countries authoritarian regimes blame the import of homosexuality by Western colonizers as the origin of all national evils. In post-9/11 international politics, the populist incitement of the xenophobic 'clash of civilizations' discourse among right-wing Western politicians as part of anti-immigration campaigns has progressed side by side with the mobilization of homophobia by authoritarian regimes in some countries of the global South (particularly in Islamic nations).

In such a hate-filled political milieu, the growth of racist ideologies in the West – sometimes in the form of 'homo-nationalism,' in which GLBT rights are portrayed as inherently Western (Puar 2007) – goes hand in glove with a growing aversion toward sexual rights in conservative regimes in the global South.

Sexual politics are about 'the moral, sexual, symbolic, cultural and political codes in which individuals, families and the nation are linked, and with the interplay between sexed and gendered bodies and the socio-political realm' (Wieringa 2003: 71–2). In contemporary China, state-driven economic changes have allowed the opening up of certain discourses on sexuality, as Huang analyses in this volume. The chapter by Ndjio details how, in Cameroon, the brutal link between the accumulation of wealth and power and shifting moral codes has resulted in the production of a hegemonic heterosexual identity and a 'natural' aversion to other sexualities. In the process, women's sexuality becomes ever more controlled, and dissident sexual identities and gender expressions demonized. Sierra Madero (this volume) recalls how, in early twentieth-century republican Cuba, the specter of male homosexuality was raised as signifier of the 'degenerate unmanliness' attributed to local intellectuals and politicians who submitted to US imperialist influence, betraying the manly honor of the heroes in national independence narratives. Accusations of female masculinity, on the other hand, were an instrument in anti-feminist campaigns. Sempol's chapter outlines how the collective construction of a political sensibility to violence as a violation of human rights in post-dictatorship Argentina mediated the emergence of gay and lesbian rights. Vasudevan's essay details how, in India, shifting discourses on women's sexuality, and the economic, social, and cultural interactions involved, deeply affected the lives of female public dance performers – an ongoing process under the influence of globalization and the rise of right-wing fundamentalist Hindu groups.

### Sexuality and the politics of location

Post-colonial authors have seldom referred to issues of sexual politics in relation to present-day processes of state formation and community-building in the global South. Authors like Bhabha (1994) have often focused more on race than on sexuality. Ever since Weeks (1981) and Foucault (1978) wrote their landmark studies on the historicity of Western sexuality, a wealth of scholarly publications have appeared on the historical relationship between imperialism and sexual domination (Hyam 1991 and Stoler 1995). Recent socio-anthropological studies have explored the effects of globalization (understood as the late-modern intensification of the transnational flow of people, capital, manufactures, knowledge, cultural goods, and symbols) on sexuality and on sexual identities (Manalansan 2003). Some of these studies (notably Altman 1997 and 2001 and Binnie 2004) are embedded within Northern-centric traditions. As Loomba (2005) points out, the focus on globalization as a Northern-centered, Northern-bound process generates some major distortions. On the one hand, it eschews the shift from colonial to post-colonial governments. On the other hand, it ignores the effects of colonialism on imperial culture. Imperial nations typically forgot that their feelings of superiority, their sexual self-images, arts, and literature, were shaped partly in relation to the oriental – an always sexualized (and racialized) other. The choice of the term 'global South' to convey the scope of the intellectual project in this book encompasses an attempt to interfere with the Northern-dominated geopolitics of knowledge instituted by western European imperialism.

The study of sexualities transnationally demands an effort to look at global South locations not merely as places where metropolitan sexual politics have been applied, and sexual subjects have been colonized, but as contexts where the sexual realm has been invented and reinvented with specific meanings (Povinelli and Chauncey 1999). This is a critical shift, not only because it allows for better-grounded analyses of sexual politics worldwide, but also for an exploration of the influence of the rest on the West. The strategy of focusing on epistemologies and pedagogies generated from one or more of the multiple locations that make up the metropolitan periphery is therefore considered a corrective to the imbalance explicit in conventional classifications such as 'First/Third World,' or 'developed/underdeveloped/developing' nations. However, like any refoundational project, this exercise risks reproducing the binaries it seeks to question, supplanting the primacy of one naturalized essence by another. In this book we are faced with the challenge of escaping the schematic reproduction of binaries such as global/local, continuity/change, tradition/modernity, and imported/ indigenous (Corboz 2009: 14). As sexuality and sexual regulations have those binaries embedded in their very conception as fields of social practice and political struggle, one important step to deconstruct them is laying out their operation, and signaling its tensions. Our objective here is neither more, nor less, than that. We address sexual politics without essentializing either sexuality or location. Rather, the geographic, social, and symbolic locations where sexuality is regulated, resisted, and reinvented are investigated as socially constructed sites in the making. As all authors in this volume show, those processes are profoundly political (shaped by power) and politicized (shaped by concrete, situated social agents).

An effect of the poststructuralist turn in sexuality studies has been the decentering of the human subject. The focus is no longer on the heterosexual couple and its homosexual others, as female, transgender, and intersex people, of multiple ethnic, class, and national backgrounds, have become the subjects of (self-)analysis (see Manalansan 2003). The authors in this book engage the global South as their primary location and as a perspective from which to interrogate the technologies of power that produce sexual morality, sexual knowledge, and sexual classifications. Rather than mapping the mosaic of 'sexual diversity' around the global periphery as cultural variants of a universal human order (Vance 2007 [1991]: 46–9), this perspective involves a fundamental decentering move toward interrogating the metropolitan assumptions embedded in the production of sexual difference worldwide, and the moralizing of colonial, post-colonial, and nationalist practices.

### Sexual citizenship and emerging identities

Sexual rights and sexual citizenship have received increasing attention in recent decades (Corrêa et al. 2008; Petchesky 2000; Weeks 2007). Discourses on demography, sexual and reproductive health, human trafficking, and AIDS have, for decades, taken center stage in sexuality studies on the global South. Meanwhile, the individuals and collectives classified as 'sexual subjects' by researchers, policymakers, and activists have been producing other narratives as well. Forms of personhood and citizenship are constructed often under difficult conditions, by articulating other markers of difference as well. Notions of sexual identity have become both more globalized and localized at the same time. As LGBT movements and communities have reached unprecedented visibility, and legal reforms provide recognition and combat discrimination as an increasingly central aspect of a broader democratization process, self-definitions like 'lesbian,' 'gay,' or 'transgender' have enabled people in the South to find a basis for solidarity with others who share similar experiences. Although partial, tentative, and not always binding at a deep subjective level, the language of rights has helped frame their experiences of discrimination. Faced by complex phenomena such as the lay appropriation of MSM ('men who have sex with men'), an originally epidemiological term, as self-identification by grassroots communities emerging in the context of NGO-sponsored AIDS-prevention projects, or the strategic use of a pathological discourse as means of accessing state-funded coverage for the transsexualization process, scholars and activists must negotiate the temptation to domesticate their subjects and constituencies by teaching them 'the right language,' as a process of purification in order to acquire true (global) sexual citizenship (Sívori 2007).

On the other hand, both in Northern and Southern countries, influential conservative religious groups often react to progressive legislation and demands of access to abortion, against discrimination on the basis of sexual orientation, for adolescents' right to sexual and reproductive information, and even to efforts to outlaw violence against women, by labeling them as foreign. 'It's not our culture,' they claim. Solid historical documentation of local experiences, and how societies have addressed gender and sexual diversity, such as the chapters in this volume provide, can be a critical resource for activists mobilizing for changes in public thinking and for policy change.

**Conclusion**

The grounded historical, material, cultural, and political analyses in this volume point to a plurality of discourses around sexuality and to the often violent 'passionate esthetics' at work in sexual politics. The education of desire as a nation-making device reveals the moral quality of politics as spectacle: policing the imagination of the community as a self-contained entity. In countries like Cameroon, post-colonial traumas run deep. While in countries like China a secular path is charted, in many others patriarchal interpretations of religion have a determining influence on the visibility and expression of sexual desires and identities. A shifting world order and the complex intermingling of people with different cultural, class, and ethnic backgrounds – as the result of migrations and diaspora, as well as peripheral, uneven appropriations of modernity (Appadurai 1996) and cosmopolitanism – create conditions in which borders between sexual cultures become porous. Multiple, hybrid, alternative modernities are being produced, with far-reaching consequences for sexual politics and studies of sexuality. The following chapters that address the sexual politics at the heart of nation-building reveal the embodied sexual nature of modern governmentality. Conversely, sexual dissidents demonstrate the capacity of sexual desire to taint or redeem a collective identity.

By displacing modern Western sexualities from the center of observation, the authors of this book interrogate the perceived hegemony of Western conceptualizations of sexuality. At the same time, the dialog between their localized accounts provokes reflections on the varied directions cultural flows might take within and beyond the global South.

## Notes

1 See Bleys (1995) on modern European representations of cultural otherness in male same-sex relations.

2 Some exceptions are Corrêa et al. (2008); Manderson and Jolly (1997); and Wieringa et al. (2007).

3 See examples in Altman (1997, 2001); Binnie (2004). For a critique, see Krishnaswamy and Hawley (2008).

4 See Wieringa (2011) for a report on violence against women in same-sex relations in Africa and Asia.

## References

Ahmed, S. (2005) *Queer Phenomenology: Orientations, Objects, Others*, Durham, NC: Duke University Press.

Altman, D. (1997) 'Global gaze/global gays,' *GLQ*, 3: 417–36.

— (2001) *Global Sex*, Chicago, IL: University of Chicago Press.

Andaya, B. W. (2006) *The Flaming Womb, Repositioning Women in Early Modern Southeast Asia*, Honolulu: University of Hawai'i Press.

Appadurai, A. (1996) *Modernity at Large: cultural dimensions of globalization*, Minneapolis: University of Minnesota Press.

Basu, A., I. Grewal, C. Kaplan and L. Malkki (eds) (2001) 'Globalization and gender,' *Signs: Journal of Women in Culture and Society*, 26(4) (special issue).

Bhabha, H. (1994) *The Location of Culture*, London: Routledge.

Binnie, J. (2004) *The Globalization of Sexuality*, London: Sage.

Blackwood, E. (2005) 'Gender transgression in colonial and postcolonial Indonesia,' *Journal of Asian Studies*, 64(4): 849–79.

Bland, L. and L. Doan (eds) (1998) *Sexology in Culture: labelling bodies and desires*, Cambridge: Polity.

Bleys, R. C. (1995) *The Geography of Perversion. Male-to-Male Sexual Behaviour outside the West and the Ethnography of Imagination, 1750–1918*, New York: New York University Press.

Brah, A. and A. E. Coombes (2000) *Hybridity and Its Discontents: politics, science, culture*, London and New York: Routledge.

Braidotti, R. (2011) *Nomadic Subjects: embodiment and sexual difference in contemporary feminist theory*, 2nd edn, New York: Columbia University Press.

Cook, N. M. and P. A. Jackson (1999) 'Desiring constructs: transforming sex/gender orders in twentieth century Thailand,' in P. A. Jackson and N. M. Cook (eds), *Genders and Sexualities in Modern Thailand*, Chiang Mai: Silkworm Books.

Corboz, J. (2009) 'Globalisation and transnational sexualities,' Melbourne: International Sexuality Studies Network, electronic document, sexualitystudies.net/files/Globalisation%20and%20Transnational%20Sexualities.pdf.

Corrales, J. and M. Pecheny (2010) 'Introduction: The comparative politics of sexuality in Latin America,' in *The Politics of Sexual-*

*ity in Latin America: A Reader on Lesbian, Gay, Bisexual, and Transgender Rights*, Pittsburgh, PA: University of Pittsburgh Press, pp. 1–30.

Corrêa, S., R. Petchesky and R. Parker (2008) *Sexuality, Health and Human Rights*, New York: Routledge.

Epprecht, M. (2004) *Hungochani: The History of a Dissident Sexuality in Southern Africa*, Montreal: McGill-Queen's University Press.

Foucault, M. (1978) *History of Sexuality*, vol. 1: *An Introduction*, New York: Pantheon.

— (1985) *History of Sexuality*, vol. 2: *The Use of Pleasure*, New York: Vintage Books.

— (1988) *History of Sexuality*, vol. 3: *The Care of the Self*, New York: Vintage Books.

Frühstück, S. (2003) *Colonizing Sex: Sexology and social control in modern Japan*, Berkeley: University of California Press.

Gagnon, J. and R. Parker (1995) 'Conceiving sexuality,' in R. Parker and J. H. Gagnon (eds), *Conceiving Sexuality: Approaches to sex research in a postmodern world*, New York and London: Routledge, pp. 3–19.

Halperin, D. M. (2002) *How to Do the History of homosexuality?*, Chicago, IL: University of Chicago Press.

Hollibaugh, A. L. (2000) *My Dangerous Desires: a queer girl dreaming her way home*, Durham, NC, and London: Duke University Press.

Hyam, R. (1991) *Empire and Sexuality: The British Experience*, Manchester and New York: Manchester University Press.

Jeffreys, S. (1985) *The Spinster and Her Enemies: feminism and sexuality 1880–1930*, London: Pandora.

Katjasungkana, N. and S. E. Wieringa (eds) (2012) *The Future of Asian Feminisms*, Newcastle: Cambridge Scholars Publishing.

Krishnaswamy, R. and J. Hawley (2008) *The Postcolonial and the Global*, Minneapolis: University of Minnesota Press.

Lemke, T. (2001) '"The birth of bio-politics": Michel Foucault's lecture at the Collège de France on neo-liberal governmentality,' *Economy and Society*, 30(2): 190–207.

Loomba, A. (2005) *Postcolonial Studies and Beyond*, Durham, NC: Duke University Press.

Manalansan, M. F. IV (2003) *Global Divas: Filipino Gay Men in the Diaspora*, Durham, NC: Duke University Press.

Manalansan, M. and A. Cruz-Malavé (2002) *Queer Globalizations: Citizenship and the Afterlife of Colonialism*, New York: New York University Press.

Manderson, L. and M. Jolly (eds) (1997) *Sites of Desire/Economies of Pleasure: Sexualities in Asia and the Pacific*, Chicago, IL: University of Chicago Press.

Mepschen, P., J. Duyvendak and E. Tonkens (2010) 'Sexual politics, orientalism and multicultural citizenship in the Netherlands,' *Sociology*, 44: 962–80.

Mohanty, C. T., A. Russo and L. Torres (eds) (1991) *Third World Women and the Politics of Feminism*, Bloomington: Indiana University Press.

Morgan, R. and S. Wieringa (2005) *Tommy Boys, Lesbian Men and Ancestral Wives, Women's Same Sex Experiences in Southern Africa*, Johannesburg: Jacana Publishers.

Murray, S. O. (1995) *Latin American Male Homosexualities*,

Albuquerque: University of New Mexico Press.

Murray, S. O. and W. Roscoe (1998) *Boy-wives and Female Husbands: studies of African homosexualities*, New York: St Martin's Press.

Peletz, M. G. (2009) *Gender Pluralism: Southeast Asia since Early Modern Times*, New York and London: Routledge.

Petchesky, R. (2000) 'Sexual rights: inventing a concept, mapping an international practice,' in R. Parker, R. M. Barbosa and P. Aggleton (eds), *Framing the Sexual Subject: The Politics of Gender, Sexuality and Power*, Berkeley: University of California Press, pp. 81–103.

Pigg, S. L. and V. Adams (2005) 'Introduction: The moral object of sex,' in V. Adams and S. L. Pigg (eds), *Sex in Development: Science, sexuality, and morality in global perspective*, Durham, NC: Duke University Press, pp. 1–38.

Povinelli, E. A. and G. Chauncey (1999) 'Thinking sexuality transnationally. An introduction,' *GLQ: A Journal of Lesbian and Gay Studies*, 5(4): 439–49.

Puar, J. K. (2007) *Terrorist Assemblages: Homonationalism in queer times*, Durham, NC: Duke University Press.

Richardson, D. (2000) *Rethinking Sexuality*, London: Sage.

Robinson, P. (1976) *The Modernization of Sex*, New York: Harper and Row.

Sívori, H. F. (2007) 'Ativistas e peritos no movimento GLTTB-Aids Argentino: ciência e política da identidade sexual,' Unpublished PhD thesis, Graduate Program in Social Anthropology, Federal University of Rio de Janeiro.

— (2011) 'Medir la discriminación: la construcción de los parámetros para el registro de percepciones y patrones de violencia por prejuicio sexual,' *Debate Feminista*, 22(43): 19–52.

Spivak, G. (1999) *A Critique of Postcolonial Reason. Toward a history of the vanishing present*, Cambridge, MA: Harvard University Press.

Stepan, N. L. (1991) *The Hour of Eugenics: race, gender and nation in Latin America*, Ithaca, NY: Cornell University Press.

Stoler, A. L. (1995) *Race and the Education of Desire. Foucault's History of Sexuality and the Colonial Order of Things*, Durham, NC, and London: Duke University Press.

Vance, C. S. (2007 [1991]) 'Anthropology rediscovers sexuality: a theoretical comment,' in R. Parker and P. Aggleton, *Culture, Society and Sexuality. A Reader*, 2nd edn, London: Routledge, pp. 41–57.

Weeks, J. (1981) *Sex, Politics and Society: the Regulation of Sexuality since 1800*, London and New York: Longman.

— (2007) *The World We Have Won*, London: Routledge.

Wieringa, S. E. (2002) 'Essentialism versus constructionism,' in P. Mohammed (ed.), *Gendered Realities: An Anthology of Essays in Caribbean Feminist Thought*, Kingston: University of the West Indies Press, pp. 3–22.

— (2003) 'The birth of the New Order state in Indonesia: sexual politics and nationalism,' *Journal of Women's History*, 15(1): 70–92.

— (2009) 'Postcolonial amnesia: sexual moral panics, memory and imperial power,' in G. Herdt (ed.), *Moral Panics, Sex Panics: Fear and the Fight over Sexual Rights*, New York: New York University Press, pp. 205–34.

— (2010) 'Gender variance in Asia; discursive contestation and legal implications,' *Journal of Gender, Technology and Development*, 14(2): 143–72.

— (2011) 'Women-loving-women,' Final report, Trans/sign Project, Amsterdam and The Hague: Mamacash and Hivos.

— (2012) 'Passionate aesthetics and symbolic subversion; heteronormativity in India and Indonesia,' *Asian Studies Review*, forthcoming.

Wieringa, S. E., E. Blackwood and A. Bhaiya (eds) (2007) *Women's Sexualities and Masculinities in a Globalizing Asia*, London: Palgrave.

# 2 | The rise of sex and sexuality studies in post-1978 China

HUANG YINGYING[1]

## Introduction

The introduction of market-based economic reforms and the Open Door policy in 1978 was accompanied by dramatic social transformations in China, including the collapse of the system of working units. The weakening of social control and the fading of traditional beliefs, together with greater social mobility and changes in residency patterns, led to the development of what local observers have called a 'society of strangers.' Later on, the availability and use of the Internet and mobile phones also played a role in this process. Against this background, marriage, family, love, and sexuality are changing (Pan 2006). This has contributed to noticeable and rapid changes in Chinese people's sexual behaviors and mores. In response to this dynamic context, sex-related research has experienced a significant rise. This contrasts with the seeming sexual austerity and discursive silence on sex that marked the Maoist period, which has been termed the 'asexual culture' of the Cultural Revolution era (1966–76), when sex was highly politicized (Pan 2006, 2008). Since the early 1980s, in response to changes in social behavior, debates around sex have exploded into public discourse. Issues including premarital and extramarital sex, concubinage, prostitution, pornography, homosexuality, sex shops and HIV/AIDS, as well as sexual health, have emerged as new and controversial foci of public attention. China's new professionals – journalists, lawyers, social workers – and scholars, as well as public health officials and gay and feminist activists, have begun to raise issues of sex and sexuality as they intervene in the public policy arena. Hence many commentators argue that China is undergoing a sexual revolution both at the level of individual practice and in the broader realm of public discourse (Pan 2008; Pan et al. 2004; Jeffreys 2006).

This chapter studies the emergence of sex and sexuality research in post-1978 China as part of that sexual revolution. Although the study of sex in China has a long history, and sex-related (public) literature in certain periods (especially the early twentieth century and since

1949) has been discussed elsewhere (e.g. Finnane and McLaren 1999; Harriet 1997; Dikotter 1995), the study of sex and sexuality as a focus of academic discipline and social intervention is a new phenomenon in the People's Republic of China (PRC). During the Maoist era, changes to China's social structure and the subordination of academic disciplines to the organizing principles of Marxism-Leninism effectively ensured that the study of sexuality became a 'non-issue,' other than in relation to the regulation of monogamous marital heterosexuality.

I draw on Foucault's *History of Sexuality* (Foucault 1990) to provide a genealogy of the emergence of sex and sexuality as objects of discourse in reform-era China. In order to examine the rise of sex and sexuality studies in contemporary China as one dimension of the broader social changes that are taking place in China today, I further draw on the 'sociology of practice,' as outlined in Pierre Bourdieu's *The Logic of Practice* (1990), and further elaborated by Sun Liping (2002) for the Chinese context as 'practical process analysis.' Sun argues for the incorporation of micro-level case studies of everyday life and power relations as a means to expand and critique the conclusions of large-scale surveys and official discourses on sexuality and sexual practice. This approach enables us to look at sex and sexuality and their emergence as public issues in contemporary China in relation to the local political and social context, rather than addressing them solely as the effects of global influences or with exclusive reference to Western systems of knowledge (Boellstorff and Leap 2004).

After a preliminary comment on terminological issues, crucial to understanding the emergence of sexuality as a concept in China's public imagination, the chapter is divided into two parts, one presenting a panorama of sexuality studies in China, and the other offering an interpretation of how this field was constituted and the challenges it faces. The first section outlines the emergence of sexuality studies since the early 1980s. In a survey-like manner, I list relevant historical and cultural research investments in sexuality in general and in specific topics such as homosexuality, prostitution, and foot binding, with a focus on academic or other influential publications. The next section presents empirical sexuality studies in contemporary China. Finally I examine particularly relevant topics: sexual rights and sex education. In the second part, I address the discursive formations shaping this field, particularly an essentialist position which is the prominent approach. I conclude by addressing some challenges currently faced by sexuality studies in China, and suggesting a way forward.

## Gender and sexuality in China: preliminary comments

A discussion on terminology is needed before addressing sexuality studies in China. Paramount to this understanding is the fluidity of the concept of *xing*, shifting between sex and sexuality. Before the end of the nineteenth century, many different local terms were used in China to refer to sex and sexuality, such as the character *se* (色). In the early twentieth century, the Chinese term for sex and sexuality was translated as *xing* (性), from the Japanese. In traditional China, just as *ren* (人, person) never referred to the individual, but rather was incorporated into the *jia* (家, family), so too *xing* (sex) was never an independent category but rather was embedded within a greater conceptual totality of the 'primary life cycle' (Pan 2006). Before the May Fourth Movement (*Wu Si Yundong*) in 1919, sexual practices were strictly restricted to the following set of social norms, which obviously refer to heterosexuality: sex for the purpose of reproduction; obeying gender roles as defined by 'women for men's use' (*nv wei nan yong*); marriage as the sphere for sex; mutual gratitude and appreciation between husband and wife (*fuqi en'ai*), a more important determining factor in a couple's sexual relations than romantic love (*langman qing'ai*); spiritual abstinence, characterized as opposed to 'pleasure seeking' (*xun huan zuo le*) to regulate sexual activities; limiting the frequency of sexual activities based on the belief that 'too much sex harms men's bodies' (*lao se shang shen*); sex as something to be done rather than something to be talked about, therefore avoiding sexual communication; the exclusion of sexuality among adolescents and the elderly, establishing an age boundary (Pan 2008).

Use of the term *xing* gained strength in the 1980s with the rise of sexology and the tide of Western publications translated into Chinese during that period. The sexological understanding of *xing* assumes that sex is universal, natural, and motivated by instinct, and encourages scientific knowledge about sex. Definitions of *xing* commonly found in mainstream dictionaries are consistent with this approach. These include: 1) 'natural' male and female attributes or 'sex' (*xingbie*); 2) biological reproduction by heterosexual intercourse (*xingjiao*); sexual desire (*xingyu*); and sexiness (*xinggan*) (Lan Dekang 1998). The underlying meaning of the concept of *xing* can be characterized as: biology focused; binaristic, organized around the male/female complementary opposition; reproduction oriented; behavior-based; and phallocentric, with penile–vaginal intercourse as the standard expression of *xing*.

This conceptual framework has been challenged in the West by a 'cultural influence model,' developed from the the 1920s on by anthropologists and sociologists such as Benedict, Malinowski, and Mead; and starting in the 1970s with a 'social construction model,' promoted by anthropologists and sociologists, as well as feminist and gay and lesbian scholars and activists, emphasizing social and cultural meanings of gender and sexuality, sexual hierarchies and power relations (Weeks 1985; Gagnon and Parker 1995; Rubin 1989). Both models were introduced to China in the 1990s by local social scientists. A few sociologists began to challenge the (until then) dominant bio-medical paradigm of sexology and the medicalization of sex. In addition to some pioneer studies and activism, there are ongoing debates about the definitions of sex and sexuality, and how sexuality should be translated into Chinese to differ from sex.

Since the 1980s, the field of women's studies has grown in China. In 1993, during the first Conference on Women and Development in China, organized by an overseas Chinese Women's Association and the Women's Study Center at Tianjin Normal University, the English term 'gender' was translated as *shehui xingbie* (social sex, 社会性别; Wang 2006). The introduction of the concept of gender in China was held to be a sign of real progress, and regarded as the outcome of debates about essentialism and social constructionism within Chinese academia at the time. The concept of *shehui xingbie* emphasizes the unequal power relationship between women and men, and is used to challenge patriarchal Chinese society. This concept, however, is strongly marked as 'female' and 'heterosexual,' neglecting its relationship with sexuality, the power relationship between heterosexuality and homosexuality, and excluding LGBTQ issues. Although, in recent years, some research on sexual violence and sexual harassment has been conducted, very few feminists in China actually look at gender and sexuality, or LGBTQ issues.

### Sexuality studies in China since the 1980s

The history of Chinese sexual knowledge is mostly unknown to the general public. Yet China saw such masterpieces as *The Art of the Bedchamber (Fang Zhong Shu)*, written 2,000 years ago. In the 1920s the country was home to the noted sexologist Zhang Jingsheng. Later on, brochures were published from the 1950s up to the early Cultural Revolution. These include *Sexual Knowledge* and *Must Read for the Newly Married*.

When Lang Jinghe published the article 'Sexual hygiene in new marriages' in the opening issue of *Scientific Pictorial*, a small number of people cheered what they saw as a breakthrough in sexual freedom

(Lang 1980). In the early 1980s, two publications activated the Chinese sexology movement: the *Sex Knowledge Handbook* by Ruan (1985) and *Sexual Medicine* by Wu (1982). With the release of these books, sex suddenly became a topic one could write and read about. This led to the first upsurge in sexology, which lasted from 1988 until 1994, when the first sizable exhibition on sexual knowledge took place. In May 1994 the China Sexology Association was registered and established. Pan et al. (2004) counted a total of 273 books (excluding articles) related to sexual knowledge and sexology that appeared between the early 1980s and October 1992. Sexual research was then gradually taken up in various fields, becoming an object of study in different disciplines: the cultural history of sexuality, the sociology of sexuality, law and sexuality, sex education, gender, and so on.

The primary focus of this sexological approach was on scientific sex education and sexual knowledge, supplemented by the study of sexual culture and sexual phenomena in modern society. Sexologists also took up research on homosexuality, building on earlier work on the topic. The focus on sexual science or sexology represented an epistemological shift away from earlier approaches to sexuality. A high regard for a positivist medical 'scientific' approach has been the preferred framework for discourses on sexuality since then, departing from the philosophical discussions of earlier times. An interest in sex reassignment surgery is an example of this new medical approach. This modern sexology introduced new linguistic tools, by translating the rather essentialist bio-medical perspective of Western sexological literature. Embedded in that were moral regulations for sexual identity and sexual behavior, in the form of messages such as 'don't have too much sex' or 'masturbation is fine, but too much of it will harm the body and have a bad influence on youth.' However, any talk about sexual issues would have been impossible without this new vocabulary.[2] In this sense, the introduction of sexology itself meant a revolution. It supplied a cornerstone for discussing sex and sexuality. The term 'make love' (*zuo ai*), for example, invented in the 1980s, meant a significant innovation in Chinese language from other existing terms, *dun lun* (conjugal practice within marriage) and *xing jiao* (sexual intercourse).

From the late 1980s and early 1990s a different sexological approach was introduced, focused on historical and cultural research, under three categories: 1) inclusive research on sexuality in ancient and modern times; 2) research on sexual cultures, such as that of Dunhuang,[3] or *The Art of the Bedchamber*; and 3) research on particular phenomena such as homosexuality, prostitution, and foot binding. A large audience was introduced to China's sexual cultures by an overseas researcher named Robert van Gulik (Gulik 1990). Local research on the history of sexuality is often identified with Liu Dalin, who started his work in the 1980s. Based on his study of historical materials, literature, and his collection of cultural relics, Liu produced a comprehensive introduction to sexual culture, including sexual meanings in prehistoric dances, the relatively open attitude toward sexuality up to the Tang Dynasty, the strict regulations and ideology of abstinence prescribed by *Li* philosophy during the Song Dynasty, and sexual suppression during the Qing Dynasty (Liu 1993).[4] *The Art of the Bedchamber (Fang Zhong Shu)* is a unique heritage related to sexual culture in China. It was recovered with the discovery of the silk manuscripts found in 1972 in the tomb of Ma Wangdui of the Han Dynasty.[5] After the Cultural Revolution was over, *The Art of the Bedchamber* was reintroduced to Chinese society. Li Ling, a researcher from Peking University, systematically researched the ancient Fangshu culture, which includes *Fang Zhong Shu* (ibid.). At the end of the 1980s Pan released his influential *The Social History of Sexuality* (1988).

Another researcher, Jiang (1995), introduced the concept of 'sexual tension' to discuss the idea of 'sexual repression' in the field of Chinese sexual history. In studying traditional Chinese literature and philosophy, Jiang pointed out that, within Chinese history, two opposing sexual philosophies coexisted. One placed importance on reproduction, valuing the son or heir, while giving space for polygyny and maintaining a positive attitude toward male human desire. *Li* philosophy, on the other hand, advocated a strict regulation of sexuality, especially following the Song Dynasty, prescribing abstinence. Jiang argued that sexual tension is the product of the interaction between these two conservative philosophies. Historical studies on sexual culture in the 1980s and early 1990s explored how sexuality was expressed and regulated in ancient times, which contributed to breaking the silence on sexuality studies and bringing sexual culture back into public discussions. However, these studies were less strong analytically and did not involve a social science approach.

Homosexuality and prostitution are two key issues in the field of Chinese sexuality studies. Zhang (2001) uses rich archival material to provide a panorama of homosexuality in Chinese history. The author believes that homosexuality is both a natural orientation (i.e. biological), and can also be influenced by culture. Although the word 'homosexual' (*tongxinglian*) was used in the title and main body of the book, he argues that there is no clear or fixed concept of homosexuality in Chinese history, nor was there a clear discriminatory attitude toward homosexuality.

Other researchers have used a gender perspective to study the preference for *nanfeng* (male fashion) in Ming and Qing Dynasty novels, concluding that 'male fashion' in fact ignored women's sexuality. They argue that the patriarchal society of the time did not suppress 'male fashion' (Wu 2002). Likewise, there is also consensus that a clear 'homosexual' identity has not existed in Chinese history, either in relation to men or to women. The key 'homosexual' studies are about men; only a few studies deal with women's homosexual behaviors and cultures.

Historical research on prostitution in China addressed both the history of prostitution (Wang 1988 [1934]) and the history of anti-prostitution (Public Security Bureau of Beijing 1998). The former addressed prostitution from a cultural perspective in Chinese history, while the latter concentrated on anti-prostitution actions conducted by the government. Prostitution in Shanghai during the late nineteenth and early twentieth centuries has been a focus of attention for overseas historians and feminist scholars (Henriot 2001; Hershatter 1999).[6]

Foot binding is another key issue in the Chinese gender and sexuality studies. Historians and folk-culture researchers often refer to foot binding as an example of control over women's bodies and the subordination of women's sexuality (Fang 1997). Using a more constructivist approach, Ko (2005) explored the subjective meanings underlying these practices. Some overseas researchers have also focused on topics like sexual texts, sexual discourse, and the historical context of Chinese masculinities and femininities (Finnane and McLaren 1999; Harriet 1997; Dikotter 1995).

## Empirical studies

By the end of the 1980s, empirical studies on sexualities in China started to appear. The sociological research of Liu, Pan, and Li, who used both quantitative and qualitative methods, represents the most influential work in this area. Research topics included a broad range of issues, including: sexual behavior; sexual norms and relationships among the general population; sexuality among specific groups such as college students, women, minorities, and the 'floating population'; and specific topics such as homosexuality, the sex industry, and the sexual body.

From 1985 onwards, research was carried out using observation, surveys, and interviews to study sexual behaviors, sexual relationships, sexual norms, and sexual satisfaction. For example, from the early 1980s, Pan observed the intimate interactions between homosexual partners in parks; he surveyed the audience visiting the first exhibition of oil paintings of the human body in Shanghai; and he studied the sexual lives and marriages of 977 Beijing locals. From the early 1990s, Li studied Chinese people's sexuality, love, and marriage in a cross-cultural context, and concluded that, unlike in the West, where certain sexual practices (such as anal sex) have historically been banned, stigmatized, and deemed sinful or pathologic, the control of sexual desire and sexual practices in China has tended to be related to health and reproduction concerns. Although Li's generalizations are problematic, her cultural approach to sexuality meant a revolution in China. Since the late 1980s and early 1990s, more sociological research has been conducted in the field of sexuality. The four surveys listed below have, in particular, created a significant social impact and instigated further debate.

From 1989 to 1990, Liu conducted the first non-randomized national survey of over twenty thousand Chinese people about their sexual behaviors, relationships, and norms. The interviewees included high school students, college students, and married people from both urban and rural areas, as well as individuals charged as sex offenders (Liu 1992). He became a well-known sexologist in China, and came to be called 'the Chinese Kinsey' by some foreign media and organizations. As with other sexologists of his time, Liu's term choices and some of his conclusions carry some heterosexist bias.

In the late 1990s, Xu and Ye (1999) studied 800 heterosexual couples in urban areas, outlining the changing situation in four areas. The study covered such issues as: choosing partners; norms and patterns of love and marriage; and the role of sex within marriage. They concluded that marriage in China was a highly stable institution, and characterized by its uniformity.

From 1999 to 2000, Pan collaborated with the University of Chicago to conduct the first population-based, randomized survey among the general population about their sexualities. This was also the first time computer-assisted methods were used for a survey in China, covering sexuality issues ranging from values, behaviors, and sexual health, to relationships and sexual expression. Based on this study, Pan concluded that there have been rapid changes in Chinese people's sexuality since the 1980s, which, taken together, can be interpreted as a sexual revolution. In 2006, funded by the Ford Foundation, the survey was repeated and compared to the 2000 data; this demonstrated that a sexual revolution was indeed taking place. These two surveys had a strong impact on the media, as well as on health programs and society (Pan et al. 2004, 2008).

Young people's sexuality is a major concern in Chinese society. There are many debates on morality related to sexuality. Sexual openness tends to be considered as a bad influence on youths, in spite of the lack of evidence or the opinions of this age group. Youth sexuality is usually discussed in the context of sex education, where major concerns are voiced around how to prevent 'early love' and abortions, causing youth sexuality to be forbidden and neglected as a topic of debate. The taboo on youth sexuality is also commonly used as a rationale to combat pornography and forms of sexual expression.

Since the 1990s, many surveys have focused on college students. Pan Suiming and his team, for instance, started a longitudinal study in 1991, the first among Beijing college students (1991, 1995), which later included college students nationwide (1997, 2001, 2006). The research covered such diverse issues as: physical growth; same-sex and heterosexual interactions; conceptions of sex and love; relationships; the need for sex education; sexual harassment; and sexual norms. Based on that data, Pan further challenged the commonly held belief in Chinese society that college students are out of control and should be governed more strictly. Instead, he recommended that greater respect be given to youth and youth sexuality, and called for the provision of sex education grounded in students' needs (Pan and Yang 2000; Pan and Zeng 1999).

Women's sexuality also became a topic for research at this time. Before Pan concluded that a sexual revolution was going on in China, Li had interviewed forty-seven Chinese women ranging from twenty-nine to fifty-five years old, from various occupational backgrounds, about their experiences and events in their sexual lives. The study embraced more than thirty topics, including: first menstruation; first experience of falling in love; sexual repression; sex education; non-marital sex; first sexual relationship; sexual frequency and patterns; sexual pleasure; sexual desire; masturbation; contraception; abortion; childbearing; and domestic violence. Li concluded that sexuality among Chinese people could be characterized as shame-based, abstinent, traditional, and lacking awareness of sexual rights (Li 1998), as compared to Western standards, although her study does not provide a detailed analysis or reflections on the latter.

After that, other studies pertaining to women's bodies and sexuality took place in China, focusing on sexual harassment and violence from a gender, legal, and rights perspective (Tang 1995; Rong and Song 2002). Women's sexual and reproductive health was another focus in population studies and the field of public health. In recent years, more research among women with a positive perspective on women's sexuality and bodies has been conducted, including such topics as: women's sexual body, sexiness, women's sexuality and the Internet, and sexual expression and identity (Huang 2008; Ren 2005; Pei 2007).

The study of sexuality among minorities has been scattered within ethnographic and folk-culture studies, including a study on 'walking marriages' among the Mosuo people (Zhan 1980; Zhou 2001)[7] and investigations on drug use, and gender and sexuality among certain ethnic groups (Weng 1996). Research on sexuality among migrant workers began in recent years in relation to the HIV/AIDS crisis. The focus has largely been on sexual behavior, perceptions of HIV/AIDS and STIs, and reproductive health (Zhang 2005; Huang et al. 2008). However, we still lack an in-depth understanding of sexualities among different categories of migrants. Generally speaking, although sexuality and sex-related studies among these specific groups have begun, there is still a lack of research, especially pertaining to women, migrant workers, and ethnic groups, from a social constructivist perspective or with a positive approach to sexuality.

Sex work in contemporary China is another key area that has been studied since the late 1990s. Sex work is illegal in China. In earlier years, popular culture portrayed prostitutes as bad women who sell their souls for 'dirty money' (*duoluo*). However, social attitudes have changed somewhat in the past ten years, as a victimizing approach (mobilizing 'poor girls' or 'forced into prostitution' narratives) has gained visibility in the mass media and in academic circles. This has resulted in some legal debates around anti-prostitution policy in China. Some argued that prostitution should remain illegal, supported by the discourse that prostitution is a social evil. Others maintained that women selling sex should be decriminalized, arguing that women in prostitution should be 'saved,' while men buying sex should be punished. This argument was supported by the discourse on women as victims. A few voices arguing for the empowerment of sex workers are also beginning to make themselves heard.

Pan was the first researcher to study contemporary red-light districts in China in depth. In 1999, he published an influential book, *Existence and Absurdity: The study of underground red-light districts in China*. His team at the Institute of Sexuality and Gender later continued to use ethnographic methodology to study female sex workers in China, visiting over fifteen red-light districts, interviewing thousands of female sex workers (FSWs), hundreds of male clients, madams, managers, and pimps. The studies exposed critical issues related to their life situation, occupational stratification, occupational practices, identities, mobility, and health, as well as to the legal situation (e.g. Pan 2000; Huang 2004; Huang and Pan 2003; Pan and Huang 2005; Zhao 2007). The findings from these studies reveal: a great diversity among sex workers; the social and cultural context of FSWs; and their own views on their work (Huang 2004). This research uses a rights-based approach and is concerned with occupational health issues involved in sex work. This stands in contrast to the 'victim' discourse most feminists employ, and the KABP (knowledge, attitude, behavior, and practice) model used by most health providers.

Additional research about FSWs has focused on commercial sex workers within re-education centres (Wang 1998 [1934]). In recent years, HIV/AIDS research related to FSWs has grown dramatically, and FSWs have been defined as one of the high-risk populations in the AIDS era.

A few studies about male sex workers have been carried out, and are worth noting here. Certain English terms – such as 'money boys,' or male sex workers (MBs), men who have sex with men (MSM), as well as FSWs – have been introduced to China by HIV/AIDS programs. The researcher Tong Ge, who conducted interviews with more than one hundred MBs in collaboration with the Beijing Gender Health Education Institute, documented details on the life stories, experiences, self-identities, and sexual practices of MBs in China from a social, cultural, and legal perspective. Based on this research, Tong pointed to the need for a holistic understanding of MBs' health and bodily care practices, rather than focusing solely on them in the context of HIV/AIDS (Tong 2007a). Another researcher carried out his fieldwork in nightclubs, looking at masculinity among male sex workers (Fang 2007). Although transgender sex work, and S/M (sado-masochistic sex play) sex work, have become more visible in recent years and are targeted by grassroots groups that provide HIV prevention services, no studies or detailed discussions have been conducted on transgender.

The study of homosexuality in contemporary China started in the early 1990s. Wang and Li's 1992 publication *Their World: A Study of Homosexuality in China* became popular. In 1993, Pan interviewed 165 homosexuals about their sexual behaviors and relationships in the context of HIV/AIDS prevention. In 1994, Zhang published his book *Same-sex Love*. In recent years, propelled by international HIV/AIDS programs and other international forces, gay issues in China have become a hot topic. Most studies in the AIDS era portrayed gay MSM with a focus on sex practices and risk of STIs and HIV infection. Yet a few voices drew attention to identities, culture, and rights. In 2005, the personal life stories and experiences of more than one hundred male *Tongzhi* (the local term for homosexuals) were presented, using a subjective perspective, by Tong and his team (Tong 2007b). Although it lacked a theoretical framework and analysis, this provided a vivid picture of homosexual culture in contemporary China, revealing detailed information on such topics as: the local terms and language used in different communities; sexual tastes and appeal in same-sex relationships; sexual behavior and relationships; love; marriage; self-identity; and relationships with family, colleagues, and friends.

In addition to issues related to gay men, researchers also began to look at questions pertaining to lesbian, queer, and transgender people. Documentary film-makers and cultural studies scholars (e.g. Cui Zi'en and Ai Xiaoming) have also become interested in LGBTQ issues, and there has also been an increase in the number of LGBTQ magazines and pamphlets, such as *Friends*, *Les+*, and *Homo-heart*.

The rise in research on homosexuality is clearly visible in the abstracts and papers submitted since 2007 to the Biannual Conference on Sexualities in China, organized by the Institute of Sexuality and Gender. More than half of the papers submitted now focus on this topic, and the numbers increase each year. These studies, most of them arising from HIV/AIDS programs, have made homosexual issues far more visible than before. However, they are usually limited to a level of exploring 'new' phenomena and with a focus on so-called risky behaviors. Generally, they suffer from a lack of in-depth analysis, combined with the absence of critical gender theories and a sufficient understanding of local Chinese cultures.[8]

### Sexuality and the law

Since the 1990s, attention has been paid to legal issues related to sexuality. Areas of concern include: virginity rights; the marriage law; sexual assault; pornography and prostitution; sexual harassment; sexual violence; and domestic violence. Sociologists, feminist scholars, and lawyers have participated in these debates. In 1993, Li Dun expanded the discussion on gender and the law to include sexuality (Li 1993). Tan focused on aspects of human evolution and the history and development of civilization as related to sex and sexuality (Tan 1998).

During the mid- to late 1990s, it was rumoured in the media that the new Chinese marriage law might limit divorce, increase the level of difficulty in obtaining a divorce, interfere with extramarital affairs, and penalize 'the third party' (*di san zhe*). As a result, lawyers and sociologists debated amendments to the new marriage law. Some scholars felt that emotions should not be regulated by law; morality-based legislation should be held in question; and divorce should be based on the principle of a broken marriage. Consequently they opposed limiting access to divorce, and proposed a divorce damage compensation system whereby the party at fault, if such exists, is liable for emotional damage compensation. This same group of scholars also advised against legislation to penalize extramarital affairs (the third party) and interfere with people's privacy. At the same time, however, other scholars advocated the sanctity of spousal rights, and called for legislation to penalize parties involved in extramarital affairs.[9]

Sexual violence and domestic violence are among the most studied areas within the field of sex and the law. Discussions about marital rape and sexual harassment have been particularly widespread and extend outside of the fields of jurisprudence. Marital rape, date rape, and sexual harassment have also been studied from a women's rights egalitarian perspective. Scholars are looking at sexual harassment as a violation of individual rights and personal dignity. In this view, sexual harassment not only violates women's rights and specifically targets women; what is threatened is something intangible yet invaluable to all human beings: our dignity (Pan 2005).

## Sex education

As mentioned earlier, China witnessed a temporary trend in promoting sex education in the first half of the twentieth century. This movement paved the way for the rise of sexology in the early 1980s, becoming one of the banners under which it flew. Research on sex education has since reappeared. *Informal Notes on Sexual Knowledge*, compiled by Hu, was published in 1980. That same year, *Sexual Knowledge*, compiled before the Cultural Revolution by Wang and others, was republished; its total circulation had surpassed 5 million by March 1981. The works by Ruan and Wu were considered the authoritative texts on sex education. The early 1980s was also the time when Shi's *Human Sexuality Counselling* was published. The journal *Sex Education* was first published in 1988; its founding contributors included such authors as Liu Dalin. Various other sex education books and articles, as well as training courses to provide a 'scientific' understanding and attitude toward sex among media workers and sex educators, also came out during that period. In 1986, *Sex Psychology* (by Henry Havelock

Ellis), translated and edited by Pan Guangdan, was republished. In the postscript for this second edition of this book, Fei wrote: 'Through the policies of opening-up and reform, China is transforming from a country that once closed its doors and refused contact with others, to a modernized society. As science and democracy spread to the masses, the formerly forbidden field of sexology is now being accepted with open hearts and arms' (Fei 1986: 549).

Starting in the mid-1990s, the Capital Normal University in Beijing began to offer Sex Education as a course of study. A series of related textbooks was published in 1998 (Zhang 1998). Another university also began to offer courses on Sexual Biology and A General Introduction to Human Sexuality and Sexology in 1990 (Peng 2002). Beginning in 1997, Renmin University of China offered a training course on Sex Education and the Media. In the last twenty years, sexuality and gender courses have been incorporated into the curricula of about twenty universities.[10] The rise of AIDS has brought a new urgency to the topic of sex education. HIV/AIDS prevention projects have advanced the integration of sex education and AIDS education. Numerous research, teaching materials, and articles about sex education have been published in recent years.

Sex education and related research efforts have been primarily concerned with issues of human sexuality. As we have explored earlier, more attention has been given to pedagogy and medicine than to social science. However, questions and concerns such as who should carry out sex education, when should sex education begin, and what kind of content should be involved have been debated. Some researchers have shown interest in current challenges facing sex education, such as: the late introduction of sex education as compared to the onset of adolescence; the scarcity of sex education teachers and teaching materials compared to growing needs; and the role of family and society in influencing students' sexual knowledge in the face of systematic school-based measures (Wang and Wang 2005). Moral concerns about youth sexuality on the part of educational authorities have resulted in conservative and regulatory-oriented education.

From the 1980s onward, researchers like Li and Pan also translated and introduced influential Western theories and thoughts on sexology, queer theories, and sociological studies on sexuality (Li 2002; Pan et al. 2004). Since the late 1990s, this body of work has been applied to help explain Chinese sexuality. However, concerns arose about its applicability to local situations. A more local culturally oriented analysis on sexuality, gender, and desire in China was advocated (Pan and Huang

2007). For example, rapid social changes in relation to sexuality in China could not be regarded merely as the result of Western influence or as following the West, as the mass media and some scholars have claimed. They should be understood against the changing background of Chinese society over the last twenty years, and the changes in the relationship between marriage, love, sexuality, kinship, and family relations (Pan 2006: 36; Jeffreys 2006).

## Discourses arising from sexuality studies

In the section above, I surveyed the rise of sex and sexuality studies in China since the 1980s. This section analyzes the major discourses they deploy. I distinguish at least four discourses (Huang 2008). The most established and dominant voice is a medicalized discourse. This rose to prominence in the 1980s and early 1990s, in the form of sexological research, as illustrated by the publication of such groundbreaking texts as the *Sex Knowledge Handbook* (Ruan 1985), *Sexual Medicine* (Wu 1982), and *Sexual Culture in Modern China* (Liu 1992). This bio-medical, essentialist discourse is driven by sexologists, physicians, and public health officials, as well as by commercial interests. It draws on early twentieth-century discourses on sexology and is predominantly conservative in orientation, concerned with health and the sexual body (Pan et al. 2004). While originally viewed as a 'healthy' counter-argument in relation to the asexual culture of the period of the Cultural Revolution, the focus of sexologists on delineating 'scientific' sexual knowledge, 'scientific' sexual health, and 'scientific' sexual behavior is now associated with the commercialization and medicalization of the sexual body. In this approach, 'sex' is a property or thing with specific standards that can be mastered and obtained (see McMillan 2006). Likewise, the work of China's sexologists, particularly over the past five to six years, has advocated stricter controls over sexuality to prevent sexually transmitted diseases, including HIV/AIDS. Rather than paying attention to the sociocultural factors underpinning China's changing sexual conduct, this approach pathologizes the (Chinese) sexual body, presenting it as something to be 'cured.' Additionally, this emphasis on disciplining bodies and dismissal of a cultural understanding of how sexuality is lived from an everyday perspective has potentially damaging consequences for the effective implementation of safer-sex health programs.

The second discourse on sexuality in present-day China is concerned with the subordination and oppression of women's bodies and sexuality. During the Maoist era, the CCP (Chinese Communist Party) claimed to have liberated Chinese women by eradicating prostitution, abolishing foot binding and concubinage, and enabling women to take part in the productive labor force. However, along with the introduction of market-based reforms, women's bodies have been commercialized as sexual objects to be consumed by men. Prostitution and 'mistress-keeping' have re-emerged, albeit in different forms. The resurgence of such 'traditional' phenomena, combined with increased rates of divorce, extramarital affairs, and domestic violence, has encouraged studies that focus on the subordinate status of Chinese women vis-à-vis Chinese men and criticize China's male-dominated culture and unequal gender relationships. Despite the evident importance of such studies, they also have the effect of focusing on 'women-as-victims' and thereby discouraging positive representations of female sexuality and autonomy. Thus, more recent studies (e.g. Huang 2008; Li 1998) suggest that it is necessary to provide accounts of how women in China view their sexuality and bodies from the perspective of women as agents, without abandoning the critical concern with gendered power relationships.

The third discourse I distinguish is that of the Chinese sexual revolution. This discourse is driven by scholars and the mass media. As numerous scholars note, the introduction of Deng Xiaoping's economic reform and Open Door policy of December 1978 has contributed to a sexual revolution in China by hastening the collapse of the former system of social control, which was exercised via the work unit and the neighborhood policing system, and by promoting a new demarcation between the public and private spheres (Pan 2006: 36; Jeffreys 2006). Over the past twenty years, this has resulted in: 1) a shift from notions of sex for reproduction to new conceptions of sex for pleasure; 2) a dramatic change in sexual behavior and practices (e.g. an increase in rates of premarital and casual sex); 3) new understandings of female sexuality; and 4) public and academic debate on sex-related issues and an associated proliferation of new terminology and concepts (Pan et al. 2004: 1–17). In the mass media, the sexual revolution discourse is often distorted to claim that China is a virtual 'paradise of sexuality' or 'liberal,' as in 'Westernized.' In so doing, the mass media often present a skewed account of exactly who is benefiting from China's 'sexual revolution' and in what way.

Taken in conjunction with the preceding three discourses, the focus on 'self-control' and 'respect for oneself' functions to reinstate 'tradition' as a means to resist what are seen as the negative consequences of 'Westernization.' This slogan features prominently in sexual health and education projects targeted at China's youth, which emphasize a 'traditional' ideology of appropriate behavior, not talking about sexuality, and avoiding casual sex, especially for girls (Huang 2008). The problem here, as other studies show, is that this approach does not correspond with social practice, since, for instance, rates of premarital and casual sex in China are on the rise (Pan et al. 2004).

In addition, Western researchers have begun to engage with issues of sex and sexuality in reform-era China, which raises additional questions regarding the politics of translation and how to generate a productive dialog between China and the West (Finnane and McLaren 1999; Jeffreys 2006). Western discourses on sexuality have been criticized for ignoring local cultures and allowing their own theoretical frameworks to predetermine their conclusions (Cook and Jackson 1999: 22). On the other hand, while we need to recognize the specificity of China's political and social context, it is equally important not to see China as a completely unique case that is somehow immune from global concerns. In short, besides documenting how 'sex' has emerged as an object of discourse in contemporary China, and with what consequences, we need to situate those changes within a truly global conversation (see Merle 2004).

## Conclusion

At present, a somatic, essentialist view of sex as a predominantly bio-medical fact is the dominant paradigm. Additionally, women are often seen as victims, for instance of prostitution, the media reinforcing this image. In the face of the HIV/AIDS crisis, within this framework, practitioners call for moral control over the sexuality of youths and self-control by men. However, owing to the rapid social changes, other perspectives have emerged. Some researchers uphold a social constructivist view and advocate a rights-based approach to sexuality and gender. Instead of seeing it as a source of oppression, or illness, they promote an understanding of sexuality as a positive force in human lives. Meanwhile, debates are also taking place on the extent to which the study of Chinese sexuality should be permeable to Western influence, vis-à-vis the value given to local and traditional understandings.

I argue for a view broader than the behavior-based concept of sex and sexuality that is currently hegemonic in China. This approach should include an analysis of gender relations (*she hui xing bie*), and take sexual diversity into account, in contrast to the genderless understanding of sex and the asexual understanding of gender characteristic of the currently dominant essentialist model. Moreover, academic practice should have a better sense of concrete local social, cultural, and political contexts, and a respect for subjects' agency and voices. In this effort, the adoption of elements of Western cultures by Chinese society should be regarded as part of those contexts and voices, a result of cultural flows between nations. American and European social theories and ideas on sexuality and gender studies should be critically examined and, if found useful, enriched with the local context.

**2 · Huang**

## Notes

1 This research received support from the Ford Foundation, Sephis; the Fundamental Research Funds for the Central Universities; and the Research Funds of Renmin University of China (10XNJ059, PI: Huang Y.Y.). Special acknowledgments go to Professors Pan Suiming and Elaine Jeffreys.

2 The first such movement came about around the time of the May Fourth Movement (1919), an anti-imperialist cultural and political movement in early modern China which promoted a re-evaluation of Chinese cultural institutions, often linked to societal changes that later became manifest in the beginnings of the Communist Party of China.

3 Dunhuang was the site of the largest complex of ancient Chinese art. About the sexual culture of Dunhuang, see Shi (1999).

4 Tang Dynasty (618–907), Song Dynasty (960–1279), Qing Dynasty (1636–1912). *Li*: Confucian concept often rendered as 'ritual,' 'proper conduct,' or 'propriety.'

5 Han Dynasty (206 BCE–9 CE).

6 For the purposes of this chapter I will not discuss the English literature in detail.

7 'Walking marriage' is a widely used misnomer for romantic and sexual relationships embedded in the culture of the Mosuo ethnic minority of China. The Mosuo call it *tisese*, which translates literally as 'walking

back and forth.' That traditional culture is predominantly matrilineal and matrilocal. Mosuo women open their doors to their lovers every evening, and the men walk home to work in their mother's household every morning. A man is responsible for supporting his sisters' children.

8 In addition, research has been carried out on swing (partner exchange), multi-sexual relationships, one-night stands and sexual narratives in villages.

9 For these debates, see Li and Ma (1999).

10 For details, see Huang et al. (2008).

## References

Boellstorff, T. and W. L. Leap (2004) 'Introduction: Globalization and "new" articulations of same-sex desire,' in W. L. Leap and T. Boellstorff (eds), *Speaking in Queer Tongues: Globalization and Gay Language*, Champaign: University of Illinois Press, pp. 1–21.

Bourdieu, P. (1990) *The Logic of Practice*, Stanford, CA: Stanford University Press.

Cook, N. M. and P. A. Jackson (1999) 'Desiring constructs: transforming sex/gender orders,' in P. A. Jackson and N. M. Cook (eds), *Twentieth-century Thailand, Genders and Sexualities in Modern Thailand*, Chiang Mai: Silkworm Books, pp. 1–27.

39

Dikotter, F. (1995) *Sex, Culture and Modernity in China: Medical Science and the Construction of Sexual Identities in the Early Republican Period*, Hong Kong: Hong Kong University Press.

Fang Gang (2007) *Nan gong guan he nv ke ren guan xi zhong de nan xing qi zhi* [Masculinities among male sex workers], Unpublished PhD thesis, Renmin University of China, Beijing.

Fang Hong (1997) *Foot Binding, Feminism and Freedom*, London: Frank Cass.

Fei Xiaotong (1986) 'Postscript,' in Ai Lishi (Henry Havelock Ellis), *Xing xinlixue* [Sexual psychology], trans. Pan Guangdan, Beijing: San Lian Publications, p. 549.

Finnane, A. and A. McLaren (1999) *Dress, Sex and Text in Chinese Culture*, Clayton, Australia: Monash Asia Institute.

Foucault, M. (1990) *The History of Sexuality: An Introduction*, Reissue edn, London: Vintage.

Gagnon, J. H. and R. G. Parker (1995) 'Introduction: Conceiving sexuality,' in R. G. Parker and J. H. Gagnon (eds), *Conceiving Sexuality: Approaches to Sex Research in a Postmodern World*, New York and London: Routledge.

Gulik, R. van (1990) *Sexual Life in China: A preliminary survey of Chinese sex and society*, Shanghai: Shanghai People's Publishing House.

Harriet, E. (1997) *Women and Sexuality in China*, New York: Continuum.

Henriot, C. (2001) *Prostitution and Sexuality in Shanghai. A Social History, 1849–1949*, Cambridge: Cambridge University Press.

Hershatter, G. (1999) *Dangerous Pleasures, Prostitution and Modernity in Twentieth-century Shanghai*, Reprint edn, Berkeley: University of California Press.

Huang Yingying (2004) *A shi yu B shi fa lang xiao jie de zhuan ye hua shi jian* [Occupational practices of hair salon FSWs in city A and B], in Sun Liqing et al. (eds), *An Anthology of Masters Theses from Peking University, Tsinghua University and Renmin University, 2002–2003*, Shandong: Shandong Renmin Press, pp. 20–45.

— (2008) *Shen ti, xing, xing gan: Zhongguo cheng shi nian qing nv xing de ri cheng sheng huo yan jiu* [Body, sexuality and sexiness: study on Chinese women in daily lives], Beijing: Zhongguo she ke wen xian Publications.

Huang Yingying and Pan Suiming (2003) 'Job mobility of brothel-based female sex workers in northeast China: from laid-off worker to sex worker,' *Studies in Sociology*, 17(3): 51–63.

Huang Yingying, Pan Suiming and Du Juan (2008) *Liudong, xing, ai zi bing fang zhi* [Mobility, sexuality, and HIV prevention: a research report], Gao Xiong: Universal Press.

Huang Yingying, Pan Suiming, Peng Tao and Gao Yanning (2009) 'Teaching sexualities at Chinese universities: context, experience, and challenges,' *International Journal of Sexual Health*, 21(4): 282–95.

Jeffreys, E. (ed.) (2006) *Sex and Sexuality in China*, London and New York: Routledge.

Jiang Xiaoyuan (1995) *Xing zhang li xia de Zhongguoren* [Chinese people under sexual tension], Shanghai: Shanghai Renmin Publications.

Kinsey, A. (1989) *Nan xing xing xing*

*wei* [Sexual behavior in the human male], trans. Pan Suiming, Beijing: Guang ming ri bao Publications.

Ko, D. (2005) *Cinderella's Sisters: A Revisionist History of Foot Binding*, Berkeley: University of California Press.

Lan Dekang (1998) *International Standard Chinese Dictionary*, Beijing: Electronic Industry Publications.

Lang Jinghe (1980) 'Sexual hygiene in new marriages,' *Scientific Pictorial (kexue huabao)*, 1.

Li Dun (1993) *Xing yu fa* [Sex and the law], Henan: Henan Renmin Publications.

Li Ling (1993) *Zhongguo fang shu kao* [Textual research on Chinese divination methods], Beijing: Zhongguo Renmin Publications.

Li Yinhe (1998) *Zhong guo nv xing de qing gan yu xing* [Sexuality and love of Chinese women], Beijing: Zhongguo jin ri Publications.

— (ed.) (2002) *Ku'er li lun: xi fang 90 nian dai xing si chao* [Queer theory: Western theories on sexuality in the 1990s], Beijing: Shi shi Publications.

Li Yinhe and Ma Yinan (eds) (1999) *Hun yin fa xiu gai lun zheng* [Debates on the revision of marriage law], Beijing: Guang ming Daily Publications.

Liu Dalin (1992) *Zhongguo dang dai xing wen hua* [Sexual culture in modern China], Beijing: San lian Publications.

— (1993) *Zhong guo gu dai xing wen hua* [Sexual culture in ancient China], Beijing: Hua xia Renmin Publications

McMillan, J. (2006) *Sex, Science and Morality in China*, New York: Routledge.

Merle, A. (2004) 'Towards a Chinese sociology for "communist civilisation,"' *China Perspectives*, 52: 4–6.

Pan Suiming (1988) *Shenmi de shenghuo* [The mysterious and sacred fire – The social history sexuality], Zheng Zhou: Henan People's Publishing House.

— (1999) *Cun zai yu huang miu* [Existence and absurdity: the study of underground red-light districts in China], Guangzhou: Qun yan chu ban she.

— (2000) *Shengcun yu tiyan, zhongguo hongdengqu kaocha* [Intensive study of a 'red light district' in China], Beijing: China Social Science Press.

— (2005) *Han wei ge ren zun yan: fan dui xin sao yao de ben zhi yi yi* [Defend individual dignity: the meaning of fighting against sexual harassment], www. sexstudy.org/article.php?id=91, accessed 3 February 2005.

— (2006) 'Transformations in the primary life cycle: the origins and nature of China's sexual revolution,' in E. Jeffreys (ed.), *Sex and Sexuality in China*, Routledge Studies on China in Transition, London: Routledge, pp. 21–42.

— (2008) *Zhong guo xing ge ming zong lun* [Sex revolution in China: its origin, expressions, and evolution], Gao Xiong: Universal Press.

Pan Suiming and Huang Yingying (2005) *Xiaojie: Laodong de quanli* [Female sex workers and labour rights in southeastern and northeastern China], Hong Kong: Hong Kong Dadao Press.

— (2007) *Zhuti goujian: Xingshehuixue yanjiu shijiao de geming yiji zai zhongguo bentu de fazhan kongjian* [Subjective construction:

revolution in research on sexuality in China], *Research on Sociology*, 127: 175–92.

Pan Suiming and Yang Rui (2000) *Dangdai dangxuesheng de xingxingwei* [Sexual behavior of all the current Chinese college students], San-lian Publications.

Pan Suiming and Zeng Jing (1999) *Zhongguo dang dai da xue sheng de xing guan nian yu xing xing wei* [Sexual behavior of all the current Chinese college students], Beijing: Shang wu yin shu guan.

Pan Suiming, Huang Yingying and Liu Zhongyi (2008) *Report on Male Clients in China: HIV Risks and Preventions*, Gao Xiong: Universal Press.

Pan Suiming, Bai Willian, Wang Aili et al. (2004) *Dangi dai zhongguoren de xing xing wei yu xing guan nian* [Sexual behaviors and sexual mores of contemporary Chinese people], Beijing: She ke wen xian Publications.

Pei Yuxin (2007) *Xu ni zi wo yu xing zi ben: shanghai nian qing nv xing de wang luo xing jing yan yan jiu* [Virtual self and sexual capital: research on young Chinese women's sexual experience on the Internet], in Huang Yingying and Pan Suiming (eds), *Sexuality Research in China*, Universal Press, pp. 317–40.

Peng Xiaohui (2002) *Xing ke xue gai lun* [Introduction to sexual science], Beijing: Ke Xue Publications.

Public Security Bureau of Beijing (1998) *Beijing fengbi jiyuan jishi* [Document on closing the brothels in Beijing], Beijing: Zhongguo he ping chu ban she.

Ren Jue (2005) 'Cybersex, *Zuo wei yi ge quan xin de xing xue yan jiu ke ti* [Cybersex: a new research topic in sexuality], in Pan Suiming (ed.), *The Start and Mission of Sexuality Research in China*, Gao Xiong: Universal Press, pp. 76–87.

Rong Weiyi and Song Meiya (2002) *Dui zhen dui fu nv de jia ting bao li: zhong guo de li lun yu shi jian* [Fighting against domestic violence against women: theories and practices in China], Beijing: China Social Science Press.

Ruan Fangfu (1985) *Xing zhishi shouce* [Sex knowledge handbook], Beijing: Kexue Jishu Wenxian Publications.

Rubin, G. (1989) 'Thinking sex: notes for a radical theory of the politics of sexuality,' in C. S. Vance, *Pleasure and Danger: Exploring Female Sexuality*, London: Pandora.

Shi Chengli (1999) *Dunhuang xing wenhua* [Dunhuang sexual culture], Guangzhou: Guangzhou Publications.

Sun Liping (2002) 'Analysis of the sociology of practice and the market transition process,' *Journal of Social Science in China*, 137: 83–96.

Tan Dazheng (1998) *Xing wen hua yu fa* [Sexual culture and law], Shanghai: Shanghai Renmin Publications.

Tang Chan (1995) *Xing sao rao zai zhongguo de cunzai: 169 ming nv xing de ge an yan jiu* [Sexual harassment in China: case study on 169 women], *Women's Research Forum*, pp. 31–4.

Tong Ge (2007a) *Zhongguo nan nan xing jiao yi zhuang tai diao cha* [Study on male sex workers in China], Report, Beijing: Ji'ande jian kang zi xun zhong xin.

— (2007b) *Zhongguo ren de nan nan xing xing wei: xing yu zi wo ren tong zhuang tai diao cha* [MSM in China: sexuality and self-identity], Report, Beijing: Ji'ande jian kang zi xun zhong xin.

Vance, C .S. (2003) 'Anthropology rediscovers sexuality: a theoretical comment,' in R. Parker and P. Aggleton, *Culture, Society and Sexuality: A Reader*, London: UCL Press.

Wang Jinling (1998) *Shang ye xing xing jiao yi zhe de xing bie fen xi bi jiao* [Gender analysis of commercial sex traders], *Zhejiang Academic Journal*, 3: 49–53.

Wang Shunu (1988 [1934]) *Zhongguo chang ji shi* [The history of Chinese prostitutes], Beijing: San lian Publications.

Wang Xiaobo and Li Yinhe (1992) *Ta men de shi jie: Zhongguo nan tong xing lian xian xiang yan jiu* [Their world: a study of homosexuality in China], Hong Kong: Cosmos Press.

Wang Xuefeng, Gao Chang and Wang Liguo (2005) *Wo guo xue xiao xing jiao yu de san chong mao dun* [The triple contradiction of sex education in the Chinese school system], *Qing nian tan suo*, 1: 46–8.

Wang Zheng (2006) *She hui xing bie gai nian zai zhong guo* [The application of gender in China], www.bdstar.org/Article/ShowArticle.aspArticleID=3565, accessed 10 September 2011.

Weeks, J. (1985) *Sexuality and Its Discontents: Meanings, Myths and Modern Sexualities*, London: Routledge and Kegan Paul.

Weng Naiqun (1996) *Gu, xing he she hui xing bie* [Gu, sexuality and gender], *Quarterly Journal of Chinese Social Science*, Hong Kong, 16: 42–54.

Wu Cuncun (2002) *Ming qing she hui xing ai feng qi* [Sexual love in the Ming and Qing Dynasties], Beijing: Renmin wen xue Publications.

Wu Jieping (1982) *Xing Yixue* [Sexual medicine], Kexue Jishu Wenxian Publications.

Xu Anqi and Ye Wenzhen (1999) *Zhongguo hun yin zhi liang yan jiu* [Research on the quality of marriage in China], Beijing: China Social Science Publications.

Zhan Chenxu (1980) *Yongning na xi zu de a zhu hunyin he muxi jiating* [A Zhu marriage and matrilineal family], Shanghai: Shanghai Renmin Publications.

Zhang Beichuan (1994) *Tong xing ai* [Same-sex love], Shandong: Shan dong ke ji Publications.

Zhang Kaining (2005) *Ying dui ai zi bing wei ji de gong gong guan li yu gong gong fuwu* [Public management and services in response to the HIV epidemic], Beijing: China Population Publications.

Zhang Meimei (ed.) (1998) *Xing lun li xue* [Ethical issues in sexuality], Beijing: China Social Science Publications.

Zhang Zaizhou (2001) *Ai mei de li cheng: Zhongguo gu dai tong xing lian shi* [Ambiguous course: homosexual history in ancient China], Beijing: Zhong Zhou gu ji chu ban she.

Zhao Jun (2007) *Chengfa de bianjie* [The boundary of punishment], Beijing: China Law Publications.

Zhao Tielin (1999) *Ju jiao sheng cun: piao bo zai dou shi bian yuan de nv hai* [Focused existence – drifting girls in the margins of the cities], Qinghai: Qinghai Renmin Publications.

Zhou Huashan (2001) *Wu fu wu mu de guo du?* [A society without father and husband?], Beijing: Guang ming Daily Publications.

# 3 | The obscene modern and the pornographic family: adventures in Bangla pornography

HARDIK BRATA BISWAS

Good looks do not matter to them, nor do they care about youth; 'A man!' they say, and enjoy sex with him, whether he is good looking or ugly. (Doninger and Smith [1991: 14])

... by running after men like whores, by their fickle minds, and by their natural lack of affection these women are unfaithful to their husbands even when they are zealously guarded ... (Ibid.: 15)

No one should sit in a deserted place with his mother, sister or daughter; for the strong cluster of sensory powers drags away even a learned man. (Ibid.: 215)

A sister was eavesdropping at her elder brother's door. Inside the room, the brother and his wife were talking amorously; ... Just as the husband and the wife had progressed to making love, that wretched sister, outside the room, was suddenly overwhelmed by a desire for sex. She no longer remembered that he was her own brother – and at such a time who, indeed, could think clearly? The door to the brother's room was not locked that day. Crazed and half-naked, the sister rushed in and embraced her brother, her mother's child. (Mitra [1884: 37–8])

## Introduction

*Manusmriti* has been the principal written source of the dominant form of Hinduism for centuries.[1] Satyacharan Mitra's book is an example of a popular Bangla genre of advice manuals from the nineteenth and early twentieth centuries, meant for educating Hindu housewives in the context of emerging nationalist thought under the British colonial regime. The two textual references, from different eras in South Asian history, cannot be missed if one is to explore the location of women and constructions of the obscene by modern Bangla erotica in the print culture. This chapter addresses the discursive creation of a 'new woman,' as expressed in nineteenth-century popular Bengal print erotica, and the form and meaning of the investment in incestuous relations within the Hindu family elaborated by pornographic books and digests published in Kolkata in the past two centuries.

According to classic anthropological scholarship on kinship (Morgan 1877; Lévi-Strauss 1977) and then on to Freud (1961 [1913]), the incest taboo marks the entrance to the order of culture (Meigs and Barlow 2002: 39). In modern societies, rules of exogamic exchange among social groups and heteronormativity maintain and reinforce social domination, particularly in the field of gender relations. Among Bengali Hindu middle classes, culturally dominant since the nineteenth century, sexual exchange is expected to begin after marriage, while marriages are not allowed within the same family or between cousins. In that context, control over women's sexuality is crucial. While divorce is not popular among the working class, contemporary middle-class legally divorced or remarried women are in conflict with notions of chastity and good behaviour.

Since the mid-nineteenth century, undivided Bengal witnessed the growth of a popular print culture, which was coeval to the rise of nationalism and women as a trope for national honor and the purity of the family household. Scores of popular pamphlets and advice manuals for women were published from the late nineteenth to the early to mid-twentieth century. In those, sex without the purpose of procreation – even between husbands and wives – was charted as morally wrong, especially for women. Love was anchored on chastity, purity, and self-restraint. The representation of women in popular print culture as the fulcrum of scandal, mystery, and erotica – underbelly of the apparently prudent Bengali *bhadramahila* (gentlewoman) – produces a stark contrast with the morally pure sartorial presentation of the latter in the Bangla public imagination since the late nineteenth century.

Deriving its meaning from the ancient Greek *porne* (whore) and *graphos* (writing, etching, drawing), the term pornography gained wide currency only in the nineteenth century (Hunt 1996: 10). The *Oxford English Dictionary* included the word in 1857, although in French the word, associated with its modern definition, was in use as early as 1769. One of the earliest occurrences of the term in print is Etienne-Gabriel Peignot's *Dictionnaire critique, littéraire et bibliographique des principaux livres condamnés au feu, supprimés ou censurés* (Paris, 1806). Pornography can be defined as the written or visual realistic rendering of genital or sexual behavior as a deliberate violation of widely accepted moral and social taboos (Wagner 1988: 6). That definition, however, raises the evident classificatory problem of making a distinction between what is received and what is produced as erotic, obscene, or pornographic; and applying it to the variety of print, written, audiovisual, or otherwise sensory representation of the human body over space and time.

The *Oxford Advanced Learner's Dictionary* (OUP 2005: 1046) defines obscenity as connected with sex or extremely large in size or amount, in a way that most people find unacceptable and offensive. It is the attribute of obscenity which qualifies a cultural object or production as pornographic, according to the moral norms and values hegemonic to the context where that production is received. In his study of banned literatures in pre-revolutionary France, Darnton (1985) refers to the pornographic underside or lowlife of Enlightenment literature as often enlisted in the attack on the *ancien régime*. According to Hunt, 'others have postulated a closer relationship between pornography and the Enlightenment's stinging criticism of clerical rigidity, police censorship and the narrowness and prejudices of conventional mores' (1996: 33).[2] The esthetics of the obscene works in ways at times antithetical to the esthetics of the beautiful, provoking a particular, individual, often bodily, response to a specific, not necessarily idealized, object of sexual desire (Pease 2000: 35).

Although popular mid-nineteenth-century erotic series originally produced in English were translated into Bangla,[3] print media investments in pornography were part of the fast growth in popular print cultures in and around Battala, north of Kolkata, and other urban centers in Bengal since the mid-nineteenth century. Bangla definitions, uses, and political meanings of the obscene and the pornographic – much like the idea of an import of Victorian conscience into the 'domesticated inner domain' of the emerging Bengali middle class – call for a more nuanced understanding of colonial modernity. Unlike their early European counterparts, Bangla print literatures classified as obscene or pornographic since the mid-nineteenth century generally did not have explicit modes of enunciation.

## Obscenity and language in nineteenth-century Bengal

The erotic domain had been integral to religious texts, mythologies, hagiographies, and performance traditions in pre-colonial Bengal cultures. As a paradox of colonial modernity, in an attempt to sanitize its cultural inheritance, the new *bhadrasamāj* of Bengal rejected this tradition,[4] and began a crusade against obscene literature as its own illegitimate child. While hardly comparable to European pornography, sexually explicit renderings in print were subject to bitter scorn in the nineteenth century. Carefully separated from the 'pornographic' as 'obscene,' erotic literatures sought acceptance in the cultural main-stream. The introduction of explicitly sexualized, desiring bodies in popular literature marked a redistribution of the erotic and the obscene in esthetic forms. In his address at a public meeting for the creation of the Society for the Suppression of Public Obscenity in Kolkata in 1873, Keshub Chunder Sen, a Brahmo reformer, claimed:

> Are we to believe that every Bengali book is obscene and comes under this Criminal Code? ... The Bidya Sundar (an amorous tale of love between Bidya and Sundar) has often been instanced in support of the arguments of our opponents and considerable anxiety seems to have been felt about the fate of that book in the hands of our society ... [N]ow ... it has been held up as a pattern of Bengali poetry and is exten-sively read as a classical work. We have, therefore, no desire to suppress that book and have made an exception in favour of all classical works of a similar character, not written with the object of satisfying impure cravings. It is however to be deeply regretted that this book blends the purest poetry with the grossest and foulest obscenity ... (Ray 1979: 193)

The earliest experimentations with print books in Bengali are attri-buted to the Baptist missionaries of Serampore.[5] By the early dec-ades of the nineteenth century, Bangla had become the language of a self-conscious generation seeking to find its place in a fast-changing colonial context (Ghosh 2006). With the molding of a new vernacular, the rift between colloquial and genteel language use and form became more prominent.[6] A clientele across caste and other social boundaries of traditional society would later become the massive consumer base of the print cultures that spread around Battala in the nineteenth century. Concerns with purity in language are connected to themes of purity in manners and culture. *Oshlilata* (obscenity) became a main criterion for the cleansing of cultural traditions by the new educated Bengali middle class, creating a sliding scale of difference from the colonizer's repertoire, constructed as alien and infectious.[7] In 1856, an Act was passed to prevent the practice of 'offering for sale to public view obscene books and pictures' that 'encouraged immorality' (Ray 1979: 199). The all-out nationalization drive in the realm of language use was also a crucial factor forcing pre-modern sensual Bengali cultures to go underground. The subaltern elite of the Western-educated, city-bred middle class responded to the ruler's critique of their culture by seeking to rectify itself along dictated lines (Banerjee 1987).[8]

The Bengali expressions branded as obscene by the colonial regime had been an integral part of the region's literary traditions. Folk religious and literary traditions of pre-colonial Bengal, often deriving from original courtly strands, made uninhibited references to the body and its physical aspects.[9] Conversely, in nineteenth-century Bengal, obscenity became more a floating epithet than a precise term of reference. The words *adirasa* (denoting the erotic) and *oshlil* (obscene) were often used interchangeably by critics. Words that became keys of reform movements in Bengal were recent acquisitions of mid-nineteenth-century emerging lexicons. Despite all odds, during the 1874 *Charak* festivities,[10] the *swangs* (bawdy performers using masks, placards, and dresses to mock others) of Kansaripada (the braziers' colony) in north Kolkata managed to bring out a procession lampooning the *bhadralok* (gentleman) and his newly found concept of obscenity. Parading around the streets of Kolkata they sang:

*Shahorey ek notun hujuk*
*Uthhechey re bhai*
*Ashleeleta shabdo mora age shuni nai*

(A new frenzy has taken the city
Never before have we heard the word obscenity)

## The obscene in print

The rise of various print genres classified as obscene was coeval to the arrival of the printing press in Bengal. Contrary to colonial and educated Bengali expectations, this technology introduced an unprecedented democratization of the printed word. Circa 1816, a publishing district began to emerge in Kolkata known as Battala, overlapping with Sonagachi, the largest community of sex workers in the Kolkata region. The popular press, unlike its missionary counterpart, produced volumes of mythological texts, hagiographies, astrological almanacs, plays, idiom horoscopes, and erotic verses roughly until the 1850s. According to a list produced by Reverend James Long,[11] biographies, moral tracts, treatises on education, natural science books, periodicals, *naksha* (satirical prose), *prahashan* (farces), and dailies were regularly published (Long 1855). Simultaneously, Battala produced novels, *kecchha* (scandals), *guptokatha* (mysteries), popular sex periodicals, and erotica. These genres were found unsuitable to the taste of the *bhadralok*, whose sensibility was cast in Victorian morality and tradition, opposed to the effeminate, hedonistic *babu*.[12]

Literature classified as obscene,[13] inspired by Victorian erotic fiction such as the works of George W. M. Reynolds,[14] did a brisk trade and was readily lapped up by readers, selling thousands of copies of books.

Only one pornographic periodical was produced, under the name of *Sambad Rasoraj* (Amatory Briefs), first published on 29 November 1849. Edited by Gaurishankar Tarkabagish, it ran for two years. The circulation of *Sambad Rasoraj* shows the split between public and private as a theme organizing middle-class *bhadralok* sexuality. Among the patrons of this periodical were well-known families of Kolkata, such as the Thakurs, Sinhas, Duttas, Shib Narayan Ghosh, Anada Narayan Ghosh, Khelat Chandra Ghosh, Rasmoy Dutta and others.[15] Stories portrayed the sexual scandals and transgression of the tabooed family ties by forbidden relationships among well-known, well-off families.

### Tracing the obscene in women

The mid-nineteenth-century nationalist project imagined the family as the inner domain of national Bengali culture, closely guarded against colonial state intervention. And women's bodies, like the home, came to be controlled as sites whose sanctity should be maintained. The issue of women's visibility, articulating colonial and pre-colonial moral classifications – including the act of veiling or exposing the face – acquired political import. An anonymous late nineteenth-century *guptokatha* (scandal digest), rather than including a graphic description of sexual intercourse, represents the woman by a series of social attributes expressed by idiomatic expressions and complex metaphors. In these, the woman stereotypically plays the role of either a victim or a coy seductress – a staple of pornography. This is a shift operated in the narratives from nineteenth- to twentieth-century Bangla print pornography.

> I lied to you when I said that he gave me medicine for stomach pain. In reality I was drunk. After you left I lay in stupor. Sometime later I heard someone come into the room. Thinking it to be Govinda I cried out his name. I distinctly remember the man replying 'yes'. I had a blackout and regained consciousness after some time. I found a man sleeping in my bed. He was turned away from me. On closer inspection I realized it was not Govinda but a drunkard. I asked loudly, 'Who are you?' The man did not answer. Instead he sat up suddenly and began to laugh. It was not Govinda nor was it a stranger. Raimoni, it was none other than my own brother, Birchandra. I was ashamed and cried out, 'What have you done brother?'

The sartorial presentation of the female body in particular becomes a powerful signifier of the success and failure of moral regulation, offering scope for controlled sexual expression, as much as for suppression

(Banerji 2001). As in model narratives of European modernity, the rights-bearing bourgeois subject is split into private and public selves. All elements not aligning with laws of public life are eventually assimilated into a structure of private repression (Chakraborty 2000: 143–4). So the private history of the bourgeois subject is constituted by all matters banned from public expression.

Of the 1,400 published Bangla books listed by Reverend James Long in 1855, about thirteen were branded as erotic. He remarked: 'These works are beastly, equal to the worst of the French school!' (Sripantha 1997: 40). A movement against obscenity, taking special issue with Battala print culture, led by respectable Hindu, Brahmo and Islamic social reformers, created the Society for the Suppression of Public Obscenity, established in 1873 at the Calcutta Town Hall. Dr George Smith, inaugurated as chair, remarked that the Society 'shall aid the executive in the suppression of one of the most subtle forms of public vice' (Ray 1979: 179). The *bhadrasamāj* elite was urged to curb the widespread subscription to 'obscene erotica' churned out by the Battala industry. On 21 January 1856, the colonial government of India passed an obscenity law prohibiting commerce in obscene books and pictures, obscene dances in public, songs, and even popular forms of expression such as *panchali*. Until then, despite great effort, censorship by the colonial government could not tame the repressed other of genteel society. Erotic works flourished in the market until the Obscene Publications Act prohibited their sale in 1856. However, from the 1860s onwards, growing numbers of Bengali citizens became sufficiently functionally literate as a result of elementary alphabetization in the vernacular to serve in city government and commerce. Thus a massive readership was ready to consume what the popular and covert press churned out. As *guptokatha* (a sub-genre of popular erotica featuring sexual scandals involving middle-class women) became popular, definitions of what was to be considered undesirable and obscene in literature were often bitterly debated. No consensus was reached.

Although the 1856 Act endeavoring to repress obscene publications did not affect clandestine sales of traditional Battala genres, their appeal fell during the last decades of the century. New tastes and demands on the part of communities exposed to urban life for the first time shaped other forms of obscene literature. Rising industrial cultures and a sexual division of labor contributed to such a process, marked by partial redefinition of family structures, which shaped sensibilities, esthetics, and reading preferences. Myths and fables spun in an earthy and colloquial language, racy and abusive dramas mocking the fallen *bhadralok*, uninhibited accounts of sexuality, were far removed from the Sanskritized and purified world of polite literature (Ghosh 2006).

In Steven Marcus's definition, 'pornotopia' is a utopian space where sexuality regularly moves toward independence of time, space, history, and language itself, where the female body becomes a decontextualized arena of consumption. As sexuality became increasingly sanitized as part of the imagination of a new national self, *guptokathas*, narratives of incestuous adventures, erotica, and sex guides were transformed into what emerged as the twentieth-century pornotopia of the Bengali *bhadralok*. Earlier sensual erotic tales gave way to narratives focusing specifically on forbidden or illicit acts, notably those of incest. Anxiety over the chastity of the *bhadramahila* (gentlewoman) at home, on the one hand, and the demonic, all-pervasive lust of the apparently tame *grihalaxmi* (goddess of wealth and prosperity, as the housewife is commonly symbolized), on the other, became a staple in the formation of twentieth-century Bangla print pornography.

> the babu came prepared to his aunt's place in the morning. His aunt quickly arranged a brunch for the babu in a quiet corner of the house ... at once the babu caught hold of a cucumber and said: 'Aunty, cucumber is delicious, why waste it by cutting it into pieces. It would have been better to have it whole' ...
> Babu: ... There is a magic bed in my garden house. Many women from my family have visited and were excited to see such a thing ... even if a beldame lies there she will be drenching the bed with her matters ... no other bed is as blissful as this ... Dayal Basak did test this with his young grandma and Raj Basak did the same with his complete family ... (Saha 2006: 609–10)

In the early twentieth century, while Battala-based print production saw a steady decline, the market did not remain vacant. As pornographic digests went underground owing to the pressure of the colonial state reformist agenda and of new Hindu nationalism, a new type of sexual literature began to emerge and gain popularity. This shift was mediated through popular sexology. The contents of popular magazines included topics such as prostitution and a scientific approach to sex, addressing issues such as the differences between male and female orgasm and child sexuality. Readers' letters sections addressed sexual problems and concerns about sexual fantasies, which were framed in sexological and psychopathological terms. From the late nineteenth century, scores of books dealing with sexual hygiene, marital sex life, prescriptions for the role and behavior of the Hindu housewife, and pamphlets about sexually transmitted diseases became popular, catering to a new literate colonial readership. Titles like *Venereal Disease* (Haracharan Sen, Kolkata, 1881), *Baigyanik Dampatya-Pranali* (Scientific Methods of Conjugality, Suryanarayan Ghose, Kolkata, 1884) were widely available and ran multiple editions.[16]

Titles like *Maharane Duronto Madan* (God of Love in the Battlefield) were quite popular. Series published around the 1940s in Kolkata fictionalized the sexual exploits of nurses, wives of soldiers on the Second World War front, military brothels, and sex crimes during war (Basu 1941). Magazines published between the late 1940s and the late 1970s were in tune with Nehruvian-era understandings of Indian democracy and development; thus carefully targeted at spicing up the love life of their adult readership. Many popular magazines from the 1950s, such as *Tomar Jiban* (Your Life), had sections on erotic literature (including translations of writers such as D. H. Lawrence) and monochrome or duo-chrome photos of semi-nude women.[17] But by the 1960s and 1970s they were becoming more adventurous. As sections on sexology and psychology faded away, there was an increase in erotic content, including narratives of incest and photo-essays on semi-nude women. Regular features on nudity, sexual frankness, and the sexual explicitness of European art, and especially French and German cinema, were a trademark. By post-emergency times[18] in the late 1970s most of these popular magazines had gone out of circulation.

Bangla pornographic digests since the 1980s show no trace of a sexological twist. Narratives stay within a set formula: a brief introduction that establishes the characters as part of the Bengali middle class, laying out relationships between the characters, which then quickly progresses to sexual intercourse, ending the narrative. The following three excerpts from porn digests between 1998 and 2005 are illustrative of how the narratives lock into a firm setting of the middle-class Hindu household:

*Bheshe Jawa* (Swept Away), by Raja Chakraborty

Rajat Sen was a well established civil engineer. Although nearing thirty he was a handsome man with a good physique. His wife Parna was twenty-four, possessing a slim and sexy figure. Their love affair began in college and culminated in marriage.

At a weak moment Parna had allowed Rajat to push his ten inch long cock into her cunt in the college common room. That first time was both intensely pleasurable and painful. After Rajat landed a good job, Parna was bound to marry him ... Rajat's financial status was no longer an issue. He was now the proud owner of a flat in a posh neighbourhood. He had been provided with a car by the company and drew a handsome salary ...

*Aristocratic Lust*, by Indra Chakraborty

A family of six lived in a beautifully furnished bungalow in CE block Salt Lake. It was a huge bungalow with separate rooms for each member. The owners Mr. Arnab Chatterjee and Mrs. Meenakshi Chatterjee were both placed in high positions in private corporate firms. Their son Kunal was a final year B.Sc (Honours) student while their daughter Sarala was studying for Higher Secondary. The other two occupants of the house were the middle-aged maid Mokkhada Devi and Sipai, the Alsatian pet dog.

No one had time for each other as each was busy in either work or with studies.

They had a colour television with combined audio-video system and CD player in the drawing/living room. The children also had their own personal portable television sets in their rooms.

The wealthy usually led immoral lives. All they ever wanted was to satisfy their cravings and lead a life of pleasure ...

*Nisiddho Abhisaar* (Forbidden Tryst), by Gautam Sadhukha

I am Sanjay Basu, a 23 year old employee of a private firm. I have recently joined this firm, which is a foreign concern ...

There are four members in my family – my mother Malabika (44), my sister Shibani, my father Sudhir (53) and myself.

We were well off. As a family we were quite modern. My father was a businessman. He dealt in iron. He had to travel for four days in a week for work.

My mother Malabika was beautiful, attractive and possessed a sexy figure. Shibani was even more attractive than my mother. Malabika liked to wear revealing clothes. I had often caught my friends staring at her abdomen and bosom which seemed not to fit in her small blouse. I realized that my mother enjoyed the attention. She would deliberately let her saree slip in front of my friends and wore sarees in such a way that her abdomen and navel were revealed. My mother and Shibani behaved like friends with each other ...

Sanjay, Arnab, and Rajat subscribe to the tropes of Bengali middle-class identity, illustrated in pornographic narratives through descriptions of specific urban professions. Acts of sexual transgression often take place in 'self-owned' houses in Kolkata, and characters commonly travel between small towns (where the male protagonist visits relatives, always fulfilling social obligations but duly finding another seductress there) and the metropolis, expanding the network of incestuous adventures by adding, for example, an aunt to a mother–son or father–daughter relationship. In narratives of incest, the woman as object of desire for the male protagonist always resists at the beginning, underlining the fact that sex is prohibited between them. But soon she will succumb to lust, generally presented as greater in the case of women, teasingly inviting her son, son-in-law, brother, father-in-law, or male domestic help to 'devour' her. This 'devouring' in most narratives goes beyond the level of enjoying each other's bodies, to include abusive language (often invited and enjoyed by the women), acting out asymmetrical power relations as means of erotic intensification.

Bandyopadhyay (1999) has noted how the female body, already tamed, gender roles internalized, becomes the proper site of pornographic language. Mid to late twentieth-century Bangla pornography subjects the female body to the double bond of presence and absence (present as a body and absent as a subject). Her subordination is foregrounded, and narratives focus on gender asymmetry by means of her subjection to grids of abuse (ibid.: 29), located within the physical boundaries of the middle-class home and its family. In the stories, the woman character is invariably presented as the eternal vile seductress who brings tension to kinship ties and family life. Such tension invariably leads to scenes of sex choreographed as abuse (*khisti*), where the woman is subject to the desire she has unleashed in the man.

In Bengali print pornography, class conventions seem comparatively more important than caste. Caste is important for marriage, especially arranged marriages, but not always or necessarily. In Bengal, inter-caste marriages, especially between Brahmins and Kayasthas (the non-Brahmin upper caste), are quite common today, although arranged marriages between lower castes and the upper-caste Brahmins or Kayasthas are not so frequent. As compared to northern and southern India, Bengal has comparatively less strict caste taboos. Although the actual rape of *sudra* (low-caste) women by upper-caste men is a common event, such violations are not to be found in most Bengali pornographic narratives, other than through the figure of the consenting voluptuous female domestic help (often depicted as in a poor economic condition, with 'useless' alcoholic husbands who feed on their income). There are almost no explicit narratives of caste taboo violations. In contrast, the figure of the virile young male domestic help or cook seduced by the rich employer's wife is commonplace. The sartorial presentation of the middle-class *bhadramahila* as a cultural fetish is illustrated by the mother, working mother, mother-in-law, daughter, and wife stereotypes.

Whereas nineteenth-century erotica used metaphorical language and symbolic references to body parts and sexual intercourse, late twentieth-century pornographic literature prods the reader's visual imagination through verbal cues, as incest re-enters the scene:

*Deher Kamana* (Lust), by Nabakumar

... He grabbed his mother's arms to prevent her from leaving the room. 'Don't get worked up mom, as I have eaten in the hotel.'

'Let me go, I must rearrange my clothes.'

'I am feeling the pain mother.'

'Everything will be fine son.'

'When will that be? I will be satisfied when I take you there with me.'

'What about your father?'

'You don't need to worry about him. He won't say no to me.'

'I will accompany you if he permits.'

'My darling,' cried he while embracing her.

'Naughty boy, stop this at once, my clothes are undone. You are such a tormentor.' ... His mother was cooking when Ramesh entered the kitchen, 'What are you staring at?'

'I am enjoying the view of the mountains.'

'Where did you find mountains here son?'

'They are here, but I won't tell you.'

'Oh! You naughty boy, go away now.'

'When will I take you to bed?'

'Why must you be so impatient? You are free to enjoy all that you desire whenever you want.'

'You know it's not the same. I want to fully possess you mother.' ...

He enfolded her in his arms and said, 'I want to guttle your bosoms.' Saying these words he began to suck at one breast while caressing the other. Soon she grew excited in his arms.

'Let me go now. The door is open.' She covered her bosoms with her hands and exclaimed, 'What are you doing son?' ... Soon both were completely naked and then ... (Panchosar, Kolkata, n.d., late 1990s)

The narratives in contemporary *panu* (apocopated form for pornography) books and *choti boi* (pocket-sized sex digests) are conceived within the grid of middle-class, educated, family relations. Popular pairings are wife/brother-in-law, mother/son, mother-in-law/son-in-law, brother/sister, aunt/nephew, uncle/niece, young boy next door/housewife,[19] wife/husband's friends, schoolteacher/student, widow/all types of available men in the family, etc. The names in the title of the narratives, as well as writers' pseudonyms, reflect upper-middle-class and caste groups. Related to this domain of discourse, right up to the late 1990s Bengali *panu* as a rule included a brief preface framing the function of sexually explicit literature within the realm of licit sexual relations:

*Preface*

Sex-stories and sex-novels play a special part in the lives of husband-wives. These stories help to overcome the boredom of daily existence. World famous sex scientists such as Dr. Chesar, Dr. Robinson, Havelock Ellis, Marie Stopes, Abul Hasanat, Dr. Swarup and others and many other psychiatrists have spoken about the positive role of such stories in overcoming frigidity in wives and low sex drive in husbands. We will feel that our toil is successful if only these come in handy to married couples.

## Female transgression and the Hindu family

Throughout the twentieth century, pornography remains the well-fed underbelly of the Bangla national male *bhadralok*. The surreptitious production, commerce, circulation, and consumption of *choti boi* (Bangla for footpath sex digests) can be seen as one of the less talked-about private tools of masculinity for a literate Bengali male clientele since the coming of print to the region. Since Battala began publishing texts with sexual overtones and innuendo in the early nineteenth century, narratives have been bound to kinship structures. Sociologist Louis Dumont (1966) has argued that the unity of Indian society lies in the special importance accorded to relations of affinity (relations by marriage) over relations of descent. However, the attempt to classify households into one or another exclusive type obscures the fact that all households undergo a cyclical process of growth and contraction, recruitment and partition. Although nuclear families have long been the predominant family unit in India, the joint family is still an empirically significant household type. Contrary to popular perceptions, it is not in a conspicuous state of disintegration. As evident in two centuries of Indian pornography and print erotica, narratives of transgression within the highly binding structures of the Indian family seem to be the primary fetish for sexual stimulation. As a contradiction at the very heart of social life, the incest taboo is systematically broken in a search for the intensification of sexual sensitivity.

The moral economy of the Indian family requires disciplining in the form of abnegation and self-control. This moral economy of family relations is based on ideals of selflessness, altruism, and duty (Uberoi 2006). In the act of surrendering a daughter to another family, the denial of conjugal love, the sublimation of parental affection, and the constraint on individual autonomy and freedom of choice are seen as sacrifices that are as ennobling of men as of women (ibid.: 32–3). In Bangla pornographic narratives, this moral economy is threatened by the insatiable 'sex-thirst' of the female. Over a span of almost two centuries, those narratives have been curiously selective in the social tensions they dramatize. No prostitutes, 'unholy public women,' take part in such narratives. Furthermore, on the one hand, stories seldom wander out of the threshold of the conjugal chamber; while on the other hand they feature incestuous relations. As evident in these narratives, the family realm – as represented by the home, the conjugal chamber, and kinship ties – acts as the primary site of sexual repression; thus its privilege as a site of moral transgression.

In the process of disciplining and regulating the sexual body that came with imagining an Indian nation, the conjugal unit was internalized – monitored and institutionalized – as the proper site for sexuality. And the burden of control rested on the woman. Naturalized gender hierarchies were projected onto a functional model of sexual intercourse, which justified alternative social roles and moral responsibilities:

> In the natural sexual act of procreation, responsibility of the man is for ten minutes, while that of the woman is for ten months. When nature itself has kept this difference of ten minutes and ten months, how can anyone suggest responsibilities of woman and man are the same? (Kannomal 1923: 34, cited in Gupta 2001: 127)

The belief in a constant, natural, and transcendent difference between the bodies and sexual urges of women and men accentuated the power of the husband over the wife. The man could get away with many wrongs but the woman could not (Gupta 2001: 126–7). A man's mischief could not cause much harm to society, while a woman's fall led to the collapse of family, community, and society (Devi 1924: 3, cited in Gupta 2001). The danger of lustful wants is also discernible in advice literature for women widely available during the same period.

The female protagonists of pornographic narratives are educated, middle-class, well behaved, cultured, caring women, in firm control of their domestic unit, who nurture the habit of reading modern Bangla literature, such as Rabindranath Thakur, but also glossy English periodicals (an 'adult' genre featuring erotic tales and nudity). Their sexual pleasure is portrayed as deriving from the act of transgression, but only by negating their own representational claims to power and authority in Hindu society. This applies to print literature from Bengal, as well as that produced in Indian cities like Allahabad, Banaras, and Agra.

The chastity of the Hindu wife, extending beyond the death of the husband, is constructed as a conscious moral choice, valued as a sign of difference and of superiority, a claim to power on behalf of Hindu communities (Sarkar 2001: 41). Conversely, the transgression of this symbolic value of the Hindu *bhadramahila* is the key to the consumption of Bangla pornographic narratives. As Bandyopadhyay has shown, in contrast to other discursive practices, pornography 'eats its cake and keeps it too': making women docile and voluptuous at the same time. Like other pornographies, and in contrast to 'obscene' nineteenth-century Bangla texts, contemporary Indian pornography does so by splitting the female body into parts which are enumerated and strictly itemized: erotic zones are over-privileged and linked in a metonymic chain (Bandyopadhyay 1999). The representation of the *bhadramahila* whore meant the vanishing of female agency.[20] In the thwarted moral economy of turn-of-the-century nationalism, the emerging *bhadrasamāj* seek discursive refuge in a world of repetitive 'sex without sexuality' (ibid.).

### Violence and the female body in pornographic language

The middle-class *bhadramahila*,[21] located inside the home, within family networks,[22] and tied to the conjugal unit, came out as the prime subject in nineteenth- and twentieth-century erotic and pornographic print. Forbidden liaisons with her kin – both blood and affine – provide a fertile ground for fantasy and lust, while other sites and configurations of sexual liaisons remain practically unexplored. The sequence followed in any given narrative begins by introducing a mother, aunt, daughter-in-law, mother-in-law, sister, or teacher, who, by the end of a narrative exploring the borderlands of sexual transgression, will have become the female embodiment of the abject.

The expulsion of the female body to the terrain of the abject, as represented by the stripping off of all *bhadramahilā* claims to personhood, is performed by means of two parallel operations. On the one hand, the body of the woman is severed into erotogenic parts,[23] which become tangible and reproducible in the form of a decontextualized body. On the other hand, as stories progress into erotically charged ground, violent language, epitomized by the iterated use of the word *khisti*,[24] punctuates the release of erotic tension. By means of repetition, in the discursive space thus created, women are allowed only one identity, that of the whore – fulcrum of unbound and unbinding transgressive desire. Insult and abuse are also a condition by which the female subject is constituted in this language. The woman, whose role as keeper of the moral economy of the family has been sacralized by narratives of national progress, is torn apart by the illocutionary power of the phenomenal violence of men's words (Austin 1976 [1962]; Davidson 1986). Pornographic lust represents women as the 'eternal whore.' Just as the carnivalesque is now missing from Bangla print erotica, the move from nineteenth-century 'modern obscenity' to the twentieth-century 'pornographic family' erased the subjectivity and sexual agency of women, now represented in a simple, repetitive narrative structure of lustful abuse.

The Bengali *bhadralok* and genteel society have, since the years of the nineteenth-century social reforms, invested a great deal of ideological labor in imagining a modern nation while keeping the colonial gendered division of (sexual) labor intact. Bangla print pornography challenges the sexual sanctity of such an apparently tranquil and stable structure. Family, like other tropes subject to interpellation in pornographic narratives, is a product of language and discourse. Just as sexual exchange within specific classes of kin is forbidden, so are particular categories of speech, especially if they threaten an existing social order or the limits of socially accepted sexuality, as represented in the female body. The arena of language in which all such operations take place is part of the discourse that fashions public culture. Social fantasies, particularly those about how one is gendered and sexed, are a basis of any society's symbolic order (Cornell 1995).

As evident in publications from the nineteenth and twentieth centuries, the primary content of Bengali pornographic narratives has been the transgression of the incest taboo. Despite its potential as the individual enjoyment of 'hidden sensations, bringing an underground stream to the surface' (Coward 1984: 97), or the ridiculing of hierarchical, dominant structures – as its early European counterparts did – Bengali pornographic literature iterates the heteronormative structures of family, marriage, and the consumption of women by men. As such there is no turning of the tables; for two centuries men have been symbolically devouring the lustful woman in Bengali pornography. Apparently libertine in its unmasking of middle-class hypocrisy, such narratives symbolize male heterosexual domination as natural and binding. The production of a South Asian pornographic eye through which men look at women's desire as a lustful threat to their dominance and fantasize their submission and desubjectification is the flip side of the rationalized investment in the modern family as the moral bedrock of the Bengali nation.

## Notes

1 Dating from the first century BCE, it was written in the form of edicts of law about a variety of spheres of domesticity. *Manusmriti* is one of the earliest textual sources conceptualizing women in religion and society in India.

2 Diderot was imprisoned in 1749 for writing pornographic prose. In one of his letters he remarked: 'There is a bit of testicle at the bottom of our most sublime feelings and our purest tenderness' (R. F. Brissenden, '*La Philosophie dans le boudoir* or A Young Lady's Entrance into the World,' *Studies in Eighteenth Century Culture*, 1972, 2: 113–41; 124.

3 The popular series 'The Mysteries of the Court of London' by George W. M. Reynolds was one of the earliest scandalous fictions translated and disseminated in Bangla (*kechha/guptokatha* – scandals/mysteries). A few of them are: '*London Rahashya*' (1871) by Haricharan Ray, '*London Rahashya ba Rajparibaraer Guptokatha*' (1898) by Ramjiban Mukhopadhyay, '*Ujir Putra*' (1872–76) by Fakir Chand Basu, '*Haridashir Guptokatha*' by Kaliprasanna Chattopadhyay, and the farce '*Phacke Churir Guptokatha*' (1883) by Shambhunath Biswas.

4 While other idiomatic uses apply to this Bangla word, by *bhadrasamāj* here we refer to the Hindu educated middle class who, since the nineteenth century, came to the forefront of the reformation,

and later of the nationalist movement.

5 In this small Danish settlement near Kolkata, a distinction was promoted between vernacular vulgar and genteel forms, which became more pronounced towards the latter half of the nineteenth century.

6 Early nineteenth-century Kolkata nouveau riche figures like Raja Radhakanta Dev, pundits like Gaurmohan Vidyalankar, and others began the project of purifying the vernacular. Societies and clubs were established to eradicate all vulgarity and baseness from indigenous language and cultures. The rapid rise of the educated middle classes became the public of such societies and readers of rapidly growing literary journals.

7 The missionaries had also sought to correct pre-colonial Bengali cultural life. Oral collective entertainment genres, such as *yatras* (indigenous drama forms), *keertans* (devotional songs), *kabir larai* (urban folk singer contests), *panchalis* (mythological narratives), *kathakata* (narration), and sensual dance forms of *jhumur* and *khemta* had all been under new scrutiny. Dialectal speech and other cultural expressions manifested a robust sense of humor, as an openly sexual and frank celebration of the sensual and the erotic.

8 Bankimchandra Chattopadhyay, a pioneer of this reformist drive,

acting as editor of *Bangadarshan*, a Bengali periodical of repute, acclaimed the efforts of the Society for the Suppression of Public Obscenity in India. The periodical became the voice of the Bengali literati. According to Ghosh, 'From 1872 onwards, it embarked firmly on a mission to shape a refined literature that could be the pride of the nation, and fit for the taste of the educated reader' (Ghosh 2006: 88).

9 Radha-Krishna love lyrics, mythical events in *Puranas* and *panchalis*, ballads spun around smallpox deities and snake goddesses, all involved the sensuous, diseased, fecund, and decaying human form. Continuing the tradition of extant manuscript traditions, the early Battala publications that assaulted the *bhadralok*'s esthetic sensibilities displayed a frank sensuality, which then came to be regarded as erotic.

10 A popular carnivalesque religious festival with a huge participation from the common, working and non-elite classes.

11 The figure of Reverend James Long was in many ways one of the most decisive influences shaping the future of Bengali literary cultures during this period. Long was an Irish missionary, a member of the Church Missionary Society. He came to Kolkata in 1840. He participated in several prominent literary societies in the city, including the Bengal Social Science Association, established in 1866, the Bethune Society, the Family Literary Club, and the British India Society. Long was also responsible for compiling several valuable reports on the vernacular press and print literature in Bengal for the government, and collecting a rare cache of rural Bengali dialectal expressions.

12 Nineteenth-century Bengal dandy.

13 Some titles were *Dyutibilash* (The Amorous Tale of the Female Messenger) (1825), *Badmashjabdo* (The Villain Treated Right), *Beshya Guide* (Guide to Prostitutes), *Beshya Bibaran* (Describing the Prostitute), *Ruptan Bibir Kecchha* (The Scandal of Ruptan Bibi), *Ramaniranjan* (Pleasuring Women), *Rasotarangini* (Amorous Waves), *Sambhogratnakar* (Sex: A Treasure Trove), *Beshya rahashya* (The Mysteries of the Prostitute), the serialized scandals of the royal family of Sobhaabazar in north Kolkata, *Amar Gupto Katha* (My Secret Stories) (1871), *Haridas er Gupto Katha* (The Mysteries of Haridas, by Bhubanchandra Mukhopadhyay), *Udashini Rajkumarir Gupto Katha* (The Mysteries of the Love-lost Princess), *Bankim Babur Gupto Katha* (The Mysteries of Bankim Babu), *Kulokalankini ba Kalikatar Guptokatha* (The Infidel Wife or the Mysteries of Kolkata), by Panchanan Roy Chowdhury (published by Tarinicharan Basu in 1900).

14 Some of Reynolds's titles were *The Mysteries of the Court of London* (1848–56), *The Lustful Turk* (1820), *Rosa Fielding, or a Victim of Lust* (1876), *The Amatory Experiences of a Surgeon* (1881) and *Randiana* (1884).

15 *Sambad Rasoraj*, 31 August 1849.

16 *A Treatise on the Science and Practice of Midwifery with Diseases of Children and Women*, by Annadacharan Khastagir (Kolkata, 1878), describes in detail the masturbatory habits of young women in rural Bengal. Considering it a morally and physically damaging practice, the publication prescribes prevention and cure.

17 The period from 1951 to 1975

saw titles such as *Tomar Jiban* (Your Life, 1950, 1951), *Sundar Jeevan* (Good Life, 1973), *Jiban Jouban* (Youth and Life, 1970, 1974, 1967), *Rangini Nayika* (Colorful Heroine, 1970), *Nayika Sangini* (Escort Heroine, 1972). These popular magazines had registration numbers from the office of the registrars of newspapers in New Delhi, a printer's page, and were bound in double demy format, including quality monochrome half-tone block photos and line drawings. Typefaces used were of average quality.

18  Under Article 352 of the Constitution of India elections and civil liberties were suspended during a twenty-one-month period in 1975–77.

19  In Bengali communities, certain neighbors are granted semi-familial relational status.

20  In a piece of nineteenth-century Bengali erotica, a female voice was represented singing:

Esho jadu amar badi,
Tomay dibo bhalobhasha
Je ashay eshecho jadu,
Purno hobe mono asha
Amar nam Hire malini
Korey randi neiko shami

(Come home, my darling, I'll show you love. You'll get, my darling, what you have come here for. My name is Hira the flower-seller. I've been a widow since I don't have any husband) (Banerjee 1989: 42).

21  *Bhadramahila*, the female equivalent of *bhadralok*, can therefore be translated as gentlewoman. Both the terms gained wide currency with nineteenth-century social reforms, which brought English education to the Bengali cultural forefront.

22  The words *kutumb*, *parivar*, *kula* and *vamsa*, as polysemic as the word 'family' in English, blur the distinction between family and lineage (Shah 1998).

23  *Buk/mai* (breasts), *pacha* (buttocks), *gud* (vagina), *pet* (torso), etc.

24  The utterance of Bangla words and phrases such as *randi* (prostitute, widow), *gudmarani maagi* (damned whore), *khankir beti* (daughter of a whore), *bokachudi* (ass-fucker), *khanki maagi* (woman whore), *kutti* (bitch), along with numerous other colloquial terms normally deemed offensive, usually punctuates the climax in pornographic narratives. Syntax and language target the woman as the focus of verbal violence. Women characters portrayed as tame creatures often solicit *khisti* (abuse) from the man, either in foreplay or during the coital climax.

## References

Altekar, A. S. (1959) *The Position of Women in Hindu Civilization: From Prehistoric Times to the Present Day*, 2nd edn, New Delhi: Motilal Banarsidass Publishers.

Austin, J. L. (1976 [1962]) *How to Do Things with Words: The William James Lectures Delivered at Harvard University in 1955*, ed. J. O. Urmson and M. Sbisa (eds), Oxford: Oxford University Press.

Bandyopadhyay, S. (1999) 'The discreet charm of the bhadraloks: an excursion into pornotopia,' *Margins: of Knowledge, Body and Gender*, August, 21–37.

Banerjee, S. (1987) 'Bogey of the bawdy: the changing concept of "obscenity" in nineteenth century Bengali culture,' *Economic and Political Weekly*, XXII(29): 1197–206.

— (1989) *The Parlour and the Streets: Elite and Popular Culture in Nineteenth Century Calcutta*, Kolkata: Seagull Books.

Bannerji, H. (2001) *Inventing Subjects: Studies in Hegemony, Patriarchy and Colonialism*, New Delhi: Tulika Books.

Bose, B. (ed.) (2006) *Gender and Censorship*, New Delhi: Women Unlimited.

Butler, J. (1997) *Excitable Speech: A Politics of the Performative*, New York: Routledge.

Chakraborty, D. (2000) *Provincializing Europe: Postcolonial Thought and Historical Difference*, New Delhi: Oxford University Press.

Chatterjee, P. (1999) *The Partha Chatterjee Omnibus*, New Delhi: Oxford University Press.

Cornell, D. (1995) *Abortion, Pornography and Sexual Harassment*, New York: Routledge.

Coward, R. (1984) *Female Desire*, London: Paladin.

Darnton, R. (1985) *The Literary Underground of the Old Regime*, Boston, MA: Harvard University Press.

Davidson, D. (1986) 'A nice derangement of epitaphs', in R. E. Grandy and R. Warner (eds), *Philosophical Grounds of Rationality: Intentions, Categories, Ends*, Oxford: Oxford University Press, pp. 157–74.

Devi, Y. (1924) *Aadarsh Pati-Patni aur Santati Sudhar*, 2nd edn, Allahabad.

Doniger, W. and B. K. Smith (1991) *The Laws of Manu*, New Delhi: Penguin.

Dumont, L. (1966) 'Marriage in India: the present state of the question III. North India in relation to South India,' *Contributions to Indian Sociology*, 9: 90–114.

Freud, S. (1961 [1913]) *Totem and Taboo*, vol. 13, ed. James Strachey, London: Hogarth Press.

Ghosh, A. (2006) *Power in Print: Popular Publishing and the Politics of Language and Culture in a Colonial Society, 1778–1905*, New Delhi: Oxford University Press.

Giddens, A. (2007) *The Transformation of Intimacy: Sexuality, Love and Eroticism in Modern Societies*, Cambridge: Polity.

Gupta, C. (2001) *Sexuality, Obscenity, Community: Women, Muslims, and the Hindu Public in Colonial India*, New Delhi: Permanent Black.

Hunt, L. (1996) *The Invention of Pornography: Obscenity and the Origins of Modernity, 1500–1800*, New York: Zone Books.

Lévi-Strauss, C. (1977) *The Elementary Structures of Kinship*, Boston, MA: Beacon Press.

Long, J. (1855) *A descriptive catalogue of Bengali works: containing a classified list of fourteen hundred Bengali books and pamphlets which have issued from the press during the last sixty years, with occasional notices of the subjects, the price, and where printed*, Calcutta: Sanders, Cones and Co.

Marcus, S. (2009) *The Other Victorians: A Study of Sexuality and Pornography in Mid-Nineteenth-Century England*, New Brunswick, NJ: Transaction Publishers.

Meigs, A. and K. Barlow (2002) 'Beyond the taboo: imaging incest,' *American Anthropologist*, New Series, 104(1): 38–49.

Morgan, L. H. (1877) *Ancient Society*, New York: Henry Holt.

OUP (2005) *Oxford Advanced Learner's Dictionary of Current English*, 7th edn, New Delhi: Oxford University Press.

Pease, A. (2000) *Modernism, Mass Culture, and the Aesthetics of Obscenity*, Cambridge: Cambridge University Press.

Ray, A. (ed.) (1979) *Society in*

*Dilemma: Nineteenth Century India*, Kolkata.

Raychaudruri, T. (2000) 'Love in a colonial climate: marriage, sex and romance in nineteenth-century Bengal,' *Modern Asian Studies*, XXXIV(2): 349–78.

Rousseau, J. J. (1991 [1762]) *Emile, or On Education*, Harmondsworth: Penguin.

Saha, A. (2006 ) 'Bhagnangsher "Jounotopia"? Ekti ashampurno pratibedan ...' *Sharadiya Anustup*, Kolkata, pp. 609–44.

Sarkar, T. (2001) *Hindu Wife, Hindu Nation: Community, Religion and Cultural Nationalism*, New Delhi: Permanent Black.

Shah, A. M. (1998) *The Family in India: Critical Essays*, Hyderabad: Orient Longman.

Sinha, M. (1997) *Colonial Masculinity: The 'manly Englishman' and the 'effeminate Bengali' in the Late Nineteenth Century*, New Delhi: Kali for Women.

Sripantha (1984) *Mohanto-Elokeshi Sambad*, Kolkata: Ananda Publishers.

— (1988) *Keyabaat Meye*, Kolkata: Ananda Publishers.

— (1997) *Battala*, Kolkata: Ananda Publishers.

Uberoi, P. (2006) *Freedom and Destiny: Gender, Family, and Popular Culture in India*, New Delhi: Oxford University Press.

Wagner, P. (1988) *Eros Revived: Erotica of the Enlightenment in England and America*, London: Secker & Warburg.

Walsh, J. E. (2004) *Domesticity in Colonial India: What Women Learned When Men Gave Them Advice*, New Delhi: Oxford University Press.

## Sources

Basu, N. (1941) *Maharane Duronto Madan: Goto Europio Mahajuddher Jouno Itihash*, Kolkata: Katyayani.

Choudhury, G. R. (1895) *Grihalaxmi*, vol. II, Kolkata: Bannerjee Dutta & Co.

— (1897) *Grihalaxmi*, 10th edn, vols I and II, Kolkata: Kedarnath Basu.

Gupta, N. (2009) *Phutonto Mallika*, Dhaka.

Jain, S. (2002) *Nayika*, Kolkata.

— (2003) *Sharadiya 2003 Tonumon – Bibahito Naranarider Jonno*, Kolkata.

Sundar Jibon (1968) Vol. II, no. IV, Kolkata.

Mitra, S. (1884) *Strir prati Sāmir Upadés*, Kolkata.

Mukhopadhyay, B. (1897) *Haridasher Guptokatha*, 4 vols, Kolkata: Biswabani Prakashan.

Panchosar (1990s) Kolkata.

Raychaudhury, P. (1900) *Kulokalan-kini ba Kolikatar Guptokatha*, Kolkata: Tarinicharan Basu.

Reynolds, George W. M. (1851) *The Mysteries of the Court of London*, vols I, III, 2nd series, London: John Dicks.

Saradiya Tanumon (2003) Kolkata.

Saradiya Ramani (2001) Kolkata.

Sambād Rasarāj, no. 12 (May 1849), no. 13 (May 1849), no. 25 (July 1849), no. 30 (July 1849), no. 31 (July 1849), no. 32 (July 1849), no. 34 (August 1849), no. 62 (November 1849), no. 63 (November 1849), no. 64 (November 1849), no. 66 (December 1849).

# 4 | Sexing the nation's body during the Cuban republican era[1]

ABEL SIERRA MADERO

## Introduction

In 1902, as Cuba became a republic after US intervention in the Cuban independence war, the old institutional structures of the Spanish colonial domination were dismantled and replaced with direct involvement in local affairs by the USA. The accelerated process of modernization of Cuban society that ensued did not go uncontested, as this new order reignited debates that had taken place over national sovereignty in the island's public sphere under neocolonial rule. Such debates were often framed in moral terms, whereby gendered and sexed representations of the Cuban nation embodied challenges to national honor faced under Spanish colonial rule before independence, and under US imperialism thereafter. The national body has been presented as analogous to the human body, with well-defined shapes and borders, with erogenous places and abject zones. Iglesias (2003: 102) highlights the role of both the internal and foreign 'other' in public-discourse articulations of the nation and its boundaries in turn-of-the-century Cuba. Visions of self originally constructed in opposition to Spanish colonialism were being reshaped, involving a new 'other' – US imperialism.

In the first decades of the Cuban republican era (1902–59), metaphors of the national body took hold as powerful symbolic markers of national sovereignty (ibid.). By analysing newspaper articles and literary works from the first decades of the twentieth century, in this chapter I examine public discourses about two particular sexual 'others': *pepillitos* and *garzonas*. The former were men and the latter were women who adopted a cosmopolitan lifestyle, modernist esthetics and unconventional gender performance. As public persons, they came to signify ideological threats to the moral integrity of the nation. I explore how gender and sexuality operated in defining and regulating notions of nationality and sovereignty in Cuba during that period. I will argue that *pepillitos* and *garzonas*, as figurations of a homoerotic subject, conceived from a hygienic perspective, represented a threat to the sovereignty, the stability, the progress, and the defense of the Cuban nation.

In the first section of this chapter, I explore the overlapping of sexual and political otherness through analysis of press representations of *pepillitos* and *garzonas*. The moral anxieties elicited by the presence of *pepillitos* in urban life illuminate the role of gender relations and (hetero)sexuality as key assets for the construction of Cuban national identity. Debates on the visibility of *garzonas* reveal the salience of feminist politics in the public sphere of republican Cuba, and how the boundary between feminist convictions and female homoerotic identities was being negotiated at the time.

Sommer (1993) has shown the workings of literature as a discursive system through which the nation is symbolically constructed by re-creating Spanish America's foundational fictions. In the second section of this chapter, I look at discursive constructions of homoeroticism in two novels published in Cuba during the same period, *Hombres sin mujer* (Men without Women, 1938) by Carlos Montenegro, and *La vida manda* (Life Commands, 1929) by Ofelia Rodríguez Acosta. Both signal the introduction of homoeroticism as a theme in Cuban literature, subject to ideological regulation by the dominant discourse on the sexuality of the national body.

## The press campaign against *pepillitos* and *garzonas*

In 1928, the Cuban press launched a campaign that connected nation, gender, and sexuality in the public sphere of the republic. Journalist Sergio Carbó used his column in the daily satirical newspaper *La Semana* while Mariblanca Sabas Alomá used hers in *Carteles* weekly magazine to appeal to the public to fight against two urban trends: *pepillismo* and *garzonismo*, which – by virtue of their campaign – were soon to become the focus of a public debate. Carbó recycled and fabricated a modern version of the nineteenth-century Cuban-style dandy: the *pepillito*. The term acquired a pejorative connotation, becoming an insult to male honor and dignity. *Pepillos*, or *yonis*, *yulis*, *cuchis*, *bebis*, *yeyos*, *vaselined hair*, *affected*, *feminine*, *dummies*, as they were also called, were harassed in the name of public morality and good customs; but above all in the name of the nation.

Carbó was chief editor of *La Semana*, a nationalist, anti-North American newspaper openly against the Machado regime.[2] In his daily satirical column *Majaderías del director* (Editor's impertinences), he implacably criticized the government and public officers. On 20 June 1928, *La Semana* started a press campaign by publishing a series of texts and images lashing out against *'pepillismo.'* Carbó described it in his column as 'a type of leprosy that threatens national dignity,' corrodes 'the social structure' and sends 'its miserable tentacles inching along the future of the country, threatening to sink institutions, smear criollo virility, and drag the nation's sovereignty to an abyss ...'(Carbó 1928b: 7). He went on: 'We have to make their air unbreathable. Let's ridicule them, let's press our palms against our mouths and squeeze the air out as an ear trumpet because by doing so we shall also be contributing to forging our homeland ...' (La Semana 1928: 19).

Carbó's morally charged description presents the *pepillito* as

a human dummy, groomed as a chorus girl, dressed in big check suits, and flaunting a clean shaved, powdered, almost livid face. He usually has no manners or hat, and rubs – and this is his most striking feature – loads of hair Vaseline on his head to facilitate the black pressed shiny hairdo which is his pride, his faith and his reason for living ... The 'pepillito' is hardly ever alone, he flocks in large groups, like the Florida ducks: he is a collective that renders its maximum efficiency belching out rude compliments, and congesting traffic in centre thoroughfares and theatre entrances ... The condition of the 'pepillito' is basically moral ... lacking in virility per se, 'virility' as a superior virtue, differentiated not only by the biological sex but also by the integrity of the spirit. They are imbued with a narcissistic almost feminine coquettish manner, and have no other concern than organizing 'tea parties,' and attending balls and sports events. (Carbó 1928b: 7)

Carbó's columns, starting with the above text, exalt the values of national masculinity and underscore his indignation at the servile assimilation of US cultural colonialism by the Cuban government and sectors of the public. 'The children of some of the most illustrious and vigorous Cuban men of our Republic are "pepillitos"' (ibid.: 7). The esthetic confrontation set up by the writer praises the autochthonous elements of Cuban masculinity, characterized by 'gallant seriousness.' Thus, wearing a hat – as opposed to a bare, greased-hair head – suggests the distinction and temperance being vulgarly usurped by those whose manners are alien to the traditional *criollo* virility, which 'shelters in its heart something more dignified than a chequered suit or a five o'clock tea party with Dorothy, Charles, Bobby and Tony ...' (Carbó 1928a: 7). With a hint of irony, Carbó calls for presidential intervention to do away with *pepillitos*, symbolic of Machado's failure to restore Cuba's national pride:

If I were the President of the Republic – this is an initiative that I allow myself to suggest to General Machado – I would suppress, in the name of public health, the practice of rowing, and tennis, but most of all the use of hair Vaseline, in order to contribute to the extermination of the *pepillitos*, those impudent dummies who are depriving our homeland of all its traditional virile energy, its fecund audacity and glory – all necessary virtues in the current, transitional and reconstructive stage in which our country is presently immersed. (Carbó 1928b: 7)

By opposing *pepillismo* to the 'regenerative' policy needed to reconstruct the country, Carbó criticized Machado's government's servile attitude toward the USA. In Carbó's view, that contrasted with President Machado's personal history as a general with the National Liberation Army. As he noted, 'The generation that founded the Republic was made up of warriors, the one that followed was made up of politicians and businessmen: the present one is splittingly *pepillistica*' (ibid.: 7).

In the aftermath of the independence wars, Carbó was the depository of a discourse that held the war hero as an ideal man. According to George Mosse (1985), such a conception corresponds to an ideal of masculinity dear to modern societies in need of order and progress.[3] Figures like the *pepillito* represent 'a countertype that would serve to increase [national] self-confidence as it emerged into the modern age' (ibid.: 77). Configuring what Mosse (ibid.: 77) called the 'militarization of masculinity,' Carbó's narrative opposes *pepillitos* – whose very existence is a threat to the future of the nation – to Cuban youths ready to get up in arms to fight for the nation:

... these ridiculous dummies of short jackets and thin well-groomed moustaches, pseudo athletes and pseudo men, are being kept within bounds by the implacable denunciations of LA SEMANA ... whose serious efforts [as usual] aim to wipe them out of the national scenario, while arousing disgust and indignation from Cuban youth, the true Cuban youth, who will take up arms in the event of another war of independence ... (Carbó 1928a: 7)

On the other hand, with reference to women, Mosse (1985: 8–9) observes:

As national symbols, however, [they] did not embody generally valid norms such as the virtues that masculinity projected but, instead, the motherly qualities of the nation, and pointed to its traditions and history. ... Woman as a public symbol was a reminder of the past, of innocence and chastity ...

*La Semana*, like other national publications, often depicted Cuba as a woman dressed in the colors of the national flag and occasionally wearing the Phrygian hat that tops the national coat of arms. In the sacralization of the nation as a feminine body performed by this image, it is man's mission to safeguard her honor and the values deposited in her. The disapproval of *pepillismo* also predicated the failure of lesser men to fulfill their duty as guardians of the motherland. '*Pepillitos*,' says Carbó, 'do not fight for or defend women ... and this is not to say that they are *effeminate in the worst sense of the word*, but rather that they are less than men' (emphasis added). Here, 'effeminate in the worst sense of the word' is a euphemism for homosexual, which, according to Carbó, 'is merely separated from all of the above by a very thin wall' (Carbó 1928a: 7).[4] He blamed such behavior on the strong attachment of certain children to their female nurturers – a narrow line indeed.

The impact of Carbó's writings on *pepillitos* was still felt some time after *La Semana* published its last editorial on the topic. On 5 August 1928, *Carteles* magazine, edited by Alfredo T. Quilez, published two pieces, one authored by Cuban intellectual Emilio Roig de Leuchsenring and the other by his alter ego, *El curioso parlanchín* ('The prying chatterbox'), one on *pepillotes*, and the other on *pepillitos*. In his texts, Roig de Leuchsenring (1928: 22) praised Carbó's prose as rare in that it 'has not yet succumbed to the big backyard of temptations that has become our island, as a result of a servile, backslapping, effeminate spirit.' Although Roig de Leuchsenring (ibid.: 22) acknowledged the pro-phylactic value of Carbó's intervention for the sake of social hygiene, he warned that 'the *pepillito* is not the most pernicious type that affects our poorly baptized Republic.' According to the Havana historian, the *pepillito* was 'no more than a poor devil, a ridiculous dummy ...' (ibid.: 22), as compared to *pepillotes*. In Roig de Leuchsenring's essay (ibid.), the superlative (*pepillote*) applied to the privileged class of lawyers, doctors, professors, and writers who had joined Machado's entourage and supported his servile policy. Whereas the *pepillito* sought to stand out in his dress and manners, what made the *pepillote* a greater threat to the future of the nation is that they passed for patriots and men of integrity. To Roig de Leuchsenring, the unmanly spirit of *pepillismo* lurked under the hypocritical façade of pro-American statesmen.

Along with Carbó and Roig de Leuchsenring, Mariblanca Sabas Alomá, a prominent Cuban feminist activist at the time,[5] joined the press crusade with a series of articles published in *Carteles* magazine in April 1928 – compiled in Sabas Alomá (2003). The first article, '*Pepillitos* and *garzonas*,' contributed to the uncloseting of female homosexuality – then referred to as *garzonismo* – and thus to the construction of a female homoerotic subject. *Garzonas* were caricatured by Sabas Alomá as 'sterile women rotted by masculinity,' and an affront to civilized progress. Recognizable by their manly manners, *sportif* in appearance, with 'hair styled in boyish bobs,' they were considered biological degenerates, 'decadent by-products of a corrupt, vicious, republican capitalist society and would disappear with the advent of socialism' (ibid.: 102).

Sabas Alomá set her feminism clearly apart from *garzonismo*. We, she said, 'are naturally suited to reproduction and have been entrusted that vital mission to preserve the species,' as feminism's main postulate is '*to make men more men by making women more women*' (ibid.: 62). The text is an expressive vehicle to articulate a nonconformist feeling by a majority that had been hurt 'in their human integrity.' The texts on *garzonismo* come as an antidote to that 'sickening sexual disease.' The writer justified a collective feeling of repulsion toward these women, 'where the man who could not be a man and the woman who did not know how to be a woman are fused and confused' (ibid.: 62). Applying the psychiatric theories of degeneration circulating at the time, which differentiated innate and acquired 'sexual inversion,' Sabas Alomá (ibid.: 62) speculated 'that 90% of our tropical garzonas are not as affected by a biological predisposition as by the poor education and instruction they received.' Likewise, the common belief popularized by psychiatrists at the time was that lesbianism was the result of unfulfilled relations with men.[6]

As Carbó's writings warned about *pepillismo*, Sabas Alomá (ibid.: 62) denounced the danger *garzonismo* represented, which had to be readily fought in the name of 'normal people' who 'repudiate a social evil that so gravely affects the good development of the human species and the collectivity.' Cuban youth in particular was to be protected from the social and political disasters caused by sexual inversion – whose seed was planted by the local acolytes of US imperialism. The future of the nation called for the preservation of the 'natural' sexual and gender order, whereby 'a masculinized woman, like an effeminized man, becomes a pathological condition' (ibid.: 62).

The debate on *garzonismo* had special value to the feminist movement, which had attained some political objectives by this time. In 1917, women were granted parental rights over their children after remarriage or widowhood, as well as the right to administer their wealth. A year later, the divorce law was sanctioned (Pichardo 1983: 339). Cuban women hosted two congresses, in 1923 and 1925, which debated suffrage, the recognition of illegitimate children, feminism, and the role of women in society.[7] Women's suffrage was a hotly debated issue in the late 1920s,[8] together with women's integration into the labor force and 'free love.' The issue of women's citizenship, raised by mostly white, elite women, was nonetheless challenged by the more conservative sectors of Cuban society, for whom progress depended on men and women sticking to their traditional roles. It was in this context that Cuban feminists launched a public vindication of feminism of homophobic overtones.

Sabas Alomá refused to consider lesbianism as a feminine sexual variant, and she disagreed with both Freud's psychoanalytical and Marañón's sexological theories about the etiology of homosexuality. Nevertheless, she shared some points of view with the latter, who had lectured in Cuba in 1927. Marañón had criticized the inequality of men and women before the law and advocated equal rights and opportunities for women. Sabas Alomá (2003: 104) cited him stating that women 'have all intellectual and social avenues opened, but above all, women have to behave in a more womanly manner every time' (Marañón 1928b: 216). For Sabas Alomá, *garzonismo* or lesbianism is primarily a socioculturally induced condition. The metaphors she used to describe what she considered a social evil evoke ideas of moral corruption associated with gender inversion. She viewed *garzonas* as 'sores,' 'escape valves,' 'pestilent viruses that corrode the entrails of humanity' (Sabas Alomá 2003: 103). By means of this discursive operation, a legitimate feminist subject was reconstructed through an exaltation of positive feminine values that mirrored the hyperbolic projection of deviant masculine features upon *garzonas*. *Garzonismo* is to feminism, she stressed, 'as antagonistic as *pepillismo* is to masculinity. The *garzona* is an inferior woman as much as the *pepillito* is an inferior man' (ibid.: 105). For Sabas Alomá, lesbianism was the equivalent of 'lust,' 'wantonness,' 'sexual deviation,' and 'social irresponsibility.' However, there was a further qualitative difference, she wrote:

> Undoubtedly, the *pepillito* can be more easily eradicated from the human scenario than the *garzona*. *Pepillitos*' masculinity lies anesthetized somewhere; under that apparently dormant, moral, mental, and spiritual decadence there still lives a man. But in the case of the *garzona*, the woman, the female for whom the sacred mission of preserving the species was commanded by nature, is dead. When the female surrendered in despair under the despotic power of *garzonismo*, she aborted all possibility of carrying the seed of a new life inside her.

If impregnated, her womb can only give birth to a creature marred by vices and sexual lewdness. Probably neither a *garzona* nor a *pepillito* will be born, because they are fashioned by what we could call 'external life,' regardless of their intimate bodily contextures. However, *candidates* will be born, who will have greater chances of being assigned those two humiliating denominations. (Ibid.: 105–6)

Journalistic writing of the period reveals, if not 'tolerance' of male homosexuality, at least not the overt repulsion against lesbianism expressed in Sabas Alomá's writing. However, public treatment of lesbian identity virtually starts with the publication of these articles. The public visibility of *garzonas* subverted the heteronormative scripts that subordinated female desire to domesticity, maternity, and the holy matrimonial institution. To Sabas Alomá (ibid.: 105), when she abandons 'the mission of preserving the species,' the *garzona* 'is murdering the woman.'

In parallel with psychiatric conceptions regarding male homosexuality, Sabas Alomá conceptualizes female homosexuality as sexual and gender 'inversion.' According to that postulate, the attributes of the opposite sex are usurped and performed in public in an exaggerated manner by the 'inverted' person. It is that public manifestation which is regarded as a challenge to social order and the progress of Cuban society. Conversely, the least conspicuous homoerotic behavior remains outside of this discursive regulation of sexuality, as it does not invade the public arena.

In his novel *La Garçonne*, French writer Victor Margueritte (1926) situated *garzonismo* historically as a post-war product, a transition between the traditional feminine and the truly emancipated woman.[9] In an effort to cleanse feminism of any trace of gender or sexual inversion, Sabas Alomá (2003: 104) refuted any possible association between the latter and *garzonismo*:

> The garzona, far from being a phase of feminism, thrives in spite of feminism. Because feminism is not, and will never be a generating matrix of that 'masculinized' woman ... Quite the contrary, feminism is the exultation of the noblest and highest attributes of femininity; it sustains the progressive betterment of the species and embraces a humanistic fidelity, essentially maternal to the full, straight and firm extent of the word.

After the article on '*Pepillitos* and *garzonas*' was published, *Carteles* began to receive and publish letters addressed to Sabas Alomá, initiating a public debate. On 5 April 1928, the same day the text was published, Leticia de Arriba de Alonso, Marquise of Tiedra, treasurer of the Alianza Nacional Feminista (National Feminist Association), wrote a note to Mariblanca Sabas Alomá thanking her for the article and supporting its postulates. The *garzonas*, said the marquise, are an assault against the progress and reasoning of the species (De Arriba, cited in ibid.: 109).

Several days later, on 13 April 1928, the journalist received another letter, signed by Flora Díaz Parrado, which – together with Margueritte's novel – reveals the diversity of perspectives at play within feminist thought at the time. The commentator distinguished between 'biological' and acquired *garzonismo*. To her, the difference between the two is evident at plain sight, and it is only the former which belongs in the pathological realm. 'I feel for them the same compassion that I feel for a mad person. Conversely, as you know, in the past the epileptic and the mad were looked down upon with moral mistrust' (Díaz Parrado, cited in ibid.: 114). Díaz Parrado has a more relativistic regard toward acquired *garzonismo*, as she admits that there are certain 'sexual needs that are simple morbid curiosities,' which cannot be cured with social repudiation. Then she goes on to further doubt moral judgments in sexual matters: 'who knows if today's repulsion won't be anathema tomorrow' (Díaz Parrado, cited in ibid.: 114). Like Margueritte, Flora Díaz Parrado regards the *garzona* as a novel creation, a revolutionary woman. To her, as much as the *garzona* is a product of the independence war, she is someone who has transgressed the new socio-sexual order. And she ponders: 'When had we seen a "pose" like this before? Never!' (Díaz Parrado, cited in ibid.: 114).[10]

### Homoeroticism in two novels

In 1928, as the debate on *pepillitos* and *garzonas* was taking hold in the Cuban public sphere, writer and feminist activist Ofelia Rodríguez Acosta (1929) published her novel *La vida manda* (Life Commands), which soon became a smash editorial success. The novel broke new ground in the representational spectrum of feminine characters in Latin American writing of the early twentieth century. Although written within the heterosexual canon, its pages exude a liberating, homoerotic discourse. The novel questions ingrained conventions related to women's sexuality and pleasure, free love, matrimonial institutionalism, and household economy.

Gertrudis, the protagonist of *Life Commands*, is not married; she does not have an aristocratic background, nor is she bound to a domestic household milieu. She is neither a virgin nor a mother; neither a nun nor a prostitute. Gertrudis is a single young female attracted to feminist and socialist ideas, open to experimentation and exploration of non-traditional intimate relations based on equality. Her life project aims at achieving socio-economic independence through salaried work. She distrusts the matrimonial institution, and has unbiased concepts about sex. Feminine desire and pleasure are given a central role, although the desiring feminine subject is inscribed within the realm of sexual aggression. Gertrudis is avid for pleasure and sexual satisfaction, but the men with whom she has had intimate relations have not been able to offer her erotic and emotional realization. In the social and political context in which the book was published, this fictional discourse performed a deconstruction and reconfiguration of the terms in which gender relations, love and sexuality, pleasure, and family and maternity, as well as the public and private, were negotiated in both literature and public life.

During the nineteenth century and early twentieth centuries, marriage had been the privileged space of reproduction, household economy, and patrimonial transmission, particularly among the higher classes, but hardly a space for sexual pleasure. In those days, women's pleasure was taboo and was associated with hysteria – a disease that was labeled as exclusively feminine, and whose causes were attributed to frigidity, lack of interest in heterosexual coitus, sexual deviations, and to 'lesbianism.'[11] Spanish philosopher Beatriz Preciado (2002: 92) has observed that the only therapeutic spaces in which to treat hysteria were the matrimonial bed and the surgical table. The construction of both feminine sexuality and pleasure took place either within the institution of heterosexual matrimony – where women were tied to their husbands – or medical institutions, where they were treated as patients. Masturbation and orgasm were proscribed by religious and bio-medical discourse as 'demonizations' or 'convulsions' (Ortiz 2005: 170), as a potentially sick, unnecessary waste of energies.

In *Life Commands* homoerotic desire is expressed and decodified mainly by way of silences.[12] Silence is a recurrent element throughout the text, alternatively veiling and unveiling sentiment and eroticism. 'How did I give myself away to you, Delia?' asks Gertrudis. 'In your silences. Your silences are irrefutably eloquent, sometimes even disconcerting. As I pay attention to them I can see you crying, craving, unashamedly thinking: loving ...' (Rodríguez Acosta 1929: 80–1) answers the other. Silence is compounded by the exchange of emotionally charged gazes between the two women friends. 'Delia trailed her up and down with her eyes' (ibid.: 35). In another part it reads: 'Gertrudis' hypnotized gaze came down to Delia's lips that were quivering voluptuously ... She agitated herself in the long, endless, sinful yet sweet gaze of the other woman. Delia smiled triumphantly. That wet, palpitating smile awakened Gertrudis' (ibid.: 94). The free, indiscreet gazes place the homoerotic eye – as a tactile vehicle – in a privileged dimension, when passing from silence to articulated love: 'I have never loved a woman as I love you,' confesses Delia to Gertrudis, 'to the limits of renunciation, to the purity of the senses, with the senses pending so much on you ...' (ibid.: 146). In the novel, the homoerotic relationship of these two women is interrupted after a series of explicit allusions to lesbian desire on the part of the protagonist, and later in the story Delia will reappear only as a vague allusion.

Perhaps for this resolution, Mariblanca Sabas Alomá gave the novel a positive review in *Carteles* magazine, and went so far as to describe it as brave. The journalist encouraged readers not to judge the text 'with the archaic and obnoxious spectacles of the customary mores because it would read ridiculous, laughable and silly. Leave that to the inept and mediocre. The intelligent reader will go through it free of prejudice' (Sabas Alomá 2003: 239). Curiously, and in contradiction with the latter statement, Sabas Alomá (ibid.: 235) conditions the readers' interpretation by reiterating and underscoring that the book should be read as 'a novel of a woman, *a full-fledged woman* and by a woman,' a recurring phrase throughout the whole review. The homoerotic liaison is not mentioned in her analysis, and it is only referred to as Rodríguez Acosta's proneness to 'spicing up her love scenes with lust,' but according to the reviewer, the writer 'managed to sort out all hurdles with graceful wit and courage,' because Gertrudis 'carries on with her life embracing a high moral stance worthy of admiration ...' (ibid.: 236–7).

Perchance for similar reasons she also praised the prison narratives by Carlos Montenegro, who won the 1928 short story award sponsored by *Carteles* magazine for his story 'El Nuevo' (The new one). Sabas Alomá interviewed the writer, who ten years later would become the author of the novel *Hombres sin mujer* (Men without Women) in the Castillo del Príncipe fortress, a penitentiary. Her review of *El Renuevo* (The Renewal) *and other stories*, published in *Revista de Avance* in 1929, anticipates the reception of *Hombres sin mujer*, as at least four stories in that book served as the backbone of Montenegro's later novel. Regarding the characters, she comments:

The social types that Carlos Montenegro has given life to will never be forgotten. He is magnificently brutal in his naked depictions; marvelously horrendous in his aggressive brutality ... Those are Montenegro's 'brothers in disgrace.' It is good that he came across them while in prison, because in the outside world, it would have been hard for him to have met them. (Ibid.: 221)

A quick look at the preliminary note 'to the reader' of *Men without Women* would have sufficed Sabas Alomá to have acquitted Montenegro of charges of offense to public morality. The note reads:

... to read it with complacency would have meant to sacrifice reality, thus restraining the possibility of achieving my goal of denouncing the prison conditions I was submitted to ... I would like to remind those who accuse these pages of depravity that everything depicted in them is part of an existing social evil and it should be this evil and not its description that ought be judged. (Montenegro 2001: 3)

This passage is Montenegro's apology – in his condition as witness – for revealing prison life in such crude tones, and for portraying homosexuality as an institutional ill, not as a manifestation of an intrinsic or naive form of pleasure, but rather as a demonic scatological expression, a functional link that supplants the deprivation of '*men* [who are] *without women*.' The reception of the novel was mediated by the assurance that the 'evil' Montenegro denounces is kept at bay within the penitentiary walls; it remains there like a prisoner sentenced to life.

The main character is a black man, Pascasio Speek, inmate number 5062. He has served eight years at the Castillo del Príncipe penitentiary. The narrator, ubiquitous witness of the events, shares the point of view of this abstinent, solitary man, bearer of an unyielding *criollo* masculinity. His personality is exalted by all 'because of the reputation of his dark skin' and because, since his imprisonment, he has stayed away from the frequent bouts of sodomy that took place between the '*leas*' and the '*bugas*.' The narrator reveals how 'every time that Pascasio came closer to someone, he discovered the shameful proclivity – in a lesser or greater degree' which 'some already brought with them from the outside world. To him, they felt like lepers who could contaminate him' (ibid.: 14). In moments of desperation, Pascasio 'dreamt of Encarnación, of Tomasa, or even of a broomstick dressed with a skirt, and those images comforted him. Then he was ready again!' (ibid.: 15). However, Pascasio felt more disgust for 'snitches' than for homosexuals.

The issue of homosexuality in prison was addressed by Montenegro as an inexorable fall or moral calamity. Speaking through Comencubo, one of his characters, he says: 'But I know that this is like a soap house: you either fall or slip. It's only a matter of time. Here, not even the old ones are spared. They go about, like cats in heat, pretending to give young people advice ... but in the end they are nothing but crotch hunters' (ibid.: 12–13). The novel makes explicit references to the Freudian notions of mourning, and homosexuality as a melancholic structure of the psyche. In another passage, a prisoner makes a direct allusion to the psychoanalyst:

> His was an inconsequential fling, a memory from the outside world that took hold of him, and the boy [referring to newly arrived inmate Andrés Pinel, who was lying down unconscious owing to a hard day's work] had nothing to do with it. Freud could say whatever he wanted, but have anyone come and convince him that that lad, regardless of his feminine looks, was weighing on his feelings. It was all a simple association of ideas, based on a sheer resemblance, because nothing in him compelled him to find satisfaction in the perverse. (Ibid.: 126)

In a passage, prisoners Manuel Chiquito and Brai comment on Pascasio's abstinence and the rumors of his alleged involvement with a homosexual known as La Morita. Sentenced to life for murder, Brai had built up a violent, macho reputation among prisoners and guards, even though he had sex with La Duquesa. He respected and admired Pascasio and did not tolerate any homosexual slander against him. To this, Manuel Chiquito said, 'Dude, don't stand for anyone. When you have been here longer than natural, your crotch starts itching and suddenly you don't know if it is time to fuck or get fucked' (ibid.: 33). Brai vigorously retorted:

> I didn't get any itch! That only happens to sissies. The motherfuckers did all they could to retain me here long enough and now I'm too old to spend my life jerking off like the American horse. But I can't blame it on the itch. The hell with them all! *I did it because I wanted to.*' (Ibid.: 33, emphasis added)

The novel reproduces the prison jargon by which the seducer or 'active' sexual performer (inserter) is called '*buga*' (represented as possessor of a hyperbolic masculinity), whereas the '*leas*' or '*mares*,' perceived as effeminate and passive (receivers in sexual intercourse), are 'spoiled,' 'put to the sword,' and 'deflowered' after giving in to sexual advances. Commenting on this state of affairs, Matienzo, another inmate, tells Andrés Pinel:

You know what the matter with all of us is? You know what's the matter with us? We are men without women. There are no degenerates here, only men without women. That's all. You are not a woman but you look less manly than the rest of us and for that reason, every now and then, you'll have your 'headaches.' (Ibid.: 69)

The issue of the sexual conquest is embedded in ethno-racial representations. The crazy mulatto man, Valentín Pérez Daysón, is constantly wielding an imaginary machete against black and mestizo men while hollering his sexual appetite toward white folks with a recurrent line: 'I want to eat white chick'n! Ouch, white chick'n!' (ibid.: 7).

Although homoerotic desire is placed outside pleasure and normality, the novel reveals a nuanced understanding of the variation within homosexual experience. As in Brai's sudden admission of guilt, other passages distance the active/passive dichotomy and the traditional economy of sexual roles. Manuel Chiquito comments: 'If only by a hush-hush, quick kiss, your heart races so fast that it wants to burst out of your chest! And you don't even know if you are playing the man's or the woman's role or both ...' (ibid.: 173).

When characters offer different views or visions on homosexuality, these are circumscribed to the perverse, scatology, and madness. However, when Pascasio Speek meets Andrés Pinel, the discourse on homoerotic desire acquires new overtones. Pascasio realizes that what 'was happening to him was what he always feared and rejected' when he became aware that 'the young man was spreading through him and putting him off track.' Pascasio feels 'that he was rolling down the hill at a vertiginous speed and was already disarticulated' (ibid.: 165). In a monolog, Pascasio convinces himself that he is in love: 'his love wandered away from the norms, as if they were also a barrier, beyond which passion became more intimate and above all laws' (ibid.: 190) and he didn't have to establish any differences 'between what was moral and wasn't; he didn't care anymore if his feelings were in or out of the natural frontiers of life' (ibid.: 188–9). In this groundbreaking passage, Pascasio Speek, a black man, expresses genuine feelings of homosexual love. It is impossible, ponders the character:

... that what he felt were similar to the feelings experienced by each one of the other inmates who had fallen victims of that abject desire. None of those beasts, rolling over and over in their own mud, had discovered that ultra human gasp of pure air that had engulfed him, driving him into an irresistible whirlwind of passion. He was cleaned of any degenerate, onerous form of lust; his unconfessed sin had a choir of a thousand voices clamoring not in his defence, which he deemed a ridiculous act, but in jubilation. (Ibid.: 190)

His agitation, he says to himself, 'was not that of a man who had lost his mind. Despite the contradictory feelings that obsessed him, what dominated him above all was a jubilation beyond his capacity to feel. Whatever it was, it couldn't be alien to him; it was a feeling beyond his understanding that was opening up unsuspected horizons in his life; tormenting him, but it couldn't be alien to him even if it felt awkward' (ibid.: 162–3).

However, after this climatic moment, the narrator begins to prepare the reader for a fatal outcome in which the homoerotic liaison will be dismembered and left uncompleted. Even though Pascasio is 'shaken by a powerful force, he understood that the whole affair was not viable':

It is not like he was giving up on his dream but he couldn't material- ize happiness, only the desperation of the unattainable ... he thought that, since he was unable to take another step in the realization of his dream, it was going to be miscarried – though still embedded in him like a remorseful feeling of a crime committed, a secret shared with no one – and so the only thing left for him to do was to drag his silence like a heavy load. (Ibid.: 191)

The romance ends tragically and violently when Pascasio kills Andrés after finding him exchanging caresses with Manuel Chiquito, and then commits suicide. The lovers have died and love with them. Thus Montenegro resolves the conflict. The ending, while consistent with the narrative of homosexuality 'not as a result of a natural pre- disposition, but due to the crimes of men and the prison circumstances that muddled his strong and sound spirit' (ibid.: 228), and also consist- ent with psychiatric theories available at the time, does not prevent the novel from portraying Pascasio overtaken by homoerotic passion with singular detail and sensibility. It is indeed a break from clinical and criminological representations.

## Conclusion

The public visibility of *garzonas* and *pepillitos* in early twentieth- century Cuba destabilized ideals of masculinity and femininity and existing gender relations. The gender and sexual ambiguity of these new subjects triggered a moral panic, acted out in the form of a press campaign by nationalist intellectuals. In the imagination of turn-of- the-century Latin American elites, imagining a nation as modern entailed gaining control over the makeup of its population. Sexual regulation had both a material function and a symbolic meaning. As Mosse observed of the genesis of modern European nations, in Cuba masculinity was conceived in the form of a self-contained, exclusive identity unit at the core of the construction of the nation.

The stigma attached to *pepillitos* relates to the concrete reality of Cuba's submission to a foreign power, namely US imperialism. *Pepillitos* were thought to embody a threat to national masculinity and sovereignty, since their effeminate traits were the result of the defeat of national virility by North American values. *Pepillitos* were framed as sexual others, portrayed as 'subservient,' pro-North American and anti-national. The specter of sexual inversion was used as a recurrent discursive resource to defend the social order and national honor. Consequently, homosexual love and sociability were perceived as threats to the country's sovereignty, stability, progress, and defense.

The campaign against *garzonas* must be read in the context of feminist debates of the time. Homoeroticism operated as a category of accusation against feminists, who, in order to legitimize their pledge, detached themselves from *garzonismo*, trying to neutralize anti-feminist propaganda. The issue of publicity and visibility connects the campaign against *garzonismo* and *pepillismo* with the representation of homoeroticism in Cuban novels of the period. *La vida manda* and *Hombres sin mujer* were praised as frank accounts of the sentimental density of the issue, which involved the effective concealment of the homoerotic drive among women, in the first case, and the enclosure of homosexuality within the walls of a men's prison in the second. The authors and reviewers of these novels managed to keep homosexuality within the boundaries of the silent and the abject, conjuring the threat they would represent to a nation struggling to consolidate itself and enter modernity.

## Notes

1 This chapter was translated from Spanish by Roberto García and corrected by Nora Gámez.

2 Gerardo Machado, member of the Liberal Party, was the fifth president of the republic from 1925 to 1933. As opposition grew, his second and third terms – including the amendment of electoral law – were won by a combination of bribes and violence. He exercised harsh repression against detractors, and

censorship of the press, including *La Semana*, which was shut down by the regime in 1930. Machado was removed by a popular revolt known as the 1933 Revolution.

3 George L. Mosse (1985: 9) explains the links between sexuality and nationalism in Western nationalist regimes using the notion of 'bourgeois respectability.' The distinction between sexual normality and abnormality was basic in

the ideal of respectability and was a control device in those societies. Nationalism, on the other hand, 'helped respectability to meet all challenges to its dominance, enlarging its parameters when necessary while keeping its essence intact.'

4 In his text, Sergio Carbó uses the term 'intersexuality,' which at the time was synonymous with homosexuality. The term was introduced in Cuba by the Spanish sexologist Gregorio Marañón (1928a), ridiculed in *La Semana* cartoons and jokes.

5 Women entered the political arena during the first decades of the republic, campaigning for universal suffrage. Between 1912 and 1913, three feminist parties were created (the Feminist National Party, the Suffrage Party, and the National Suffrage Party). In 1920, the Cuban Feminine Club was founded, as was the National Federation of Feminine Associations one year later.

6 See, for example, Pardo y Suárez (1932).

7 See also Memorias del Primer Congreso Femenino 1923, Dolz (n.d.), and Pichardo (1983).

8 The right to vote was granted to Cuban women in 1934.

9 Margueritte's argument would be recovered by the lesbian feminism of Monique Wittig during the 1960s in France.

10 From a present-day perspective, the term 'pose' could be read – thanks to the contributions of feminist and contemporary postfeminist theory – as masquerade or gender performance.

11 See, for example: Blackwood (1986), De Laurentis (1993) and Rubin (1975, 1984).

12 As Nina Menendez (1997: 267) has pointed out, this codification should not be understood as a lesbian textual strategy, which was theoretically consolidated decades after the novel was written, but as keys and codes used by the author.

## References

Blackwood, E. (1986) 'Breaking the mirror: the construction of lesbianism and the anthropological discourse on homosexuality,' in E. Blackwood (ed.) *The Many Faces of Homosexuality: Anthropological approaches to homosexual behavior*, New York: Harrington Park Press, pp. 1–17.

Carbó, S. (1928a) 'Aclarando lo del pepillismo,' *La Semana*, Year 4, 8 July.

— (1928b) 'Los "pepillitos,"' *La Semana*, Year 4, 20 June.

De Laurentis, T. (1993) 'Sexual indifference and lesbian representation,' in H. Abelove, M. A. Barale and D. Halperin (eds), *The Lesbian and Gay Studies Reader*, New York and London: Routledge.

Dolz, M. L. (n.d.) *El progreso del feminismo* [The progress of feminism], Vol. Leg. 41, Archivo Nacional de Cuba.

Iglesias, M. (2003) *Las metáforas del cambio en la vida cotidiana* [Metaphors of change in everyday life]: *Cuba 1898–1902*, Havana: Ediciones Unión.

La Semana (1928) Year 4, 4 July.

Marañón, G. (1928a) *Los estados intersexuales del hombre y la mujer*, Havana: Imprenta Mercaderes.

— (1928b) *Tres ensayos sobre la vida sexual* [Three essays on sexual life], Madrid: Biblioteca Nueva.

Margueritte, V. (1926) *La Garçonne*, Paris: Flammarion.

Memorias del Primer Congreso

Femenino [Proceedings of the First Feminine Congress] (1923) Havana: Imprenta La Universal.

Menendez, N. (1997) 'Garzonas y feministas in Cuban women's writing of the 1920s: *La vida manda*, by Ofelia Rodríguez Acosta,' in D. Balderston and D. J. Guy (eds), *Sex and Sexuality in Latin America*, New York: New York University Press.

Montenegro, C. (2001) *Hombres sin mujer y otras narraciones* [Men without women and other stories], Havana: Editorial Letras Cubanas.

Mosse, G. (1985) *Nationalism and Sexuality. Respectability and abnormal sexuality in modern Europe*, New York: Howard Ferting.

Ortiz, F. (2005) *Brujas e inquisidores* [Witches and inquisitors], Havana: Fundación Fernando Ortiz.

Pardo y Suárez, V. (1932) *Lesbianas. Apuntes para un estudio de psico-sexualidad femenina* [Lesbians. Remarks for a study of feminine psycho-sexuality], Havana: Cultural, S.A.

Pichardo, H. (1983) 'La liberación de la mujer I y II' [Woman's liberation], in H. Pichardo (ed.),

*Documentos para la Historia de Cuba* [Documents of Cuban history], vol. 2, Havana: Editorial Ciencias Sociales.

Preciado, B. (2002) *Manifiesto Contra-sexual. Prácticas subversivas de la identidad sexual* [Contra-sexual manifesto. Subversive practices of sexual identity], Madrid: Ediciones Opera Prima.

Rodríguez Acosta, O. (1929) *La vida manda*, Madrid: Biblioteca Rubén Darío.

Roig de Leuchsenring, E. (1928) 'Los pepillotes,' *Carteles*, XII, 5 August.

Rubin, G. (1975) 'The traffic in women: notes on the "political economy" of sex,' in R. Reiter (ed.), *Towards an Anthropology of Women*, New York.

— (1984) 'Thinking sex: notes for a radical theory of the politics of sexuality,' in C. S. Vance (ed.), *Pleasure and Danger: Exploring Female Sexuality*, Boston, MA: Routledge and Kegan Paul.

Sabas Alomá, M. (2003) *Feminismo*, Santiago de Cuba: Editorial Oriente.

Sommer, D. (1993) *Foundational Fictions. The National Romances of Latin America*, Berkeley: University of California Press.

# 5 | Government and the control of venereal disease in colonial Tanzania, 1920–60

MUSA SADOCK

## Introduction

Since the nineteenth century, 'venereal disease' (henceforth VD) has been deemed one of the greatest human health risks.[1] The fight against sexually transmitted diseases linked an emerging concern with the composition and welfare of ethnic groups, which was informed by racist ideologies at the height of modern nationalism and colonial domination, to debates about moral reform. In Africa, focus on the control of sexual relations involved interventions on behalf of colonial power-holders to regulate the sexuality of the local population with a particular focus on prostitution – believed to constitute the main site of VD transmission. Yet historical studies on government intervention against VDs in Africa, especially in Tanzania, have been lacking.[2] This chapter assesses colonial government strategies to control VD in Tanganyika,[3] based on historical sources from the district of Mbozi, an area with a long history of settlement, labor migration, and other forms of population mobility. A historical understanding of the political dynamics, ideological assumptions, and socio-demographic implications of VD control under British 'indirect rule' may shed light on sociocultural aspects of current efforts in the fight against sexually transmitted diseases (STDs), including the HIV/AIDS pandemic.

This chapter draws from a theoretical framework that sees disease and societal responses to health crises as a function of interactions between bio-medical and social conditions (Nguyen and Sama 2008: 244; Brandt 1987: 4). Colonial state responses to disease, including medical interventions, are analyzed as events of a political nature. In the case of VDs, they targeted the sexuality of social groups that the authorities perceived as the transmitters of the diseases to the general population. VD control strategies are an expression of modern 'biopolitics,' whereby sex becomes the object of state policing and interventions concerned with the bodily and moral welfare of human populations (Foucault 1981). To this end, medical science and state administration established an intimate collaboration to control marginal sexualities and treat 'diseased populations.'

This study is largely based on archival research conducted at the Tanzania National Archives (TNA) in Dar es Salaam, Mbeya Zonal Archives (MBZA), and in the Mbeya (Mbozi) district between 2008 and 2009. VD registers and medical reports from the period under British administration were examined, complemented by interviews with experts in the Mbozi district. Historical sources were analyzed using a comparative approach. The chapter is organized into seven sections. The first three introduce the population and STD history of colonial Mbozi. The others address colonial government efforts to control marginal sexualities and review colonial government hygiene and medical policies.

### Mbozi

The Mbeya district (to which the current Mbozi district belonged) was established in 1926 under British rule, in the Iringa Province, in current southwestern Tanzania, bordering Zambia and Malawi. Mbozi is mainly inhabited by Bantu-speaking peoples; especially the Nyiha and Nyamwanga, who are said to have migrated into the district two millennia ago from the Congo basin west of Lake Tanganyika.[4] The district was settled by agriculturalists as far back as the first millennium AD (Knight 1974: 12). During the early colonial period, Mbozi experienced a large influx of people of diverse ethnic origins from within the region and other parts of the territory; the Nyakyusa and Ndali from Rungwe and Ileje districts constituted the largest groups of immigrants. These immigrants were attracted to the district by the availability of land and employment opportunities in white settler coffee estates, which were established in the 1920s (ibid.: 6). The plantations also attracted migrant laborers from neighboring territories, the current Malawi and Zambia. Mbozi also exported migrant laborers to the Lupa gold fields in the Chunya district, the Zambian copper belt, the South African gold fields, and the sisal plantations of the coast of Tanganyika. It also served as a transition point for migrant laborers from Central Africa to the coast of Tanganyika and from Tanganyika to central and southern Africa. Labor migration decreased after independence, but the region continued to act as a gateway between central and southern Africa.

The territory of Tanganyika was governed by the British under 'indirect rule,' through traditional chiefs, also known as 'the native administration,' who, in practice, acted as agents of the colonial administration. Between 1926 and 1931, Sir Donald Cameron, then governor, carried out a policy of unifying the native authorities. Under this system, local authorities had a mandate to provide social services to the citizens. Indeed, many local authorities built their own native schools and dispensaries. This system continued after independence until 1963, when chiefs' administrative functions were abolished and most former chiefs and village headmen were integrated into the new local government and became salaried employees (Miller 1972: 149, 153). Under this structure, policies and directives were centralized.

Mbozi has a long history of massive interaction among peoples of diverse ethnic origins and cultures, which has impinged on sexual relations, as well as the sexual aspects of cultural contact, migrant labor, and colonial relations. These conditions had an impact on the spread and prevalence of STDs in the district. In turn, the material and symbolic standing of the region as a hotbed for VDs generated specific responses from colonial governments in terms of law, education, and health policy, including the regulation of prostitution, and the internment of infected members of specific social groups, such as female sex workers and mobile persons. How governments responded to the diseases are issues worth investigating. The district is still, today, the worst affected by STDs, especially gonorrhoea, syphilis, and HIV/AIDS, in the Mbeya region.

## Discourses on the prevalence of STDs

Medical reports of the 1920s and mid-1930s in colonial Tanganyika showed a high prevalence of VDs in urban areas, as well as in specific populations: sex workers, migrant laborers, soldiers, and African women doing domestic work for Europeans. The only exception to this general trend was the Bukoba district of northwestern Tanganyika, where VDs were prevalent in rural areas as well.[5] In the 1920s, a medical officer from the Rungwe district (to which Mbozi belonged before 1926) stated that VDs were brought to the Tukuyu township by 'native prostitutes,' mainly from Nyasaland (Malawi).[6] As elsewhere in Tanganyika, sex workers were blamed for the spread of venereal diseases to the general public and soldiers (*Askaris*).[7] Domestic servants, especially in Dar es Salaam, were also seen as reservoirs of the diseases that could transmit them to their European employers.[8]

This perception of venereal diseases as concentrated in specific populations in urban areas changed during and after the Second World War, when they came to be seen as a general epidemic in both urban and rural areas.[9] Nonetheless, migrant laborers, soldiers, prostitutes, drivers, and other mobile groups continued to be apportioned the greatest share of the blame for transmitting the diseases to the general public in both urban and rural areas.[10] In 1957, a medical report pointed out that venereal diseases continued to flourish in Mbeya district.[11]

Assessments of the prevalence of VDs were molded according to colonial medical authorities' and administrators' preconceived and exaggerated notions of African sexuality. They regarded Africans as victims of excessive sexual desire, which led to promiscuous behavior, understood to be the cause of the high prevalence and the spread of VDs. In 1947, Oldaker, the Provincial Commissioner of Mbeya, noted that:

> There is a difference in the conception of sexual morality between Palaearctic and Tropical peoples. The term social evil is applicable to Great Britain, not Tanganyika where no stigma attaches to promiscuity or venereal infection. The prostitute and promiscuity are integral parts of indigenous tropical society.[12]

Another official noted: 'There is no lever within the tribal system to restrict promiscuity.'[13] Such 'levers' should come from outside through education.[14] This view was common to colonial administrators across the tropics. In Uganda, according to Tuck, colonialists attributed the prevalence of venereal diseases to the promiscuous nature of Africans (Tuck 2001: 194). Leibing shows that early nineteenth-century doctors believed warm climates favored debauchery. According to that narrative, Africans who had been taken to Brazil from tropical Africa by the slave trade added sexual excess as they had 'the fire of concupiscence in their very blood' (Leibing 1997: 90). These factors, went the argument, explained why syphilis was so widespread in Brazil.

Apart from being mistaken, the argument of an unrestrained sexuality was ignorant of African sexual customs. Hunter (2003) has argued that, first, polygamous behavior is verifiable in societies across the globe, and secondly, colonialists failed to recognize local customs that restricted sexuality. In pre-colonial and colonial Mbozi society, a man could divorce his wife if she engaged in extramarital relationships (Brock 1966: 10). While biased against women and silent on men, this custom performed the function of regulating sexuality in general, and women's sexuality in particular.

## VD prevalence in colonial Mbozi

The few available statistics for the Southern Highlands province show a high prevalence of venereal diseases. Rungwe district records from the year 1920 show eighty-two cases of VD among Africans,[15] for an estimated total population of 237,200.[16] Of those cases, fifty-three were of syphilis, twenty-three of gonorrhoea, two of gleets, and four of orchitis. Compared to other districts in Tanganyika, the incidence of VD in Rungwe was small: Bukoba and Tabora had totals of 253 and 237 VD cases, respectively. This prevalence was attributed to labor migration, the effects of the First World War, and increased urbanization, among other factors.[17] Syphilis was always the leading ailment. Mbeya district records from the 1940s still show a high prevalence of VDs. Disease returns from Mbeya hospital in 1947 show sixty-nine admissions on account of VDs among Africans, and four cases among European males,[18] for a district population of 185,265 (that included 772 Asians, 421 Europeans, and 19 'colored').[19]

These statistics should be treated with caution. With the exception of those from health centers that had laboratory services, VD prevalence data were unreliable and often exaggerated. This was due to a combination of misdiagnosis and misconception regarding African sexuality. During the colonial period, the lack of testing facilities led to improper diagnostic procedures and high indices of false-positive serology. A 1958 medical report from Mbeya commented that many native dispensaries in rural areas reported any sore on genitalia as syphilis.[20] Similar observations had been made elsewhere in the territory in the 1930s.[21] As Young observed in the 1940s, in the African environment, penile sores could result from trauma,[22] among other factors. Additionally, in the 1930s, medical staff, especially in the rural areas, did not follow proper diagnostic procedures when treating outpatients (Young 1948). Quite often a patient would enter the 'doctor's' room asking for an injection (*Sindano*);[23] the doctor would ask which disease, and the patient would reply syphilis (*Kaswende*). Eventually the patient would receive the injection.[24] For those patients that were tested, Young noted that many Africans in the 1940s were misdiagnosed with syphilis because various tropical diseases, such as early age residuals of yaws, tested positive in adults (ibid.).

All those flawed cases went into the records, thus inflating VD figures. Notions of an exacerbated African sexuality contributed to the exaggeration of VD prevalence. However, STD statistics are significant for two reasons. First, they show the existence of the diseases, although their extent is debatable. Secondly, the figures enlisted governments' responses in terms of prevention policy, education, and medical intervention. In order to better understand the relevance of VDs in colonial East Africa, we need to look into the socio-economic, political, and cultural contexts conducive to the spread of, and responses to, the diseases.

## Colonial responses to VD

In line with other colonial policies, the medical policies on VD in Tanganyika served colonial state interests (Mihanjo 2004: 103–5). These included preventing the spread of VD to the white population (as it was assumed that the source of infection was in the African population) and among Africans employed in the government and other sectors: soldiers in the King's African Rifles – KAR division, clerks, messengers, mine and plantation migrant workers, to name but a few. In the 1920s, confronted with the perceived threats of VD, the colonial authorities adopted a policy of voluntary treatment at Early Treatment (ET) Centers and hospitals, mostly located in urban centers. Towns were seen as hotbeds of venereal diseases, and it was there that the efforts of the medical department were concentrated.[25] 'Prostitutes' and other social groups 'at risk' were encouraged to attend the services.

This voluntary policy was a sharp departure from the preceding German policy of licensing and compulsory medical examination of sex workers in towns.[26] In the assessment of British health administrators, the German policy had a number of weaknesses.[27] First, the medical examination applied only to professional female sex workers; it left out amateur prostitutes who outnumbered the full-time professionals. Secondly, only females who performed the sexual services were examined. The policy did not reach the male customers. Thus female sex workers were bound to be reinfected. Additionally, in Europe, the experience of licensing brothels had failed to prevent the spread of VD.

The British adopted the voluntary treatment policy partly as a response to the failure of the regulated prostitution. But the new policy did not entice many Africans to attend the health facilities, for two reasons.[28] On the one hand, Africans tended to use alternative means of treatment, by traditional healers. On the other hand, the stigma and shame associated with VDs led those who had contracted them to conceal their condition. In the shorter term, the diseases did not impair the sick from performing their daily duties, though this changed during the acute stages of the diseases.

The British, however, were not consistent in the implementation of the policy. Owing to the prevalence of venereal diseases among *Askaris* and the police force in 1925 in Dar es Salaam, there was a roundup and compulsory medical examination of sex workers.[29] Ostensibly, the sex workers bore the blame for spreading the diseases to the security forces not only in Dar es Salaam but also in other parts of the territory, including the Mbozi district. Compulsory examination persisted during and after the Second World War. In 1945, a Native Authority

Order for compulsory treatment of VD patients was in place in Mbeya. The order stated:

> Any person who has the disease must report to a dispensary or hospital and must continue any treatment until he is pronounced cured. When he first attends a treatment centre he is given a chit telling him when to return and showing a record of his visits ... Any failure to attend as directed would be reported to the Native Court who would then call upon the man to produce evidence of attendance, failure to do so would render him liable to punishment.[30]

Other colonial states in Africa implemented similar policies, which eventually included internment. The Belgian Congo's colonial administration ordered compulsory registration and medical examination of African female sex workers and detention of the sick among them until they were cured of the diseases (Hunt 1998: 115).

The British also developed a treatment policy dubbed the 'Public Health Cure' (as opposed to the 'Clinical Cure') for VDs. The Public Health Cure entailed administering the 'simplest and shortest course of treatment of venereal cases' to render the disease non-infective.[31] In Tanganyika, the recommended treatment to render syphilis non-infective in 1935 was six injections of bismuth.[32] This dosage, however, fell short of the clinical cure recommended by the League of Nations Health Organization at the time; which stipulated a minimum of thirty-two injections of bismuth for a syphilitic male adult, followed by serological and a clinical observation for not less than three years.[33] The Public Health approach was a response to a shortage of drugs, medical staff and laboratories.[34]

In most instances, the Public Health Cure policy failed to render venereal diseases non-infective. Instead, it resulted in chronic illness.[35] Moreover, relapses were common among treated patients. In addition, owing to the high cost of drugs and lack of facilities, the policy was weakly implemented. Penicillin, which, by the 1940s, was the proven means of control, was considered too expensive and was freely given only to pregnant mothers and infants. Additionally, the drug required refrigerators, which were unavailable in most rural dispensaries.[36]

## Controlling marginal sexualities

As noted earlier, STDs were widespread in all social groups, including whites. Despite this reality, colonial authorities instituted measures aimed at controlling the sexuality of specific social groups perceived as transmitters of the diseases to the public. That included female sex workers, mobile unmarried women, and labor migrants. Following gender and racial hierarchies in the colonial order, Europeans, as well as African male customers in the sex trade, were excluded from the measures. The colonial authorities believed that migrant laborers and prostitutes were the main channels for the spread of VDs to the public.[37] In Dar es Salaam, arrests were common and well documented. In 1925, fifty-six female sex workers were detained and forced to undergo medical examination for VDs; thirty-five were found to be suffering from gonorrhoea, and three from syphilis. They were treated at Sewahaji Hospital.[38]

In any case, the strategy of rounding up female sex workers was ineffective, as only a small number – especially those who worked the streets – were arrested. Moreover, prostitutes devised strategies to resist colonial government control. In the 1920s, one official in Rungwe noted that it was difficult to control prostitutes in the Tukuyu township because prostitutes resided with old women, but they did not use the houses for prostitution. They had established a reputation, so they did not need to solicit or ply for hire, as clients sent for them and received them in their homes.[39] Additionally, the colonial police lacked the resources to patrol extensive areas.[40]

Laws and regulations were also used to enforce hygienic controls on sex workers. Section 32, paragraphs 2, 3, 4, 5, and 6 of the Defence Amendment for the Compulsory Treatment of Venereal Diseases of 1944, empowered any police officer to arrest without a warrant any person loitering near or around railway stations and military camps, reasonably suspected of undertaking prostitution, to undergo medical examination for venereal diseases by the government medical practitioner. If the arrestee was infected with VD, the officer had to issue a written notice instructing her to undergo treatment at a named medical center. Failure to comply with the requirements of such a notice empowered the medical practitioner to report the matter to the magistrate, who would order detention to impose such treatment. Any person who contravened or failed to comply with those provisions was 'liable to a fine not exceeding one thousand shillings, or to imprisonment for a period not exceeding six months.'[41] In Mbeya, the regulations were applied along the Great North Road, which ran from Cape Town to Cairo and was dotted with numerous military camps during the war. The Mbozi Division was situated along the road, so native prostitutes were subject to this policy (Mihanjo 2004: 103). Nevertheless, given the lengthy procedures and discretionary powers of police officers, enforcement was most likely subject to corruption by police officers and medical practitioners.

Migrant laborers were also subjected to hygienic control. In the 1950s, migrant laborers from Mbozi seeking employment in the coastal areas of Tanganyika and the gold mines of South Africa had medical checkups for VDs during recruitment and at the time of returning home. Those who were diagnosed as positive were either not recruited or, at the end of their contract, detained until cured.[42] However, in order for this control to be effective, laborers had to be re-examined in transit or immediately after returning home. In the late 1950s, no such examinations were carried out on migrant laborers returning from South Africa, Zambia, coastal areas of Tanganyika, and the Lupa gold mines.[43] Laborers thus contracted the diseases in transit. As one informant noted, 'many migrant labourers returning to Mbozi from South Africa had sex with prostitutes while on transit at Francistown in Botswana, and a great number of them contacted many venereal diseases [there].'[44]

In general, the strategy of targeting specific social groups had little effect in controlling the diseases. It was partly because of this failure that measures to control the diseases among all Africans were put in place, as attested to by the Mbeya District Native Order cited earlier. Educational campaigns were introduced aimed at imparting preventive knowledge to the general public.

## VD prevention campaigns

Educational campaigns were one of the pivots of the battle against venereal diseases in Tanganyika. Colonial authorities agreed on the need for education to fight the diseases, but disagreed on the content of such education. One group advocated moral education, whereby sexual morals such as continence, chastity, a social code of ethics, and abstinence were to be emphasized.[45] The other group emphasized epidemiological education. This had to be scientific, and concentrate on how venereal diseases were transmitted, how they could be prevented, their consequences (such as sterility and death), and the need to seek medical treatment.[46] To impart these messages to Africans, various media were used, including posters, film trailers, and pamphlets. Schools and colleges were also avenues for disseminating VD information. Indeed, school and college curricula included sex education.[47]

Nevertheless, colonial government efforts to disseminate information on VD were not very successful. The written content of posters and pamphlets had a very limited audience among Africans, who were mostly illiterate in Western scripts. That is why some officials suggested that Western-educated Africans should be used to influence others by disseminating information to their fellow Africans.[48] Additionally, posters were not widely distributed in the territory. The few that reached their intended audience were outdated and in pathetic condition.[49] VD treatment campaigns were also unsuccessful. The Mbeya Annual Medical Report of 1958 noted: 'There are no venereal disease treatment campaigns in the province as practice has shown that these have no effects.'[50]

## Medical interventions

The colonial administration in Africa strove to conquer diseases in a manner analogous to the military conquest of the continent, in this case by medical means. Medical facilities were established and Africans were persuaded to seek treatment voluntarily or enticed and coerced to submit to it. Although many Africans were treated at health facilities, medical interventions against venereal diseases faced a number of obstacles, including deficient diagnosis and treatment, lack of funding and personnel, and inadequate medical facilities.

Treatment of venereal-disease patients required a steady supply of drugs. The drugs commonly used for treating syphilis in the 1920s included bismuth salts (sodium titrate and potassium titrate), mercury, salvarsan, and arsenic;[51] and for gonorrhoea they were mercurochrome, calcium chloride, and sulphonamide.[52] Apart from their being toxic, the use of these drugs posed a number of logistical problems. Treatment had to be administered over a long period and was interrupted owing either to shortage of drugs or to low adherence by patients.[53] Moreover, even when treatment was completed, the drugs were not efficient.[54] Relapses were common.[55]

In the 1940s, penicillin became the indicated drug, as it proved effective for the treatment of venereal diseases. However, like some of the earlier drugs, it was not available to every African patient owing to its cost.[56] Native authorities' budgets could not afford those drugs. Drug supply was problematic as well. In the 1940s, it was reported in Mbeya district that medical supplies were erratic and inadequate owing to delays in their arrival at medical facilities.[57]

Another problem was the lack of medical personnel. In general, Tanganyika was chronically short of medical staff, but this shortage was more acute in the case of venereal disease specialists. It was only in 1945 that a venereologist, Dr W. A. Young, was appointed to coordinate VD control in the colony. His work was affected, though, by a lack of junior medical staff.[58] In 1947, it was reported that although the medical staff was adequate for urban areas in Mbeya, it was insufficient to address the venereal diseases in rural communities, where communication was hampered by long distances.[59] Female medical staff was even scarcer, causing women to shy away from attending medical facilities for VD treatment,[60] as male doctors' access to their genitalia was culturally unacceptable.

Lastly, the medical facilities in Tanganyika were not only inadequate, they were also in a dilapidated condition.[61] There were too few government hospitals and dispensaries to serve too many people. In the Mbozi Division in 1947, four native authority dispensaries, Igamba, Ndalambo, Kamsamba, and Msangano,[62] served a total of 57,423 Africans.[63] This meant that, on average, one dispensary served approximately 14,356 people. Apart from the four dispensaries, Mbozi residents used two other medical facilities: the Mbozi Moravian Mission Hospital and Mwenzo Mission dispensary in northern Rhodesia, which was located eight kilometers from the Tanganyika border town of Tunduma.[64] But even with these mission facilities, medical facilities in the area remained insufficient. In addition, government dispensaries lacked medical supplies and equipment. In the 1950s, Mbeya Hospital was the only facility that had a laboratory.[65]

Some additional observations can be made regarding the treatment of VDs in colonial Tanganyika. First, to a large extent, Western medicine was not the main means used to treat VD cases among the African population. Many cases were treated with traditional medicine. Secondly, some of the obstacles faced by Western medicine in the treatment and prevention of VDs during the colonial regime persisted in post-colonial Tanzania. Both topics are worth addressing in further research.

### Conclusion

In his correspondence to the Director of Medical and Sanitary Services, a Principal Medical Officer (PMO) complained about the presence of domestic African servants who stayed in European officials' homes and traveled with them, who had not undergone VD medical examination, thus posing a danger of transmitting the diseases to the officials.[66] Prevention and care, carried out by a native administration under indirect colonial rule, were devised as an effort to contain a 'diseased population.' Racist, gendered views of good and bad sex within the black population and between colonizers, colonized, and in-betweens (Asians and 'coloured') blinded health authorities to the fact that transmission in the context of the sex trade included both the female sex worker and the male client; the black female servant and the white lord.

In addition, lack of facilities, of appropriate equipment, of trained personnel, and the insufficiency of available supplies doomed any efforts to curb the spread of infections, while the racial ideology that regarded VD as the disease of blacks foreclosed any comprehensive prevention programs targeting all races. The obstacles faced by educational campaigns also raise the critical issue of language and access by the target population, as well as the structural challenge of literacy in colonial Africa. Africans' access to the languages used in education campaigns against VDs was limited by the fact that few Africans were literate in those languages.

Finally, the detention of sex workers for testing, as well as internment and other forms of coercion imposed on individuals to complete their treatment, backfired, prompting a variety of forms of resistance and illegality.

## Notes

1 The term encompassed a variety of infections transmitted through sexual contact, including gonorrhoea, syphilis, genital herpes, genital warts and chlamydia. See National Guidelines for Management of Sexually Transmitted and Reproductive Tract Infections, United Republic of Tanzania, Ministry of Health and Social Welfare (March 2007), p. 2, Interview with Dr E. Mwitula, Dar es Salaam, February 2009. See Tanzania National Archives (hereafter TNA) Accession (Acc.) no. 3, 'Venereal Diseases,' a circular from the Principal Medical Officer, Dar es Salaam (DSM), to the Chief Secretary to the Government, 22 March 1920.

2 A few exceptions are Kaijage (1993) and Iliffe (2002), who focused on the Bukoba colonial district. See also Mihanjo (2004).

3 Tanganyika, the current Tanzania mainland, became independent in 1961. Prior to this, the territory was under German (1891–1919) and then British (1920–61) colonial rule. Tanganyika, the denomination

adopted during the British period, was abandoned in 1964, following the unification of two earlier independent states, Tanganyika and Zanzibar; hence the current name Tanzania.

4 See Hall (1990: 20–4) and Knight (1974: 32–40).

5 TNA Acc. 450 no. 3, 'Venereal Diseases.'

6 TNA Acc. 450 no. 3, 'Venereal Diseases,' a circular from the District Commissioner, Rungwe, to the Provincial Commissioner, Iringa province, 4 March 1927.

7 TNA Acc. 450 no. 3, 'Venereal Diseases,' a circular from the Principal Medical Officer, DSM, to the Director of Medical and Sanitary Services, dated 25 October 1928.

8 Ibid.

9 TNA Acc. 450 no. 1401/15, Annual Report Southern Highlands 1946, a circular from the Senior Medical Officer to the Director of Medical Services (henceforth DMS), DSM, 19 May 1947.

10 TNA Acc. 450 no. 3, Minutes of Meeting held in Palace Chambers

(London), 3 February 1948. The meeting was convened to discuss the problem of venereal diseases in East Africa. TNA Acc. 450 no. 3 77/26/5, 'Venereal disease in Bundali and Bulambia,' a circular from the District Commissioner (Tukuyu) to the Medical Officer, Tukuyu, 3 March 1945.

11 TNA Acc. 450 no. 3, Annual Report for 1957 of the Provincial Medical Officer, Southern Highlands Province, Mbeya.

12 TNA Acc. 450 no. 3, a circular from the Provincial Commissioner, Mbeya, to the Chief Secretary to the Government, DSM, 10 October 1947.

13 TNA Acc. 450 no. 3/2, a circular from the Provincial Commissioner, Northern Province, Arusha, 'Control of Venereal Diseases,' to the Chief Secretary to the Government, DSM, 1 November 1947.

14 Ibid.

15 TNA Acc. 450 no. 3, Return of Venereal Diseases for Six Months ending 31 December 1920.

16 TNA Acc. AB 424, Reports: Tanganyika Territory 1922–1923.

17 Ibid.

18 TNA Acc. 450 no. 3 1423/19, Annual Report of 1947, Return of Diseases in non-European male patients with totals for females. Return of Diseases in European males with totals for females.

19 TNA Mbeya District Book II, Tanganyika Territory Population Census 1948.

20 TNA Acc. 450 no. 3 1623/9, Annual Report of the year 1958 for the Provincial Medical Officer, Southern Highlands, Mbeya.

21 TNA Acc. 450 no. 3/ 2, a letter from the Acting Senior Medical Officer, Mwanza, to DMS, 'Venereal Diseases Differential Diagnosis,' 28 November 1935.

22 TNA Acc. 450 no. 3, W. A. Young, 'Notes on Attitude Towards Cases of Possible Treponematoses in East Africa,' 25 November 1947.

23 In Tanzania all medical practitioners are called 'doctors.' During colonial times, the term applied to any practitioner with some medical training, or in charge of a medical facility. That included Tribal Medical Assistants (TMAs), who were granted a government certificate after three years' medical training in a government training institution. Government-certified Tribal Medical Aides undertook training shorter than three years; while Tribal Dressers received other training apart from the aforementioned.

24 TNA Acc. 450 no. 3/2, a letter from the Acting Senior Medical Officer, Mwanza, to DMS, 'Venereal Diseases Differential Diagnosis,' 28 November 1935.

25 TNA Secretariat AB 424, Report of Tanganyika Territory 1922–1923.

26 TNA Acc. 450 no. 3, a circular from the Principal Medical Officer, DSM, to the Director of Medical and Sanitary Services, DSM, 25 October 1928.

27 TNA Acc. 450 no. 3 10340, a letter from the DMSS to the Chief Secretary, DSM, 28 April 1927.

28 TNA Acc. 450 no. 2 M. 87, a circular from the Medical Officer-in-Charge, Sewahaji Hospital, DSM, to the Principal Medical Officer, Civil Administration, DSM, 3 March 1920.

29 TNA Acc. 450 no. 2, Extract from Monthly Report of MOHT for June 1925.

30 TNA Acc. 450 no. 3 77/26/5, a letter from the District Commissioner, Mbeya, to the Provincial Commissioner, Southern Highlands Province, Mbeya, 16 October 1945.

31 TNA Acc. 450 no. 3, a letter

from the Medical Officer of Health, DSM, to the DMS, DSM, 5 April 1948.

32  TNA Acc. 450 no. 3/2, 'Venereal Diseases Differential Diagnosis,' a circular from the Acting Senior Medical Officer, Mwanza, to DMS, DSM, 28 November 1935.

33  Ibid.

34  TNA Acc. 450 no. 3, Extract from Minutes of the Advisory Committee on Public Health, 14 April 1947.

35  TNA Acc. 450 no. 3, a circular from the DMS to the Chief Secretary, DSM, 24 November 1945.

36  TNA Acc. 450 no. 3, a circular from the Medical Officer, Sukumaland, to the Provincial Medical Officer, Mwanza, 5 April 1948.

37  TNA Acc. 450 no. 3/2, a letter from the Medical Officer, Government Hospital, Mbeya, to the Senior Medical Office, Southern Highlands Province, Mbeya, 6 April 1948; TNA Acc. 450 no. 3/2, Minutes of the Meeting Held in Palace Chambers, London, 3 February 1948; Extract of the Summary of the Proceedings of the Second Conference of Provincial Medical Officers held at Medical Headquarters, DSM, 26–30 August 1946; TNA Acc. 450 no. 3, a letter from the Principal Medical Officer, Tanganyika Territory, to the Chief Secretary to the Government, DSM, 23 March 1922; TNA Acc. 450 no. 3, a letter from the District Officer (Rungwe) to the Provincial Commissioner, Iringa Province, 4 March 1927; TNA Acc. 450 no. 3, Report of the Minutes of Recent Meeting on the Advisory Committee on Public Health from the DMS to the Chief Secretary, DSM, 25 May 1948.

38  TNA Acc. 450 no. 2, Extract from Monthly Report of MOHT for June 1925.

39  TNA Acc. 450 no. 3, a letter from the District Officer (Rungwe) to the Provincial Commissioner, Iringa Province, 4 March 1927.

40  TNA Acc. 450 no. 3, a letter from Lieutenant General, Officer Commanding-in-Charge, East Africa Command, Nairobi: 'Subject VD,' to His Excellency the Chairman, Conference of East Africa Governors, Nairobi, 5 April 1945.

41  Tanganyika Territory Ordinances Enacted during the year 1944, with an Appendix containing Proclamations, Rules, Regulations, Orders and Notices (Dar es Salaam: Government Printers, 1945).

42  TNA Acc. 450 no. 3, a letter from the Medical Officer to the Government Hospital, Tukuyu, to the Senior Medical Officer, Mbeya, 14 April 1948; interview with M. Mgogo, 24 October 2009, Mpanda village, Mbozi district.

43  Interview with H. Myala, Mbozi, 18 October 2008. The interviewee spent a number of years in South Africa and Tanga as a migrant worker.

44  Interview, M. Mgogo.

45  TNA Acc. 450 no. 3, 'Venereal Diseases,' a letter from the Senior Medical Officer, Lindi, to the DMS, DSM, 13 April 1946.

46  TNA Acc. 450 no. 3, 'Re: Venereal Diseases,' a circular from the Acting DMS to Senior Medical Officers to all Provinces (n.d.).

47  TNA Acc. 450 no. 3, 'Venereal Disease,' Extract from Agenda for consideration by Members of the Advisory Committee on Public Health, 9 February 1948.

48  TNA Acc. 450 no. 3, 'Re: Venereal Disease,' a letter from the Senior Medical Officer, Lindi, to the DMS, DSM, 22 March 1948.

49  Ibid.

50  TNA Acc. 450 no. 3, Annual

Provincial Medical Report of 1958, Southern Highlands Province, Mbeya.

51 TNA Acc. no. 3 10024, 'Dr A. J. Boase's Report on the use of Bismuth Salts for the Treatment of Yaws and Venereal Diseases,' a circular from the Secretary of State for Colonies to the Governor, Tanganyika, 4 December 1928.

52 TNA Acc. 450 no. 3, Tanganyika Territory Annual Report 1925.

53 TNA Acc. no. 3 10024, 'Dr A. J. Boase's Report on the use of Bismuth Salts for the Treatment of Yaws and Venereal Diseases.'

54 TNA Acc. 450 no. 3, a circular from the Principal Officer, Tunduru, to the Chief Secretary to the Government, 7 May 1921.

55 TNA Acc. no. 3 10024, 'Dr A. J. Boase's Report on the use of Bismuth Salts for the Treatment of Yaws and Venereal Diseases.'

56 TNA Acc. 450 no. 3, a circular from the DMS to the Senior Medical Officer, Dodoma, 20 October 1945; a circular from the DMS to the Chief Secretary, 24 November 1945.

57 TNA Acc. 450 no. 3/1401, Annual Medical Report 1946: Southern Highlands Province, 19 May 1947; TNA Acc. 450 no. 3/1401, Annual Medical Report: Southern Highlands Province 1945.

58 TNA Acc. 450 no. 3/193, a circular from the Chief Secretary to the Government, Tanganyika, to the Chief Secretary to the Governors' Conference, Nairobi, 16 June 1945; TNA Acc. 450 no. 1098, a letter from the Lieutenant General General Officer Commanding-in-Charge East Africa Command, Nairobi, to His Excellence, the Chairman, Conference of East Africa Governors, Nairobi, 5 April 1945.

59 TNA Acc. 450 no. 3/140, Annual Medical Report Southern Highlands Province 1947.

60 TNA Acc. 450 no. 3, a letter from the Medical Officer of Health, Tanga, to the DMS, DSM, 29 April 1948.

61 TNA Acc. 450 no. 3/1179, 'Post War Medical Policy 1943–1945,' a letter from the Medical Officer, Government Hospital, Mwanza, to the DMS, 20 October 1944.

62 TNA Acc. 450 no. 3/1401/15, Annual Medical Report: Southern Highlands Province 1947.

63 Mbeya District Book II East African Population Census, 1948, Mbeya District, African Population as at 23 August 1948.

64 TNA Acc. 450 no. 3/1401/15, Annual Medical Report: Southern Highlands Province 1947.

65 TNA Acc. 450 no. 3/1623, Annual Medical Report 1958.

66 TNA Acc. 450. no. 3, Principal Medical Officer (PMO), Dar es Salaam, to the Director of Medical and Sanitary Services, Dar es Salaam, 25 October 1920.

## References

Brandt, A. (1987) *No Magic Bullet: A Social History of Venereal Diseases in the United States since 1880*, New York: Oxford University Press.

Brock, B. (1966) 'The Nyiha of Mbozi,' *Tanzania Notes and Records*, 65.

Foucault, M. (1981) *The History of Sexuality*, vol. I: *An Introduction*, London: Penguin.

Hall, M. (1990) *Farmers, Kings and Traders*, Chicago, IL: University of Chicago Press.

Hunt, N. (1998) 'STDs, suffering and their derivatives in Congo – Zaire: notes towards a historical ethnography of diseases,' in C. Becker et al. (eds), *Experiencing* and *Understanding AIDS in Africa*, Dakar: Codesria.

Hunter, S. (2003) *Black Death: AIDS in Africa*, New York: Palgrave.

Iliffe, J. (2002) *East African Doctors: A History of the Modern Profession*, Cambridge: Cambridge University Press.

Kaijage, F. (1993) 'AIDS control and the burden of history in north-western Tanzania,' *Population and Environment: A Journal of Inter-disciplinary Studies*, 14(3), January.

Knight, C. (1974) *Ecology and Change in an African Community*, New York: Academic Press.

Leibing, A. (ed.) (1997) *The Medical Anthropologies in Brazil*, Berlin: VWB.

Mihanjo, E. (2004) 'Colonial policy on sexually transmitted diseases and other infectious diseases in Tanganyika, 1900–1960,' in Y. Lawi and B. Mapunda (eds), *History of Diseases and Healing in Africa*, Dar es Salaam: History Department.

Miller, N. (1968) 'The political survival of traditional leadership,' *Journal of Modern African Studies*, 6.

— (1972) 'The political survival of traditional leadership', in L. Cliffe and J. Saul (eds), *Socialism in Tanzania*, vol. 1, Nairobi: East African Publishing House.

Nguyen, V. and M. Sama (2008) 'Social determinants of HIV transmission: lessons from Africa,' in V. Nguyen and M. Sama (eds), *Governing Health Systems in Africa*, Dakar: Codesria.

Tuck, M. (2001) 'Venereal disease, sexuality and society in Uganda,' in R. Davidson and L. Hall (eds), *Sex, Sin and Suffering: Venereal Diseases and European Society since 1870*, London: Routledge.

Young, W. (1948) 'Notes on attitude towards cases of possible treponematosis in East Africa,' *East African Medical Journal*, 25(12), December.

## Archival sources

Tanzania National Archives (TNA), Accession 450 no. 3, Venereal Disease

Mbeya Zonal Archives (MBZA), Health Department Accession no. 13, and 16, Labour Department Accession no. 1

Colonial Secretariat file AB 424, Reports Tanganyika Territory 1922–1923

## Interviews

Dr E. Mwitula, Dar es Salaam, 18 February 2009

M. Mgogo, Mbozi, 24 October 2009

H. Myala, Mbozi, 18 October 2008

# 6 | Violence and the emergence of gay and lesbian activism in Argentina, 1983–90

## DIEGO SEMPOL

Gay and lesbian activists were pioneers in establishing close relations between the discourses of human rights and sexuality, confirming the power of the notion of human rights to politicize social action, and enable the emergence of new subjects and issues (Pecheny 2001b; Brown 2002). However, events during the 1980s in Argentina show there is no linear relation between the formal functioning of a democracy and democratization of society at large (O'Donnell 1996). In that decade, gay and lesbian (GL) organizations were attempting to expand the notion of citizenship itself. Recent studies of the emergence and development of gay, lesbian, bisexual, and transgender (GLBT) social movements (Fillieule and Duyvendak 1999; Epstein 1999; Brown 2002; Pecheny 2001b; Facchini 2005) have paid little attention to the role of violence as a mobilizer, and its impact on organizational forms and political strategies. In this chapter, I address the emergence of gay and lesbian activism in Argentina during the 1980s, analyzing the links between the political structure and the role that violence against gays and lesbians played in this configuration.

### Political actors, GL rights and 'democratic consolidation'

Although the Argentinean Criminal Code of 1886 did not mention the crime of sodomy, sexual dissidents have suffered police persecution and harassment throughout the 200 years of this liberal republic in South America. This repression of homosexual activity by law enforcers acquired legal status by means of vaguely worded Police Decrees applied to the control and regulation of prostitution and homosexual sociability, often involving bribery, extensive violence, detention, and torture.[1] With varying intensity during the twentieth century in Argentina, gays, lesbians, and transgendered persons suffered periods of state persecution under legislation that expressly discriminated against them.

This system of legal and illegal repression was in force in 1983, when constitutional guarantees were restored after the last military dictatorship (1976–83). During the transition process triggered by the defeat in the 'Falklands War' (1982), among the arc of opposition groups the human rights movement stood out, reporting the enforced disappearance of 30,000 people at the hands of state forces during the military regime. The human rights movement managed to influence both the political opening process and the ethical context of the new democratic regime. In Argentina, to a larger extent than in other Latin American transitions, human rights were a key element in the new democracy (Jelin 1994: 46). The new government attempted to construct a democratic culture adopting human rights as its basic framework and leading a cultural modernization program which included a revision of the education system and family law (Barros 2002: 111). A Shared Parental Rights Act was passed in 1985, and a Divorce Act in 1987.

During what has been termed 'democratic consolidation,'[2] organizations for the defense of gays and lesbians emerged in Buenos Aires,[3] thus defining 'framing processes' (McAdam et al. 1999: 40) that would become a reference for the future GLBT movement and society as a whole. Coordinadora Gay was formed in 1982, Comunidad Homosexual Argentina (CHA) in 1984, Grupo Autogestivo de Lesbianas (GAL) in 1986, and *Cuadernos de Existencia Lesbiana* (*Cuadernos*) in 1987. A similar process was also taking place in other Southern Cone cities (Montevideo, São Paulo, Rio de Janeiro), and in all cases contacts can be traced between the local groups, groups in other countries, and international LGTB organizations.[4]

Studies on democratic transition and consolidation have focused on institutional aspects and negotiation among elites (Fox 1990; Waylen 1994), paying little attention to the social aspects of democratization processes, particularly to gender (Waylen 2000) and sexuality. Addressing these issues, I argue that gay and lesbian movements introduced new notions of citizenship, and debated definitions of democracy and its reach. From their point of view, the goal of full democratization was not being accomplished. The rights of gays and lesbians continued to be systematically violated during this period. In this chapter I address two key aspects which illuminate such disjuncture. First, the reasons that explain the emergence of gay and lesbian organizations in the 1980s, and the relation between their strategies and organizational forms, and the various forms of violence to which gays and lesbians were subjected during the period. Secondly, the challenges these groups faced during the 1980s, as they sought to become a unified social movement, emanating from differentials in how their identities were configured in relation to the experience of specific forms of violence.

**Violence and the emergence of gay and lesbian organizations**

Academic and activist discourses on the Argentine GLBT movement have tended to naturalize the definition of CHA as a human rights organization.[5] This group was a pioneer in the Latin American and international context in linking sexuality and human rights, but that innovation did not take place among lesbian feminist organizations. In this period both GAL's and *Cuadernos'* concerns were focused on identity issues. How are these differences explained?

The human rights movement was a key player in the democratic transition process. CHA followed closely the interpretation frameworks of the human rights movement, imitating its organizational form (as a civil association, outside of the political party system) and strategies (police complaints, judicialization, public visibility in media and street protest, alliance with other social movements). The consolidation of human rights as a basic framework explains the expansion of political opportunities for gay and lesbian organizations. But CHA – not without resistance from and tensions with other organizations – also introduced sexuality as an issue in the human rights field. CHA's slogan, 'The free exercise of sexuality is a human right,' expresses the struggle to legitimize sexual matters as worthy of state guarantees and protection.

President Alfonsín's secularizing impetus caused a confrontation with the Catholic Church, opening a political opportunity to introduce the debate and legal reforms toward gender equity. This process, however, did not include the gay and lesbian rights agenda. CHA found no allies in any fractions of the major political parties during the period. That key absence would, to a certain degree, prevent an expansion of opportunities. The emergence of CHA in 1984 can be explained only as the outcome of a complex combination of factors. A positive one is the expansion of cultural opportunities opened by the renegotiation of the sexual order effected in changes in legislation regarding the legal status of women, thanks to the alliance of women's organizations with the Unión Cívica Radical party since the early 1980s (Htun 2003: 120). A negative one is the permanence of forms of state repression against homosexuals.

GAL and *Cuadernos* were created within the feminist movement under the local influence of Latin American feminist conferences and the independent lesbian struggle that was taking place at the time in Mexico, Chile, Peru, the Dominican Republic, and Costa Rica (Mogrovejo 2000: 357). Feminist lesbians challenged the universalism and individualism inherent in the liberal ideology of human rights.

Their critique incorporated gender difference as a constitutive aspect of their struggle.

I will argue that the role of violence is key to understanding the strategies and organizational forms displayed by GL movements during the period. Robben and Nordstrom (1995: 4) point out that violence is formative because it modifies individuals' perception of who they are and what they are fighting for across space and time, as well as the identities they construct. Jelin (2002: 100-3) has argued that the interpretational frameworks of the phenomenon of violence differ, in general, for men and women, as they hold different positions in the gender system, which imply clearly different vital experiences and hierarchical social relations. These notions lead to a differential analysis of the types of violence faced by gays and lesbians.

Records show that, during this period, gays were the predominant victims of police repression against sexual dissidents, and murders publicized in the press,[6] while symbolic violence prevailed in the case of lesbians. This model distinction, akin to Weberian 'ideal types,' is not intended to imply that other forms of violence were not operating in both cases; or to deny the symbolic dimensions in physical violence: as Cardoso (2005) points out, a moral dimension is indispensable in order to conceptualize physical violence as such. Indeed, the object of this discussion is to locate the paradigmatic role of specific definitions of violence in relation to the pragmatic and expressive content of gay and lesbian struggles for recognition, and how nuances in those definitions were reflected in different trajectories.

Although records are fragmentary and not systematic, the scope of the problem can be measured by comparing data produced by the CHA and press reports. Between June 1982 and September 1983, nineteen gays were murdered – in most cases tortured and executed in their homes – in Buenos Aires. The police never found the perpetrators. Only two people were arrested. Their identities were withheld, although they were finally prosecuted for two homicides. In 1982, the self-named Commando Cóndor had spread threats in public media calling for the killing of homosexuals. In the context of state terrorism exercised by the military dictatorship, such events can be understood under the doctrine of National Security, which linked the integrity of national society to Catholic values and defence of the 'traditional family.' Revolutionary politics, youth culture, and sexual liberation were constructed as threats, epitomized in the figures of 'Marxists,' 'homosexuals,' and 'drug addicts' (Filc 1997: 44).

Also alarming are the figures for police detentions in the city of

Buenos Aires: between 20 December 1983 and 21 March 1984 (the first three months of constitutional rule under Alfonsín), the police arrested 21,343 people under the Criminal Records Act (Jáuregui 1987: 187). It is not clear how many were homosexuals. According to Jáuregui, after being detained, men were often threatened with a phone call to their workplace or families to explain the reasons for their detention. The call could be avoided if the person signed a 'confession' acknowledging he was gay. The number of detainees rose once again in 1986. Police raids had two 'epicenters' within the city (Precincts 17 and 19), corresponding to gay cruising areas, where gay discos and bars were also located. In early 1987, the main newspapers (*Clarín*, *Crónica*, *La Nación*) confirmed more raids at gay venues and sites. CHA records for 1989 register twenty-eight reports of anti-gay raids within a period of six months, some of which seized up to two hundred people. According to gay activists who kept records of police repression during that period,[7] in the early 1990s the focus of police repression gradually retreated from gay sites, became more intermittent, and started to focus on the transgendered population, whose presence in the Federal Capital was becoming more overt.

In the case of the CHA, since raids took place in gay areas and sites, but not against its activists, I believe it is more relevant to include it as a dimension, rather than an indicator, of political opportunities.[8] As Tarrow (1997: 157) has pointed out, collective action is more likely in systems characterized by a mix of open and closed factors. This duality between democracy and human rights as a founding framework on the one hand, and police repression on the other, is key to understanding the expressive content of the gay movement and its mobilization structure. In the Argentine political and social tradition, police repression against subaltern social sectors was not new; neither was the recognition among these sectors of the absence of certain rights. What was new was the emergence of gay activism, whose focus on sexual freedom was in fact redefining 1980 vernacular, as well as global notions of citizenship. According to Della Porta (1999: 100), one of the consequences of repression is the granting of political connotations to everyday actions.

CHA records make almost no mention of women. What was happening with lesbians then? Low lesbian visibility in the public realm is due to gender patterns that, materially and symbolically, relegate women to the private realm (Mason 1996; Fuskova and Marek 1992). Lesbians were excluded from public discourse. That pattern is confirmed by Fígari and Gemetro (2009) in their account of women who desired other women in Argentina before 1970. In public media and state discourse, lesbians existed only by omission. Their existence is not enunciated, so lesbians are accorded the status of non-being, as non-women. If women can only exist, according to predominant social values, to fulfill the project of caregiving and motherhood, subordinated to a man, the absence of those elements is a problem that merits debate. Traditional family models still exerted their hegemony in the 1980s: from the 'familism' of the human rights movement, to the rejection of divorce by the Catholic Church (Filc 1997; Jelin 2002). Thus, violence in this case operates less as the conspicuous use of physical power, and more as a way of configuring the limits of an intelligible existence. In the lesbian perspective, everyday life becomes a prison sustained by society as a whole.

### CHA: a response to state repression

CHA was founded on 16 April 1984 as a coordination space for several homosexual groups created in 1982 and 1983 as social networks, which came to form the collective basis of this new organization.[9] Since then, the activist group has attained strong institutionalization and inner specialization. This process was closely related to the impact of police repression and conceptions regarding state violence. The need for this new space of articulation was explained as follows by Carlos Jáuregui, the first CHA president:

> During the first months of the government of Raúl Alfonsín there were no repressive acts, until in March 1984 a disco was raided and 300 homosexuals were detained. After this raid, the Federal Police conducted a policy of continuous repression that led to the unity of several of the groups that worked in isolation, and others that emerged at the time. The civil association CHA is thus formed in a crowded meeting. CHA becomes a human rights organization that advocates for the free exercise of sexuality and gives the association a legal framework, leaving behind the previous hidden and clandestine forms, to defend the individual rights of homosexual people.[10]

CHA thus became the first organization to make sexual identity a public, political, and citizenship issue. The founding group chose the civil association format as the first strategic step to ensure associationism and provide an anchor for the struggle against police repression in the format of a legal collective. Bylaws were approved on 21 May 1984, defining the election of authorities (president and vice-president),[11] and an operational structure. From the start, CHA generated organizational routines, administrative tasks, electoral procedures, internal documentation (bylaws, commission reports, position papers), and media releases, as well as print publications.

The goal of fighting police repression and discrimination, advocating for human rights, influenced how CHA was organized and how its work was understood by its members. Early on, the organization created a Legal Service. A lawyer was hired to give free legal counsel and was in charge of seeking the release of detainees, and their defence. A Solidarity Commission was formed, to provide the 'moral support needed by detainees and those who [are put on] trial.'[12]

CHA's recruiting routines involved the 'realization' of sexual identity through an ideological matrix focused on human rights. This generated a social conflict which was considered a step toward achieving an individual merger with the struggle carried out by CHA. Indeed, 'realization' implied a 'rite of passage' to become a 'homosexual militant.' In this process the organization promoted a significant learning process (Schütz 1993: 192–200) which enabled a reconstruction of individual identity under non-stigmatized parameters, informed by political commitment. The notion of rights on which this process was based implied an idea of victimization that enabled the new member to become a mobilized player, relating responsibility and pain. 'Social cooperation incentives' (Gamson and Meyer 1982) were created, which activated individuals' willingness to raise their voices against authority.

Both the goals of 'realization' and of 'letting yourself be known' worked toward increasing and developing CHA's ability to mobilize so as to make their public interventions and social influence more effective. Mobilization was considered by leaders like Carlos Jáuregui as a tool that encouraged members' politicization, as well as their coming of age as activists. This notion of mobilization as key to defeating repression was closely aligned with a call for 'citizen participation' by the Alfonsín administration, aimed at modifying a prevailing authoritarian culture, in place partly as an inheritance of the military regime. This 'mobilizing' model – which left a strong impression on the institutional dynamics (resources, training, yearly timetable of activities) of the organization – was in conflict with another model, based on the idea of 'service' and 'community.' The latter encouraged a more self-referential institutionalism, and was focused on the consolidation of sociability spaces and the construction of grassroots solidarity links. Alejandro Zalazar, CHA president for several periods, outlined in 1986 what he termed the excessively 'political' nature of the organization, and he proposed making its human rights policy more flexible in order to 'adapt to the social circumstances the country lives in.' He suggested transforming the working groups into spaces open to participants' spontaneous demands: 'It's about channeling through these groups all of those homosexuals that come to CHA with other concerns that are not exclusively political.'[13]

Police repression became significant to explain the transformation of 'discrete identities' (Pecheny 2002), the politicization of gays, and the development of the representation mechanisms of a strategically construed 'community.' Although in Buenos Aires police repression against gays did not generate spontaneous acts of collective resistance during the detentions,[14] reports of police raids increased the public exposition of gay activists, made CHA known, and provided alternative models to traditional media coverage of law enforcement and gay sociability. The issue of visibility led to a debate within the CHA on the most appropriate way to appear before the media, resulting in a trend to homogenize the existing diversity within the gay community (Rapisardi and Modarelli 2001). CHA members made explicit recommendations as to what could legitimately be made public in order to achieve political goals.

The recommendations defined parameters of what behaviors were acceptable, and an explanatory framework about disruptive differences. For Jáuregui, the *marica* (fag) and the *bombero* (fireman) were two 'social characters resulting from repression.'[15]

### The state and sexual politics

In the 1980s, CHA developed an integrationist approach, minimizing the differences between homosexuals and the rest of society, making their presence visible in all social and professional spheres. For instance, CHA talked about 'homosexual dignity,' stressing adherence to universal humanistic values, as opposed to 'gay pride,' which was understood as an unwanted promotion of group distinctions. This interpretational framework, based on legality, characterized CHA's political strategy and was a springboard to demanding rights and legal reform.

Grimson (2007: 39) has argued that Argentine social formation is based on a rejection of diversity. That is why in this country social conflict acquired a language of direct political engagement. This long-term trait was reinforced by the Alfonsín administration's project of cultural modernization, which sought to develop a democratic culture and rules above particular demands. CHA took part in this transformation process by developing demands based on equality. In the Argentine movement, identity becomes the foundation for an assimilation strategy that relativizes its significance and consequences. The notion of homosexuality as a fixed condition was an efficient way to challenge medical and religious discourses that stated that homosexuality was a reversible condition.

CHA demands were aimed at the state and sought to revoke laws and decrees repressing homosexuals, seeking protection from institutionalized forms of violence and discrimination. To these demands CHA also added the legalization of abortion, birth planning methods, the decriminalization of prostitution, sex education, and adequate care for people living with HIV/AIDS.[16] In order to achieve these goals CHA designed a political strategy that privileged high media visibility. CHA's presence legitimized the organization as a political player in the eyes of the media, politicians, and the general public. However, although CHA leaders managed to establish fluid contact with representatives from various political parties and government authorities, they rapidly detected that there was no political will to solve the repression problem. In an interview with a national publication, Antonio Tróccoli, minister of the interior (head of internal security) in the Alfonsín government, stated:

> Homosexuality is an illness, so we shall treat it as such. If the police have acted it is because there have been exhibitions or attitudes that publicly compromise what could be called the rules of the game of a society that wants to be preserved from manifestations of this sort, so there is no such persecution. On the contrary, I believe it has to be treated like an illness.[17]

Tróccoli's downplaying of repression against homosexuals fueled CHA's investment in judicial strategies. During those years, the association faced a series of negative rulings. In 1985, an attempt to include discrimination based on sexual orientation as an offense contemplated in the Anti-Discrimination Act 23,592 ('Open letter to legislators') failed. In 1986, a campaign to repeal Police Decrees signed by 2,000 petitioners also failed. In August 1986, a criminal appeals court ruled in favor of the constitutionality of regulations that allowed the Federal Police to make an arrest without a court order. Facing a substantial number of social demands and corporate pressure, the Alfonsín government implemented a policy that crystallized a notion of human rights associated exclusively with the issue of crimes committed during the dictatorship. This configuration and CHA's weak capacity for mobilization during those years enabled the state to ignore or minimize CHA's demands.

CHA also sought to implement alliances with other organizations in order to expand its action front. CHA activists attempted to approach the feminist movement and other homosexual organizations in the country. It managed temporary alliances, but never the consolidation of a common agenda. They also attempted to join the human rights movement. CHA's first public appearance was staged on 20 September 1984, during a human rights march in support of the Report of the National Commission for the Disappeared, delivered to the Argentine president. The first stand-alone appearance would come only in late 1986, in a demonstration in front of Buenos Aires Cathedral, against a letter on homosexuality released by the Vatican that year. During the 1980s CHA activists, banners, and slogans were present in most public demonstrations organized by the human rights movement.

In 1987, CHA managed to participate as a guest in 'organ meetings' (a caucus of human rights organizations) that brought together the 'historical' organizations of the Argentine human rights movement. State violence against homosexuals implied that, among the available repertoires at the time, human rights organizations constituted the political and ideological articulation closest to the reality lived by homosexuals in Argentina. This interpretational framework also permitted a reinterpretation of persecution against homosexuals as 'repression' and 'discrimination.' One of the terms mobilized to refer to the repression of homosexuals was 'psychological torture' during detention.[18] This articulation is one of the most significant theoretical achievements of the Argentine homosexual movement, which managed to intertwine sexuality and human rights almost a decade before the international GLBT movement.

The theoretical connections between (homo)sexuality and human rights varied over time in the trajectory of CHA as an organization. Members occasionally supported the idea of a progressive transformation of human rights. At other times, they claimed a person's right to free use of their body. In 1986, a CHA assembly on human rights produced an internal paper supporting the theory of indivisibility of human rights;[19] while during the same period the International Gay and Lesbian Association (ILGA) still talked about sexual rights and sexual freedom (Correa et al. 2008: 167-8). Feminist and GLBT transnational networks tried to link sexual rights with human rights for the first time in the UN sphere, in the mid-1990s (ibid.: 167-71).

### 'Patriarchal oppression' and lesbian feminism

The feminist and women's movements in Argentina were empowered during the democratic transition by a favorable framework of political opportunities. The local scenario was vast, distributed among various organizations working in multiple layers (political, social, health, academic, and grassroots), interacting with each other and with other social players in the form of a complex network.

During this period, feminists and women activists created a number of spaces, such as Comisión Pro Reforma del Ejercicio de la Patria Potestad (Commission for the Reform of Parental Rights) and the Multisectorial de la Mujer (Women's Multi-sector Group), where they pursued a common agenda: the struggle against violence, legalization of divorce, and shared parental rights. In 1986, the First National Women's Meeting took place, and it has been repeated annually since then with a constantly growing attendance.

In this section I analyze the Grupo Autogestivo de Lesbianas (GAL) (Self-governed Lesbian Group) and *Cuadernos de Existencia Lesbiana* (*Cuadernos*) (Notebooks on Lesbian Existence), the two groups that politicized their erotic-affective specificity, identifying themselves as 'lesbian feminists.' Both were born within feminism and under the influence of Latin American international feminist networks (Mogrovejo 2000: 357). GAL was founded in 1986 at Lugar de Mujer[20] (Woman's Place), operated until 1989, and published *Codo a Codo* (Side by Side) and *Sin Candado* (No to Padlocks). *Cuadernos*, a publication with a staff of variable size, was founded in 1987 with support from ATEM,[21] but in 1992 it underwent a transformation to become Convocatoria Lesbiana (Lesbian Call).

Although the notion of 'lesbophobia' had not been appropriated, and its use began only in the early 1990s, violence became an important (among the notions mobilized by Argentine feminism in the 1980s)[22] and recurrent issue in the life of organizations and their publications. It was presented as an extensive problem, affecting culture, family, and economy, and causing social subordination and oppression under 'compulsory heterosexuality,'[23] which imposed the roles of 'woman, wife, daughter, and mother.'[24] The patriarchal system was the central problem, it was said, and the final explanation for a life of violence and submission. The notion of violence, from this perspective, not only applied to physical means of overcoming resistance, but to any type of domination practiced on another person, which took different forms and modes according to circumstances and power relations.[25]

As Chejter (1996) recalls, the first actions on the issue of violence were determined by the articulation of very different groups. According to Chejter, at the beginning of the 1980s understandings of violence became fragmented, as state recognition tended to compartmentalize health and judicial claims. In lesbian feminist groups, a comprehensive reading and a systemic cultural critique of violence against women prevailed, although this vision would be mitigated in the following decade. This comprehensive view can be related, as Mason (1996) argues, to the fact that anti-lesbian violence often operates under a network of prejudice where gender, sex, and sexuality categories are not perceived. Mason (ibid.) found that victims interviewed for her work in Australia very rarely believed that the verbal aggression they had suffered had its origin exclusively in their sexual orientation. Most could not determine whether they had been verbally abused or assaulted for being lesbians or simply for being women. This feature, which also appears in the testimonies of Fuskova and Marek (1992) in Argentina, could help explain why lesbian-feminist organizations were formed in this period within feminism and not outside it. Gender violence and violence against lesbians are deeply intertwined in social life, and feminism offered an optimal space in which to understand the matter politically.

In organizational terms, GAL and *Cuadernos* – in contrast to what happened with a good part of the feminist movement – did not seek to formalize their existence or define bylaws to regulate their internal operations. They were basically horizontally managed, autonomous spaces, without formalized representation mechanisms. This organizational mode was directly linked to their goals: taking lesbians out of their invisibility, and facing the symbolic violence of a social discourse which denied and silenced their existence. Therefore they formed thought-action groups and crafted their own publications and other communications media. Under this approach, seeking any form of state mediation was interpreted as an unnecessary compromise: 'with small legal reforms we will be back to trusting the husband-state. And we distance ourselves from the only possible solution, trusting ourselves and other women and together reversing the colonization of our bodies and our minds.'[26] The weapons to be used were 'desire, possibility, dreams, and metaphor.'[27]

Although, in the 1990s, lesbian organizations aimed their visibilization strategies at society as a whole, taking part in television shows, in gay pride marches, and in publishing projects of all kinds, in the 1980s the goals were humbler; targeted, above all, within feminism and the women's movement. In 1987, the editorial of the publication *Cuadernos de Existencia Lesbiana* called for lesbians to 'break with isolation, get away from the alienating ghetto ... and address these women's problems from a feminist analysis.'[28] Visibility implied 'pride,'[29] and was understood as a way to break with oppression, to challenge patriarchy in order to gain freedom, and to recover the body 'colonized by the system' by enabling the redirection of eroticism toward other women.[30] Their struggle also aimed at constructing a political lesbian identity, as 'feminist lesbians.' Lesbianism, according to members of GAL and *Cuadernos*, was not therefore just a 'sexual preference,'[31] but first of all a form of resistance to patriarchy and male oppression. This became a form of political struggle and confrontation with patriarchal violence, as it allowed for the creation of new forms of relations and affect.

Apart from the issue of visibility, in this period both feminists and lesbian feminists insisted on stressing the relations between cultural, economic, and political forms of subordination. Discrimination, from this point of view, was not a formal issue between equal individuals, which could be corrected through education and legal reform. In the 1980s, this led lesbian groups to reject the development of strategies seeking legal reform. They sought, instead, a countercultural alternative: 'The formation of lesbian thought-action groups opens up the possibility of building a counterculture, with alternative values and operating ways, a seed for a counter-system in sharp opposition to the dominant system.'[32]

The emergence of 'lesbian feminism' is the clearest example of sexual identities forged in the mobilization and participation process, rather than a pre-existing condition. Most lesbian feminist activists were women who had worked for years within feminism until this process finally transformed them and encouraged them to expand their spaces and their ways of participating, and conceptualized their activism; discovering and politicizing their erotic-affective particularity. The politicization of their identities was related to the stigmatization lesbians suffered within feminism. The formation of lesbian groups allowed them to confront the stigma and introduce a debate.

This confrontation within feminism can also help explain the stress on identity on the part of GAL and *Cuadernos*, as well as their strong essentialist and trans-historical stand, which led to reflection about and investigation of the history of humanity in order to retrieve landmarks in the 'collective memory' of non-patriarchal societies.[33] In this sense, there was a major divergence from CHA, whose activists insisted on talking about 'homosexual dignity,' and developed integrationist strategies. CHA's claims at the time were not located within any movement; instead they developed in an almost opposite direction: to achieve effective integration within the human rights movement and to influence the Alfonsín government.

Of course, not all women who felt erotically and affectively attracted by other women developed the same type of role. As Mason (1996) points out, the experience of violence implies events and an interpretation, a type of knowledge at the time of performing the act of interpretation. Analyzing the form these instances of violence take and the repertoires used to explain and justify them enables understanding of the form in which these episodes are interpreted. An interesting example of this complexity is the role of CHA women, a group of activists who participated in this organization and identified themselves as 'homosexual women' instead of 'lesbian feminists.'[34]

In this case, violence against lesbians was regarded as similar to that suffered by all homosexuals, since the interpretational emphasis was placed first on sexuality, and then on gender. The specificity of homosexual women was acknowledged, but at the same time relativized, and could become part of a comprehensive integrationist agenda that claimed the recognition of sexual orientation as a human right. CHA women were sharply criticized by lesbian feminist organizations, since CHA was considered an organization regulated and controlled by men, which hardly included the needs of lesbians.

CHA minutes from elections and membership rosters reveal a very small number of women during the 1980s, as well as a major difficulty in retaining them. This situation changed in the early 1990s. In 1992 the board of directors had a majority of women.[35]

### GL rights and the 'democratic deficit'

During the 1980s, organizations that politicized sexual identity, making demands and generating a public debate on their situation of social subordination, appeared in the public scenario for the first time in Argentina. The violence suffered by homosexuals and other subaltern subjects at the hands of state agents was seized on by CHA in its public campaigns and judicial actions. In the cycle of contention and the political opportunity structure provided by the emergence of the human rights discourse and the establishment of a human rights movement, violence performed an important role for the configuration of CHA's claims, which explains the creation of a community in the political sphere represented by the gay activist. This transformation, which implied a relocation of the right to a sexual orientation in the political arena, had major effects, as it enabled the development of a political subject that, for the first time, talked about its problems in the first person, and the social circulation of a non-heteronormative model of sexuality.

During the 1980s, the Argentine government engaged with CHA as a player but ignored its demands and even questioned the existence of the problems reported. Only in 1992 did the government, for the first time – and owing to strong international pressure – recognize a homosexual association as legitimate and grant CHA its legal identity. Thus, it started down a path where discrimination and violence toward homosexuals and lesbians progressively gained status as an object of state policy, leaving behind its condition as a 'social problem.' Two events are benchmarks on this path: the inclusion of protection against discrimination due to sexual orientation in the City of Buenos Aires Constitution in 1996; and the revoking of the Offense Code, which included discriminatory clauses toward homosexuals and transgender persons, in 1998. According to Pecheny (2001a), the HIV/AIDS impact was key in this process, and forced the state to integrate gays – and, to a lesser degree, lesbians – in its discourse.

But the Argentine case is theoretically productive in another way. An analysis of the origin of the Argentine gay movement empirically confirms the need to include cultural transformations and the development of interpretational frameworks as significant elements, along with a modification of political opportunities.

The history of lesbian-feminist organizations also raises two important caveats. First, the importance of not considering political opportunities as something objective, since their perception depends on the creation of interpretational frameworks (Gamson and Meyer 1999). Secondly, the need to historicize processes, instead of reproducing the interpretations and common sense of the players. Male chauvinism and discrimination against lesbians within a male-dominated gay movement have often been singled out as the reasons that explain the permanence of lesbian organizations within feminism, and the absence of a joint agenda with gay organizations in the 1980s. But did discrimination against lesbians, as analyzed above, not exist also within the feminist movement? That reasoning does not explain the motives for the scarce articulation between CHA and lesbian feminist groups in the 1980s. Perhaps the explanation lies in the fact that the agendas of gay and lesbian groups were shaped differently, as each category occupied different spaces, and was subject to predominantly different types of violence. This, and the way they interpreted the phenomenon of violence, led to types of participation and political priorities that were difficult to articulate in a united movement.

On the one hand, CHA activists faced the problem of police raids, attempted to defend the human rights of homosexual men and women, and developed interventions addressing the AIDS crisis, conceiving their struggle in juridical terms: judicialization of cases, parliamentary change, and building of legal capacity. On the other hand, GAL and *Cuadernos* struggled against lesbian invisibility and patriarchal domination by means of criticism and reflection on culture, institutions, and the role of the mass media, adopting an anti-systemic and countercultural discourse anchored on identity, which precluded organizational formalization.

Changes in the 1990s enabled a different social configuration when the possibility of building a united front became possible. By that time, lesbian-feminist organizations had gained strength and started to develop a mixed agenda: they sought to balance 'inside' and 'outside,' training activists to take a stand in the public sphere. The fact that most of these organizations began a slow but persistent process of revaluation of the potential found in the struggle for legal recognition would also prove decisive. Lastly, in the 1990s, a proliferation and diversification of gay and lesbian organizations took place, and transgendered women and men joined the movement, bringing in a more complex engagement in a burgeoning field which would no longer be hegemonized by CHA. That all of these organizations agreed on encouraging visibility through the coordination of a pride march as an ideal space – because it was open enough and able to integrate many specificities and institutional paths – was key to consolidating this first articulation of the whole movement.

A detailed analysis of this process exceeds the scope of this chapter, but confirms the efficiency of the gay and the lesbian-feminist movement in the 1980s. CHA, GAL and *Cuadernos* show that, on occasion, opportunities themselves can become the goal sought by social movements, and can be the object of strategic intervention processes. The work of activists in these three organizations sought the construction of interpretation frameworks that would enable them to expand the structural framework of opportunities: the end of the closet and guilt, and the struggle to depathologize male homosexuality and lesbianism, as well as the expansion of the notion of citizenship.

That is why the demands of the three organizations can be understood as part of a wider social debate about the meaning of democracy and the definition of its contents. Their demands challenge the state and other political actors to link institutional changes to the expansion of democratic practices. During this process, it became clear that the discourse of human rights entails a great potential of politicization for social action, as well as great flexibility to embrace new subjects and issues. This ability is due, at least in the Argentine case, to its close relation to democratic values, which transformed it into an indicator of democratic quality.

## Notes

1 Federal Police Decrees sanctioned 'those who exhibit themselves on a public road or public places dressed or disguised in clothing of the opposite sex,' and 'persons of one or the other sex that publicly encourage or offer themselves for carnal knowledge.' Although homosexuality is not mentioned, the Federal Police often applied it to detain homosexuals. The Special Procedures Code of 1949 expressly addressed homosexuals: 'precinct stations, upon the knowledge that in certain homes or locales under their jurisdiction, homosexuals meet with objectives linked to their immorality, beyond the preventive and repressive measures that may correspond, shall communicate this fact to the Superintendence of Criminal Investigations for its intervention.' Additionally, one of the main legal means to detain – or threaten – homosexuals (as well as youths and political dissidents prior to the 1980s) was the Criminal Records (Averiguación de Antecedentes) Act of 1958, which empowered the police authority to detain citizens for up to forty-eight hours pending confirmation of their identification.

2 I refer to the compliance with democratic rules by political parties and organized interests, subordination of the armed forces to the government, and the alternation from one elected administration to the next.

3 The first gay organizations appeared in Argentina in the late 1960s: Nuestro Mundo in 1968, and Frente de Liberación Homosexual in 1971. These were semi-clandestine organizations, which sought contacts mainly with leftist movements and political parties. The *coup d'état* of 1976 forced their disappearance, but early experiences remained in the memory of gay and lesbian activists in the 1980s.

4 In 1979 the first global organization of homosexual groups was formed, called International Gay Association. Latin American gay and lesbian organizations joined this international network and participated in campaigns that granted it a growing visibility. CHA, several Brazilian organizations (Grupo Gay da Bahia and Triangulo Rosa, among others), and Uruguayan groups (Escorpio, Somos) joined this international circuit early in the process.

5 Pecheny (2001b) and Sívori (2007) addressed the history of the Argentine GLBT movement partially in their PhD theses; Rapisardi and Modarelli (2001) focused on the gay issue during the military dictatorship. Brown (2002) analyzed the history of the Argentine GLBT movement in 1970–2000.

6 Research was conducted at the CHA archive of press clippings (1982–90) and case reports records (1988–90), including public denunciations and news stories on police raids against gay venues and cruising sites.

7 Three GLBT activists interviewed wrote reports on police persecution in Buenos Aires during the 1990s.

8 For McAdam et al. (1999) the emergence and success of social movements rely, to a great extent, on opportunities found by nonconformists, generated by changes in the institutional structure and the ideological conceptions of the groups in power. They analyze four dimensions of political opportunities: the political system's degree of relative openness, the stability or instability of alignments among the elites, the presence or absence of allies among the elites, and the government's capacity and tendency to repress.

9 Eight groups were formed in Buenos Aires during the democratic transition, gathered briefly under Coordinadora Gay, which did not withstand heated debates on struggle strategies.

10 CHA document *Discriminación y sexualidad en la Argentina* (December 1987), p. 6.

11 CHA informative document (1984/85).

12 First General Report of CHA Civil Association, 13 August 1984, p. 2.

13 Alejandro Zalazar, Work plan for the April–December 1986 period.

14 Jáuregui was arrested at the disco Contramano on 13 July 1984. He resisted and called, unsuccessfully, those present to do the same. *Tiempo Argentino*, 14 June 1984.

15 *Libre*, Year 1, no. 23, 19 June 1984.

16 CHA document *Política y sexualidad en un estado de derecho* (1986).

17 *Radiolandia 2000*, 2911, 1 June 1984.

18 CHA document *Homosexualidad y Derechos Humanos* (1985).

19 CHA document *Plenario sobre Derechos Humanos* (1986).

20 Lugar de Mujer was founded in 1983 as a space for the participation and debate of women and feminists. From 1987, their work was focused on domestic violence.

21 The Asociación de Trabajo y Estudio de la Mujer-25 de noviembre was formed in 1982 and became a central point for meetings and debates for several feminist groups.

22 In 1982 and 1984, ATEM held conferences that included the subject centrally. Also, in 1983 the Tribunal de Violencia contra la Mujer 'Mabel Montoya' was formed.

23 *Cuadernos de Existencia Lesbiana*, 9, March 1990, p. 11.

24 *Cuadernos de Existencia Lesbiana*, 8, July 1989, pp. 5–6.

25 Ana Rubiolo, Grupo Autogestivo de Lesbianas, 'Articulaciones entre política sexual y lesbianismo desde la perspectiva feminista'; Chejter (1996: 143).

26 *Cuadernos de Existencia Lesbiana*, 13 May 1992, p. 4.

27 Ibid.

28 *Cuadernos de Existencia Lesbiana*, 2, May 1987, p. 1.

29 *Cuadernos de Existencia Lesbiana*, 5, March 1988, p. 15.

30 *Cuadernos de Existencia Lesbiana*, 13, May 1992, p. 2.

31 *Cuadernos de Existencia Lesbiana*, 9, March 1990, p. 12.

32 Ana Rubiolo, Grupo Autogestivo de Lesbianas, 'Articulaciones entre política sexual y lesbianismo desde la perspectiva feminista'; Chejter (1996: 144).

33 See, for example, *Cuadernos de Existencia Lesbiana*, 17, November 1996.

34 The presence of women in CHA dates back to its foundation, but the section formed in 1989.

35 The publication *Vamos a Andar* (19 March 1992) states that the

CHA executive committee in 1992 was formed by eight women, out of eleven members.

## References

Barnes, A and P. Ephross (1994) 'The impact of hate violence on victims: emotional and behavioural responses to attacks,' *Social Work*, 39.

Barros, S. (2002) *Orden, Democracia y Estabilidad*, Córdoba: Alción.

Brown, S. (2002) 'The lesbian and gay movement in Argentina,' *Latin American Perspectives*, 29(123).

Cardoso de Oliveira, L. (2005) 'Direitos, insulto y cidadania. (¿Existe violencia sem agressão moral?),' *Serie Antropologia*, 371.

Chejter, S. (1996) 'Feminismo por feministas. Fragmentos para una historia del feminismo argentino,' *Travesías. Temas del debate feminista contemporáneo*, 5.

Correa, S., R. Petchesky and R. Parker (2008) *Sexuality, Health and Human Rights*, New York: Routledge.

Della Porta, D. (1999) 'Movimientos sociales y Estado: algunas ideas en torno a la represión policial de la protesta,' in D. McAdam, J. McCarthy and M. Zald (eds), *Movimientos sociales: perspectivas comparadas*, Madrid: Istmo.

Ehrlich, H. (1990) 'The ecology of anti-gay violence,' *Journal of Interpersonal Violence*, 5(3).

Epstein, S. (1999) 'Gay and lesbian movements in the United States,' in B. Adam, J. Duyvendak and A. Krouwel (eds), *The Global Emergence of Gay and Lesbian Politics*, Philadelphia, PA: Temple University Press.

Facchini, R. (2005) *Sopa de Letrinhas?*, Rio de Janeiro: Garamond.

Fígari, C. and F. Gemetro (2009) 'Escritas en silencio. Mujeres que deseaban otras mujeres en la Argentina del Siglo XX,' *Sexualidad, Salud y Sociedad. Revista Latinoamericana*, 3.

Filc, J. (1997) *Entre el parentesco y la política. Familia y dictadura, 1976–1983*, Buenos Aires: Biblos.

Fillieule, O. and J. Duyvendak (1999) 'Gay and lesbian activism in France. Between integration and community-oriented movements,' in B. Adam, J. Duyvendak and A. Krouwel (eds), *The Global Emergence of Gay and Lesbian Politics*, Philadelphia, PA: Temple University Press.

Fox, J. (ed.) (1990) 'The challenge of rural democratisation,' *Journal of Development Studies*, Special issue.

Fuskova, I. and C. Marek (1992) *Amor de mujeres. El lesbianismo en Argentina, hoy*, Buenos Aires: Planeta.

Gamson, W. and D. Meyer (1999) 'Marcos interpretativos de la oportunidad política,' in D. McAdam, J. McCarthy and M. Zald (eds), *Movimientos sociales: perspectivas comparadas*, Madrid: Istmo.

Gamson, W. A., B. Fireman and S. Rytina (1982) *Encounters with Unjust Authority*, Homewood, IL: Dorsey.

Garnet, L., G. M. Herek and B. Levey (1990) 'Violence and victimization of lesbians and gay men. Mental health consequences,' *Journal of Interpersonal Violence*, 5.

Grimson, A. (ed.) (2007) *Pasiones nacionales. Política y cultura en Brasil y Argentina*, Buenos Aires: Edhasa.

Herek, G. M., J. R. Gillis, J. C. Cogan and E. K. Glunt (]1997) 'Hate crime victimization among lesbian, gay and bisexual adults: prevalence, psychological correlates, and methodological issues,' *Journal of Interpersonal Violence*, 12.

Htun, M. (2003) *Sex and the State. Abortion, Divorce, and the Family under Latin American Dictatorships and Democracies*, Cambridge: Cambridge University Press.

Jáuregui, C. (1987) *La homosexualidad en Argentina*, Buenos Aires: Tarso.

Jelin, E. (1994) 'The politics of memory. The human rights movement and the construction of democracy in Argentina,' *Latin American Perspectives*, 21(81).

— (2002) *Los trabajos de la memoria*, Buenos Aires: Siglo XXI.

Mason, G. (1996) 'Are you a boy or a girl? (Hetero)sexism and verbal hostility,' in C. Sumner, M. Israel, M. O'Connell and R. Sarre (eds), *International Victimology*, Australian Institute of Criminology.

McAdam, D., J. McCarthy and M. Zald (eds) (1999) *Movimientos sociales: perspectivas comparadas*, Madrid: Istmo.

Mogrovejo, N. (2000) *Un amor que no se atrevió a decir su nombre*, Mexico: Plaza Valdéz.

O'Donnell, G. (1996) 'Ilusiones sobre la consolidación,' *Nueva Sociedad*, 144.

Pecheny, M. (2001a) 'La salud como vector del reconocimiento de derechos humanos: la epidemia de sida y el reconocimiento de los derechos de las minorías sexuales,' in A. Domínguez, A. Federico, L. Findling and A. Mendes (eds), *La salud en crisis. Una mirada desde las ciencias sociales*, Buenos Aires: Dunken.

— (2001b) *La Construction de l'Avortement et du Sida en tant que Questions Politiques: le Cas de l'Argentine*, Villeneuve d'Ascq: Presses Universitaires du Septentrion.

— (2002) 'Identidades discretas,' in L. Arfuch (ed.), *Identidades, sujetos y subjetividades*, Argentina: Prometeo.

Rapisardi, F. and A. Modarelli (2001) *Fiestas, baños y exilios. Los gays porteños en la última dictadura*, Buenos Aires: Editorial Sudamericana.

Robben, A. and C. Nordstrom (1995) 'The anthropology and ethnography of violence and sociopolitical conflict,' in C. Nordstrom and A. Robben (eds), *Fieldwork under Fire*, Berkeley and London: University of California Press.

Schütz, A. (1993) *La construcción significativa del mundo social. Introducción a la Sociología compensiva*, Barcelona: Paidós.

Sívori, H. (2007) 'Ativistas e peritos no movimento GLTTB-AIDS argentino. Ciência e política da identidade sexual,' Unpublished PhD thesis, Universidade Federal do Rio de Janeiro.

Tarrow, S. (1997) *El poder en movimiento. Los movimientos sociales, la acción colectiva y la política*, Madrid: Alianza.

Waylen, G. (1994) 'Women and democratization: conceptualizing gender relations in transition politics,' *World Politics*, 46(3).

— (2000) 'Gender and democratic politics: a comparative analysis of consolidation in Argentina and Chile,' *Journal of Latin American Studies*, 32.

## Archival sources

CHA Archives, First General Report of CHA Civil Association, 13 August 1984

— Informative document (1984/85)

— Jáuregui and Zalazar, 'A los miembros de la Comunidad,' 1 April 1985

— *Homosexualidad y Derechos Humanos* (1985)

— Alejandro Zalazar, Work plan for the April–December 1986 period

— *Política y sexualidad en un estado de derecho* (1986)

— *Plenario sobre Derechos Humanos* (1986)

Cuadernos de Existencia Lesbiana:

2 (May 1987), 5 (March 1988), 8 (July 1989), 9 (March 1990), 13 May 1992

— 'Discriminación y sexualidad en la Argentina,' December 1987

— Newsletter, *Vamos a Andar*, 19 March 1992

**Newspapers**

*Tiempo Argentino*, 14 June 1984

*Libre*, 23, 19 June 1984

*Radiolandia 2000*, 2911, 1 June 1984

# 7 | Sexuality and nationalist ideologies in post-colonial Cameroon

BASILE NDJIO

## Introduction

In his seminal *Nationalism and Sexuality*, George Mosse (1985) shows the crucial role of nationalism and moral respectability in the making of sexuality in modern Europe. The value that Western nationalist thought of the nineteenth and twentieth centuries put on regulating sexual desire as a condition of the progress of modern capitalist societies was seen as one of the devices most easily and uncritically transferred to a variety of other national political regimes, regardless of their affinity with the source of this modern Western invention. Likewise, the value attributed to respectability by the emerging capitalist bourgeoisie, who regarded control over sexuality as vital to the stability of modern society and the maintenance of its dominance, would later be assimilated even by regimes that abolished class stratification (see also Evans 1993; Weeks 1981).

In contrast to this Western tradition, the historical link between nationalism and sexuality in anti-colonial liberation movements in Africa has been poorly studied. Indeed, the absence of any reference to nationalism in the mainstream literature on African sexuality is striking. It is all the more surprising that, across the continent, the refoundational aspirations of pan-Africanist thought and Afrocentrist philosophies sustained the nationalist ambition to constitute an exclusive African sexual identity. They also provided an ideological justification for the exclusion by many African post-colonial states of a variety of sexual experiences, expressions, and desires from the realm of respectable citizenship.

Recent studies on same-sex orientation in sub-Saharan Africa have demonstrated how Western colonialism, contemporary African popular culture and media, and the two dominant religious traditions (Islam and Christianity) have contributed to construct a singular African sexual selfhood (Epprecht 2008). These forces have also helped achieve a naturalization of heteronormativity as a central aspect of post-colonial African governmentality. In Cameroon, as in many African countries, the control of the bodies and sexuality of the local population has been a central governmental concern since the creation, by the Ahidjo regime (1960–82), of the United Republic of Cameroon in 1972. Indeed, the post-colonial Cameroonian government implemented various administrative practices and judicial procedures aimed at homogenizing the sexualities of the masses. Through this sexual governmentality, Cameroonian officialdom also aspired to suppress the plurality of the country's sexual past (Ndjio 2010). As a result, homosexual men and women, as well as men judged effeminate and women considered mannish, came to be seen by holders of political and administrative power as threats to the post-colonial sexual and gender order.

In this chapter I address the issue of sexuality and nationalist ideologies in post-colonial Africa. I focus on the question of how a dominant heterosexual identity has come to be constructed by post-colonial nationalist leaders in Africa. I reflect on sexual governmentality in post-colonial Africa in relation to pan-Africanist ideologies that have legitimized the establishment in many African countries of phallocratic, patriarchal, and heterosexist social structures that urge African men to assert their masculinity through the sexual submission of women (cf. Biaya 2001: 71–85; Mbembe 2001; Toulabour 1991: 55–71). I focus on the bid by post-colonial nationalist elites in Cameroon not only to fabricate heterosexual subjects promoted as good citizens in opposition to homosexuals generally misrepresented as 'uncivic' citizens and 'alien' Africans, but also to 'Africanize' the sexuality of the masses in a global context that dramatizes the uncontrolled flow of desires and pleasures, and especially the proliferation of unconventional sexual practices and expressions perceived as a challenge to the stability of the dominant genital order.[1] In line with this concern, the present study tries to answer the question of how a hegemonic heterosexual identity has come to be constructed or internalized in post-colonial Africa, and how both African men and women have come to believe that to be 'good' citizens or 'real' Africans, they have to become oedipalized subjects,[2] to borrow Deleuze and Guattari's concept (1983 [1972]).

Four 'strategic units' (Foucault 1981 [1978]) mark the deployment of this sexual politics in post-colonial Cameroon, tracing major shifts in dominant discourses on sexuality and the way sexual dissidence is addressed by the state. The first unit is the sublimation of procreative and reproductive sexuality, accompanied by the fetishization and ritualization of heterosexual relationships. This has helped maintain a longue durée of male sexual supremacy as the foundation of post-colonial political power in the continent at large. The second unit is the essentialization and racialization of native Africans' sexuality. These primordialist conceptions of sexuality are based on the theory of an original African sexuality, rooted in local custom and tradition, and are premised on the idea of an original distinctive African *sexe propre*. This led to the reconstruction of racialized sexual typologies defining Africans as fundamentally and naturally heterosexual, reinventing a native history of exclusively heterosexual pleasures. Symptomatic of this racialized sexual ideology is the political invention of the Muntu – the libidinous African male heterosexual.

The third strategic unit is the segregation and symbolic 'othering' of homosexuals. Homoeroticism and the emergence of homosexual identities are regarded as the effect of alienation due to Western influence. Homosexuality is simultaneously represented as an un-African phenomenon, a disease or evil brought to Africa by whites, the most dangerous vestige of Western colonialism, and the most insidious form of neocolonialism.[3] As a result, gays and lesbians are largely depicted as 'uprooted' and 'acculturated' Africans, and especially as agents of the perpetuation of Western imperialism in the black continent. The fourth unit is the criminalization and demonization of homoerotic practices and other unconventional forms of sexual longing and expression. The anti-homosexual policy currently deployed by the different law enforcement apparatuses of the Cameroon state, and amplified by sensationalist local media, treats gays and lesbians as sexual delinquents, and brands them as sorcerers or witches – dangerous sources of moral impurity.

### State sexual policy: from criminalization to the demonization of homosexuals

In Cameroon, as in many African countries (see Epprecht 2004), gay people are generally seen as a threat to the very foundation of the nation's moral and social order (Ndjio 2009). They are also viewed as potential destroyers of all that is considered, by both the masses and the elite classes, as the African way of life, which is generally contrasted to so-called perverse and decadent modern Western lifestyles. In addition, these sexual minority groups are the object of vilification and stigmatization by the conservative Biya regime (in power since 1982). Apart from using homosexuals as scapegoats for the social and economic meltdown of the country, this regime has also committed itself to eliminating these 'enemies from within,' who 'stand in the way of the nation being united and pure as one body,' as Werbner (1996: 13) would put it. It is in line with this homophobic policy condoned by the Cameroonian government through the repressive sodomy law of 1972 that, since 2005, representatives of the state have launched what looks like a crusade against men and women politically and juridically construed as gays or lesbians. These crusades, often supported by the masses, have been accompanied by the intensification of both juridical and administrative persecutions of men and women rightly or wrongly branded as homosexuals by new inquisitors of modern times.[4] The following episodes illustrate how this modern-day inquisition is deployed by the state in Cameroon.

On 22 May 2005, the police raided Elysée Bar, a popular bar in the Essos neighborhood of Yaoundé (the political capital), a spot where trendy youths regularly congregated. In a storming operation, eleven men aged between sixteen and thirty-two were arrested and taken into custody, suspected of being homosexual. After several weeks in police custody during which they endured all sorts of mistreatment and humiliation, the unfortunate men were transferred to the infamous Nkondegui prison, where they spent over a year awaiting trial. Just a few days after his release from custody, one of the detainees died of AIDS-related complications. He reportedly contracted HIV/AIDS as a result of sexual abuse by his fellow inmates, to whom free rein was given to abuse homosexual detainees (see ADEFHO 2009).

Two years after the Elysée Bar raid, in the middle of the night four heavily armed gendarmes broke into the room of two young men who had been reported by neighbors as having a homosexual relationship and arrested them. At gunpoint, the men were coerced into admitting that they had performed homosexual acts. During the trial, the defense attorneys claimed that while their clients were held in a disciplinary ward for several days, they were denied the right to be assisted by a lawyer or to receive family visits. Although all prosecution charges were disproved by the defendants, they were nevertheless sentenced to one year's imprisonment for sodomy and offenses to public decency (ibid.).

Between February 2007 and November 2010, I witnessed seven cases involving homosexual offenses at the Douala High Court, generally involving young men and women from underprivileged backgrounds. One case involved six young men (aged between twenty-five and thirty-nine), who were arrested between 19 and 21 July 2007 by members of a special unit of the 3rd Branch of the Douala Central Police, and charged with 'sodomy practice' and 'gross indecency.' Their arrest and detention followed the discovery of their telephone numbers in the documents of one of two teenagers who had been reported for being part of a homosexual ring. In their statements, the accused disclaimed any close connections with the two teenagers presented by the prosecutor as the victims of their immoral sexual practices. However, they were found guilty of the homosexual offenses, and sentenced to six months' imprisonment.

In another case, two young hairdressers and a street vendor from the popular neighborhood of Deido in Douala were prosecuted for 'flagrante delicto of homosexuality,' based on a denunciation by a neighbor. As in the previous case, the accused were arrested and detained in a special cell. After several days, they were sent for pre-trial detention for almost five months at the notorious New Bell prison. During the trial, the prosecutor regularly made use of expressions such as sexual crime, sinful sexual practices, animalistic sexual behavior, or unnatural passions, to denounce the defendants' behavior, which, according to him, undermined moral and ethical values. He ended his accusation by calling for severe actions against those he characterized as moral perverts and dangerous pederasts. When the main prosecution witness was called to the witness box, he claimed to have overheard a sordid conversation between two of the defendants and another young man about their permissive sexual activities. This was indecent enough to convince him that the young men were *mademoiselles* (passive gay males) who traded their bodies to Western foreigners in exchange for gifts and money. The defense lawyer dismissed the claims of the prosecution witness as baseless and pure fabrication, causing the prosecutor to request a medical expert who could examine the rectum of the accused, seeking proof of acts of sodomy. This request was finally conceded by the judge, despite the protestation of the defense. The degrading examination was conducted, but the results were never sent to court. Although there was no consistent evidence of the defendants' actual involvement in homosexual acts, they were nonetheless convicted on a charge of 'homosexuality attempt,' and sentenced to six months' imprisonment.

The deployment of police raids, the staging of court proceedings, and spectacular forms of punishment reveal an inquisitive power that has made magistrates and gendarmes the main instrument of its institutionalized homophobic violence. All this aggressive deployment of 'bio-power' (Foucault 1981 [1978]) goes along with the exuberant production of moralizing discourses on unconventional sexualities by these law enforcers and magistrates who make new use of Cameroon's sodomy law of 1972 to abusively arrest and detain young Cameroonians – generally from underprivileged backgrounds – suspected of crimes against national sexual morality. Indeed, the vague and imprecise terms of Article 347 Bis of this sodomy law, which criminalizes homosexuals as sexual delinquents, allow for the arbitrary interpretation of a broad range of behavior as *outrage à la pudeur* (offense to public decency), or *contraire aux bonnes moeurs* (contrary to good morals).[5] To the existing sodomy legislation, which acknowledges only *flagrant délit d'homosexualité*, judges have incorporated controversial and morally loaded notions of 'unnatural sexuality' and 'sexual perversion' in their rulings as part of a crusade against homosexuals suspected of plotting to turn Cameroon into a biblical Sodom and Gomorrah.

Additionally, since 2005, many magistrates and police officers have moved homosexual offenses from the juridical logic of crime and misdemeanor to the vocabulary of sorcery, occultism, and devilry. In this imagery, lesbianism and male pederasty are interpreted as forms of sexual malevolence associated with witchcraft. This shift has led to a demonization of homoeroticism and same-sex relations. As a result, several gays and lesbians have been publicly accused of being danger-ous witches or sorcerers, capable of absorbing their victims' vital force, and motivated by economic ambitions.[6] In a recent case revealed by a Cameroonian online newspaper, three lesbian women from the district of Ndikinimeki in the Centre Region of the country[7] were charged with homosexual offenses and the practice of witchcraft, which is a criminal offense in the Cameroonian penal code.[8] This example, like many other cases recorded by local gay organizations, shows how representatives of the state power are now actively drawing upon the language of witchcraft and sorcery to generate a new political imagery of same-sex relations. It also reveals the engagement of the entire legal system (judges, prosecu-tors, and police) in the administrative and juridical invention of the gay and lesbian witch, responsible for the moral decay of the country.

The state's practices of categorizing, naming, stigmatizing, blaming, criminalizing, and especially demonizing people branded as gays or lesbians expose new developments in sexual governmentality in Cameroon. This chapter offers an interpretation of this disciplinary deployment of sexuality by the Cameroonian state through its anti-gay rhetoric as a tepid reaction to the association, in the popular imagination, of the big men's economic and political power with their alleged involvement in 'homosexual sects,' as reported in the Cam-eroonian press.[9] According to this popular narrative, the conspicuous enrichment of politico-bureaucratic elite classes was the result of the subjugation of the *derrières* (backsides or buttocks) of disempowered men as their sexual toys. The anti-homosexual state campaign, which started in late 2005, can also be interpreted as a political response to popular dissatisfaction with the Biya regime, often mocked as *pouvoir sodomiseur* ('sodomite power') or *anusocratie* ('rule by anus'). In this sexualized representation of the Cameroon government, the rectum of the disempowered is imagined, not only as a place for perverse pleasures and sexual fantasies, but also as a privileged site for the expression of political domination and supremacy by the members of the dominant classes (Ndjio 2009). The pervasive notion of an 'anal politics' sublimates the practice of pederasty and sodomy as a means of upward mobility, and a means to gain access to state resources (see Kemogne 2006: 5–6). Thus, by launching a crusade against gays and lesbians, state agents have attempted to thwart the accusation that the Cameroon government was promoting an alleged 'homosexualization of the society.'

## The nativist construction of African sexuality

The repressive sexual policy of the Cameroon government toward sexual inverts or dissidents suggests that in this country, as in many contemporary African countries, sexuality has become a political and social landscape of privileged intervention by the post-colonial state seeking to purify the body of the nation, to paraphrase Richard Werbner (1996). It has also become a key site where the myth about African cultural unity is enacted by those who see a complex continent and its diverse populations through the lens of homogeneity and uniformity.[10] In addition, sexuality has been made a cultural tool through which Africanity is expressed, and nativist ideologies are dramatized. Moreover, in this part of the world, sexuality is increasingly appearing as a marker of citizenship, and especially a critical mode either for claiming one's citizen's rights or denying other people their rights as citizens (see Mkhize et al. 2010). This is because, since the independence period, the sexuality of Africans has been developed in an axis of the inclusion of so-called heterosexual citizens and the exclusion of homosexual subjects (see Gaudio 2009; Terroirs 2007). In so doing, many African leaders made the sexuality of the masses both a 'locus of categorical purity' (Malkki 1995: 4), a space for the construction of 'defensive identities based on communal principles and parochial solidarity' (Castells 1997: 11), and a bastion of exclusion of those represented as culturally different from other members of the community (Germond and De Gruchy 1997).[11]

Indeed, since the early 1960s, many post-colonial African leaders have taken up the duty of reconstructing an authentic African selfhood perverted by colonialism. In this reformative project, an African 'imagined community' was forged: first, by the political annihilation of any kind of (sexual) difference that could constitute an obstacle to the achievement of nation-building (see Epprecht 2008); secondly, by the means of violent exclusion from the post-colonial public sphere of the embarrassing presence of those sexual 'aliens' whose unconventional sexual desires and practices problematize the very ontology of the African subject (see Johnson 2007). In all this process, both African history and culture are selectively reshaped, revised, and even reinvented by nativist discourses through a deliberate amnesia concerning earlier forms of African sexualities, including male and female same-sex relations.[12]

In other respects, the obsession of many post-colonial African leaders with 'normalizing' or 'policing' the sexual desires and expressions of the masses might suggest that these nativist elites have supported rather than challenged the Victorian view of sexuality. They have assimilated the modern framework of respectability and civilization disseminated during the colonial period. In contrast to post-colonial India's experience, discussed by Chatterjee (1993), many post-colonial African nationalist leaders did not break with colonial practices of monitoring the sexual behavior of African subjects or policing their sexual desires and fantasies. Nor did they depart from mythological colonial representations of black people as prone to sexual excess and promiscuity. Indeed, post-colonial nativist conceptions of sexuality replicated the colonial essentialist representation of African sexuality. While placing African carnal urges outside the boundaries of Western civilization, the latter had also created a number of myths about both the hyper-virility of native men and the lasciviousness of native women.[13] More importantly, pan-Africanist projects have perpetuated the fables of African sexual exceptionalism first invented by Western colonial administrators, travelers, and thinkers in the late nineteenth and early twentieth centuries.[14]

The 'civilizing mission' of the colonial powers entailed among other things transforming the sexualities of the African natives, by taming what they viewed as licentious behavior and immoral sexual practices from an early age. This reformative project promoted heterosexuality, monogamous marriage, conjugal virtue, child-rearing, and family life as values essential to social order and progress of the colonial society. To achieve this project, colonial administrators enacted a series of laws and regulations which – with the aid of missionaries – taught Africans to discipline and channel their sexual desire exclusively toward the preservation of life and the increase of the population (White 1990). The degree of decency, respectability, civility, and good manners attained became the means of assessing the natives' headway toward civilization and modernization. Conversely, unconventional sexual practices and desires, deemed unnatural, therefore immoral, were seen as the dark side of modernity and an obstacle to progress.

Post-colonial African elites developed a pan-African nationalist ideology, expressed in the racializing discourse of negritude or African personality (see Nkrumah 1964; Senghor 1964, 1977), which locked up the African imagination in narratives of alienation, loss, and dispossession (Mbembe 2002: 239–40). This nativist ideology led to the elaboration of a metaphysics of difference by post-colonial intellectuals, who took up the 'redemptive mission,' aiming to recover the lost African self and, along with it, an African Eros perverted by Western colonialism.[15] In line with this narrative of redemption and liberation, sexuality has become one of Africa's modes of transcendence and its main touchstone of purity (White 1980: 282). Within this moral economy of alterity, which cultivates homogeneity and dramatizes authenticity, homosexuality and other transgressive desires have been denounced as influenced by neocolonialist forces attempting to realienate or reacculturate the minds that African nationalists set free of such burdens and 'purified.' If colonial agents have tended to interpret African homosexuality as a 'vice of natives' (Bleys 1995), post-colonial nationalist elites have rather attributed the pervasiveness of homoeroticism in Africa to the sexual alienation that came with colonization – epitomized by the case of native men emasculated by some perverse Western colonialists who made them their boy-wives.[16]

In many respects, the African post-colonial deployment of sexuality appears distinctive from what Foucault (1981 [1978]) has noted for modern western Europe for two main reasons: first, it is through the 'nationalization' of the sexuality of its citizens that, in many African countries, the post-colonial state has managed to draw boundaries between Africans and Westerners, insiders and outsiders, citizens and strangers, authentic and deracinated Africans, good and bad citizens, loyal and disloyal subjects. This is the case with countries such as Cameroon, where stigmatizing homosexuality as an alien, un-Cameroonian phenomenon has become a crucial element to emphasize one's belonging or rooting. In this country, there is also a growing tendency among the local population to equate heterosexuality with patriotism, localism, and Africanness, while homosexuality is generally associated with globalism and strangeness. For example, in the course of June 2009, I witnessed at the Douala High Court a trial of two young men accused of homosexual offenses. The prosecutor requested severe penalties against the offenders on the grounds that they were 'acculturated' Africans who were deliberately perverting traditional African culture. He ended his arguments by calling on the Cameroonian government to resist the forces of alienation. A similar rhetoric is mobilized in Nigeria, where, according to one social activist, political and religious leaders tend to alienate those who engage in same-sex relations by deploying discourses of 'otherness' (Aken'Ova 2009: 16–18).

Secondly, pan-Africanist thought, which played a significant role in (re)shaping the contours of the modern African sexual regime, constructed the sexuality of African men and women on the basis of dominant sexual codes establishing heterosexual relationships as the sexual norm. Indeed, in the heyday of African nationalism during the 1960s and 1970s, heterosexual acts were idealized – often fetishized – as an efficient means of achieving the nationalist project of increasing the size of African populations. This 'normalization' of heterosexuality was accompanied by the suppression of other sexualities, construed as contrary to the nation's sexual order or morale. In Cameroon, for instance, where both the regimes of Ahmadou Ahidjo (1960–82) and Paul Biya did their best to enforce one type of sexuality as a norm, the claim of a deep authentic African subjectivity was first embedded in the promotion of what can be called *heterotitude*. This concept accounts above all for a ritual celebration of heterosexual relationships, which has led to the prohibition and condemnation of male homosexuality and lesbianism.[17] As a nativist imagination of sexuality and bodily pleasures, this heterotitude ideology has also resulted in this country, as in many African countries, in the political invention of the Muntu. The (re)making of this sexual category has served to establish a demarcation between what is considered pure or authentically African on the one hand, and what is seen as foreign or unauthentic on the other.

### Muntu: the idealized African male heterosexual

In his famous *La Crise du Muntu*, published in 1977, the Cameroonian philosopher Fabien Eboussi-Boulaga defined the Muntu as 'a man in his African condition, who has to assert himself by overcoming what contests his humanity and puts it in danger.'[18] In a 2006 interview with one Cameroonian magazine called *Potentiel*,[19] he described the Muntu as an African man concerned with '*la reprise de soi*' (self-recovery); that is, 'the desire to attest for his contested humanity,' and 'the desire to be by and for himself.' In his view, both colonialist and post-colonial nativist discourses were partly responsible for what he referred to as the 'crisis of the Muntu.' If the former denied Africans their humanity, the latter deprived them of their subjectivity and agency. Thus the Muntu ('black stallion'), as the icon of African post-colonial masculinity, needs to fight in order to recover his own self and free himself from what the Ghanaian historian Emmanuel Akyeampong calls 'the intellectual rigidity of pan-Africanism' (2006: 310).

Eboussi-Boulaga (1977) argues for an understanding of the Muntu as an 'invented' subject, a by-product of historical contingency. But, contrary to Mudimbe (1988) and other pan-Africanist thinkers, who tend to limit the genealogy of the African subject either to the colonial imagination or to Western discourses on Africa and its people, Eboussi-Boulaga sees the Muntu as a by-product of both colonialism and African post-colonial ideologies of identity. In the post-colonial ethno-philosophical imagination of masculinity and African sexuality, the (re)making of the Muntu, idealized as a metaphor of the African (male) subject, marks a particular mode of self-representation. Like Eboussi-Boulaga (1977), in this study we define the Muntu not as a fixed character type, but rather as what R. W. Connell would call 'configurations of practice (and desire) generated in particular situations in a changing structure of relationships' (2005 [1995]: 81). More explicitly, the Muntu expresses an emerging form of the so-called African masculinity in a context dominated by essentialist conceptions of selfhood, national identity politics, discourses on autochthony, and a nativist vision of the African self. This context is also marked by the *retour en force* of anti-European sentiments, Afrocentrist philosophy, and pan-Africanism.

From another standpoint, the Muntu can also be read as a repressed subject whose sexuality is caught in an authoritarian heterosexist ideology. This is because, since the independence period, many African men have been led to believe that 'a real man is a good lover' (*un vrai homme est un bon démarreur*) and that 'without his sex, a man is nothing in the eye of the woman' (*sans son sexe, l'homme n'est rien devant la femme*), as one of my elder cousins used to remind me when I was a teenager. According to this popular notion, it is only by sexually asserting his masculinity by means of sexual command and violence that an African man can (re)gain his authority and respect (Biaya 1999: 41–6; Nyamnjoh 2005: 295–324).

Besides being a sexually saturated figure of the African heterosexual male (see Friedman 2001), the Muntu is also the iconic representation of a libidinous African man to whom Boris de Rachewitz (1964: 37) once referred as an 'eternal deflowerer of women.' In her insightful novel *Une*

*Nuit dans le Sissongo* (2009), which sheds light on the popular notion of phallocratic power, the female Cameroonian writer Elise Mballa Meka uses the term *bitocrate*[20] to characterize these lustful African men who conquer and subdue African women by the authoritarian power of their voracious and insatiable *bite* (phallus).[21] Two forms of sexual aggression particularly characterize the Muntu *bitocrate*: first, the entanglement of African women of all ages and classes in a moral economy of rape and adduction[22] through which the disempowerment of their bodies and personhood is achieved by violent means, as several reports on sexual and gender-based violence in Africa have forcefully demonstrated.[23] Secondly, the transformation by ruse or mischief of the bodies of African women into a space of sexual transactions between economically marginalized women and powerful men.

The above observation suggests that the violent masculinity of the Muntu often incarnates three different but related figures, that of the rapist, of the pedophile, and of the polygamist. These three categories embody dominant forms of masculinity as a tool for male domination over women. A Muntu-rapist makes use of violence and brutal force to get sexual favors from his female victims. Wars, political unrest, ethnic conflicts, and other upheaval situations provide the *bitocrate* with an opportunity to appease his sexual desires. Combatants, soldiers, 'freedom fighters,' and rebel groups are key figures of the Muntu rapist, playing an important role in the moral economy of rape nowadays rampant in many African countries (see Campbell and Sefl 2004; Mugawe and Powell 2006).

The Muntu-pedophile gains sexual access to teenage or pre-pubescent girls by means of ruse and cunning, often taking advantage of his dominant social position to entice his naive victim. Whether a schoolteacher or university lecturer (Smith 2007), a priest who baptizes the backsides of his young female followers with his big phallus (Ndjio 2005: 265–94), or a big man who honks his car horn behind schoolgirls (Mbembe 2001), a Muntu-pedophile has a propensity to turn teenagers, adolescents, and immature girls into an object of his unlimited sexual fantasies. In his conflicting relationships with his victims, a Muntu-pedophile can turn from 'sugar daddy' to 'bogeyman,' from protector to predator.

The polygamist is a Muntu whose material means enable him to have control over several women. He is the 'king of the bush' who reigns over a harem of women subjugated to the whims and caprices of his insatiable phallus (Ombolo 1990). This was the case with the late Cameroonian singer and diviner Mongo Faya, who was married to seventy-five women and had allegedly fathered more than a hundred children.

All the three versions of the Muntu *bitocrate* share the desire to assert the hegemonic power of the phallus, dramatized by a compulsive passion for women, embodying what Connell (2005 [1995]: 5) has referred to as 'hegemonic masculinity,' defined as 'exclusive, anxiety-provoking, internally and hierarchically differentiated, brutal, and violent.' According to her, misogyny, homophobia, racism, and compulsory heterosexuality are also determinant characteristics of this hegemonic masculinity (ibid.).

The revelation made by Ndoumbe, an undertaker at the Douala Laquintinie Hospital mortuary, shows that in his violent expression of manliness, the Muntu has no qualms about turning even dead bodies of young women into sexual fantasies or objects of pleasure. Indeed, on a radio talk show broadcast in mid-March 2009, the notorious undertaker revealed that he regularly performed sex on young deceased women while washing them. The middle-aged man explained further that these beautiful dead women had irresistible vaginas, which could leave no normal man indifferent, and took pride in having 'tasted' about one hundred of them. He added that his 'lovers' often smiled at him as he was taking possession of their dead bodies. In response to one caller who dismissed him as psycho-pathologic, the undertaker-cum-necrophile replied that the government had given him unlimited power to take care of the deceased. Thus, as 'the king of the realm of the dead,' he had 'the right to sexually possess the bodies of deceased women who belonged to his kingdom,' as he put it. Ndoumbe's narrative of unlimited access to women, and his argument of authority, are telling of the sexual expressiveness of post-colonial power in sub-Saharan Africa, not only as brutal and forceful, but also staged as immoderate, intemperate, and extravagant.[24]

If erudite depictions of the Muntu re-enact and reinforce colonial racist stereotypes about an African Eros,[25] its political invention embodies the nationalist effort to rewrite colonial narratives about African bodies and sexuality. This new writing of the African self positions itself as a counter-narrative to colonial sexual policy, which led to the feminization and emasculation of the native men who had been made available to Western expatriates in the colonies (see, e.g., Aldrich 2003; Hyam 1990).[26] Thus the virilized and energetic body of the Muntu was initially meant to counter the emasculating effect of the sexual violence that colonial power exerted upon native men. It was especially intended to move the African's phallus from a condition of impotency and devirilization in which it had been encapsulated by the colonial *ars erotica* to a situation of liberation in which the black phallus recovered its lost sovereign power.[27] In this liberation process that implied a new *art d'aimer*, a new use of body and sex, and a new use of pleasure, a cathartic role was assigned to the African's phallus: re-energizing and revitalizing the African male body at large, or giving to it a new form of life.

Often in Africa, local people cast doubt on the manliness of a male adult who is not able to make his female partner faint during sexual intercourse, or who has not fathered children. For example, when I was growing up in the popular neighborhood of Kassalafam in Douala, one neighbor was disdainfully called *eau glassée* (cool water), or 'Darryl Cool.' Even women from the neighborhood often mocked the middle-aged man, implying that he was not a real man, that he was a *faiblard* (weak, passive person) in bed. His alleged 'cool' and feebleness made reference to sexual impotency which, according to the locals, explained why he did not have any children, and why he had never succeeded in making his wife cry with pleasure at night, as was common in the neighborhood.

The case of 'Darryl Cool,' whose masculinity was questioned by his neighbors, shows how the often taken-for-granted virility of the Muntu is as precarious as that of African men under the colonial regime, as the former is always at risk of losing his authoritative power over the bodies and the will of native women. Likewise, African men make heavy investments in reinvigorating their sexual potency as an attempt to make up for its slow degradation as they age. Elsewhere (see Ndjio forthcoming), we described how, in Cameroon, an increasingly popular brand of Chinese medicine offers clients the promise of turning a sexually impotent male into a real stallion. While some stayed loyal to the local pharmacopeia and traditional doctors, whose aphrodisiac plants made for a prosperous business in times of sexual crisis, others took the risk of losing authenticity by turning to foreign therapeutic practices.

### Homosexuality, masculinity, and homophobia in post-colonial Africa

The history of homosexuality in Cameroon, as elsewhere in Africa, can be narrated as the history of a collective homophobic hysteria that went along with the morbidification, demonization, and condemnation of gays and lesbians as a public enemy by modern inquisitors. It is also the chronicle of the proliferation of moralizing discourses and regulations against sexual dissidents. Yet the contemporary history of homoeroticism and homosexual desires is the narrative of the public gaze that both post-colonial bureaucratic elites and common people in this country have been turning on gays and lesbians since the early 1970s. The Cambridge *Advanced Learner's Dictionary* (2003) defines a gaze as 'an act or fact of looking at something or someone for a long time, especially in surprise, admiration or because you are thinking about something else.' But in this study, we rather understand a gaze as a panoptical regard of the post-colonial state whose agents have been granted unlimited rights to watch, survey, monitor, and spy on gay people, as well as inspect their bodies – including the examination of their intimate parts and underwear in search of the presumed marks of sodomy. This mystifying gaze has played a critical role in the creation and dissemination of categories such as *ndepso*, *mademoiselle* and *tata*, iconic figures of effeminate gay men in Cameroon.

Lesbians are conceived as *femmes-hommes* who have lost their feminine sensibility, and gays as *hommes-femmes* who have been deprived of their phallic power as a symbol of authority. Thus their critical status vis-à-vis the post-colonial sex/gender regime is characterized as the enemy in narratives of national healing and recovery. As a result of widely publicized anti-homosexual policies since 2005, lesbians and most notably gays are viewed as aliens to the nation, as people *sans identité fixe* (without a stable identity): the reverse of the Muntu. By this process of uprooting, alienation, and estrangement, gays and lesbians become lesser persons, deprived of their most basic rights as citizens.

This official gaze has been instrumental in the development of both erudite and popular knowledge about homosexuality. In this country, the will to know all about homosexuals has resulted in the proliferation of 'facts,' 'truths,' and 'revelations' about gays and lesbians in the local media. It has also led to an exuberant production of tales, legends, myths, and stories about the lives of homosexuals. According to these beliefs, homosexuals have plotted to make Cameroon a '*paradis terrestre*' (heaven on earth) for sodomy, pederasty, and homosexuality, as the prosecutor claimed at one of the trials for homosexual offenses I observed in the Yaoundé High Court in September 2009. Gays and lesbians are also believed to be diseased in body and spirit, usually pictured as pale, hollow-eyed, and weak.[28]

While vilifying gays and lesbians, the state gaze also scrutinizes what are assumed to be their hidden secrets. For example, in another trial for a homosexual offense I attended in February 2009, one gendarme, who was a witness for the prosecution, claimed that he knew that the defendant was a homosexual because he had observed him for a long time. According to him, *mademoiselles* and *tantouses*, as effeminate gay men and mannish lesbians are commonly called in Cameroon, were widely recognized by their speech patterns, mannerisms, appearance, and behavior. Yet he focused on the protuberance of the defendant's backside, as incontestable proof that he was gay. He further explained to the court that the defendant's prominent buttocks were the first thing that drew his attention to him, as they looked like the buttocks of gay people. In his indiscretion, he also mentioned that he had suspected that the defendant was wearing nappies. Despite the defense's refutation of this witness's testimony as irrelevant (*leger*), it was admitted as valid by the judge.

If the attributed lack of masculinity and femininity justifies, under a regime of institutionalized homophobia, multiple violations of the rights of African men and women branded as gays or lesbians, the rhetoric of monstrosity strips them of their bare humanity. For example, during a public debate on homosexuality in Cameroon organized in Yaoundé in March 2006 by the Kaba Ngondo cultural association, Celestin Lingo, then chairman of the Union des Journalistes du Cameroun (Cameroon Journalists' Association), claimed that homosexuals were 'less than animals' because they engaged in sexual practices avoided by even the less intellectually developed creatures.

There are several reasons why *mademoiselles* and *tantouses* are the main concern of many African post-colonial leaders, and why, for example, the Cameroonian penal code has endorsed the Judeo-Christian conservative view about homosexual acts and desires. First, echoing nineteenth-century European psychiatric theories, homosexuality is understood as a form of sexual inversion, which transgresses the '*bonnes moeurs*' and 'natural' sexual drives of the model African citizen. Claims of public visibility for sexual dissidence encourage a 'proliferation and subversive play of gendered meaning' (Butler 1990: 33), exposing the narrowness and arbitrariness of gender sexual roles, and undermining the dominant heteronormative sexual order. Moreover, they are a reminder that the taken-for-granted masculinity of the Muntu's sexuality is nothing more than a comedy, a parody of self. Secondly, the specter of a 'homosexualization of Africa' challenges nativist narratives and the regulation of desire, passion, emotion, and pleasure in post-colonial Africa. At another level, it demystifies an essentialist representation of African sexuality as inherently heteronormative. In other words, gays and lesbians confront the post-colonial power with the unpleasant truth that 'African sexuality,' long fantasized and invested in by the post-colonial bourgeoisie as essentially and exclusively heterosexual, is complex, ambivalent, and elusive.

In other respects, the male *'mademoiselles'* who prefer the passive role in sex with other men, and renounce their 'natural' right over women, lay bare the dilemma of African masculinity as a 'precariously held, endlessly tested, unstable condition' (Rochlin 1980: 91). Likewise, mannish, sexually active lesbians who overtly exhibit the signs and symbols of masculine power and identity, and claim the masculine role in sex acts with other women, also put at risk the foundation of post-colonial power, which rests on male sexual supremacy. That is why, in many African countries, state officials and social reformers are increasingly concerned about women who no longer accept submission to men's aggressive sexual power, or to be the containers of male desires. Indeed, if *tantouses* and *tapettes* (mannish gay women) have been placed under state surveillance, it is because they symbolize what can be called unsubmissive African women who reject the passive role African patriarchal society has imposed on women. These 'mannish' dominating African women do not content themselves with challenging the myth of female sexual passivity. They also assert their right to sexual freedom and pleasure, even if this implies contesting the supremacy of the male's phallus.

If the Muntu is the figurehead of an 'oedipalized, conditioned subject' (Deleuze and Guattari (1983 [1972]: 15) who has renounced other forms of sexual desire and fantasy, and unconditionally surrendered his sexuality to 'the nativist ideologies of patriotic and a civic heterosexuality' (Watney 1989: 15), the *ndepso* or male *mademoiselle* incarnates a 'schizophrenic subject.' In Deleuze and Guattari's definition, a schizophrenic subject is an 'anti-oedipalized subject,' liberated from the agency of post-colonial power. He is also a courageous subject who escapes from, disrupts, and contests the state project of totalizing and unifying desires and pleasures (ibid.: 341). Thus, as an 'anti-Oedipus,' the African male homosexual has released himself from a dominant phallic economy (Irigaray 1985). As the reverse of the Muntu, he willingly or unwillingly breaks the link of sexual submission of women by men, and subverts the moral economy of gender-organized sexual exchanges. By so doing, he positions himself as an uncaptured subject who is delighted to ridicule and betray the long-established myth about the Muntu's virility.

## Conclusion

While the recent radicalization of the state's repressive policy toward homosexuals in Cameroon resonated as a reaction to popular representations of the Biya regime as established on the basis of a '7 · Ndjio'

representations of the Biya regime as established on the basis of a 'sodomite power,' it also came as a backlash to the public visibility that gays and lesbians had acquired over recent years. In order to assess the historical, political, and cultural conditions for this kind of institutionalized homophobia, in this chapter I aimed at reconstructing the master narratives of gender and sexual relations in post-colonial Africa, which provide meaning to the construction of the homosexual representing a state of radical alterity or Other. Indeed, a regime of compulsory exclusive heterosexuality that naturalizes aversion toward other sexual desires has formatted the national identity of men and women as oedipalized subjects. I have argued that this sexual ideology is constitutive of the nativist discourse of (pan-)Africanism, which played a critical role in streamlining and policing the sexual desires of the population. Operating through rules of exclusion and categorization, the discourse of a genuine African identity locked up the post-colonial erotic imagination in a metaphysics of difference and differentiation, stressing the idea of an exceptional character of African sexuality. The fetishism of this regime created a civil cult of the Muntu, the hyper-virile African heterosexual male. The flip side of the coin was the suppression or negation of other forms of sexuality such as homosexuality and female lesbianism, generally misrepresented as un-African sexual practices. In a country such as Cameroon, the nationalist project of the post-colonial leaders has resulted in the state's exuberant production of moralizing discourses that not only categorize gays and lesbians as sexual perverts, but also criminalize them as sexual delinquents. In addition to their criminalization and pathologization, in recent years both male and female homosexuals have also become the objects of a process of demonization. Symptomatic of this demonization of sexual inverts is the pervasive figure of the gay/lesbian witch, which now permeates both the official and popular discourses on homosexuals in contemporary Cameroon, as a further justification for a politics of radical exclusion and persecution.

### Notes

1 On the effect of global processes on African sexuality, see Arnfred (2004); Nguyen (2005: 245–67).

2 Deleuze and Guattari (1983 [1972]) define 'oedipalized subjects' as repressed or sexually emasculated subjects. In this contribution we understand 'Oedipalized subjects'

as those who express aversion to any form of sexuality other than heterosexual.

3 For a critique of this perspective, see Murray and Roscoe (1998) and Morgan and Wieringa (2005).

4 Between 2007 and 2010 Alternative Cameroon and ADEFHO

(Cameroonian association for the defence of gay rights), two of the most influential gay organizations in Cameroon, have recorded about sixty cases of homosexual offenses brought to different state courts throughout the country. In addition, the same organizations claim to have provided legal assistance to more than a hundred young men and women prosecuted for similar sexual crimes (see ADEFHO 2010).

5 Article 347 Bis of the Cameroonian Penal Code punishes anyone who performs homosexual acts with six months to five years' imprisonment, in addition to a fine ranging from 20,000 to 200,000 CFA francs (15–150 euros).

6 On the link between same-sex relations and occultism, see Abega (2007: 95–112); Geschiere (1997); Ndjio (2010).

7 One of the co-accused was detained in a cell at the police station together with her nine-month-old son. See www.camer.be.org (accessed 16 October 2008).

8 For example, Article 251 of the Cameroonian criminal code punishes anyone involved in witchcraft-related practices with five to ten years' imprisonment.

9 See L'Anecdote, 256, 9 February 2006, p. 4. See also Le Messager, 2059, 7 February 2006, p. 2.

10 This exercise of cultural homogenization is found in the works of some prominent African scholars and political leaders, such as Diop (1978 [1964]), Ndaw (1983), and Senghor (1964, 1977), to name a few. In many countries, it has led to the institutionalization of one-party system, the authoritarian imposition of a pensée unique and a quasi-religious devotion to a charismatic leader, embodying the figure of

a godly 'father of the nation' or 'Enlightened Guide' (Bayart 1985, 1993; Mbembe 2001).

11 On sexuality and the closure of ethnic barriers, see Nagel (2003).

12 For a critique of this amnesia in the reading of African history, see Wieringa (2005).

13 For a critique of colonial representations of African sexuality, see Bleys (1995); Fanoudh-Siefer (1968); Stoler (1995, 2002).

14 See De Pedrais (1950); Evans-Pritchard (1951, 1971); Herskovits (1937); Malinowski (1941 [1929]).

15 See Terroirs' special issue on homosexuality in Cameroon (issue 1/2, 2007).

16 For a critical discussion of the role played by colonialism in spreading homosexuality in Western colonies, see Aldrich (2003: 201–18).

17 The maintenance of Article 347 Bis of the Penal Code and the endorsement by the Biya regime of anti-gay policies inherited from its predecessor suggest that there is a strong continuity between the nationalist projects of the 1960s and 1970s, and present-day state-sponsored homophobia.

18 Translation from the French original: 'L'homme dans sa condition africaine, qui doit s'affirmer en surmontant tout ce qui conteste son humanité et le met en danger.'

19 Potentiel, 23 May 2006.

20 A play on words of the French term 'bite' (phallus or penis) and Greek 'kratos' (power), referring to the lustful man who advocates bitocratie – that is, the power of the phallus.

21 On institutionalized phallocracy in Cameroon, see Sindjoun (2000).

22 On the literature on sexual and gender-based violence in sub-

Saharan Africa, see Barker and Ricardo (2005).

23 See, for example, the UNFPA Sub-regional Analysis Report on Gender Based Violence (GBV) and on Behavior Change Communication (BCC) in eastern and central Africa, published in 2007, which focused on thirteen francophone and anglophone African countries, including Cameroon. In addition, recent research conducted by a coalition of NGOs in Cameroon has revealed that every year more than four thousand young girls and boys are victims of sexual abuse (see *Le Messager*, 22 March 2011, p. 4).

24 See Mbembe's (2001) seminal work on the esthetics of vulgarity and banality of the African post-colonial power.

25 Symptomatic of this colonial representation of African sexuality is De Rachewitz's Black Eros (1964).

26 See Mbembe's devastating critique of the imagination of the African self in nationalist writing (2002: 239–73).

27 On the sexual impotency of African men, see Miescher (2005).

28 Since 2006, many local sensationalist dailies and weeklies have echoed rumors and fables of gay people as degenerates, witches, and delinquents. See, for example, *L'Anedocte* (12 May 2006); *Le Popoli* (23 June 2007).

## References

Abega, S. (2007) 'La Presse et l'état: l'exemple des procès sur l'homosexualité au Cameroun,' *Terroirs*, special issue on 'L'Homosexualité est bonne à penser,' 1/2: 95–112.

Adams, V. and S. Leigh Pigg (eds) (2005) *Sex in Development: Science, sexuality and morality in a global perspective*, Durham, NC, and London: Duke University Press.

ADEFHO (2009) *Rapport sur les violations des droits des homosexuels au Cameroun*, Report no. 1, October.

— (2010) *Rapport narratif des affaires judiciaires engagées et défendues par ADEFHO sur les procès pour homosexualité au Cameroun*, Report no. 2, October.

Aken'Ova, D. (2009) 'State-sponsored homophobia: experiences from Nigeria's struggle for equality: sexual orientation and gender identity and human rights in Africa,' *Perspectives*, 10(4): 16–18.

Akyeampong, E. K. (2006) 'Race, identity and citizenship in black Africa: the case of the Lebanese in Ghana,' *Africa*, 76(3): 297–323.

Aldrich, R. (2003) *Colonialism and Homosexuality*, London and New York: Routledge.

Altman, D. (2001) *Global Sex*, Chicago, IL: University of Chicago Press.

Arnfred, S. (ed.) (2004) *Rethinking Sexualities in Africa*, Uppsala: Nordiska Afrikainstitut.

Barker, G. and C. Ricardo (2005) 'Young men and the construction of masculinity in sub-Saharan Africa: implications for HIV/AIDS, conflict, and violence,' Social Development Papers: Conflict Prevention and Reconstruction no. 26, World Bank.

Bayart, J.-F. (1985) *L'Etat au Cameroun*, Paris: Presses de la Fondation Nationale des Sciences Politiques.

— (1993) *The State in Africa: The Politics of the Belly*, trans. M. Harper, London and New York: Longman.

Bayart, J.-F., A. Mbembe and C. Toulabor (1992) *Le Politique par le bas en Afrique noire:*

contributions à une problématique de la démocratie, Paris: Karthala.

Biaya, T. K. (1999) 'Eroticism and sexuality in Africa: directions and illusions,' CODESRIA Bulletin, 3(4): 41–6.

— (2001) 'Les Plaisirs de la ville: masculinité, sexualité et féminité à Dakar (1997–2000),' African Studies Review, 44(2): 71–85.

Bleys, R. (1995) The Geography of Perversion: Male-to-male sexual behaviour outside the West and the ethnography of imagination, 1750–1918, New York: New York University Press.

Butler, J. (1990) Gender Trouble: Feminism and the subversion of identity, New York: Routledge.

Campbell, R. and T. Sefl (2004) 'The impact of rape on women's sexual health risk behavior,' Health Psychology, 23(1): 67–74.

Castells, M. (1997) The Power of Identity, Malden, MA: Blackwell.

Chatterjee, P. (1993) The Nation and Its Fragments: Colonial and Postcolonial Histories, Princeton, NJ: Princeton University Press.

Connell, R. W. (2005 [1995]) Masculinities, London: Polity.

De Pedrais, D. P. (1950) La Vie Sexuelle des Africains, Paris: Payot.

De Rachewitz, B. (1964) Black Eros: Sexual customs of Africa from prehistory to the present day, trans. Peter Whigham, London: George Allen & Unwin.

Deleuze, G. and F. Guattari (1983 [1972]) Anti-Oedipus: Capitalism and schizophrenia, trans. B. Hurley et al., preface by M. Foucault, New York: Viking.

Diop, C. A (1978 [1964]) The Cultural Unity of Black Africa, Chicago, IL: Third World.

Eboussi-Boulaga, F. (1977) La Crise du Muntu: authenticité africaine et philosophie, Paris: Présence Africaine.

Epprecht, M. (2004) Hungochani: The history of a dissident sexuality in southern Africa, Montreal: McGill-Queen's University Press.

— (2008) Heterosexual Africa?: The History of an Idea from the Age of Exploration to the Age of AIDS, Athens, OH, and Scottsville: Ohio University Press and University of KwaZulu-Natal.

Evans, T. D. (1993) Sexual Citizenship: The material construction of sexualities, London and New York: Routledge.

Evans-Pritchard, E. E. (1951) Kinship and Marriage among the Nuer, Oxford: Oxford University Press.

— (1971) The Azande, Oxford: Clarendon Press.

Fanoudh-Siefer, L. (1968) Le Mythe du nègre et de l'Afrique Noire dans la littérature française: de 1800 à la deuxième guerre mondiale, Paris: Klincksieck.

Foucault, M. (1981 [1978]) The History of Sexuality, vol. I: An Introduction, Harmondsworth: Allen Lane.

Friedman, D. M. (2001) A Mind of Its Own: A cultural history of the penis, New York: Palgrave.

Gaudio, R. (2009) Allah Made Us: Sexual outlaws in an Islamic African city, Hoboken, NJ: Wiley-Blackwell.

Germond, P. and S. de Gruchy (eds) (1997) Aliens in the Household of God, Cape Town: David Philip.

Geschiere, P. (1997) The Modernity of Witchcraft: Politics and the Occult in Postcolonial Africa, Charlottesville: University of Virginia Press.

Gevisser, M. and C. Edwin (eds) (1994) Defiant Desire: Gay and lesbian lives in South Africa, Braamfontein: Ravan Press.

Gilmore, D. (1990) *Manhood in the Making: Cultural concepts of masculinity*, New Haven, CT, and London: Yale University Press.

Hanry, P. (1970) *Erotisme Africain: le comportement sexuel des adolescents Guinéens*, Paris: Payot.

Herskovits, M. J. (1937) 'A note on "woman marriage" in Dahomey,' *Africa*, 10: 335–41.

Hyam, R. (1990) *Empire and Sexuality: The British experience*, Manchester: Manchester University Press.

Irigaray, L. (1985) *This Sex Which Is Not One*, Ithaca, NY: Cornell University Press.

Johnson, C. A. (2007) *Off the Map: How HIV/AIDS programming is failing same-sex practicing people in Africa*, New York: International Gay and Lesbian Human Rights Commission.

Kagame, A. (1956) *La Philosophie Bantu-rwandaise de l'être*, Brussels.

— (1976) *La philosophie Bantu comparée*, Paris: Présence Africaine.

Kemogne, J.-B. (2006) 'La Dynamique anale de la politique au Cameroun,' *Le Messager*, 17 February.

Lindsay, L. A. and S. F. Miescher (eds) (2003) *Men and Masculinities in Modern Africa*, Portsmouth, NH: Heinemann.

Malinowski, B. (1941 [1929]) *The Sexual Life of Savages in Northwestern Melanesia*, New York: Halcyon House.

Malkki, L H. (1995) *Purity and Exile: Violence, memory, and national cosmology among Hutus refugees in Tanzania*, Chicago, IL: University of Chicago Press.

Mballa Meka, E. (2009) *Une Nuit dans le Sissongo*, Cameroon: L'Harmattan.

Mbembe, A. (2001) *On the Postcolony*, Berkeley: University of California Press.

— (2002) 'African modes of self-writing,' *Public Culture*, 14(1): 239–73.

Miescher, S. F. (2005) *Making Men in Ghana*, Indianapolis: Indiana University Press.

Mkhize, N., J. Bennett, R. Vasu and R. Moletsane (2010) *The Country We Want to Live In: Hate crimes and homophobia in the lives of black lesbian South Africans*, Cape Town: HSRC Press.

Morgan, R. and S. Wieringa (2005) *Tommy Boys, Lesbian Men and Ancestral Wives: Female same-sex practices in Africa*, Johannesburg: Jacana Publishers.

Mosse, G. L. (1985) *Nationalism and Sexuality: Respectability and abnormal sexuality in modern Europe*, New York: Howard Fertig.

Mudimbe, V. Y. (1988) *The Invention of Africa: Gnosis, philosophy, and the order of knowledge*, Bloomington and London: Indiana University Press and James Currey.

Mugawe, D. and A. Powell (2006) *Born to High Risk: Violence against girls in Africa*, African Child Policy Forum.

Murray, S. O. and W. Roscoe (eds) (1998) *Boy-Wives and Female-Husbands: Studies of African homosexualities*, London: Macmillan.

Nagel, J. (2003) *Race, Ethnicity and Sexuality: Intimate intersections, forbidden frontiers*, New York: Oxford University Press.

Ndaw, A. (1983) *La Pensée Africaine: recherche sur les fondements de la pensée négro-africaine*, Preface by L. S. Senghor, Dakar: Nouvelles Editions Africaines.

Ndjio, B. (2005) 'Carrefour de la Joie: Popular deconstruction of the African postcolonial public sphere,' *Africa*, 75(3): 265–94.

— (2009) 'Homosexuality, power and domination in contemporary Cameroon,' George Mosse Lecture Series (working paper), ASSR, University of Amsterdam.

— (2010) 'If you are a gay you are a witch: homosexuality, sorcery and the political invention of the "other" in postcolonial Cameroon,' SEPHIS research report, Amsterdam.

— (forthcoming) '*Tanshi* or the success-story of traditional Chinese medicine in Africa.'

Nguyen, V.-K. (2005) 'Uses and pleasures: sexual modernity, HIV/AIDS, and confessional technologies in a West African metropolis,' in V. Adams and T. Leigh Pigg (eds), *Sex in Development: Science, sexuality and morality in a global perspective*, Durham, NC, and London: Duke University Press, pp. 245–67.

Nkrumah, K. (1964) *Consciencism*, London: Heinemann.

Nyamnjoh, F. B. (2005) 'Fishing in the troubled water: disquettes and thiefs in Dakar,' *Africa*, 75(3): 295–324.

Ombolo, J.-P. (1990) *Sexe et société en Afrique Noire*, Paris: L'Harmattan.

Otutubikey Izugbara, C. (2004) 'Patriarchal ideology and discourses of sexuality in Nigeria,' Understanding Human Sexuality Seminar Series no. 4.

Rivkin-Fish, M. (2005) 'Moral science and the management of sexual revolution in Russia,' in V. Adams and S. Leigh Pigg (eds), *Sex in Development: Science, sexuality and morality in a global perspective*, Durham, NC, and London: Duke University Press, pp. 71–94.

Rochlin, G. (1980) *The Masculine*

*Dilemma: A psychology of masculinity*, Boston, MA: Little, Brown.

Senghor, L. S. (1964) *Liberté1: négritude et humanisme*, Paris: Seuil.

— (1977) *Liberté3: négritude et civilisation de l'universel*, Paris: Seuil.

Sindjoun, L. (ed.) (2000) *La Biographie sociale du sexe: genre, société et politique au Cameroun*, Karthala, Dakar and Paris: CODESRIA.

Smith, D. J. (2007) *A Culture of Corruption: Everyday deception and popular discontent in Nigeria*, Princeton, NJ, and Oxford: Princeton University Press.

Stoler, A. L. (1995) *Race and the Education of Desire: Foucault's history of sexuality and the colonial order of things*, Durham, NC: Duke University Press.

— (2002) *Carnal Knowledge and Imperial Power. Race and the intimate in colonial rule*, Berkeley: University of California Press.

Terroirs (2007) 'L'Homosexualité est bonne à penser', Special issue, 1/2.

Toulabor, C. M. (1991) 'Jeux de mots, jeux de vilains. Lexique de la dérision politique au Togo,' *Politique Africaine*, 3: 55–71.

Watney, S. (1989) *Policing Desire: Pornography, AIDS and the Media*, Minneapolis: University of Minnesota Press.

Weeks, J. (1977) *Coming Out: Homosexual politics in Britain from the nineteenth century to the present*, London: Quartet.

— (1981) *Sex, Politics and Society: The regulation of sexuality since 1800*, London: Longman.

Werbner, R. (1996) 'Multiple identities, plural arenas,' in R. Werbner and T. Ranger (eds), *Postcolonial Identities in Africa*, London: Zed Books, pp. 1–26.

White, E. (1980) *States of Desire*, London: André Deutsch.

White, L. (1990) *The Comforts of Home: Prostitution in Colonial Nairobi*, Chicago, IL: University of Chicago Press.

Wieringa, S. L. (2005) 'Postcolonial amnesia in Indonesia and southern Africa and sexual rights,' Presidential address, V IASSCS conference, San Francisco.

**7 · Ndjio**

# 8 | The 'lesbian' existence in Arab cultures: historical and sociological perspectives

IMAN AL-GHAFARI

## Introduction

This chapter examines the possibility of 'lesbian' existence in Arab cultures from a lesbian perspective that analyzes the varying degrees and types of socio-political control exercised over the female body in Arab history. Most Arab writers and historians treat Arab history as a sacred realm, repeating the same stories in a manner that either sustains heteronormativity or defends the Arab culture against its Western critics. With the help of gender analysis, I re-examine both essentialist identity formations and constructed sexual politics, outlining the ambiguous position of the lesbian as an innate orientation and as a female body in Arab cultures. I use various sources, ranging from medieval Arabic texts to modern writings, Arab-Islamic writings, biographies, novels, orientalist views and contemporary views. I rely on a Western lesbian and feminist discourse because it provides me with the needed tools, terminology, and methodology to examine the perplexing position of lesbian subjectivity, and the perils of 'coming out' of Arab closets. I find Rich's (1972) approach of 'revision' useful. With reference to Foucault's *The Birth of the Clinic* (2007 [1963]), I examine the paradoxical position of the lesbian in the biological approach adopted by some male writers who view the lesbian as a pathological case, transforming the lesbian body from a dangerous clitoral body into a vulnerable vaginal body, or even an anal one. Sedgwick (1990) reveals that the 'lesbian' is not 'a recent invention,' but is incorporated in a long history marked by certain homosocial practices that conceal homo/heterosexual identities in private and in public. Drawing on Butler's (1993, 2004) theories, I expose how 'gender performativity' in Arab cultures obscures the already invisible lesbian identity instead of making it visible.

The dilemma between naturalizing the lesbian essence as a mere bodily desire and politicizing it as an identity is a major issue; both attitudes suppress any ethical proposition for a recognized lesbian truth within the moral norms of Arab cultures. I show how the essentialist and constructivist approaches have their limitations that forbid the coming out of any subjective truth that does not comply with the 'Truth' promoted by Arab history. Meanwhile, I discuss the problematic position of the lesbian as a female body and as a socio-sexual construct in contemporary Arab cultures in which 'one can discern a shift from an essentialist to a constructionist perspective' (Khalaf 2006: 192).

My main concern is not the material practice of 'lesbian sex,' but 'the inclination, even if it is not translated into action' (Foucault 1980: I, 43). I use the term 'lesbian' as an expression of an inherent self-awareness of an integrated lesbian identity, whether the practice of 'lesbian sex' is involved at the moment of self-identification, or not. What is at stake here is not the temporary practice, the momentary attraction, or the chosen relationship, but what I see as the tenacious lesbian soul that steadily defends its lesbian specificity throughout her entire life. I perceive the lesbian as an infinite sensual, mental, spiritual, and sexual awareness that is incarnated in a female body; an absorbed conscious-ness that exists prior to sex, love, language, gender representation, and history. Hence, the lesbian that I am trying to uncover is not a 'dead or sleeping consciousness [or even] a common consciousness' (Rich 1972: 18, 24) of a woman having a temporary sexual relationship with another woman, a woman-identified woman, or a female experiencing an interim emotional or erotic attraction toward another female.

What concerns me is not the bodily pleasure, but the spiritual essence of a lesbian identity as a genuine identity that endures invis-ibility, silence, alienation, oppression, and subordination. The lesbian existence is not just about sex; it is about 'the desire to persist in one's own being [within] ... norms of recognition' (Butler 2004: 32), and the right to defend one's autonomy within enormous complex-ities and contradictions. Since homoerotic passion, spiritual feelings, and physical sensations already exist in the desiring soul before one can convey meaning to them, the lesbian passion remains invisible, unvoiced, and unintelligible if it is not accompanied by a subtle process of self-identification. It is a thorny process that requires standing up against heterosexual expectations and homosocial norms, and a re-examination of the gendered issues of identification that might turn the female body from a desired heterosexual object into a desired homosexual one. In this chapter I explore the need to liberate the lesbian from the historical texts that stabilize her, either as a body void of any soul and sexuality, or as an over-sexualized relational presence without any spiritual essence.

The concept of identity in Arab culture has usually been politicized as a unified core that signifies shared values, beliefs, and dreams on all levels. Different voices, ones that do not repeat the symphony of a harmonious culture, are marginalized on the presupposition that they are not part of 'our' culture. Hence, remapping Arab culture requires a re-examination of the epistemological position of the woman in a hegemonic culture that treats the female body as a receptive body whose sexuality is determined according to a woman's enforced relations with both men and women in man-made and woman-made closets. Since the patriarchal structures of power in Arab countries are mainly established through history and literature, I discuss a number of historical and literary texts. The numerous marks of history over the female body are exposed by revisiting the same historical realms that increase the invisibility of lesbian subjectivities.

## The dilemma of rereading Arab history in Arab feminist discourse

Arab history provides rich material about the lives of men – as political leaders, prophets, lovers, philosophers, physicians, poets, writers, and fighters. Women have been glorified as wives of sultans, beloved of poets, wives and daughters of prophets, and very rarely as queens who follow the advice of a wise man, or even as reporters who glorify men's achievements in the private and political domains. Hardly ever does Arab history refer to a female figure except within the context of her relations with men. Arab history is mainly written and documented from a male-oriented perspective that treats women as the 'guardians of tradition and of the collective identity ...' (Bouhdiba 1998: 232). These assumptions create ignorance of the existence of a lesbian female with an independent subjectivity who has no desire for men and who does not follow the gender roles expected of her.

Since works written by self-defined lesbians do not seem to exist in Arab history, revisiting history may help remove some cultural stereotypes that surround the lives of women in general and the female body in particular. In such a context, it is not enough for women to remember their 'common history' to be able to free themselves from the prison of Arab history. What is needed is a 're-vision' which is defined by Rich as 'the act of looking back, of seeing with fresh eyes, of entering an old text from a new critical direction – [it] is for us more than a chapter in cultural history: it is an act of survival' (Rich 1972: 18). And, she continues, we need to 'know the writing of the past, and to know it differently ... not to pass on a tradition but to break its hold' (ibid.: 19).

Alice Walker's *In Search of Our Mothers' Gardens* (1984) reveals the need to return to the legacy of the mother as a source of inspiration. Though many feminist Arab writers adopted this rereading strategy as a means of liberation and overcoming patriarchy, they ended up trapping women in another woman-made, heterosexual tradition. Al-Mernissi (1997), for instance, extols the matriarchal system of marriage, disregarding the fact that this kind of so-called matriarchy essentialized all women as being heterosexual. Apparently, the feminist thinking of Arab women writers revolves around promoting the power of the heterosexual woman as leader, wife, or mother. In *Forgotten Female Sultans: Female Presidents in Islam* (1994), Al-Mernissi tries to establish the important political roles women played in Arab history by stating that Aisha, the Prophet's wife, was the first woman to cross borders between male territory and female territory by participating in a battle (Al-Mernissi 1994: 117). The choice of Aisha as a role model to be examined and re-examined fixes the historical figure as an archetypal example for all females, and makes her a unique model that Muslim women must identify with. The social position of Aisha, as the wife of the Prophet and 'the mother of believers,' establishes marriage and motherhood as the truest signs of women's authority in Islam. Thus, many feminist readings of Arab history entangle the woman in a story which is not necessarily every woman's story. Rather, it is merely a new version of the same story renarrated by a female writer. As Foucault reflects in *The Archaeology of Knowledge* (1969), the 'alleged truism' of history is rarely questioned (cited in Gutting 2005: 35).

In addition, Nawal El-Saadawi, a renowned Egyptian feminist physician and writer, reflects upon female sexuality in some of her works. However, El-Saadawi's reflection on 'foreplay, orgasm, and the rights to pleasure' from a political perspective establishes heterosexual desire as the only norm, shared by all women throughout history (El-Saadawi 1958). Her concentration on the materiality of the female body and its pleasurable sensations establishes woman in the singular as a common body that has a common desire.

The realization of Foucault in *The Birth of the Clinic* (2007 [1963]) that the 'gaze is not faithful to truth [because] the gaze that sees is the gaze that dominates' (ibid.: 45) can be applied to El-Saadawi's medical gaze that dominates the female body and re-exposes it to the doctor's knife, both physically and metaphorically. Hence, El-Saadawi's return to history restores the same historical woman who has no independent voice, private emotions, or unique sensations. In *Anil Mara'a* (About Woman), El-Saadawi praises the 'matriarchal system in which lineage and heredity are traced back to the mother' (El-Saadawi 1988: 26). This subversive discourse that attempts to replace the dominant hetero-patriarchal authority with a hetero-matriarchal authority assumes that all women share the same maternal and heterosexual tendencies.

Accordingly, Arab feminism became 'prey to new normative exclusions' (Chanter 2006: 88) that lacked self-assertive voices. Because Arab history was merely retold in a manner that asserts singularity and unity, all identities had to dissolve into what was constructed as the 'Arab identity' with many of the male-oriented, misogynist, heterosexual, political concepts associated with it. Despite the fact that Arab history offers some seeds of transcending imposed gender roles, the return to it remains a tricky process, especially when several modern writers deploy it as a political means of silencing any visible lesbian existence.

### Rereading women's biography: female friendships or lesbian secrets

A major gap in Arab feminist scholarship concerns lesbian issues. Most works on lesbians are subsumed under studies of male homosexuality or included in men's erotic literature about women (see also El-Rouayheb 2005). Thus, lesbians in Arab history are not only 'deprived of a political existence through "inclusion" as female versions of male homosexuality' (Rich 1980: 649); they are also denied their existence within heterosexual women's narratives. This might be attributed to the fact that Islamic traditions in Arab cultures do not conceive of intimate female same-sex relations as being lesbian in the lesbian-feminist sense. The lesbian as 'a woman [who] refuses male sexual access and lives outside traditional family structures' (Cameron 1993: 246) does not exist in the collective cultural memory.

Rejection of marriage on the part of Arab women is one of the main causes of social prejudice, because such a lifestyle 'challenges a male-dominant social order in a way that is not true for gay men' (Richardson and Seidman 2002: 4). A single woman is liable to experience different types of discrimination, not because her celibacy might suggest an implicit lesbian tendency, but because the woman's independence subtly defies the patriarchal system. The only case where the rejection of heterosexual marriage is traditionally admired is in the case of Sufi women. 'Sufism offered women a life of independence and autonomy otherwise certainly impossible for women of Rabi'a's class' (Ahmad 1991: 68). Paradoxically, Sufism enabled female figures to transcend gender restrictions, lead rebellious lifestyles, and become 'erotic' in their own way. In the Islamic tradition, society is not allowed to stand against the will of the woman to fulfill her duties toward God. Hence, a socio-spiritual rebellion based on Sufism was the only sound moral practice that enabled a woman to cross borders.

A closer look at the life of the female Sufi mystic Rabi'a Al-Adawiyya, who was glorified as the one who 'invented Divine love' (Sakakini 1994: 39), shows that this woman managed to survive as a single person in a male-oriented society through Sufism, which she probably adopted as a defensive act against the norms of heterosexual love. Refusing to be distracted from her devotion to maidenhood and worship of God, Rabi'a rejected marriage proposals in an austere manner that might convey a separatist feminist spirit. Her female biographer, Widad Sakakini, regards Rabi'a's indifference to men, and preference for a single life, as an example of 'asceticism ... which has its roots in pre-Islamic Christian traditions' (ibid.: 32). In an attempt to justify Rabi'a's relentless rejection of male suitors, Sakakini quotes Rabi'a: 'be your own guardian and do not let men be your guardians' (ibid.: 35).

Aware of the risks of placing a minority culture at the center of her biography, Sakakini was keen on criticizing both Rabi'a and her female companion, Hayouna, for their lonesome lifestyle. Hayouna is described as a sarcastic worshiper who wrote symbolic Sufi poems that reflect upon the 'ideology that drove them away from social life' (ibid.: 65). Though Sakakini shed light on this relationship, she did not explain why Rabi'a received more critical attention than Hayouna, who is included in 'Al-Nisabouri's book on *Okala'a Al-Majanin* (The Sane of the Lunatics) at the beginning of the fifth hijra century' (ibid.: 63–4).[1] Rabia'a's 'unwomanly' attitude is first despised by Sakakini as 'a dissent of her nature and instinct' (ibid.: 42). Nevertheless, Sakakini finds Rabia'a worthy of respect on the basis that 'God had granted some women what men are granted; knowledge, reasoning, faith and piety' (ibid.: 65). Hence, 'had another woman [abandoned her natural roles], she could have been accused of abnormality, because a woman's refusal of what she is born to, i.e. to preserve [the] species ... is a deviation from the law of God and Nature' (ibid.: 42).

Obviously, even when a female Arab biographer tries to give clues to some unspoken secrets, she reduces the level of intimacy between women, reinventing them within the framework of the accepted gender and heterosexual norms. Given the fact that '[We] now can never understand the past as it was understood by those who lived it' (Stanley 1992: 210), it is difficult to identify whether same-sex relations among women in Arab history were constructed as a result of slavery or whether they were an expression of an invisible lesbian love with its erotic undertones, combined with passion for God and poetry.

## Searching for the lesbian in Arab women's closets and literature

Many cultural historians have been sensitive to the use of the term 'female homosexuality' and 'lesbian identity' to describe erotic and passionate relations between women in pre-modern cultures in general and in Arab cultures in particular. This can be attributed to the perception of homosexuality as 'a distinctly modern construction' (Bristow 1997: 5). The American classical scholar Halperin declares: 'It may well be that homosexuality has no history of its own outside the West or much before the beginning of our century' (cited in ibid.: 5). In a similar spirit, Weeks (1986) argues, 'what we define as 'sexuality' is an historical construction ... and a "fictional unity", which once did not exist' (cited in Bristow 1997: 5). In this section, I search for literary traces of a lesbian identity in homosocial spaces, such as a fantasy harem and *hammam*. Ironically, it is this homosociality which confines the lesbian subjectivity in a woman-made closet, and makes any attempt to come out from a woman-made closet to a man-made closet seem to be motivated by a presumed 'heterosexual' desire to seduce men, or to identify with men. By subsuming the lesbian into the category of the historical woman, Arab women writers made it more difficult for the lesbian to assert her difference from her historical 'grandmothers'.[2]

Writing about lesbianism from a heterosexual perspective, contemporary Arab writers maintain the logic of the fantasy harem. By repeating the orientalist perspective of the harem as a safe haven for lovemaking among women, they give the impression that lesbianism is merely constructed in the private sphere. In Yazbek's *Smell of Cinnamon* (2008), the Damascene public bath is re-created as a homoerotic space where same-sex encounters can take place smoothly without being noticed. Yazbek's portrayal of the sexual encounter between the bride who 'pulls Hanan's trembling hand, and puts it on her right breast, where a large pink nipple flashes between the little fingers' (ibid.: 119) is analogous to Lucie-Smith's description of Ingres' painting *The Turkish Bath* (1862) in which 'the woman on the right side of the picture tickles the breast of her girlfriend' (cited in Al-Mernissi 2004: 175). Yazbek's re-creation of Ingres' Turkish harem, as a homoerotic space for the 'pleasure of the male voyeur' (cited in ibid.: 174), goes hand in hand with the predominant presumption of many male writers that 'a whole area of sexual life is organized around the hammam' (Bouhdiba 1998: 196).

When the orientalist obsession with the harem as an exotic space forbidden to men is repeated by a female writer, it carries more credibility, especially when there is an assumption that the woman has access to it based on her sex. According to Brown, 'works understood to be based on the woman artist's visit to a harem were universally understood to bear traces of her privileged access to the forbidden site' (cited in Jones and Stephenson 1999: 59). Hence, Yazbek's depiction of the Damascene bath as a homoerotic space confirms the orientalist view that 'the harems of Syria [are] active centres of "sapphism"' (Kabbani 2008: 93).

Yazbek's *Smell of Cinnamon* seems to re-create Al-Nafzawi's medieval text, *Perfumed Garden*, in which female vaginas are smelled and fantasized by the desiring male for the desiring male gaze. However, when the vagina is objectified by a female gaze, for the sake of an absent but 'omnipresent' male gaze, the woman writer becomes the doctor in Al-Nafzawi's clinic. According to Foucault, 'Doctor and patient are ... bound together, the doctor by an ever-more attentive, more insistent, more penetrating gaze' (Foucault 2007 [1963]: 16–17). In Arab women's literature, male doctors and female doctors are bound together by the same penetrating gaze. The scene in which Hanan faints at the sight of the woman's vagina and at the orgasmic sensations she experiences with her newlywed neighbour who 'put her in her lap, pressed her, and opened her thighs by force' (Yazbek 2008: 120) makes the vagina 'the locus of various dialectics ... political struggles, demands ... and social confrontations' (Foucault 2007 [1963]: 17). Here, vaginas are exposed for the female viewer, not to satisfy a lesbian desire or to give voice to a lesbian identity, but to provoke the absent male figure who set the rules of the 'game' in the first place, and who probably assigned a woman to be his fellow doctor or informant in the private domain.

In such a homosocial context, 'lesbian' desire is portrayed as a masochistic desire to return to the first intoxicating smell of the vagina, mixed with the smell of 'tea with cinnamon,' 'laurel oil with mud,' and inherent in the smells of female bathers in the *hammam*. Ironically, the homosocial space, in which the bride is ritually prepared to lose her material virginity on the wedding night, becomes a parody of heterosexuality in which the bride metaphorically deflowers the younger female. This type of discourse, which essentializes the lesbian desire as a systematic return to the first sexual experience, sight, touch, and olfactory sensations, is not liberating to the lesbian desire that exists prior to any sort of experience or spoken word. Quite the opposite, it presumes that knowledge of one's sexual identity springs from one's past experience.

The sexual relationship between the Damascene lady of the house and her Palestinian maid is portrayed as a sort of an obsession and a habit that is practiced out of sexual deprivation on the part of Hanan Al-Hashimi, the well-off Damascene woman who is married to an impotent man, and out of economic need and homelessness on the part of Alya, the young Palestinian girl living in a refugee camp in the poor suburbs of Damascus. Both of them are portrayed as sexual victims in one way or another. By creating an arbitrary association between the first experience and sexuality, Yazbek's discourse turns women into prisoners of an imposed experience. Hanan remains sexually attached to the vagina after her first sexual encounter with a woman, while Alya remains attached to the penis after being raped by one of the street boys she used to work with collecting plastic bottles from the garbage. Here, sexualities are not seen as identities. Rather, they are perceived as epidemics that stem from the first experience which is not chosen but imposed by women's circumstances. Seen in this light, both homosexuality and heterosexuality appear to be constructed by women's imposed experiences within the homosocial closet and the heterosocial one. Apparently, any presumed tolerance toward the fluidity of women's sexual practices within the homosocial fabric is traditionally driven by the need to sustain gender hierarchy and the dominance of heterosexual politics.

The Damascene bath is more or less a homosocial terrain for matchmaking between mothers and potential brides; it is a place where 'women lead their daughters to be watched by other women, in the hope of finding a bridegroom' (Yazbek 2008: 122). The female body is smelled, touched, and exposed to the gaze of women who seek brides for their sons. Here, female nudity is seen as an agent to heterosexuality; it is tolerated as long as it sustains a heterosexual end for women wanting to arrange marriages. In this context, the invisible lesbian, who does not want to be objectified by the female servants of heterosexuality, is put at odds with herself and with other women who do not even recognize her existence as a lesbian. Even while realizing the function of the public bath in the local culture, Yazbek's invocation of the orientalist vision, which treats the public bath as a sexualized space, generates voyeurism and invites lesbiphobia to a homosocial space.

Because female same-sex relations are traditionally homosocialized in the private sphere, they do not necessarily denote homosexuality in heterophobic Arab cultures where heterosociality arouses more suspicion than homosociality. The private sphere is subject to heterophobia on the basis of a commonly repeated 'Hadith' which demands that 'a man should not be alone with a woman in privacy, unless he is *Muhram*' (Al-Bukhari, cited in Al-Karmi 1998: 1035).[3] This religious saying came to be interpreted to mean that heterosociality between a male and a female stranger in privacy will invite the devil to seduce them. Hence, heterophobia is more intelligible to many people in Arab cultures than homophobia. Clearly, 'lesbianism has not made its way into the thinkable, the imaginable, that grid of cultural intelligibility that regulates the real and the nameable' (Butler 1991: 20). Whereas heterophobia is usually justified on the basis of biological differences, and is solidified by family laws in the Islamic system, homophobia is not similarly integrated in the web of intelligibility in Arab societies.

By ignoring the thin line that distinguishes homosexuality from homosociality, many contemporary Arab women's writings play a role in creating homophobia, deforming visibility, and restricting the lesbian existence as an identity. The concentration on the sexual dimension of female same-sex relations leads to distortions and oversimplifications. Instead of liberating the imprisoned lesbian subjectivity, Arab women's literature seems to be directed toward doubling the stigma or investing it for 'a so-called feminist cause.' Homoerotic practices are exaggerated by Arab women writers in a manner that suggests that women will necessarily turn to other women if men ignore their heterosexual needs. Set against the background of the Lebanese civil war, Elham Mansour's *Ana Hiya Anti* (I Am You) (2000) depicts all women as potential 'lesbians' who get involved in homosexual affairs while their men are busy making wars.

Indeed, the normalization of homosociality in Arab cultures might facilitate temporary same-sex attractions, but it also creates weak female relationships that are built around the concept of the 'absent male lover,' to which many women remain silently committed. In *Al-Akharoon* (The Others) (2006), the intimacy between the inborn lesbian who regards herself as having been created by God in that way (Al-Harz 2006: 178), and her beloved female friend whose erotic relations with women were for her 'an expression of a lustful desire for a man who will not come' (ibid.: 179), is frustrating for both of them. The predetermined lesbian lover is expected to show sympathy and concern over the interests of her beloved, who maintains emotional detachment while satisfying her lust.

Substantively, the socio-psychological structure of female same-sex relations in most Arab cultures makes it difficult to develop an intimate friendship which contains an intrinsic element of emotional attachment on both sides. Women's representations of female same-sex relations reveal the complexity of asserting a lesbian identity both in public and in private. The impermanent desire for 'physical gratification or release without emotional entanglements' (Abramson and Pickerton, cited in Jankowiak and Paladino 2008: 11) is less frowned upon in Arab cultures than a permanent same-sex attachment that totally excludes heterosexual 'options.'

### The lesbian body in between the biological discourse and the social one (medieval and modern views)

According to Judith Butler (1993), bodies do matter, but the way they matter is a social phenomenon. Seen in this light, the lesbian body has to be approached as a female body, without gender markings, as a virgin body that exists on the threshold of femininity and masculinity, prior to heterosexuality, homosexuality, patriarchy, and matriarchy; as a body that does not adhere to the traditional expectations and historical definitions of a woman's body. Because the 'pen is a metaphorical penis for male authors' (Gilbert 1986: 486), the female body is historically and biologically treated as a 'white page' on which men write whatever they want. The virgin female is not allowed to write her body using her own body, because she is treated as a waiting heterosexual body, rather than as a desiring lesbian body. Before the entry into the heterosexual system, female same-sex practices are traditionally seen as a prelude to heterosexuality. Socially speaking, it is the male who is supposed to explore the uncharted territories of the female body and to orient it toward hetero-erotic pleasures. Historically speaking, the materiality of the lesbian body was scrutinized by male scholars and preachers who tried to find ways to ensure the stability and the legitimization of the existing heterosexual regimes. Hence it is important to reread these texts that entangle lesbian subjectivity in debates between biological and social interpretations of lesbian sexuality. Below, I discuss two texts in which women's (same-sex) sexuality is portrayed.

In *Sexuality in Islam* (1998), Bouhdiba quotes a lengthy paragraph from *Al-Rawd al-Ater fi Nuzhat al-Khater* (The Perfumed Garden) by Sheikh Al-Nafzawi (died 1253/651) (ibid.: 154–5) that makes a distinction between the vaginas of women coming from different races and cultures: 'Byzantine, Spanish, Indian, Chinese, Slav, Negresses, Arab, Iraqi, Syrian, Persian, Nubian, Turkish, and Egyptian women.' The variety of the female vagina – their sizes, smells, visual and olfactory sensations and capacity to provide pleasure – is exposed in a manner that suggests different ways of controlling female bodies. By subjecting the private parts of the female body to a meticulous male gaze that scrutinizes their sizes and capacity for arousing desire, Al-Nafzawi's text exposes all female bodies to various forms of surveillance, in which 'the homosexual body becomes the focus of a supposedly scrupulous medical gaze' (Bristow 1997: 36). In this vein, the female body is not treated as '*aura*' or a sacred territory; rather Al-Nafzawi's detailed inspection of female vaginas exposes this '*aura*' to the public gaze, and subjects all women from various cultures to various forms of surveillance that range from circumcision to controlling women's affection, passion, and movement.

The second text I explore is Ahmad Ibn Yousef Al Tifashi's (died 1254/651) chapter on female same-sex relations in *Nuzhat Al-Albab fima La Yujad fi Kitab* (1992), which can be translated as 'The excursion of minds in what is non-existent in a book.' This text contains a humorous collection of erotic titbits of gossip, gimmicks, and poems told by anonymous judges, sodomites, 'grinders,' prostitutes, male and female pimps, adulterers, and hermaphrodites. Al-Tifashi devotes a chapter to the sexual practice of '*suhuq*' or '*suhaaq*,' which has been translated by Habib as 'grinding' (Habib 2008: 69); a term which describes the sexual act of crushing two female genitals together; a term which I will abide by at the beginning, and debate later on.

Most of Al-Tifashi's stories about 'grinders' appear to be narrated by a male voyeur, rather than by a self-assertive lesbian subjectivity. In one of the stories, a conversation takes place between some chiefs who ask about '*suhaaq*': '(I would really love to know how women "grind" each other) [the answer was] (If you like to know that, just sneak discreetly into your house)' (Al-Tifashi 1992: 241). This suggests that female same-sex relations were envisaged by the male public as commonly practiced among all women in the private sphere. In another story, 'Hobba Al-Madaniyya' is described as a woman who 'never let a man escape her wickedness' (Al-Nuaimi 2007: 85), and who is also renowned for being one of the highest-ranking 'grinders.' She teaches her daughter to 'know how to grunt and snuffle while shaking up and down' (Al-Tifashi 1992: 238). Here, 'grinding' is seen as a taught act that is transmitted from one generation to another. However, the mother's sexual advice cannot be seen as exclusively 'lesbian,' because the kinetic images of 'shaking up and down' and the nasal sounds of 'grunting and snuffling' were used in a previous chapter to depict anal sex between a man and a female maid (ibid.: 228). Here, sexuality appears to be taught, rather than inborn, because the strategy of teaching the application of sound effects during sex seems like teaching the woman how to fake orgasm.

Though Al-Tifashi makes a medical distinction between the inborn *'suhaqiyya'*/grinder and the constructed one, his distinction reveals a tendency to regard the lesbian body from a pathological perspective as suffering an inborn malady. His biological narrative presents a detailed analysis of the debates among doctors with regard to the cause of this 'inborn "instinct" in women':

> For example; if the length of the vulva was short, and the man's penis was long, she got hurt by it, so she hated men and loved *'suhaaq'*/grinding. Or, if a man had a short penis and her womb was long, she could not be gratified by men, unless the man had a very long organ.
>
> Hence, the kind of *suhaaq*/grinding that is due to the short length of the womb makes the hatred of men for its owner permanent and the ailment inherent. (Ibid: 235)

Thus lesbianism was viewed as informed by a permanent and inherent 'hatred of men' that springs from the length of the woman's womb, which is measured in heterosexual terms. In Al-Tifashi's discourse, the lesbian body is fantasized as a penetrated vulva, or a womb that tried different sizes of penises that did not fit well, so the woman ended up hating men and replacing them with women. Such an essentialist view incarnates a socially constructed one which presumes that it is the sexual experience which delivers the woman's knowledge of her sexuality, rather than the inner sensations that exist prior to any presumed 'physical measuring of the size of the womb vis-à-vis the male penis.'

Concomitantly, *'al-suhuq'* is interpreted from another pathological perspective as a remedy for the itching clitoris that needs 'grinding,' as the patient needs medicine to recover. In this light, lesbian desire is seen as springing from the 'labia,' which are magnified as an erotic zone where each part plays a role in the sexual drive of the female body toward another female body. Al-Tifashi narrates the words of 'wise men,' saying that,

> *Al-suhuq* is a natural lust, for there is between the labia a reflex like an inverted dimple which emanates vapours that incite heat and itchiness in the roots of the labial hair, and that cannot dissolve or cool down, without being rubbed and ejaculated on by another woman. Once that happens, the itching sensation cools down and turns off, because the water/liquid of the woman that springs from 'grinding' is cold, whereas the water of the man is hot, so the woman cannot gain any profit except from the water of the woman. (Ibid.: 236)

By making an association between itching and grinding, the inferred 'medical truth' presented by Al-Tifashi gives the impression that the lesbian body was examined as a patient at a certain time in history. The naturalized depiction of '*suhaaq*' desire, as springing from the female genitals, turns the lesbian body into a pragmatic one that bears a mere utilitarian philosophy, void of any love, emotion, or devotion. Al-Tifashi makes a clear-cut distinction between the biological 'grinders' who have 'itching' genitals, and the constructed 'grinders' who are fond of women as the result of 'habit.' This type of 'grinding' is seen as 'the result of [women's] infatuation with the use of female maids in youth, and they mature on this habit, so they keep on craving for it as in the case of "prostitution"' (ibid.: 236). Al-Tifashi suggests that 'any "grinding" that is constructed by practice can be easily eliminated and shifted, unlike the inborn one which is hard to be cured and can never be treated' (ibid.: 236). Al-Tifashi's clitoral interpretation of '*suhaaq*' desire came to be invested as a pretext for justifying female circumcision; the potential lesbian sexuality which is seen to be lurking in all 'pre-modified' female bodies had to be subdued.

### Are 'grinders' lesbians?

How to define lesbianism, especially in Arab history, where female same-sex relations are normalized as part of a supposedly 'tolerant' homosocial structure? Emphasizing the sexual dimension of female same-sex practices within the private sphere can lead to misunderstandings, while playing it down can lead to over-politicization. Thus a lesbian is not necessarily a woman who prefers socializing with women in the private sphere, but she is a female to whom 'nearly all relationships with women must be coloured by the possibility of love ...' (Hallett 1999: 158).

Medieval Arabic literature contains many love poems between men, but it lacks a female poet who writes her own body in her own language and who openly expresses her love of women. Most of the erotic literature and love poems seem to be written by men who underestimate women's choice of female lovers as being 'imposed,' but they sometimes encourage it for 'fear of pregnancy' or to reassert 'male potency.' In one of Al-Tifashi's narratives, 'When a man was told that his wife was engaged in "grinding", he said: As long as she spares me the burden of getting pregnant in her womb, let her do whatever she wants' (Al-Tifashi 1992: 242). Grinding appears as a practice that used to take place within the heterosexual institution of marriage as a means of avoiding the threat of having illicit heterosexual relations or unwanted pregnancies.

However, in an attempt to prove 'the existence of female homosexuality, at least as a category, in the pre-modern Arabian imagination' (Habib 2008: 4), Habib perceives the debates between grinders who have no desire for the penis and grinders who prefer the penis as an example that 'lesbian and bisexual identities begin to take shape,' and suggests that 'we should not be discouraged from labelling them as such for fear of anachronism' (ibid.: 75). Yet 'grinder' as a label cannot be used to describe a woman who has an emotional attachment to another woman before the sexual act of 'grinding' takes place. This act does not describe the intimate love between two independent and equally desiring subjectivities. Indeed, grinding is akin to 'tribadism [which] was and is a sexual practice, not a sexual identity' (Halberstam 1998: 61). The debates between grinders prove that the concept of sexual identity did not exist in the Arab history as a separate identity. Most narratives revolve around the advantages of sex with men over 'grinding,' which is mocked as 'a house without a pillar in the middle of it' (Al-Tifashi 1992: 246). In one of Al-Tifashi's stories, 'grinding' is compared to masturbation, which is perceived as a naive way of self-gratification. Hence, 'when a grinder looked at a man who has a big penis, she said: there is such a hammer in the world and I still hammer my clothes with my hand. Nay, it will never be. So, she got married' (ibid.: 246). In short, 'grinders' are not necessarily lesbians; for they do not expose a genuine and predetermined lesbian spirit that exists prior to the material practice of 'grinding,' nor do they seem to have the loving spiritual core of a female who is passionately and exclusively attached to another female.

Apart from the 'inborn grinder' who has an 'itching clitoris,' the inherent message in Al-Tifashi's text is that 'grinding' is mainly acquired by experience; women are portrayed as willing to practice any kind of sex, depending on their circumstances. Even the most devoted grinders do not regard themselves as having a different nature from other women, and the fact that they were so keen on converting the so-called 'bisexual women' to match their desires and expectations proves that they did not regard themselves as having an essentially different sexual orientation. By insisting on the beauty of 'grinding' once practiced, the defence of Al-Tifashi's grinders of grinding turns all women into potential 'grinders,' and all 'grinders' into potential 'heterosexuals.'

Though 'grinding' in Al-Tifashi's book is justified on several socio-sexual grounds, these justifications cannot be seen as a sign of tolerance. Rather, they confirm that the lesbian subjectivity was denied the possibility to speak. The symbolic debates between 'grinders' seem to assert that 'grinding' is an 'insufficient' practice that will be abandoned once women enjoy the penis. In another story, a female 'grinder' writes to her beloved woman, who 'tasted a man and got stuck to him,' trying to convince her in a metaphorical manner to return to the 'true path,' but her beloved woman metaphorically asserts that she cannot return to the 'taste of the onion' after having tasted 'the damask rose' (ibid.: 245). This debate is another blatant example of the conflict between a semi-essentialist discourse which regards the practice itself as a 'true' expression of the self, and the constructionist discourse which regards it as imposed owing to the lack of a 'better' alternative, thus stabilizing lesbian love as an alternative mode of pleasure, or 'the second best' (Bouhdiba 1998: 200).

Most of the stories told about female relations in Al-Tifashi's chapter, even when 'grinding' is praised, are didactic ones that insist on revealing the merits of heterosexuality. The only story that appears to be 'confessional' and more self-assertive than the rest of the stories is narrated by a 'grinder' who is most probably nicknamed Warda *'Al-Suhhaqiyya'*. Al-Tifashi's citation of Warda's lengthy, vivid, and eloquent description of lesbian orgasmic sensations presents 'grinding' as an 'instinct' for the natural beauty of the female body. Sensuous love among women is perceived as being heavenly, utopian, majestic, and beyond men's comprehension. Hence, Warda challenges 'philosophers' and 'the gods of fun and mirth/rapture' to understand the nature of their ecstasy (ibid.: 242–3). Warda's perception differs from that of other 'grinders,' who resort to 'grinding' as a means of avoiding 'fornication, adultery and an unwanted pregnancy' (ibid.: 244). For the other anonymous 'grinders,' *'suhaq'* is an imposed safe sex, while for a proud and a self-assertive 'grinder,' such as Warda, it appears as a gratifying bodily objective.

Warda's defence of the materiality of clitoral and labial pleasures, in which the female body is eroticized to encompass all natural and feminine beauties, might locate an early tendency to expose a same-sex desire within the context of a repressive phallic philosophy. Nevertheless, Warda cannot be considered as a 'modern lesbian subject,' as Habib suggests (Habib 2008: 82). Warda's words embed the possibility that she is the mouthpiece of a group of 'grinders' whose main concern is to have sex with a perfect female figure:

we are a community of 'grinders' in which the *one of us is joined with the one* who is soft, white, coquette, youthful, with delicate skin just as a bamboo cane, with a mouth like the daisy rose, and ringlets like blackish beads, and a cheek like the anemone flowers and the apples of Lebanon, and breasts like pomegranates, and a four-folded belly, and a vulva in which fires lurk, with a genital labia that is thicker than the lips of the Israelites' cow, and a crotch as prominent as the hump of Thamud's she-camel ... (Al-Tifashi 1992: 242, translation and emphasis mine)

Warda's words imply that there is an anonymous matchmaker, who facilitates the sexual encounter between the desiring grinders and the desired female bodies. Here, grinding is not portrayed as an identity with a spiritual core as discussed above, but as an idealized end. Warda's grinders might appear 'lesbian' in their adoration of the female form, and enjoyment of labial pleasures. However, their attraction toward the objectified female body imposes a heterosexual mechanism of an active grinding subject versus a silenced grinded object. By identifying the adored female with 'the feminine,' Warda becomes a gleeful informant who embellishes her lustful tale with an ideal form of female beauty that thrills the public imagination.

The parody of the slave–master relation that is obvious in men's relations with women, pretty boys, and effeminate young men is re-created in the sexual dynamics of the desiring grinders. Al-Tifashi's depiction of the *'tharifa'* or the 'witty woman' as wealthy, 'excessively clean, perfumed, wearing the best of clothes, eating the best of food, and having the best of furniture ...' (ibid.: 237–8), shows that only the rich, generous, and independent grinder was seen as 'witty' by virtue of her distinguished social status. Consequently, only the witty grinder is entitled to play the role of the active male lover, and is given the upper hand in her relation with her beloved women.

The story that is narrated by an Egyptian judge peeping at two women making love in the graveyard reveals the socio-economic power relations that exist between women. In his narrative, 'the woman on bottom is a Turkish maid who makes the full moon shy away,' for she is 'white, youthful, with full grown and prominent breasts' (ibid.: 239). The woman on top is described as being 'fat, good looking, cleanly dressed ... but she is not as beautiful as the bottom woman' (ibid.: 239). Apparently, the upper woman is the one who complies with the image of the witty woman and who controls the relationship. In offering the Turkish maid to the judge to prevent him from 'inviting pedestrians' to punish them, the 'witty lover' subjects her beloved to the threat of being raped. Despite the fact that the 'witty' woman eventually invents a trick to make the judge leave the scene before his erect penis penetrates the vagina of the maid, her inconsiderate attitude does not reveal enough respect for the woman who is easily presented as a sex object to a male intruder. Al-Tifashi's description of the terms of lovemaking between two female bodies fantasizes the witty woman as a master and a lover, even when her pimp-like attitude does not convey enough love.

Al-Tifashi's 'grinders' ended up subverting the dominant ideal of womanhood by merely internalizing, imitating, and re-creating the misogynistic ideal of manhood, male chauvinistic attitudes, and the oppressive heterosexual mores that were available for them at that time. The 'witty ones'/'*tharifat*' were seen by Habib as constituting a 'transgression against orthodox Muslim ideals of womanhood as well as subversion of those ideals' (Habib 2008: 70). Indeed, it is a transgression against the 'ideals' of womanhood which transforms them into the ideals of manhood, rather than a deconstruction of these essentialized ideals.

The presentation of various perceptions of 'grinding' cannot be taken as proof that same-sex practices were tolerated at a certain time in Arab history, as Habib's reading might suggest. In a letter written by a judge to his deputy in Alexandria, he warns him against tolerating 'grinders' and their practices lest they should be preoccupied with it as the norm and 'forget their obligation' (Al-Tifashi 1992: 206). The indulgence of Al-Tifashi's grinders in the practice was permitted as long as it did not make the woman forget her 'wifely duties.'

Al-Tifashi's 'grinders' appear to be the double agents of hetero-patriarchy, because they obscure the innate differences among females as subjectivities. When applied transhistorically, the term 'grinder' invokes an essential linkage between grinding and rubbing practices on the one hand, and grinding, rubbing, and lesbianism on the other hand. Such a connection is very faint, because it includes all women who practice grinding as part of their relations with their husbands, children, or other women; and the connection is extended in Salwa Al-Nuaimi's *Burhan Al-Asal* (Evidence of Honey) (2007) to include male rubbers. By identifying grinders with the rubbers who have different sexes and sexualities, Al-Nuaimi deprives Al-Tifashi's grinders of any essential sense of lesbian selfhood.

## Re-examining female masculinities

'What is it like to be a lesbian?' is a difficult puzzle, especially within the complicated socio-political components of the Arab cultures.

Because awareness of one's self as being 'something' is an intuitive core that precedes intentionality but which cannot be articulated without situating it within the socio-political structures of the culture, I feel obliged to re-examine the superficiality of behavioral criteria and its incapacity to define the essence. Historically speaking, behavior is seen as 'an outer shell,' rather than as a reliable guide to one's innate tendencies. Because behavior is imitative, it can rarely be seen as a spontaneous expression of one's true self; thus it is inaccurate to define the lesbian subject as a woman who merely appears to be 'intimate' with women, or as a woman who acts in a 'mannish' manner.

I will now discuss some historical narratives on cross-dressing women. Since masculinity and femininity as imagined social constructions do not seem to compose an identity, cross-dressing is rarely regarded as an attempt to assert a lesbian identity. Rather, it is mainly seen as an attempt to socialize freely with men, to seduce them, or to be able to play roles that are only permitted for men, as is the case in *Banat Al-Riyadh* (Daughters of Al-Riyadh) (Al-Sane'e 2006), where some females tend to cross-dress to be able to drive a car and to invade a male-dominated public sphere in Saudi Arabia.

Female masculinity in many Arab cultures is rarely conceived as a transgendered identity or as an expression of lesbian sexuality. This could be attributed to the fact that female masculinity was at times seen as a means of subverting the attention of male sodomites from pretty boys and direct it to females. 'Faced with competition from boys, Arab women sometimes tried to resemble them. The Abbasids, for example, even preferred a tomboy type of woman, with hair cut very short and a manly stride' (Bouhdiba 1998: 142). Because the femininity of a beautiful and beardless young man was seen as more dangerous and seductive to men – 'it is more criminal to look at him than to look at a strange woman' (ibid.: 119) – the boyish female *'gulamiyya'* did not seem to constitute a threat to the heterosexual system. In Al-Tifashi's chapter that revolves around sodomites, *'Allata'* (men who have sex with men), there is a story that suggests that the tomboyish maid can be bought by some well-off male sodomites as a substitute for effeminate males. That option was proposed to men as being 'less sinful' than sex with men (Al-Tifashi 1992: 182). Preoccupied with male homosexuality and subverting it toward heterosexuality, female masculinity was seen as a replacement for the practice of sodomy among men.

Al-Tifashi narrates some reflections upon *the physical* (or intersexual) sense of hermaphroditism, which implies being born with both male and female organs. Al-Tifashi returns to anatomy to show that there are females who have penises and there are males who have wombs (ibid.: 303). Here, the body of the *'muthakkara'* – masculine woman – is not only defeminized, it also appears as 'an odd body' that has some of the physical attributes of males, such as 'moustaches and beards, or even a penis in some rare cases' (ibid.: 303). This argument turns the mannish woman into an androgynous body; a third gender that can also be sodomized or heterosexualized for the desiring male. In such a context, the lesbian subjectivity becomes invisible as it dissolves into an 'intersexual body' that might be seductive to male sodomites, heterosexual men, and even heterosexual women. Certainly, the various options available on the basis of intersexuality and transgenderism expose an awareness of multiple sexual practices, but they also reveal latent heterosexism.

Clearly, the centrality of the penis vis-à-vis the female body is more tolerated than in the intercourse between two male bodies. In Al-Tifashi's chapter 'On penetrating females as males,' anal sex within the institution of marriage is justified by some Islamic jurisprudents who base their argument on a verse in the Qur'an which says: 'Your women are your farm that you can cultivate wherever you want' (cited in ibid.: 226; *Surat al-Bakara* [The Cow Sura], verse 223). For them, the verse implies that men are permitted to enter women from diverse sides. According to the official jurisprudence in Islam, penetrating the female from the anus is described as a 'minor *liwat*/sodomy' as opposed to the 'major *liwat*/sodomy' in which males penetrate other males (see Juma'a's introduction in ibid.: 31). Analyzing 'The penis-centred masculinity in a Lebanese village' (Hage 2006: 117), Hage uses some ethnographic details that reflect the boys' entry into heterosexuality through a 'minor' homosexual encounter with a girl. In a taped conversation, his informant describes the early experience of *'a'sit el-dabbour'* (ibid.: 120), which literally translates into 'the sting of the wasp'; an experience which made him explore his erection as a boy on a girl's buttocks. Despite the fact that the interviewer was suspicious of the credibility of his story, it remains an ethnographical example of how the female body is fantasized by some as an anal object.

Obviously, Arab history does not offer many examples of masculine women who openly expose a lesbian identity. Judith Halberstam rightly suggests that 'there are many examples of masculinity in women that resonate within a complex of heterosexualities' (1998: 57). When female masculinity is perceived as seductive to male sodomites, rather than as a transcendence of gender representation, it becomes rather absurd to define the lesbian as a transgendered female. Since there is no inherent harmony between gender identity and sexual orientation, transgendered behavior does not in itself provide the lesbian subjectivity with the means to create a comprehensible means of self-assertion. Rather, the masculine-looking lesbian may assume an illusive visibility that might create more borders that separate her from men who regard her as 'a potential vagina,' or maybe an 'anus,' and from women who might come to regard her as a dangerous penetrative body. In *Banat Al-Riadh* (Al-Sane'e 2006: 57), the lesbian is depicted as a woman 'rapist' who hunts her female victims in an old building in the university. Ironically, the newly fantasized image of the lesbian is negatively impacted by the historical image of the 'male sodomite who rapes boys.'

Gender appears as an act or unstable role that can be performed by either males or females to fulfill; the multiple desires of the male. Since the female body is seen as an object for various types of bodily pleasures sought by males, transgendered behavior on the part of some females cannot be totally relied on as a proper means of identity assertion.

### Conclusion: a virgin body, an unwritten history

My analysis of the perplexing position of women as writers, feminists, grinders, rubbers, Sufis, and invisible lesbians in the opaque closets of Arab history proves that Arab history was not totally innocent of medical and sociological inscriptions that misinterpret the female body and oppress lesbian subjectivity. The return to Arab history tells many told, retold, and untold stories which show the need to denaturalize the past and re-examine its truth. Since 'the cohesion of the moral body requires the cleaning up of language and the woman at the same time' (Rose 1986: 115), the cohesion of the lesbian body in Arab history requires the cleaning of the female body of successive historical marks. Trapped in history, the independent lesbian subjectivity in the Arab cultures cannot exist transparently, without liberating the female body from the heterosexual essentialism and the socio-political interpretations imposed on it.

Though the homosocial context provided plasticity for homosexual practices, it did not give the female the freedom to identify the self as being lesbian. Since 'grinding' describes playful practices among heterosexually married women, mothers, daughters, and ex-grinders, who usually abandon the practice once they become heterosexually gratified wives, the lesbian identity is socio-historically muted and denaturalized as a temporary form of pleasure. As it is difficult to locate the lesbian within the codes of womanhood or manhood, or within fantasized/performed masculinities or femininities, it is only the 'unmarked' female body which would help delocate the lesbian subjectivity from the conflicting socio-political means of signification, while making it trans-culturally 'plausible' and anticipated.

In order to avoid being produced and reproduced by the consumers of history, the lesbian body needs to be approached as a body that exists prior to written history, as a spiritual body that exists prior to the material practice of sex, as a sensual body that speaks a different body language, as a mental body that has its own ethics, and as a virgin autonomous body without inscribed spaces, marks, or sites. The genuine core of the lesbian subjectivity in the modern Arab cultures cannot be exposed, without remapping the female body, and over-throwing the heterosexist assumptions that besieged it in the closets of history books and meaning-makers. When political boundaries are imposed as cultural boundaries, crossing borders cannot be achieved without liberating the female body from the ties that fix it in the bottle of an imagined, collective, anonymous closet called History.

## Notes

1 According to the Christian calendar, approximately the tenth century.

2 In *Burhan Al-Asal*, Salwa Al-Nuaimi (2007: 86) says: '[our] grandmothers were better than "us"; they combined the two glories,' referring to sex with men and sex with women.

3 A *mukhrim* is a male relative; the level of kinship is clarified in Surat Al-Nisa'a (Women Sura), verses 22–4.

## References

Ahmad, L. (1991) 'Early Islam and the position of women: the problem of interpretation,' in N. R. Keddie and B. Baron (eds), *Women in the Middle Eastern History: Shifting Boundaries in Sex and Gender*, New Haven, CT, and London: Yale University Press.

Al-Harz, S. (2006) *Al-Akharoon* [The others], Beirut: Al-Saqi.

Al-Karmi, A. S. (ed.) (1998) *Sahih Al-Bukhari*; *Imam Abi Abdullah Mohammad Ibn Ismail Al-Bukhari*, Al-Riadh: International Ideas Home for Publishing and Distribution.

Al-Mernissi, F. (1994) *Forgotten Female Sultans: Female Presidents in Islam*, trans. A. H. Abbas, Damascus: Dar Al-Hassad.

— (1997) *Beyond the Veil: The Dynamics of the Masculine-Feminine in Modern Islamic Society*, trans. A. Saleh, Damascus: Dar Houran.

— (2004) *Are You Immune against Harem? A Test for Men Who Adore Women*, trans. N. Baidoon, Beirut: Al-Fank Publications.

Al-Nafzawi, Sheikh (1993) *Al-Rawd Al-Attir fi Nuzhat al-Khater* [The perfumed garden], ed. J. Juma'a, London: Riad El-Rayyes (based on the medieval Arabic manuscript).

Al-Nuaimi, S. (2007) *Buhan Al-Asal* [Evidence of honey], Beirut: Reyad El-Rayyes Books.

Al-Sane'e Abdullah, R. (2006) *Banat Al-Riyadh* [Daughters of Al-Riyadh], 4th edn, Beirut: Al-Saqi.

Al-Tifashi, S. E. A. (1992) *Nuzhat Al-Albab fima La Yujad fi Kitab*, ed. J. Juma'a, London: Riad El-Rayyes Books (based on the medieval Arabic manuscript).

Bouhdiba, A. (1998) *Sexuality in Islam*, trans. A. Sheridan, London: Saqi Books.

Bristow, J. (1997) *Sexuality: The New Critical Idiom*, London and New York: Routledge.

Butler, J. (1991) 'Imitation and gender insubordination,' in D. Fuss (ed.), *Inside/Out: Lesbian Theories, Gay Theories*, New York and London: Routledge.

— (1993) *Bodies that Matter: On the Discursive Limits of 'Sex'*, London: Routledge.

— (2004) *Undoing Gender*, New York and London: Routledge.

Cameron, D. (1993) 'Ten years on: compulsory heterosexuality and lesbian existence,' in S. Jackson et al. (eds), *Women's Studies: A Reader*, Essex: Pearson Education.

Chanter, T. (2006) *Gender: Key Concepts in Philosophy*, London: Continuum International Publishing Group.

El-Rouayheb, K. (2005) *Before Homosexuality in the Arab-Islamic World, 1500–1800*, Chicago, IL: University of Chicago Press.

El-Saadawi, N. (1958) *Mozakkerat tabiba* [Memoirs of a woman doctor], Cairo, www.arabwomenwriters.com/index.php?option=com_content&view=article&id=87&Itemid=91, accessed 26 February 2010.

— (1988) *Anil Mara'a* [About woman], Cairo: Dar Al-Mustaqbal Al-Arabi.

Foucault, M. (1980) *The History of Sexuality*, vol. 1: *An Introduction*, New York: Vintage.

— (2007 [1963]) *The Birth of the Clinic: An archaeology of medical perception*, trans. A. M. Sheridan, London and New York: Routledge.

Gilbert, M. S. (1986) *Critical Theory since 1965*, Florida State University Press, www.english-e-corner.com/comparativeCulture/etexts/more/feminist_reader/literarypaternity.html, accessed: 7 December 2009.

Gutting, G. (2005) *Foucault: A Very Short Introduction*, Oxford: Oxford University Press.

Habib, S. (2008) *Female Homosexuality in the Middle East: Histories and Representations*, New York and London: Routledge.

Hage, G. (2006) 'Migration, marginalized masculinity and dephallicization: a Lebanese villager's experience,' in S. Khalaf and J. Gagnon (eds), *Sexuality in the Arab World*, London: Saqi Books.

Halberstam, J. (1998) *Female Masculinity*, Durham, NC, and London: Duke University Press.

Hallett, N. (1999) *Lesbian Lives: Identity and Autobiography in the Twentieth Century*, London and Sterling, VA: Pluto Press.

Jankowiak, R. W. and T. Paladino (eds) (2008) *Intimacies: Love + sex across cultures*, New York: Columbia University Press.

Jones, A. and A. Stephenson (eds) (1999) *The Body: Performing the Text*, London and New York: Routledge.

Kabbani, R. (2008) *Imperial Fictions: Europe's Myths of the Orient*, London: Saqi Books.

Khalaf, S. R. (2006) 'Breaking the

silence: what AUB students really think about sex,' in S. Khalaf and J. Gagnon (eds), *Sexuality in the Arab World*, London: Saqi Books.

Mansour, E. (2000) *Ana Hiya Anti* [I am you], Beirut: Dar El-Rayyes.

Rich, A. (1972) 'When we dead awaken: writing as re-vision,' *College English, Women, Writing and Teaching*, 34(1): 18–30, National Council of Teachers of English, www.jstor.org/stable/375215, accessed 11 September 2008.

— (1980) 'Compulsory sexuality and lesbian existence,' *Signs: Journal of Women in Culture and Society*, 5(4): 631–60, links.jstor.org/sici?sici=0097-9740%28198022%295%3A4%3C631%3ACHALE%3E2.0.CO%3B2-2, accessed 11 December 2009.

Richardson, D. and S. Seidman (eds) (2002) *Handbook of Lesbian and Gay Studies*, London: Sage Publications.

Rose, J. (1986) *Sexuality in the Field of Vision*, London: Virgo.

Sakakini, W. (1994) *Al A'Ashika Al-Mutasawifa: Rabi'a Al-Adawiyya* [The Sufi female lover: Rabi'a Al-Adawiyya], 2nd edn, Damascus: Dar Tlas.

Sedgwick, E. K. (1990) *Epistemology of the Closet*, Berkeley: University of California Press.

Stanley, L. (1992) 'Romantic friendship? Some issues in researching lesbian history and biography,' *Women's History Review*, 1(2): 210.

Walker, A. (1984) *In Search of Our Mothers' Gardens*, London: Women's Press.

Yazbek, S. (2008) *Ra'ehet Al- Kirfa* [Smell of cinnamon], Beirut: Dar Al-Adab.

# 9 | 'Public women' and the 'obscene' body: an exploration of abolition debates in India

NITYA VASUDEVAN

## Introduction

> As with other aspects of human behaviour, the concrete institutional forms of sexuality at any given time and place are products of human activity. They are imbued with conflicts of interest and political manoeuvring, both deliberate and incidental. In that sense, sex is always political. But there are also historical periods in which sexuality is more sharply contested and more overtly politicized. In such periods, the domain of erotic life is, in effect, renegotiated. (Rubin 1992)

This chapter deals with the regulation of female performance entertainment in the Indian context, in the form of the public and 'sexualized' performances of three communities of dancers at different moments in history – the *devadasis*, the *lavani* dancers, and the bar dancers. I posit the relationship between sexuality and publicness as a grid through which to understand these practices, which range from the nineteenth-century to the contemporary. Three basic questions frame this exploration: What is it about 'sex' or the sexualized body on display that causes such extreme levels of anxiety and outrage? How does 'prohibition' work in regulating this field of 'visibility' – that is, what can be seen and not seen, what is considered productive or nurturing and what is considered dangerous? What constitutes an obscene body? Is it a characteristic inherent to the body and practice (like nudity, or the sexual act), or is it something else?

The early 1990s, the decade of liberalization in economic policy, was a period in which 'new' freedoms were sought and equally 'new' forms of backlash to this seeking were generated (in the form of the ultra-virulent and violent right-wing proliferations). It has therefore been cast as the era of proliferations, of excess – of sexual freedom, of the desire for sexual freedom, of right-wing mobilizations in the name of a respectable Indian culture, and, alongside this, of changes in levels and modes of consumption, relationships with technology, and forms of mobility. Interestingly, the contemporary moment (in popular discourse) is set against an undefined past, ranging from colonial times to the Nehruvian[1] socialist era to the period of Hindutva expansion[2] in the country, in which these freedoms were not available to people, especially to women. And more importantly, it is during this era that 'liberation' or 'freedom' comes to be equated with a particular desire for, and certain knowledge of, 'sexuality.'

The present moment is also witnessing a set of disturbing trends in relation to sexual or sexualized practices in the public space.[3] The contestations involving public space are now more than ever demanding that they be explored in relation to anxieties around the (gendered) body and sexual subjectivity.

## Publicness and the field of visibility

There is something that happens when a text or a body is sexualized in the public domain. This something may manifest itself in the form of state censorship demands, right-wing outrage and violence, or even celebrations of sexual freedom and media attention. It cannot be explained away by saying that 'sex' is a private matter in the Indian context and that when it leaves its private context, it causes controversy. On the contrary, sex is a public concern, and the distinctions between public and private are precisely blurred by sexuality. Also, it is not so much that the Indian context is repressive when it comes to sexuality – rather, one has to read the practice of censorship or prohibition or abolition as a set of transactions involved in the condition of being 'public.'

'Publicness' as a concept is therefore defined as the condition of being-in-the-public-eye. This includes a range of things – what is done in the name of 'public interest,' what is said to and on behalf of the collective termed 'the public,' the lines that seem to divide the public and the private spheres, the idea of a right to privacy, and laws against public display. The idea of a 'field of visibility' is linked to publicness, and its significance derives from the difficulties involved in explaining why there seem to be such frenzied and public reactions to sex and the (female) body when these are usually thought of as relegated to the sphere of the private-intimate. Visibility here is read as a transaction rather than a static condition. The field of visibility is a field of transactions, and this is established through an exploration of the publicness of the body or sexuality. This is also seen as of concern particularly to the form of the modern democracy. Gurpreet Mahajan quotes Habermas on the notion of publicity – 'While various forms of visual displays continue even in the present day, the public-ness has taken on a new meaning in modern democracies. It is now linked to political communication, legitimation and accountability of authority – aspects that were absent from previous bodies' (2003: 18). In this chapter I argue that visibility is very much a part of this grid of 'political communication, legitimation and accountability of authority.'

I examine the idea of the 'obscene object' in terms of two modes – the mode of social reform (late nineteenth and early twentieth century) and the mode whereby modernity is seen (in a particular context) as a stage of sleaze, with various until now innocuous objects being drawn into this theater of corruptedness (Rajadhyaksha 2005).

## Sexuality and nationhood

Post-colonial and feminist scholars and historians[4] have argued that the idea of the nation in the nineteenth century rested on a particular imagination of the Indian woman (an upper-caste subject who inhabited the private domain, which is where her education and intelligence were to be put to use). There were certain ways of negotiating the public–private divide that accompanied nation-building. Chatterjee (1989) argued that, in late nineteenth-century Bengal, the 'home' became the domain of the spiritual Indian identity, a feminine sphere, while the 'world' became the domain of politics, technology, and economy, a masculine sphere.

The term 'public' also became crucial to the framing of the constitution. When the constitution for the new nation was being drafted, the term 'public' changed from meaning simply the services rendered by a state, to connote something in the realm of the imagination, something much more meaningful to the newly independent nation.

This newly meaningful 'public' was closely tied to sexual practices and the representational arena, especially in terms of female sexuality and the ways in which it was regulated. Tropes of degradation, demoralization, excess, and desire were all tied to bodies and how they performed. Concepts like the dignity of women or female modesty have their roots in colonial law, and are embedded in the Indian constitution. Whether it is the sexualized image of the woman, which is discussed as early as in the 1927/28 Report of the Indian Cinematograph Committee, or the ways in which 'public women' were slowly marginalized and rendered illegitimate through the colonial and anti-colonial era, there is historical evidence to show that publicness and sexuality were and are inextricably bound in the narrative of the nation-state. Through the idea of the obscene body practice, I argue that it is not in fact the 'content' (sexuality as a positive set of attributes)

which renders a body obscene. It is the transaction that takes place
in entering the domain of the public, and an involvement in the very
technology, economy, and politics that are considered the stronghold
of (nationalist) masculinity, which render that body obscene. Therefore,
the declaration that something is violating Indian culture or morality, rather than being read as a call to maintain some inner core of
conservatism, should be read as a repeated enactment that tries to
regulate the movements between private and public spheres.

## What constitutes public interest?

The idea of the 'public' as a collective body has changed from
the era of colonial rule to the post-colonial nation-state. The colonial
rulers viewed the public as subjects they were ruling, whose moral
education they had to foster. In the post-colonial period, the public
has gained the added aspect of being the body that elects or votes,
and to which the government is accountable. There has therefore
been a shift from the notion of a public morality that involved the
colonial authorities dictating what was necessary for this morality to
be maintained, to 'public interest,' which indicates a more inclusive
and benevolent, though not less regulatory, approach to the collective.

The public is that body collective which is always known to be
'watching' or seeing or participating and therefore always acting,[5] but
also static in the strange way of not being a differentiated body, instead
having a uniformity imposed on it. Members of this public (who have
supposedly been led astray by their politics/obsessions/sexual perversions) are also prone to acts of violence, unthinking and irrational
behavior, and disruptions of law and order.

I am interested in what comes to constitute public interest, what
the condition of being 'public' means for a particular female body or
subject. In the Indian context, birth, death, reproduction of life and
labor, and the service of women are not rendered private. The division between public and private spheres and the relegation of 'sexual
life' to the latter does not quite take place. Kosambi argues that the
public–private divide was introduced by British rule (2007). Whether
owing to the colonial underpinnings of anthropology or the nature
of the colonial context itself (as a time-space of contestation centered
on 'difference'), sexual life is staged as 'a concern for everyone,' and
as 'implicated in the idea of the common good.' The central aim of
this chapter is to explain precisely how sexual life and the body are
public concerns.

## 'Slipped sisters'

> If the notions of the State as to dancing are to be accepted, we would
> have reached a stage where skimpy dressing and belly gyrations, which
> is today the Bollywood norm for dance, will have to be banned as inher-
> ently or invariably pernicious. We think as a nation we have outgrown
> that, considering our past approach to dancing, whether displayed as
> sculpture on monuments or in its real form. (Extract from the Dance
> Bar Judgment)[6]

This section deals with the idea of the 'public woman' as it pertains
to histories of the performing arts and live entertainment. I refer
here only to those forms that have been decidedly 'female,' by which
I mean various things – only women have performed them; they have
constituted a source of livelihood for large numbers of women; and
they have been 'sexualized' in ways that have brought them under
the scrutinizing eye of the colonial state, the social reformer, or post-
colonial democratic institutions.

I juxtapose the three instances – *devadasi* abolitionist campaigns
in the late nineteenth century and finally abolition in 1947; the ban
imposed on *lavani tamasha*, in the late 1940s; and the dance bar ban in
2005 – in order to lay out the continuities and discontinuities between
these instances, and to explain the relationship between publicness
and female sexuality in this context. In order to talk about the female
dancer and the abolition of her practice, I argue that the idea of the
public woman structures the debates on abolition in the case of the *devadasi* system in southern India, and the ban on *lavani tamasha* and bar
dancing in Maharashtra. The public woman emerged precisely because
of the nationalist construction of the educated, politically informed,
but nevertheless private middle-class and upper-caste woman. The
private woman had no consistent access to official economic policy and
to modern technologies. The public woman, on the other hand, was
constantly in contact with men outside the familial sphere, occupied
public spaces, and was outside the bounds of private family law (as
these communities of women had their own codes of marriage and
inheritance). These women introduced the kind of ambiguity that the
discourse of modernity, whether the colonizer's notions of a morally
educated and enlightened body of subjects or the nationalist notions
of the divided realms of domesticity (where sexuality was supposed
to be contained) and politics, could not deal with easily.

Commerce governs the discourse on dancing. It is not the dance
itself which is the problem; it is the way in which the dance and the

dancer are placed in an economy of pleasure, sexual relations, service, and entertainment. This combination of pleasure and commerce is important here because that is what differentiates, in the dance bar judgment, for instance, the dancer from the waitress working in the same bar. The former is a publicly sexualized figure in ways that the latter is not. In the case of the abolition of dancing, the charges of 'sex,' 'obscenity,' or 'immorality' actually referred to this realm of ambiguity where the lines between public and private, sex and art, entertainment and labor or livelihood, sexuality and property relations, were proved fragile and contingent, the underpinnings of both (colonial) rule and (anti-colonial) resistance thereby rendered problematic.

The currency this section has for the present moment in India derives from the judgment relating to the ban on dance bars in Maharashtra, which came into effect on 21 July 2005. A case was filed with the Bombay High Court by the Bar Owners' Association, the newly formed Bar Girls' Union, and a group of feminist NGOs that were interested in the lives and livelihood of the dancers and their right to practice their profession. The case was fought against the state, which, through Sections 33A and 33B of the Bombay Police Act 1951 (as amended by the Bombay Police Amendment Act 2005), had banned dancing as an activity in all bars in Maharashtra and canceled the entertainment licenses that these establishments had acquired. The bill was passed by the Legislative Assembly on 21 July 2005 and by the Legislative Council on 23 July 2005. The ban was lifted following the judgment in 2006.

At this juncture, we need to differentiate between 'abolition' and 'ban' as modes of prohibition. Abolition is a legal term that is no longer in circulation. It derives its charge from the period of colonial rule, particularly the late nineteenth and early twentieth centuries, when the colonial state participated in the social reform of Indian society through the eradication of 'social evils' that had supposedly led to its degeneration. The *devadasi* practice (which will be explained below) was one of many that were targeted to be done away with. Abolition therefore addressed practices of a certain kind – film-making, for instance, was censored rather than abolished, for it was born of modernity and was a part of the theory of progress and Western rationality in ways that sati,[7] hook-swinging[8] and the *devadasi* practice could never be. Even though film censorship was being discussed at the same time as *devadasi* abolition (the late 1920s), the two were not brought into the same conceptual realm of colonial governance. There was therefore a range of practices that were seen as regressive and not in line with Western ideals of a civilized life. The 'ban' on bar dancers, on the other hand, is aligned more with forms of censorship that are enacted in a contested moment (this moment possessing its own history) than with a lengthy period of reform of a practice. A ban is not as much motivated by ideas of backwardness and irrationality as by ideas of immorality and obscenity.

## 'A thing that is vanishing tomorrow': the *devadasi* system and the abolitionists

The dedication of young girls to the service of the temple was a practice prevalent from the eleventh century right up to the late colonial period, when it was abolished by the British government in 1947. 'Dedication' in this instance meant that they were 'married' to the deity, and did not live like other women, marrying into domestic life. They were expected to dance and perform other services in the temple. The practice had its patrons among the rulers, landlords, and wealthy merchants (see Chakravarti 1989; Nair 1994).

The problem the colonial state identified with the practice of the *devadasis* did not attach to the performance itself. The *devadasi*, who performed her services in the temples and for patrons, was never classified as 'obscene.' It was her relationships with the men who were her patrons, the dedication of young girls to the temple (and to sexual services in exchange for patronage), and her position as a woman whose economic and public position challenged structures of masculinity and inheritance which brought her under the eye of the colonial legal system. She was charged with procuring and disposing of minors for purposes of prostitution under Sections 372 and 373 of the Indian Penal Code (IPC) (Kannabiran and Kannabiran 2003).

The *devadasi* system was in many ways an institution in itself – the women who were part of it were not '*sadharan stri*' (ordinary women). 'Because of the fact of its entrenchment in caste society and its legitimacy in the caste order, *devadasi* women could not be treated on [a] par with "degraded women" in the matter of their inheritance rights, notwithstanding their equation to prostitutes in legal discourse' (ibid.: 26). The *dasis* had their own rules of inheritance, with property passing on from mother to daughter, not from father to son. They were given land under the Bombay Rent-Free Estates Act 1852, and the Exemptions from the Land-Revenue Act 1863. This land (the *inam*) was attached to the temples in which they performed and became central to legal battles fought by them during and after abolition. The Devadasi Protection Act 1934 had to not only abolish the practice, but also decide on this question of property.

What the later nineteenth- and early twentieth-century period witnessed was not a debate surrounding an obscene practice, but the recasting and gradual eradication of an institution that functioned according to particular social and economic codes that went against the grain of the standardized systems of law, property relations, and marriage that were being instituted during nineteenth-century colonial rule. It was not only the colonial legal system which was involved in this process. Muthulakshmi Reddi,[9] famous for her battle against this system, was part of a social reform campaign that sought to eradicate all the ills in Hinduism, thereby revealing its inner strength and glory. Curiously also fighting for abolition, but differing in its position from Reddi and the Brahmin social reformers, was the Self-Respect Movement,[10] which saw the *devadasi* system as representative of the dominance of Brahminism within Hindu religion.

### The *devadasi* becomes an 'age-old peculiarity'

For the colonial authorities in the late nineteenth century, 'public morality' was aligned with the Penal Code, and the *devadasi* system, which had not faced a problem of illegitimacy till then, seemed to embody a contradiction to public law. 'The initial exercise of the courts in privileging the textual tradition over the customary or oral tradition now shifted to the privileging of Penal Law, which was based on 'universal principles of the science of legislation ...' (ibid.: 11). The early twentieth-century cases on land inheritance involved extensive discussions on textual authority, with ancient Hindu legal texts being consulted in order to decide the status of the *devadasi* in relation to the institution of the family, particularly the division of property between the children born to the wife and to the *dasi*. Was she a slave, a concubine, a second wife, or a mistress? The peculiarity of the *devadasi*'s position in social relations is demonstrated by this code – 'to enable an illegitimate son to lay claim to a share in his father's property, his mother must be a *Sudra*, must have been unmarried and must have been kept by the putative father as a continuous concubine.'[11] The positions of the various Hindu texts were examined and a conclusion was reached about the right of the *dasi*'s son to inherit property. Though this indicates the dependence on Brahmin scriptural text, there was still no moral judgment on the *devadasi* system, and no rigid polarization of the codes of the *devadasis* and the legal system. It is only later, with the onset of the abolitionist movement and social reform on a large scale, that the *devadasi* came to represent a 'problem' for both the colonizer and the nationalist. This was obviously the point of the shift toward a 'public law.'

The emphasis on the universal principles of the science of legislation is significant because it points to the way in which the *dasi* system was being positioned, as inherently occupying the realm of habit, tradition, and regressive custom as opposed to the realm of progress, enlightenment, and scientific rationality. 'A blind adherence to usage, which was against public interest and in the process of extinction, would work to the detriment of "social progress". The court therefore reserved the right to overrule a custom that violated "natural reason"' (ibid.: 13). The Penal Code, or 'public law,' represented movement toward a future, while personal law was described as stagnant and lacking the dynamism of the former. In the Constituent Assembly debate (1948), T. T. Krishnamachari said, '... I wish most my honourable Friends in this House will not try to import into these fundamental rights age-old peculiarities of ours that still persist ... This system of *Devadasis* obtaining in India has been abolished by legislation in Madras ... I think public opinion is sufficiently mobilized for all provinces undertaking legislation of that type. Why then put it into the fundamental rights, a thing which is vanishing tomorrow?'[12] The *devadasi* system suddenly took on the nature of the obsolete, and came to be positioned this way in the abolition debates – as opposed to 'public' law and morality; whether as that which represented the degeneration of Hinduism (in the discourse of the Brahmin social reformers), or as that which kept in place Brahminical Hinduism and stood in the way of secular and rational citizenship (in the discourse of the Self-Respect Movement). In other words, it came to be positioned as habit or tradition.

There are clearly contradictions in the positions taken up by the colonial authorities, the social reformers and the self-respecters. The link between them seems to be that sexuality was a significant arena in which the discourse of colonial rule, nationalism, and anti-caste politics was produced. As Nandy suggests,

> ... once the two sides in the British-Indian culture of politics, following the flowering of the middle-class British evangelical spirit, began to ascribe cultural meanings to the British domination, colonialism proper can be said to have begun. Particularly, once the British rulers and the exposed sections of Indians internalised the colonial role definitions and began to speak, with reformist fervour, the language of the homology between sexual and political stratarchies, the battle for the minds of men was to a great extent won by the Raj. (Nandy 1983: 6)

This homology seems to structure the ways in which the abolition debates took place. For the self-respecters, on the other hand, it was a question of putting in place an anti-erotic ethic, in order that the unequal structures of Brahminism could be undone, and conjugality based on comradeship and companionship, not casteist distribution of resources or 'public lust,' could be established in its place.

## The *devadasi's* claim on publicness

The *devadasi* occupied the outer margins of respectability in the independent national imaginary. In an environment where the division between private and public was rigid, women's entry into public life was far from easy. *Devadasi* women entering public-political spaces alongside 'respectable' women threw up more dilemmas that were not easy to resolve. There was the 'tendency among men to assume that only "slipped sisters" could participate in public functions in public places' (Kannabiran and Kannabiran 2003: 36). This is in reference to the *devadasi* women's participation in the freedom struggle, claiming political citizenship as a right. They could not be co-opted by the nationalist struggle as women who by their very chastity and refusal to sexualize their bodies defied the white rulers. These women could not be easily deployed as 'private' bodies in the nationalist discourse. The *dasis* who resisted abolition and claimed political citizenship sidestepped the moral question being raised as central to their lives, 'asserting instead, that the centre was the public space they inhabited, on the stage and in temples, and the art they embodied, their "private" lives being completely marginal to questions of citizenship as they saw it' (ibid.: 37). Unlike the middle-class, upper-caste women who were positioned as figures whose sexuality was consigned to the private realm and whose political participation depended on this consignment, the *dasis* were there precisely as women whose sexuality was seen as public.

## The recasting of the *lavani* performance in Maharashtra

A certain arena of entertainment and performance, a domain of women with its own production of knowledge and pleasure, was acted upon by both colonizer and Indian nationalists in the process of modernizing India. This brings us to yet another practice that was recast and eroded as a result of colonial and nationalist discourse and the problem of public sexuality – the *lavani* tradition of the Kolhati women of Maharashtra. *Lavani* is a form of eroticized song-and-dance that is performed by women in Maharashtra. The *shringarik lavani* speaks of love and sexual desire and is considered the most bawdy of the *lavani* performances.

With the rise of the middle classes, existing forms of performance came to be recast, resulting in the marginalization of those elements which were considered obscene or not in tune with a certain idea of art, dance, or theater. Nandy points to the emulation and internalization of British Victorian middle-class culture that this period found in the Indian middle classes, even in their resistance to colonialism (1983: 6). His position seems to imply a homogeneously emulative resistance to colonialism, deriving fully from 'an attempt to explain the west in Indian terms and to incorporate it in the Indian culture as an unavoidable experience' (ibid.: 22).

The *lavani tamasha* is carried out by women, usually of the lower castes. Rege, writing about the *lavani* performers of Maharashtra, points to the major changes that took place in the 1850s in the Deccan region as a result of colonialism and British market forces; two new social categories, the middlemen and the middle classes, came into being, affecting 'the face of the *lavani tamasha* and its construction of female sexuality' (1995: 28). She argues that the first Marathi play by Vishnudas Bhawe of the court of the Raja of Sangli was popular among the audiences of Bombay and Pune and, with this, the middle-class, upper-caste theater was placed in opposition to the folk *tamashas*. This had its impact on existing forms of theater and performance.

> The female roles in the plays were performed by males dressed as females. The patrons of the theatre were the new, Western-educated middle classes, modelling themselves on the lifestyles of the British officers. Between 1860 and 1880, several English and Sanskrit plays were translated into Marathi. The *nachee* (dancing girl)/*nartaki* (dancer), *tamasgir* (performer)/*kalakaar* (artist) dichotomies intensified as the upper castes displaced the lower castes from their hereditary sphere of the performing arts. (Ibid.: 29)

According to Rege, a hierarchy was established, with Victorian theater being the most highly respected, followed by Marathi theater, and then by the form of the *tamasha*.

Viewed within the overall perspective of the intersection of caste and gender, the *shringarik lavani* became one of the modes of constructing the bodies of lower-caste women as constantly either arousing or satiating male desire. This construction was crucial to the pre-colonial state appropriation of the labor of lower-caste women through the institution of slavery. With the *embourgeoisement* that followed the establishment of colonial domination in Maharashtra, the *tamasha* of the *Mahar* and *Mang* castes began to center around the *vag* or spontaneous folk theater, thereby marginalizing the performance of *shringarik lavani*. New kinds of troupes emerged, composed of women of the Kolhati caste and devoted to the performance of the *lavani*. These troupes, known as *sangeet barees*, soon came to be labeled as obscene and immoral (ibid.: 25). The Kolhati women were the breadwinners of their families, dancing and prostitution being their caste-based profession. They were nomadic, which meant that they constantly engaged with public spaces in ways that other women (and even men) did not. They did not marry, and the men of the community depended on the women for sustenance. The women were also reputed to possess knowledge of cures for sexually transmitted diseases and impotency. It was not an isolated 'obscene' practice that was involved in this shift, but a certain kind of social formation, with a unique relationship to the public domain, which was appropriated.

The viewing of the *lavani tamasha* as obscene and immoral led to the Bombay state imposing a ban on *lavani tamasha* immediately after independence (late 1940s), after the then chief minister of Maharashtra (Sri Kher) received complaints on the obscene nature of these performances. The public presence of the *lavani* dancer was being regulated in tune with state censorship policy.

While the *lavani* troupes were being marginalized, the *tamasha* became a popular form in the new Marathi cinema that was trying to compete with the new national form of the Hindi cinema. In this cinema, *lavani* was a packaged representation, using the skills of the actual *lavani* performers in order to produce representations of them as lascivious and titillating objects of male desire. The dancers themselves had no control over these representations, which seemed to necessitate their marginalization as women who previously actively occupied the public sphere and public spaces. The *lavani* practice was seen as closely linked to, and in fact leading to, 'realized' or 'concrete' sexual practices, in the form of prostitution, whereas the cinematic representations of them were seen as controlled by censorship and therefore not tied directly to commercial sex. In fact, as the troupes fell into the hands of middlemen contractors, the women were expected to imitate the dances and movements and songs found in the films in order to please crowds. This resulted in their alienation from their own art form (ibid.).

The dance bar ban did not apply to *tamasha* theaters. By this time, *tamasha* theaters had gained enough respectability to be considered a site for cultural activities by the state government (Abrams 1975).[13] In the state's efforts to refine what was previously a 'bawdy' form of entertainment in order for it to then serve the purposes of nation-building lies the crucial idea of publicness. Erotic dancing was therefore no longer formally associated with the *tamasha* theater, or, rather, the central commercial element in the *tamasha* was no longer the *lavani* or any other form of dancing that was the prerogative of women.

A link between the *lavani* and today's dance bars is the fact that women migrated to the cities in search of livelihood and employment after the delegitimization and ban imposed on several of the older forms of dancing. Historically, the setting up of dance bars in Maharashtra, specifically Bombay city, to serve the purposes of entertaining the large labor force of migrants, seems to coincide with the gradual decline in patronage suffered by established communities of dancers such as the Kolhati women, over the nineteenth and twentieth centuries (Agnes 2005). 'Women are the primary breadwinners in these communities. But after the zamindari system[14] introduced by the British was abolished, they lost their zamindar patrons and were reduced to penury. Even the few developmental schemes and welfare policies of the government bypassed many of these communities ... The dance bars provided women from these communities an opportunity to adapt their strategies to suit the demands of the new economy' (ibid.: 4).

### The obscene object of amusement? Banning the dance bar

The dance bar came to occupy its position as the underbelly of the era of industrial development in the context of Bombay, taking its place in the 'playhouses' that were meant not only to entertain the male customers of bars, but also to boost liquor sales and therefore the revenue the government collected through taxation on the sale of liquor. Agnes suggests that the bar dancer is somehow more dangerous a figure than the sex worker in how she threatens notions of culture and publicness (ibid.: 10). Sex workers are seen as always already delegitimized, while the bar dancers are part of licensed establishments but are at the same time offering their bodies to be sexualized.

Agnes's article refers to the ban imposed on 21 July 2005, as a result of which dancing was prohibited in all bars in Maharashtra, and in one stroke 75,000 bar girls lost their jobs. She notes the language with which the dancers were discussed in the House while the bill was being discussed, placing emphasis on the disrespect with which those who uphold the 'dignity of women' discuss the dancers, their bodies, and profession. It is also a moment when the ruling Congress Party members, the BJP, members and those from the left-wing parties all seem to hold the same view – that bar dancing is obscene and degrading to women.

The final judgment was issued in April 2006, and it lifted the ban on dance bars. Looking at parts of this judgment enables us to understand not only the processes of legal change, but also the relationship between obscenity and performance in the current moment.

The dance bar case represents an example of how the language of rights now informs charges of obscenity in the Indian context. The parties opposing the ban argued on these counts in relation to the bar dancers: a) the right to freedom of expression; b) the right to life; c) the right to livelihood; d) that the distinction drawn between dance bars and other establishments is arbitrary and not justified by the evidence presented. The court, while it denied the validity of the first two arguments, upheld the latter two, and declared that the state had not established any nexus between the object of the petitions (to ensure the dignity of women and the maintenance of public morality), and the ban on the dances performed by these women. Interestingly, the closing statements of the judges included references to the history of dance as a form of entertainment and livelihood in India, as part of 'cultural tradition.' The judgment also makes specific mention of the *lavani* performances – 'Undertaking dance performances by ladies for a living, is not and cannot be said to be inherently pernicious or harmful to the general public. In fact ladies undertaking dance performances for the entertainment of men, is part of the cultural tradition of Maharashtra e.g. *Lavnis, Tamashas*, etc.'[15]

Women dancing to entertain is also framed as a state-sponsored activity, dance bars in particular having been in existence for two decades.

> The Government of Maharashtra expressly permitted/licensed and even encouraged the establishment of such dance bars ... The number of such licensed dance bars had increased from 24 in 1985–86 to 210 in 1995–96 to 2500 in 2005; 75,000 women earned their livelihood by undertaking dance performances in such places of public entertainment. These women supported families, children and dependents ... The direct and immediate effect of the impugned legislation would be to totally prohibit this lawful profession/calling of undertaking dance performances in places of public entertainment and thus deprive these women of their livelihood.[16]

The judgment also raises the question of why it is at this particular juncture that the ban has been called for, the case therefore not being treated as an atemporal scrutiny of a possibly obscene practice. 'Neither the Act nor its objects and reasons nor the Government's affidavit indicates what changed in April 2005, or why it was suddenly decided to totally prohibit dance performances which had been specifically permitted for the past twenty years.'

The combination of these elements leads us to believe that the processes of the law do not treat the practice of dancing in isolation from the economies it is embedded in, whether of state-sponsored commercial activity, or of the independent lives of the women concerned. To add to this, the case is denied any relevance to the category of 'public order' – 'Inebriated men, whether in dance bars or other bars are a known source of nuisance. The State has not cancelled the liquor permits to remove the basic cause of the problem ... If drunk men fight or involve themselves in criminal activity, it cannot result in denying livelihood to those who make a living out of dance.' Public order is therefore not to be defined lightly. Curiously, the phrase 'public morality' does not seem to play a significant role in the final reckoning. Public morality is taken care of as long as the dances that are performed are not of an obscene nature.

## Placed on the 'stage of sleaze'

What explains the way the law treats the bar dancer, in comparison with the *devadasi* and the *lavani* dancer? While the state that filed the case did so precisely on the grounds that the dancing was obscene, the fact that a total ban on all dancing was being sought made it impossible to scrutinize the dances performed and point to those that were 'obscene.' The legal system therefore loses a clear focus of the object in question, the bar dance, and is consumed by questions of whether a complete ban on dancing is warranted, this question constantly slipping past the object itself. This seems to be a characteristic part of obscenity law cases, the slipperiness of the object. In the case of censorship, the evasiveness derives from the fact that the real concern lies not in the text or image but elsewhere. While the cases of *devadasi* abolition and of the ban on *lavani* dancing historically occupy slightly different positions (one embedded in social reform discourse, the other undergoing a recasting at the time of the rise of the middle classes in Maharashtra), the dance bar ban rests on a par with censorship cases in its slipperiness vis-à-vis the charge of obscenity. Of course, the dance bar involves the lives and the practice of 75,000 women, and one cannot overlook the role that feminist groups have played in opposing the ban and bringing in the question of rights as central to this case. What is different in this case from the *devadasi* abolition context is the ground on which the bar girls staked their claim. The *Devadasi Sangams* and the Madras Presidency Devadasi Association, which opposed the abolition, had to portray themselves in a role that was both sanctioned by religious custom and acceptable to the changing ideology. The sanctity of marriage became a central issue, with rituals and the dedication to the deity being held up to demonstrate this sanctity at the centre of the practice – '... the *devadasi* way of life beginning to speak for itself, to demand that its legitimacy be recognised and acknowledged using the same vocabulary and categories by which it was being increasingly denounced and denigrated' (Kannabiran and Kannabiran 2003: 32).

The dance bar ban is not a case of abolition, it is not part of a bid to reform society. While the period of social reform in the nineteenth century saw specific practices labeled and classified as degenerate and as backward, the last few decades have seen practices that are seemingly innocuous charged with obscenity by political ideologues, concerned citizens, or organizations. In the case of the bar girls, there is no context of ritual, scripture, or marital relations that the practice is embedded in, which is why one is tempted to compare it to contemporary censorship cases rather than to other practices that are surrounded by debate, such as hook-swinging or body-piercing, practices that accompany religious and community belief, and which the law does not interfere with beyond a point. It has more to do with political communities and their relationship with the state. There is no realm of the sacred that the bar dancer can possibly occupy. Rajadhyaksha argues that in the writings of the former minister of culture in Maharashtra, Pramod Navalkar, modernity becomes a 'stage of sleaze' where there is a split between the one viewing this society as a critic and an ideologue, and the other participating in this shameful modernity. The bar dancer firmly belongs to this 'morbid stage of sleaze' (Rajadhayksha 2005). This kind of position seems to have become possible only in the post-independence era, where there is the conspicuous absence of the colonial ruler whose subject the Indian man or woman is.

To push this farther, these instances of ban or censorship seem to lack the historical narrative depth that the *devadasi* dedications and the *lavani* performances possess. There is no traditional form that the bar dance lays claim to in its defence (though it might draw on various dance forms in practice). It lays full claim to the 'modern' itself, to its own contemporary moment and the practices that abound, such as the item numbers of Bollywood, the sweaty and sexualized nights in which young boys and girls dance together during the *Navratri* festival in western India, and the discotheques full of dancing bodies. In the case of the bar girls, what is being claimed is that, in the Indian context, women dancing to entertain is in itself a tradition that has been supported by the state in the past. There is no possible moral stand in this case, and no textual authority to fall back on.

## Conclusion

This chapter delineates the various ways in which 'public women' and their practices have been regulated by the colonial and the post-colonial legal system. It establishes that in all these cases immorality or obscenity are not 'positive' qualities or attributes of the body or performance of the dancers. They are embedded in a field of transactions – economic, social, and cultural relations. It is not just a static body or a sexualized performance which has been the target of legal regulatory measures and public debate. It is the mobility of the dancer, her claim to the public domain, her speech, her sexual relations, her economic transactions. She disturbs easy divisions of commerce from pleasure, performance from sexuality, and politics from the private-intimate. What are now called 'moral panics' (Herdt 2009) are not a desire to maintain an inherent and always fixed morality; rather, they are reactions to this field of transactions that makes up the dancer's life and livelihood.

## Notes

1 Jawaharlal Nehru was India's first prime minister.

2 'Hindutva' is the ideological self-description of a number of organizations referred to as 'right-wing.' It stands for the belief that India is a Hindu nation, and argues that Indian culture is currently being threatened by Westernization, Islam, Christianity, communism, obscenity in the representational field, and degenerate ideas on sex and women.

3 For instance, the attack in 2009 on a group of women in a pub in Mangalore (Karnataka) by members of the Sri Ram Sene, a Hindutva organization; and the series of attacks against hijras in 2010, when they were accused of soliciting and were evicted from their houses.

4 See, for the position of women in the nineteenth century, Sangari and Vaid (1989) and John and Nair (1998).

5 For an exploration of this idea of this 'live' public with respect to censorship, see Liang et al. (2007).

6 *Indian Hotel and Restaurants Association (Ahar), An ... vs. The State of Maharashtra through the Hon'ble Minister ...* , on 12 April 2006.

7 The practice of wives joining their husbands on the funeral pyre.

8 A devotional practice which involves inserting hooks into the body, which then swings from heights. It is a mark of one's devotion to the deity in question.

9 Muthulakshmi Reddi was a social reformer in the late nineteenth century in South India.

She was the first woman to practice law and is hailed as the leader of the abolitionist campaigns against the *devadasis.*

10 The Self-Respect Movement was founded in 1925 by Periyar E. V. Ramasamy in Tamil Nadu. The movement sought to abolish caste inequalities.

11 *Soundararajam, Minor, by his Mother and Next Friend ... vs. TRMARRM Arunachalam Chetty (Deceased) and Others,* on 14 October 1915.

12 Constituent Assembly, vol. VII (1948). See www.indiankanoon.org.

13 In 1940, the Tamasha Sudhar Samithi was set up by Balasaheb Kher, and it framed the rules, regulations, aims, and objectives to be followed while performing the *tamasha.* See Kumar (1996).

14 The zamindars were landlords who collected revenue on behalf of the state from the cultivators of the land.

15 *Indian Hotel and Restaurants Association (Ahar), An ... vs. The State of Maharashtra.*

16 Ibid.

## References

Abrams, T. (1975) 'Folk theatre in Maharashtrian social development programs,' *Education Theatre Journal*, 27(3): 395–407, Baltimore, MD: Johns Hopkins University Press.

Agnes, F. (2005) 'Hypocritical morality,' www.indiatogether.org/manushi/issue149/bardance.htm.

Chakravarti, U. (1989) 'Whatever happened to the Vedic Dasi? Orientalism, nationalism and a script for the past,' in K. Sangari and S. Vaid (eds), *Recasting Women: Essays in Colonial History*, New Delhi: Kali for Women.

Chatterjee, P. (1989) 'The nationalist resolution of the women's question,' in K. Sangari and S. Vaid (eds), *Recasting Women: Essays in Colonial History*, New Delhi: Kali for Women.

Herdt, G. (ed.) (2009) *Moral Panics, Sex Panics: Fear and the Fight over Sexual Rights*, New York and London: New York University Press.

John, M. E. and J. Nair (eds) (1998) *A Question of Silence?: The sexual economies of modern India*, New Delhi: Kali for Women.

Kannabiran, K. and V. Kannabiran (2003) *Muvalur Ramamirthammal's Web of Deceit: Devadasi Reform in Colonial India*, New Delhi: Kali for Women.

Kosambi, M. (2007) *Crossing Thresholds: Feminist Essays in Social History*, Ranikhet: Permanent Black.

Kumar, P. (1996) 'Origin of Tamasha folk theatre,' in *Tamasha Fols Theatre of Maharashtra*, Doctoral thesis, Osmania University, ch. 3.

Liang, L., N. Malhotra and M. Suresh (2007) *The Public Is Watching: Sex, Laws and Videotape*, New Delhi: Public Service Broadcasting Trust.

Mahajan, G. (2003) 'The public and the private: two modes of enhancing democratization,' in G. Mahajan and H. Reifeld (eds), *The Public and the Private: Issues of Democratic Citizenship*, New Delhi: Sage Publications.

Nair, J. (1994) 'Devadasi, Dharma and the state,' *Economic and Political Weekly*, 29: 50.

Nandy, A. (1983) 'The psychology of colonialism: sex, age and ideology in British India,' in *The Intimate Enemy Psychology: Loss and Recovery of Self under Colonialism*, Delhi: Oxford University Press, pp. 1–63.

Rajadhyaksha, A. (2005) 'Is realism pornographic?' in S. Poduval (ed.), *Re-figuring Culture: History, Theory and the Aesthetic in Contemporary India*, Sahitya Akademi, pp. 180–93.

Rege, S. (1995) 'The hegemonic appropriation of sexuality: the case of the Lavani performers of Maharashtra,' *Contributions to Indian Sociology*, 29(1/2).

Rubin, G. (1992) 'Thinking sex: notes for a radical theory of the politics of sexuality,' in C. Vance (ed.), *Pleasure and Danger: Exploring Female Sexuality*, London: Pandora, pp. 267–319.

Sangari, K. and S. Vaid (eds) (1989) *Recasting Women: Essays in Colonial History*, New Delhi: Kali for Women.

Sarkar, T. (2001) *Hindu Wife, Hindu Nation: Community, Religion and Cultural Nationalism*, Delhi: Permanent Black.

# 10 | Male homoeroticism, homosexual identity, and AIDS in Mexico City in the 1980s[1]

ALBERTO TEUTLE LÓPEZ

## Introduction

Male homoerotic sociability in Mexican urban settings has been the object of a few ethnographic studies published since the late 1980s (Carrier 1995; Carrillo 2005; List 2006, 2009; Guttmann 2000; De la Dehesa 2010).[2] In this chapter, I aim to develop an ethno-historical perspective to address the transformations in the organization of male homoerotic sociability (Fry 1982) that took place in Mexico City between the late 1970s and the late 1980s, which imprinted the social construction of a homosexual subject. This timeline roughly follows the events since the first Mexican gay and lesbian pride march in 1979, and the formal acknowledgment by health officials of AIDS as a public health issue affecting homosexual men in 1988. I analyze public representations of male homosexuality in local newspapers, magazines, cinema, and literature of the period, along with recollections about their reception by men interviewed in 2009. This reconstruction is guided by the hypothesis that the vindication and visibility promoted by the emerging gay and lesbian social movement,[3] along with the establishment of commercial venues publicly identified as homosexual, generated a context where men who participated in different forms of homoerotic sociability became more readily identified as '*homosexuales*' or, later on, '*gays*'. In Mexico, both the creation of commercial gay venues and the formation of a political identity facilitated such identification, whereas formerly clandestine cruising in public places and private venues informally adopted for that purpose favored a regime of secrecy (Pecheny 2002).

For this account, I will identify three different moments in the construction of a public male homosexual subject,[4] marked by the mobilization of representations of male homosexuality by the homosexual and lesbian movement, state policy, and the national press. The first moment of public visibility opens with the first *Marcha del orgullo homosexual* (so named according to press records from the period) in June 1979. The second moment encompasses the construction of

AIDS as a 'homosexual plague' in the public imagination as news of the disease spread in the early 1980s. The third moment involves the public representation of male homosexuals as bodies with AIDS until 1988, when a first formal response to the epidemic was formulated by public health officials.[5] Such representations deeply influenced public health policies against HIV/AIDS during that period.

My discussion will focus particularly on the evolution of the terminology by which dissident sexualities were named in public discourse during the period under consideration. The rise of terms such as 'homosexuales' evokes dispute over notions and narratives about the nature of homoerotic desire; its etiology as a sin, a crime, a disease, or its legitimacy as a sexual variety or a lifestyle choice.[6] I will suggest that the use of the label homosexual played an important role in a historical process of interpellation,[7] by which the development of a gay culture, the densification of gay networks, and an increase in public representations of homosexual men in mass media and specialized press contributed to the configuration of the male homosexual as a public sexual identity. In this chapter, I am interested in how this new visibility impacted on local understandings of homoeroticism and sexuality, and how it affected the lives of those who participated in semi-clandestine male homoerotic sociability at cruising spots and 'public sex' venues (Leap 1999). Omar, now a prominent LGBT activist in Oaxaca, inscribes the transition in terms of the replacement of one naming system by another, from a semi-clandestine, euphemistic terminology to a public one:

> I wasn't an activist before and, in fact, when I started [entré al ambiente; 1986] I only knew that gay men were called 'putos' or 'lilos.' I wasn't involved in activism and the fact that some people went to marches and rallies or just said proudly, 'I am gay or homosexual' was too daring for me ... We had different names to avoid that, that thing of calling yourself 'gay.' We used to say, 'Look, that one, he's de ambiente, or Juanito es de mucho ambiente.[8]

## Early visibility: 1979–82

By the late 1970s, Mexico was going through the ninth presidential period under the Partido Revolucionario Institucional (PRI). In power for most of the twentieth century, the party had developed a mix of corruption and violence to retain political control. It is in the context of the national debt crisis and of an increase in police repression in response to growing left-wing political opposition that the voices of a publicly visible gay and lesbian movement started to make themselves heard in the national media and gay press. *El Universal*, one of the main Mexican papers at the time, featured a few articles about '*homosexuales*' then. In addition, gay-oriented magazines, novels, and poetry started to circulate among people *de ambiente*, and openly homosexual characters became common in Mexican cinema.

For decades, law enforcement and social control mechanisms had created an atmosphere of persecution and surveillance toward what was publicly termed '*homosexualismo*,' forcing men seeking sexual or romantic involvement with other men to gather in secret. As revealed in newspaper coverage from the period, the General Department of Transit and Police (known as DGPT for its Spanish initials) routinely raided what they called 'red spots' in Mexico City. The raids, nicknamed *razzias*, were featured as scandals in local and national media. In that coverage, the 'male homosexual' was a delinquent who could be easily identified because of his effeminacy. In June 1979, the newspaper *El Universal* twice reported police procedures against men singled out as homosexual. The first article was illustrated with photos showing individuals wearing Afro wigs, scarves and makeup being arrested by the police. The article stated they had been 'captured' because of their 'unusual habits.' According to the press account, they 'assaulted people ... in places of vice and prostitution.' The second one links homosexuals to drugs and prostitution. Homosexuality was invariably associated with sordid places and a landscape of vice.[9]

Men met other men at inexpensive bars and saloons in working-class neighborhoods. Although studies of homosexuality in Mexico affirm that the *ambiente* originated in middle-class neighborhoods, one gay magazine article on police raids on gay hangouts of the period claims otherwise: 'You never heard of *razzias* taking place in fancy areas of the city, such as Pedregal de San Angel, Lomas de Chapultepec or Coyoacán. You hear lowlife in places such as Anahuac and *Colonia Obrera*.'[10]

Testimonies from that time tell stories of police extortion and harassment, threatening homosexuals with exposing 'their secret' to relatives. As Jos recalls: 'they are just security guards at department stores pretending to *ligar* someone,[11] say, in La Alameda park, and then extorting him in other places.' Before the creation of gay-exclusive venues, homosexual sociability developed secretly in public places in both middle- and working-class neighborhoods. Cruising and hooking up with other men linked the promise of pleasure to the constant threat of both formal and informal police repression; either under the form of detention and official reporting, or bribery and random violence.

However, an alternative to discreet cruising in public places emerged as gay venues began to proliferate, as the magazine from the Frente Homosexual de Acción Revolucionaria announced:

> With this we start a series of articles that aim to analyze the 'alternatives' for homosexuals and lesbians in Mexico. Can we include cruising sites among them? Streets, cinemas, public restrooms, and parks. Entertainment venues: bars, saloons, and nightclubs *de ambiente*. Social groups: *Xóchitl, Yet set gay, Blanco y Negro, Regine's de Paris*, etc.[12]

The text discusses how different spaces are appropriated by sexual dissidents, and their significance from an economic point of view. They are seen as an expression of a new group consciousness, providing sexual dissidents with names of their own, which work as an interpellation to their sexual subjectivity. With the question 'Can we include cruising sites among them?' readers are invited to reflect upon the meaning of cruising and public sex.

However, discreet forms of cruising spots and meeting men at baths and saloons provided a way to socialize and access pleasure for any male, regardless of whether they identified as homosexual or not. Another text from the period describes those dynamics:

> A large part of the male homosexual nucleus prefers to exercise their sexual preferences avoiding any commitment other than the satisfaction of their own elemental, instinctive needs. This leads them to the search for circumstantial partners and ephemeral relationships. Such double need drives them toward areas and places that are frequented by others who share their preferences: saloons, public restrooms, cinemas, cafés; key places in the city, schools and universities that have already acquired a reputation as places for cruising.[13]

Men seeking safe havens to exercise their pleasure chose deserted areas that lacked surveillance, and tipped guards and janitors, among other strategies.

Other public representations of homosexuality in the city included homosexual film, where effeminate males characters were frequent in the genre of 'Cinema of Ficheras,'[14] as well as in foreign films such as *La Cage aux Folles* and *Cruising*, labeled 'homosexuality films,'[15] their topics addressed as controversial in newspaper reviews. These characters were often featured as sidekicks for macho characters who played '*albures*' in a game of masculinity.[16]

A literature labeled as 'gay' was also emerging at the time. The milestone of gay novels was Luis Zapata's *El vampiro de la colonia*

*Roma* (1979). The novel is about the experiences of a young working-class self-identified homosexual in Mexico City. It caused a sensation among homosexual men, who still remember the precise descriptions of *ambiente* sites and ways, and contributed to the establishment of a different perspective on homosexuality at the time, particularly among gays themselves, as one interviewee recalls:

> *El vampiro* was very important, but it was gay or homosexual people who consumed it. Meanwhile, society was opening up and I think many people didn't read it because they thought it was meant for homosexuals. (Adrián)

In 1980, *El vino de los bravos* marked the emergence of a 'manly,' male-identified homosexual whose sexuality is identified with 'the passion of the fierce.' The book focused on men cruising in different landscapes and various cities, sex among men in bathhouses, parks, and public restrooms; identifying a difference between two models of homosexual liaison: 'the immediate sex of the world of men with no considerations' of secret sites in public places; and the ceremonious atmosphere of '*joteria*' in gay bars and nightclubs (González 1994: 22).

Toward the early 1980s, the mainstream press started to report on the visibility of homosexual men and lesbians in a reluctantly 'politically correct' manner, conceding gays and lesbians the right to come out in public, but still affirming that homosexuality was an intrinsically flawed condition. Reporting on the 1982 pride march:

> People show respect ... The traffic is insane, horns are blowing and the march does not shock the drivers. They display their education, they accept the 'gay' movement. They came out to the streets to prove that the mistakes of Nature are not meant to be hidden by day and be flaunted by night.[17]

The newspaper article quoted above refers to a homosexual subject and a gay movement – the latter marked by quotation marks signaling contempt or estrangement – without further explanation. It seems as if explaining who they were was no longer necessary. A process of identification was taking hold, toward the goal of being recognized by others through well-defined stereotypes.

### Before the panic: 1983–86

The early 1980s brought a more diversified production of public discourses on homosexuality. Different voices – gay-identified and mainstream – addressed homosexual life and its relationship to society. It is in this period that the foundations of the relationship between AIDS and homosexuality were established in public culture. Male homosexuality was becoming more visible as a result of gay and lesbian public actions, which were received by public voices that presented themselves as more tolerant and acknowledging of homosexuals' place in society.

The broader national context was marked by a change in presidential office and a deepening of the debt crisis. Inflation and a devaluation of the Mexican currency increased pressure on people's pockets and was reflected in a rise in criminality in Mexico City. This chain of events provided arguments for promoters of adjustment policies. In 1985, an earthquake brought immense hardship to Mexico City. The reconstruction effort catalyzed political mobilization and civil society organizing. Until then, AIDS had received a little media coverage, mainly as a medical issue, still disconnected from its social context.

Public images of the homosexual man take shape in three different fields of representation: gay-oriented cultural production;[18] mass media; and medical literature, as a medical discourse, addressing the link between homosexuality and AIDS. Connections between those fields and the broader arenas of gay sociability and national urban public culture were fragmentary at the time. I will begin to explore them in order to have a closer look at the reception accorded to HIV/AIDS and its impact on male homoerotic practices in Mexico City.

The 1983 march came along with greater visibility. Newspaper coverage included a half-page article in the main news section of *El Universal*. Apart from the leap in scale, the coverage also represented a subtle change of tone in its interpretation of homosexual and lesbian public visibility as a political event:

> Breaking with clandestine ways, rebel homosexuals and lesbians claimed their sexual freedom in front of the eyes of the citizens, who looked in great surprise at the effeminate faces of the men and the virile features of the women who walked through the main avenues towards the Hemiciclo a Juarez and the México City Zocalo.[19]

'Citizens' are interpellated by 'homosexuals and lesbians,' as a group evident by their gender-bending performance that, united in great number, has by now developed considerable social influence.

That same year, the link between AIDS and homosexuality began to be established, with the 'first homosexual death from AIDS.' Adrián recalls that on the TV journal *24 horas*, the news show with the largest audience at the time, Jacobo Zabludowsky, the most influential journalist at the time, announced 'homosexual cancer hits México.' Talk shows and commentary sections also displayed an interest in the subject.[20]

In 1984, the San Francisco gay pride parade hit the news in Mexico. The headline read, 'The power of US homosexuals and lesbians, [marching] in front of Saint Patrick's Cathedral.' Although the caption accompanying the article read 'AIDS Fund,' the topic is not mentioned in the body of the text.[21] Neither is it in the coverage of the Mexico City pride march, which still offered a stereotypical image of gays and lesbians: 'They looked like women but they were men. And women did not look like such, but they were women indeed. In this march, most of them are still "in the closet."'[22]

Homosexuality was also the topic of theater, whose consumption had grown significantly. *Kiss of the Spider Woman*, based on Manuel Puig's novel, ran for three years with success.[23] Mexican researcher Antonio Marquet considered this play a landmark of gay culture in Mexico. The most interesting aspect of this was the launch of the production of dialogue about homosexual life. Drag shows (*show travesti*) from this period presented drag as a variant of homosexuality.

Literary fiction presents a variety of perspectives, horizons, and idealized forms of gay lifestyles. The novel *Utopia Gay*, by José Rafael Calva (1983, reprinted in 1984), shows a model of gay normativity being developed at the time. In the novel, two male characters live as a couple and one of them gets pregnant. One topic that the novel addresses is the departure of its characters from the 'traditional' model of discreet homoerotic sociability (Fry 1982; Pecheny 2002) to embrace the aspirations of a gay identity:

> You are no longer what you had been, because you go to the bathhouse to take a bath and nothing more, you go to *Samborns* for a cup of coffee without checking out anyone at the bar, you go for a drink without looking for the sparkle of a stare amidst the dark ... Francisco is not a better bottom nor a better top who had and still has a crude moral take ... who could not love me, nor could I love him, who to this day does not accept his homosexuality and cheats on his wife with contractors and carriers in La Merced [a popular market in Mexico City], whose mouths he keeps closed with money so that he can say he is not gay ... Francisco, who was never happier than when I guided him, with no previous experience, to the steam room at the Ecuador Bathhouse and he found himself surrounded by horny gays and machos from Tepito. (Calva 1983: 79–80)

The enigma of men who are attracted to other men and take part in different forms of homoerotic sociability without identifying as gay or homosexual is a recurrent theme in fiction and testimonials. In his book *Malas compañías*, and the poem on this, '*De hombre a hombre*,' Luis González de Alba (1984) evokes liaisons at men-only venues such as public bathhouses and saloons. He suggests the tragic destiny of a love that cannot be conceived beyond sex.

> The guys at the motor shop mess with me
> Cause they see all the time you with me
> Soon I'll have to start a fight
> Or they gonna think they got it right
> The boss's daughter picks me up
> And I gonna give her a go
> Cause – said he, staring at his beer –
> It's been a year and, ya' see ...
> – He lost his voice a little
> And his black and pretty eyes
> Sparkled with incipient tears –
> Don't wanna get caught up in ya'
> Let's leave it there and cut it off.

(Ibid.: 27)

This kind of despair surrounding homosexual life appears in other novels, such as *Púberes canéforas* by José Joaquín Blanco (1984), which was reprinted four times. The novel is a representation of homosexual men who stay inside the closet and seek refuge in spaces that allow them to engage in sexual relationships with other men safely: '*La Gorda* and Guillermo were kind of the same age and for twenty years they had been to certain streets, cafés, restaurants, cinemas and bathhouses.' At one point, one of the characters is harassed and falls victim to extortion by the police who guard the bathhouse (ibid.: 38, 143).

During the same period the gay fanzine *Macho Tips* also appeared, featuring male nudes, letters from homosexual readers, personal ads, and short fiction. It presented itself as 'a magazine for people de *mucho ambiente*.' From its first issue, the magazine dealt with the relationship between AIDS and homosexuality. An article on the topic in that issue announced in its heading: 'This article could save your life.' The fanzine advised against intercourse with *gringos*, as Americans are known throughout Latin America.[24] Valterio, reader of the fanzine at the time, reports that AIDS was in fact scarcely covered, and was always surrounded by speculation.

In Mexico, it was a long time before AIDS became a topic of public discussion. National medical authorities disseminated little information. It was mainly from foreign media that a restricted audience received news of the new disease. Those who were closer to and more active within the gay movement had earlier access to key information. Antonio, who knew about AIDS thanks to reading about homosexuality in American sources, reports: 'It was in 1983 that the *New York Times* reported a disease that could not be identified yet. Until then I never did, but from then on I started to wear a condom.'

By 1985, some homosexual men knew of this 'new disease' that reportedly was killing gay men in the USA, as reported by the National Institute of Nutrition in the *Salud Pública* magazine, but about which what anyone could say was mere speculation. However, AIDS was not to become a public health issue until late 1986. This might be connected with the meanings of sexually transmitted diseases (STDs) at the time.[25] Three of the interviewees (Omar, Adrián, and Valterio, respectively) recalled that STDs were not openly discussed, nor a cause of concern to homosexual men:

> Venereal diseases weren't so serious. Gonorrhoea, for instance, was the most common and it took only a couple of shots. Only a week without sex and that's that.
>
> ... People started talking about AIDS in 1985, but no one took precautions ...
>
> I talked about AIDS, but with the entire stigma. Remember, I was a pharmaceutical chemistry student and, well, we were assigned to present the case to other students. Back then people called it the 'pink cancer.' We were training to work in pharmacies and, of course, we knew about contraception and stuff like condoms, but back then they were kind of toys for straight people, I didn't think of them as something to be used by me or my sexual partners. It was thought of as a means to avoid getting knocked up and, obviously, I never saw it in the places I used to go to.

Ideas of emotionally detached sexuality, despair surrounding a gay life, and feminization as a distinctive trait of the homosexual man were all elements that laid the foundation for an even closer association between AIDS and homosexuality in later years.

### AIDS and the homosexual body: 1986–88

In his essay on 'the reconstruction of the homosexual body in times of AIDS,' Ricardo Llamas has pointed out the relevance of AIDS as a 'phantasmatic incarnation of the homosexual man' (Llamas 1995: 179). Within the span of one year, the specter of a 'gay disease' had reached great proportions in the public imagination, echoing global representations of AIDS and homosexuality:

> I remember a movie that was too much because there were many cases like that among my friends in Mexico. It tells the story of a group of friends that have sex in the time of AIDS, but such is the impact that some of them keep fucking all the same, thinking that it must be a government plot. There's one couple living together, but they sleep on extreme opposite sides of the bed because they don't know where the disease sneaks out from, so they'd rather not touch each other. In Mexico I knew people who behaved like that when we heard about the virus. (Omar)

*Salud Pública* magazine, the main public health professional source in the country, started addressing HIV/AIDS in 1984/85, when an invitation to a world AIDS conference was published in two consecutive issues.[26] In 1986, the first full review on the topic was published: '*El sindrome de inmunodeficiencia humana en México.*'

In 1986, *El Universal* published a series of articles on the life of Rock Hudson, who died of AIDS in 1985. The articles focused on Hudson's homosexuality and the deterioration of his once athletic body, as marks of the disease.[27] The article was published prior to that year's Gay Pride march; however, there was no coverage of the march itself. This type of coverage generated a specific body for the specter of AIDS. Even though some of the articles reported that people other than homosexuals could get infected, it was upon 'risk groups' that such a body was constructed.

By 1986, Antonio, like other interviewees, had stopped cruising, as many of his friends and acquaintances from bathhouses had started to die because of AIDS. Others, like Jos, turned to different strategies:

> In 1985 I got married. It was a stupid thing to do, I thought I'd done all that could be done and I decided to settle down. That was before AIDS, but even then there was talk about something wrong among homosexual men. I stopped going to the Rocio Bathhouse, which was one of the few places I used to go to. I knew that contact was one of the things that could get you infected, so I went from time to time to the cinemas, but only to watch. That could not get me infected. Finally, I found out that anyone could get AIDS; it was through a friend who had attended workshops and stuff. So, eventually, there were many guys I didn't see around any more, I guessed they'd died. Well, I started to go to the

Rocio Bathhouse again, with my condom and a lot of fear, but that was in the 1990s ...

Many people who were just entering the gay scene knew that there was talk about AIDS, but they still met their first sexual partners in cruising sites:

I worked at La Merced. My parents and other workers said that there was a bathhouse there in which people had sex. That was the first bathhouse I went to, but not for sex, just to browse around and there actually was sex. The first place I had sex in was in La Alameda and later the Mina bathhouse, but I ended up making a lot of friends, with whom I attended the Facultad de Filosofía once I moved to México City for school. Of course, I got to know the main restrooms and the main building, the restrooms at the Facultad de Arquitectura and others that I don't remember any more. AIDS was known, but back then we thought of it as something very distant from us.

When Omar talks about his experiences, he claims he was more afraid of being caught than of being infected with AIDS. He and his friends did not think AIDS would affect them, as they were young and presumably healthy:

O: Look, what you had to keep an eye on was, I think, who you fucked with. If he was too skinny or had spots on his skin or anything, anything that wasn't right to you, then you should be careful. And, besides, back then we used to think that the illness was 'gringo'. If you didn't fuck with foreigners then everything was OK, according to us.
A: Who were 'gringo' to you and your friends?
O: Well, the *güeros* [blond or white people], tall men, men who cruised at tourist spots. There were many in La Alameda, for instance. That's why you went Mexican.

Homosexual-oriented magazines produced an image of 'bodies with AIDS,' which influenced people's sorting out who might or might not have it. In 1986, an article in *Macho Tips* featured one of these first portrayals of 'high risk groups.'[28] Under the heading 'AIDS, a threat to Mexicans?' it related that the chances of getting AIDS were limited to people who belonged to particular groups such as 'immigrants,' people who visited 'AIDS concentration areas, prostitutes, and people in marginal communities.' The bottom line was that AIDS was not a threat to Mexican society, which played down not only the number of documented cases during that year, but also its relevance as a serious public health issue.

The first research tests in Mexico were carried out with homosexual men, who had been labeled a high-risk group. But what was a 'homosexual man' for medicine; who fell into the category and who fell outside the research target? New definitions of 'gay' and 'homosexual' guided the targeting of information, medical monitoring, and preventive messages.

The link between AIDS and homosexuality has distinct subjective impacts. Testimonies show that different elements – sexual practice, ethnicity, and age – created different ways of interpreting body signs and constructing sexual risks. Those meanings informed how men related to each other in cruising sites, according to prevalent ideas of infection and disease.

> First they said it was a disease that was killing old men. And since it was old men and me and my pals were young, inexperienced ladies … right? Well then, it was like 'Get away from the old men 'cause they're dying and taking you with 'em!' I think it was a year later that it turned out that was wrong, young people got it too. One of the things that happened was that you lost weight, so it was that first, and then you'd just stop seeing them around. Someone you didn't see hanging around for a while and then … bam! There they were with a lot of pounds less, then … bam! You didn't see them again but this time they were gone for ever. (Dante)

By 1987 news on AIDS in newspapers, sending panic messages, had reached the level of three articles a day. One alarming piece of news on the front page of *El Universal* was that Mexico was the fifth-ranked country in America in terms of recorded cases of AIDS.[29] The article prompted panic shopping for syringes.[30] AIDS was associated with cultural images of 'homosexuals,' 'promiscuity,' and men displaying Kaposi's sarcoma lesions, who would soon die in great numbers of infections that increased at a terrifying pace. It was a fertile ground for right-wing, conservative, religious groups which campaigned against homosexuality. Organizations such as the National Parents Association become more visible and gained influence in later years through campaigns against condom use and homosexuality.[31] That year, Bishop Arteaga claimed that 'preventive actions meant to benefit some individuals who have violated human nature will be harmful to others who have nothing to do with the matter, one does the harm and another bears the blame.'[32] A flyer campaign warned: 'stay away from homosexuals, they propagate AIDS' (Salinas 2008: 74).

By 1987 AIDS had become a popular topic. It was featured everywhere, echoing global controversies around the disease. It was central to the coverage of the Venice summit in 1987. A headline read: 'Ronald Reagan was unable to impose his opinion and lost international allies.' The 'devastating pandemic' was at the top of the agenda, as 'President François Mitterrand received great applause when he proposed the creation of an international ethics committee for AIDS.'[33]

Concomitantly, homosexuality continued becoming more visible as a way of life. In 1987, *Doña Herlinda y su hijo*, a film by Jaime Humberto Hermosillo, portrayed a love triangle under a controlling mother. Dramatic tension and humor pivot upon homosexuality as a voiced secret, or silenced evidence. The film played in theaters around the city for over a year, tagged as 'a very wholesome mother with a fruitcake for a son in this witty and delicious comedy.'[34] That same year, several film comedies featured parodic portrayals of homosexual characters, including characters who played 'false' homosexuals in the *ficheras* films, generating comic situations. In *Un macho en el salón de belleza*, a hyper-masculine character claiming to be gay becomes the protégé of a flamboyant gay beautician. In order to avoid contact with his mentor, he claims to have AIDS. Every time they touch, he sprays himself with alcohol to avoid contagion. In another scene, the macho says, '*Mi problema "si da" de qué preocuparse.*'[35] They refer to AIDS as 'the twentieth-century plague.' Eventually, the 'true' homosexual man decides to take the risk and have sex with the false one because there is news of a probable cure.

By then, information about the world AIDS epidemic was still sparse and inconclusive, mainly fixed upon scrutinizing the bodies of suspected homosexuals. Omar, who then thought that he could be saved by staying away from foreigners and from 'thin and weak' bodies, added to his list of precautions, 'always acting as top' in sexual intercourse, among other things:

Some people, myself included, thought that the ones who penetrated could not be infected. There were well-established roles in our way of thinking. Machos, all virile and stuff, probably weren't very gay but at the same time we thought that all of them were tops. And I always chose my sex partners very carefully, or at least I thought I did. Until 1988 when a sex partner wanted to wear a condom – that was inconceivable to some of us. The one who wore a condom probably did because he was sick and no one wanted to mess around with him any more. He told me we had to use the condom and I kept saying no. We did it twice with the condom but I didn't want to, so he said: 'Look, let's go to the Condesa Clinic, they do the testing there, we have the

tests done, we come out clean, and then we fuck without the condom.'
We did, my results said that I had AIDS and I couldn't think of anything
else any more. (Omar)

The panic was projected upon body signs in the context of homoerotic sociability:

> If you look at my neck, I'm always very fidgety, this spot I have, well, it
> was bigger because I studied and I scratched it so much that it became
> bigger and bigger. I understood why no one would come near me in the
> bathhouse. But in other bathhouses the lights were dim and there was
> no problem. (Dante)

By 1988, a series of episodes expressive of the size of the epidemic,
and the mobilization of civil society actors – notably homosexual
organizations – had raised public awareness about AIDS as a public
health issue. An issue of the journal *Salud Pública* was dedicated to
the topic, referring to homosexual men and immigrants as high-risk
populations, priority targets for intervention. While, at that stage,
inconsistent information about how to prevent the transmission of
the HIV virus contributed to further stigmatizing of homosexual men
and people in poor living conditions, the Catholic Church and other
conservative groups used the opportunity to campaign for sexual
abstinence. *El Universal* reported on those.[36]

Another news report referred to the refusal by La Raza Hospital,
Mexico City's main state-run healthcare provider, to treat '*sidosos,*'
a derogatory term used to label persons who contracted the infection, owing to the cost of their specialized treatment. The news story
mentions that patients – mostly poor – came to Mexico City from
other states, 'to meet their inevitable ending.'[37] This event generated
a protest by gay activist groups. Following that, a series of articles
reported on the mobilization of the 'gay community,' demanding a
more considerate treatment for homosexual people and everyone infected with AIDS.[38] Meanwhile, violence against people thought to be
homosexual grew, as a casual acquaintance who attended cinemas
where 'public sex' took place recalled: 'Those were hard times for
your people. There was a great fuss against homosexuals and by the
late 1980s this cinema would be shut down and they were beaten up.
They thought homosexuals were the cause of that evil.'[39]

Salinas (2008) links the consolidation and global visibility of the
sexual dissidence movements to civil society responses to the AIDS
epidemic. Likewise, Bersani (1996) stresses AIDS' inalienable associa-

tion with public representations of male homosexuality. Homosexual men, who had become part of the portrayal of AIDS, also became the focus of health regulations dedicated to curbing the spread of the disease. Their framing as a high-risk group was crucial in bringing AIDS and homosexuality so close together in public representations. Homosexual activist associations faced the challenge of undoing such paralyzing symbolic connections, while demanding access to proper care and prevention in recognition of a health crisis that threatened the lives of homosexuals.

## Conclusions

This chapter has addressed different aspects of the public visibility of male homoeroticism in Mexico City during the 1980s, particularly in relation to the impact of the AIDS epidemic. The social dynamics and gender regime prevalent at sites of more secret or discreet homoerotic interaction labeled as 'homosexuals' those men who openly identified as such, who were assumed to play the 'feminine' role in sexual intercourse, often transgressing conventional forms of masculinity. Being 'obvio' – where 'obviously' gay stands for effeminate – meant being subject to violence and discrimination, and singled out as likely to become 'sidoso.' This context drew men who were likewise involved in homoerotic relations away from the spaces and social milieus that, during this decade, came to be publicly identified as 'homosexual.'

As the decade progressed, the increasing public visibility of homosexuality in mainstream, as well as specialized, media, and political mobilizing, and the establishment of new commercial entertainment venues, was expressive of the expansion of a new sexual regime, of male-identified gays. This new 'gay' milieu also meant a more diversified social profile, in terms of gender, class, color, and ethnic identity, as well as lifestyles and understandings of sexuality. In this new spatial economy, in the advent of the AIDS panic, new representations of public gayness, in coexistence with older forms of homoerotic sex and sociability, established new forms of social regulation. These involved judging each other's bodies, reading certain signs – as the public would judge 'the gay body' – as symbols of risk.

AIDS contributed to the heteronomous identification of homosexuals, in this case as carriers of a deadly disease. However, within the homoerotic milieu, risk was broken down according to a vernacular hierarchy, presumed vulnerability, and immunity to AIDS: younger men, 'activos' (the inserter in penetrative sex), Mexicans (as opposed to gringos and immigrants), and monogamous (as opposed to promiscuous) men were assumed to be in a safer position regarding the risk of contracting AIDS.

List has pointed out that there are ways of being gay in Mexico: 'There is a scarce development of a collective gay identity that would allow for subjects to acknowledge themselves before others in a way positive enough as to become a priority for social and community involvement' (2006: 88). The increase in public visibility of homosexual identities during the 1980s in Mexico City, as well as the advent of the AIDS crisis, represented an intense process of interpellation for men who took part in homoerotic sociability. Sites and bodies were reorganized. Public and private discrimination mechanisms developed a new, refined sensibility – as a new esthetic – which meant the rejection of certain bodies, as evident in the ecology of cruising sites. The conscientious scrutiny and cataloging of homosexual bodies translated moral anxieties into popular forms of medical knowledge.

## Notes

1 I thank Sephis and all the participants in its Sexualities in the South project, as well as my home advisors, Mauricio List and Elsa Muñiz, for their guidance and comments. Special thanks to Horacio Sívori for his contributions and patience, and to Marina de Regt and Jacqueline Rutte at Sephis for their advice and great coordination. This work entailed research in a number of archives. I would particularly like to acknowledge the Centro de Información y Documentación de las Homosexualidades en México, Ignacio Álvarez, and Hemeroteca Nacional de México.

2 Unlike terms such as 'gay' or 'homosexual,' whose uses refer to social identities, in this chapter I use 'homoeroticism' to refer to same-sex attraction and intercourse, as proposed by Núñez (1999), and 'homosexual' to refer to individuals and collectives who during the documented period self-identified with or were attributed that term in public contexts.

3 Public visibility was promoted by activist organizations struggling for the rights of *homosexuales* and *lesbianas*, as expressed in the names chosen at the time: FHAR (Frente Homosexual de Acción Revolucionaria); OIKABETH – Movimiento Lésbico Feminista; and Grupo Lambda de Liberación Homosexual (De la Dehesa 2010: 89).

4 In sources from the period, the word homosexual refers only to males. For women, the term of choice is *lesbiana*.

5 In 1985 the National Council of AIDS (CONASIDA) was created. This council defined homosexuals as a 'risk group.'

6 Nineteenth-century Mexican texts create an inextricable connection between male effeminateness and homosexual desire. List (2009) analyzes the influence of late nineteenth- and early twentieth-century health and hygiene manuals in establishing a gendered notion of personal development embedded in the project of a modern nation. In

that narrative, effeminacy in males constituted a sign of 'illness' or 'perversion.' Muñiz (2002), analyzing interpersonal relations at the time of the Mexican Revolution, recounts the rejection of effeminacy in men as a key element in the normative model of gender relations. Male effeminacy threatened the heterosexual norm intrinsic to the project of a modern Mexican society.

7 Teresa de Lauretis defined 'interpellation' as the process through which a social representation is accepted and incorporated by an individual as their own (De Lauretis 2004: 249). In the same form, the feminist said social representation is a 'distilled discursive.' I share this idea, because I think that my sources are a reflection of these discourses.

8 The word *ambiente* in urban Spanish America literally reads as 'environment' or 'atmosphere,' referring to the qualitative attributes of a venue at a given time, as well as to the milieu of a group or network (*ambiente tribunalicio*, 'court milieu,' as defined by those who are formally or informally admitted as part of it), which can be defined by a given social attribute, such as a profession (*ambiente docente*, 'teaching milieu'), stylistic feature (*el ambiente artístico*, 'the performing arts milieu,' *ambiente fashion*, meaning 'trendy'), or a moral attribute (*ambiente criminal*, crime mileu). It was adopted in gay and lesbian doublespeak as a euphemism denoting people and places identified as non-heterosexual.

9 *El Universal*, 28 June 1979.

10 *Ovaciones*, 8 October 1979.

11 The verb *ligar* and the noun *ligue* in Spanish refer to both cruising for sex and 'hooking up' with someone.

12 'Nuestro cuerpo,' *Lenguaje y Opresión*, 2/3, FHAR, 1980.

13 Unpublished manuscript submitted to *Nuestro Cuerpo* magazine, in Archivo Digital del Movimiento Homosexual.

14 *Cine de ficheras* is a B-class local film comedy genre, featuring life in brothels and saloons. *Fichera* is a vernacular name for female lap dancers, whose numbers used to be paid for with tokens (*fichas* in Spanish).

15 *Cine del homosexualismo* in the original. On the controversial nature attributed to the topic: 'Homosexuality is very old but not even the word has ever been mentioned before, yet now nobody is outraged by its featuring in films such as *Cruising*, which portrays homosexual life in New York.' *El Universal*, 11 June 1981.

16 *Albur* is a type of a sexual pun popular in working-class male culture in Mexico. For example, in *La pulquería*'s banner about a homosexual character (1980), we can read: '*Gusta del pulque de platano y nunca la hace de tos*' ('She likes banana juice and never coughs' or 'He drinks the cum and won't ever choke on it').

17 *El Universal*, 27 June 1982.

18 Owing to size constraints, the survey of literature, theatre, and cinema in this chapter will be brief and limited, to concentrate on gay-oriented magazines and fanzines.

19 *El Universal*, 27 June 1983.

20 According to Salinas (2008), this coverage 'brought more visibility than a hundred marches.'

21 *El Universal*, 23 June 1984.

22 *El Universal*, 1 July 1983.

23 Cinema and theater announcements featured in *El Universal*, 11 June 1983. The ad reads:

'The dialog between two convicts, one for his political ideals, the other for his sexual preferences.'

24 *Macho Tips* (1985), Year 1, no. 1, July.

25 I have found no mention of sexuality in the coverage of AIDS by health journals prior to 1985. Camargo (2008) comments that at the time there was no discussion of sexuality as the first policies were being implemented to research and fight AIDS – which is, ironically, a sexually transmitted infection.

26 Between 1979 and 1989, the journal *Salud Pública de México* does not feature any articles on sexual or reproductive health. Neither homosexuality nor AIDS is addressed prior to 1985, when the first world AIDS conference in the United States was announced, and 1986, when the status of AIDS in Mexico was reviewed.

27 *El Universal*, 22–24 June 1986.

28 *Macho Tips* (1986), no. 11.

29 *El Universal*, 11 June 1987.

30 Ibid.

31 As documented by González (1994) and Salinas (2008), conservative groups declared AIDS prevention campaigns to be immoral and influenced advertisers to pull their contracts with Televisa (the largest national TV network) unless the network canceled State Health Authority ads promoting the use of condoms.

32 *El Universal*, 11 June 1987.

33 *El Universal*, 21 June 1987.

34 Ibid.

35 The line includes a play on words with 'AIDS' in Spanish. It refers to the character's problem, which is AIDS. The play on words may be roughly reproduced in English as 'My problem doesn't AID Society at all.'

36 *El Universal*, 11 June 1988.

37 *El Universal*, 17 June 1988.

38 *El Universal*, 24 June 1988.

39 Field notes, 23 April 2009.

## References

Agustín, J. (2006) *Tragicomedia Mexicana*, vols 2–3, Mexico: Océano.

Bersani, L. (1996) *Homos*, Cambridge, MA: Harvard University Press.

Butler, J. (2001) *El género en disputa*, Mexico: Paidos/PUEG/UNAM.

Camargo, K. (2008) *Políticas y sexualidades*, Mexico: 1° Encuentro Latinoamericano y del Caribe: La sexualidad frente a la sociedad.

Carrier, J. (1995) *De los Otros: Intimacy and Homosexuality among Mexican Men*, New York: New York University Press.

Carrillo, H. (2005) *La noche es joven*, Mexico: Grijalbo.

De la Dehesa, R. (2010) *Queering the Public Sphere in México and Brazil. Sexual Rights Movements in Emerging Democracies*, Durham, NC: Duke Press.

De Lauretis, T. (1991) 'Tecnologías del género,' in C. Ramos Escandón (ed.), *El género en perspectiva*, Mexico: UAM Xochimilco.

— (2004) *Technologies of Gender*, Bloomington: Indiana University Press.

Foucault, M. (1992) *La historia de la sexualidad*, vols 1–2, Mexico: Siglo XXI.

— (2000) *Tecnologías del yo y otros textos afines*, Barcelona: Paidos/UAB.

Fry, P. (1982) *Para inglês ver*, Rio de Janeiro: Paz & Terra.

Galván, F., R. González and R. Morales (1991) 'Del Sida en México. Aspectos del gobierno y la sociedad,' in I. Lumsden, *Homosexualidad, sociedad y Estado en México*, Mexico:

Solediciones – Canadian Gay Archives.

Giménez, M. (2005) *Teoría y análisis de la cultura*, Mexico: CONACULTA/ICOCULT.

González, E. (1994) *Conservadurismo y sexualidad*, Mexico: Rayuela.

Guttmann, M. (2000) *Ser hombre de verdad en la ciudad de México*, Mexico: PIEM/COLMEX.

Le Bretón, D. (2007) *El adiós al cuerpo*, Mexico: La cifra.

Leap, W. (ed.) (1999) *Public Sex, Gay Space*, New York: Columbia University Press.

List, M. (2006) *Jóvenes corazones gay*, Mexico: Fondo editorial BUAP.

— (2009) *Hablo por mi diferencia*, Mexico: EON/Fundación Arcoíris.

Llamas, R. (ed.) (1995) *Construyendo Sidentidades*, Madrid: Siglo XXI.

Muñiz, E. (2002) *Cuerpo, representación y poder: México en los albores de la reconstrucción nacional*, Mexico: M. A. Porrúa/UAM-A.

Núñez, G. (1999) *Sexo entre varones. Poder y resistencia en el campo sexual*, Mexico: M. A. Porrúa/COLSON.

Pecheny, M. (2002) 'Identidades discretas,' in L. Arfurch (ed.), *Identidades, sujetos y subjetividades*, Buenos Aires: Prometeo Libros.

Peralta, B. (2007) *Los nombres del arcoíris*, Mexico: Nueva Imagen, CONACULTA/INBA.

Pollack, M. (2007) 'La homosexualidad masculina o ¿La felicidad de ghetto?' in P. Aries et al., *Sexualidades occidentales*, Mexico.

Rubin, G. (1989) 'Reflexionando sobre el sexo: notas para una teoría radical de la sexualidad,' in C. Vance (ed.), *Placer y peligro. Explorando la sexualidad femenina*, Madrid: Revolución.

Salinas, H. M. (2008) *Políticas públicas de disidencia sexual en México*, Mexico: CONAPRED.

## Archives

Miano, Hernández y Marmolejo, Archivo Digital del Movimiento Homosexual-CIDHOM y archivo hemerográfico RUIIDO, CONACYT/ENAH, Mexico, 2004

## Interviews

Arturo, 46 years old, informal conversations

Omar, 42 years old, 17 February 2009

Adrián, 39 years old, 22 February 2009

Jos, 52 years old, 27 April and 3 May 2009

Dante, 38 years old, 29 June 2009

Valterio, 55 years old, 14 June and 2 July 2009

Antonio, 45 years old, 20 July 2009

## Films

*Doña Herlinda y su hijo*, Jaime Humberto Hermosillo (dir.), México Colour, 1984

*La Pulquería*, Cinematográfica Calderón, 1981

*Un macho en el salón de belleza*, Víctor Manuel Castro (dir.), Cine de México, 1987

## Fiction and chronicles

Blanco, J. J. (1978), *Función de media noche, crónicas de la ciudad*, Mexico: Era.

— (1984) *Púberes canéforas*, Mexico: Cal y arena.

Calva, J. R. (1983) *Utopía Gay*, Mexico: Oásis.

De Alba, L. G. (1984) *Malas compañías*, Mexico: Cal y arena.

Shilts, R. (1993) *En el filo de la duda*, Spain: Ediciones B.

Zapata, L. (1979) *El vampiro de la colonia Roma*, Mexico: Grijalbo.

— (1981) *El vino de los bravos*, Mexico: Cal y arena.

# 11 | Canons of desire: male homosexuality in twenty-first-century Keralam

RAJEEV KUMARAMKANDATH

## Introduction

I came to know about these places when I was in college. I was not very sure as to what exactly happens in these places although everyone seemed to know of their existence. For us terms like *flute* and *kuntan*[1] were part of our daily vocabulary. But then I had my first sexual encounter. ... I then knew what happens there and the implications of those terms. Once you know that this exists and have experienced it then you see it everywhere or you will look for it wherever you go. The feeling of shame shudders through me sometimes. However, since then I never missed an opportunity to come here although I know it is very risky. Vipin[2] (interviewed 17 September 2008)

This chapter discusses clandestine same-sex intimacies between male-bodied individuals in Keralam, in the southern tip of India, using a critical ethnography[3] of cruising sites where they pursue their homoerotic desires. As intermediate spaces – public, yet appropriated for intimate affairs, secret detours from other daily routines – cruising sites configure symbolically powerful locations, where homoerotically inclined men are metonymically constituted as 'sexual' subjects and interpellate dominant gender hierarchies. I focus on their subjectivities and agency, within the discursive politics of gender and heteronormativity, which they simultaneously conform to and transgress. In this introduction I discuss the theoretical paradigms that have addressed same-sex orientation as related to post-colonial situations. In the next section, I explore the use of social semiosis by individuals pursuing hidden same-sex desires and examine the metonyms and metaphors associated with homoeroticism in the Kerala public imagination. In the third section, homosexuality is analyzed as an issue in relation to family and reproduction as major investments in the larger cultural politics of modernity in Keralam.

I use the tools of critical post-colonial historiography to explore the meanings of same-sex desire in a context of intense policing of gender conformity and national family values. Those who challenge the dictates of public morality and sexual regulation place themselves at the crossroads of heteronormative structures and sexual dissidence. Their subjectivities, as Johnson stated, 'are produced, not given, and are therefore the objects of inquiry, not premises or starting points' (1986: 6). The subjects involved are the anonymous, invisible bodies that have recently come under the term 'men who have sex with men' (MSM), an epidemiological construct developed as part of medical efforts to curtail the spread of HIV/AIDS, particularly in Third World countries. As a response to social regulations organized around the politics of reproduction, these men contrive to preserve their dissidence from gender norms and beliefs.

In India, as in other global South contexts, Seabrook advocates the use of MSM over terms like gay, lesbian, bisexual, transgender, and queer, as these terms are inherently Western. For him, 'to impose such categories – except upon a small minority who have been much influenced by western gay experiences – is to bring alien concepts to the people involved,' and it would be 'arrogant and disregarding for other cultures' (1999: v). While concerns about reading 'Indian sexuality' or sexualities with the help of Western theories are common, to imagine its reverse would be equally problematic. That is, an Indian sexuality or an Indian sexual self as radically distinct from its Western counterparts. As John and Nair articulated, 'the very conception of the other of the west as being something to which western concepts do not apply (or only as an act of violation from which one must be redeemed) is itself a western legacy' (1998: 6). Hence, accounts of subjective formations in the context of same-sex desire have been theorized amid constructions of transnational homosexual subjects, such as gay and lesbian, informed by cultural differences. While the former results in the 'flattening' of categories, 'erasing the differences and nuances among same-sex desiring peoples' in the non-West (Collins 2005: 182), the latter leads to 'de-historicized and exoticized depictions of the non-western other' (Hindley 2001: 117).

In an attempt to explain the impact of rapid changes 'on lifestyles and an identity politics' (Altman 1996: 78), theories about the expansion of an 'existing western category' have been contradicted by 'heterogeneous understandings' of homosexual persons that exist in non-Western societies (Jackson 1997: 55). In relation to debates about the pertinence of 'modern gay' and 'traditional *Kothi*' models in Hyderabad, in south India,[4] Reddy argues that the post-Foucauldian distinctions between nineteenth-century homosexual and twentieth-century gay, as well as between subjectivity and behavior, have tended 'to elide the receptive/penetrative sexual distinction so common in parts of Latin America and Asia' (Reddy 2004: 148).[5] Reddy stresses the 'trans-local' nature of gay subjectivities, which disproves 'the universal gay identity ... and an explicit non-universal, local particularity' (ibid.: 149). In her work on gay hosts in the tourist district of Mallate, Philippines, Collins argues that 'Transnational analyses provide an alternative to globalization approaches; they shift the emphasis away from western mobility and its consequences and consider sexualities as the product of a hybrid reworking of identities, languages, and desires' (2005: 189).

The literature on sexual identity, cultural contact, and transnational flows has often ignored the dynamics of the interaction between the subjective formations and local regulatory apparatuses. The subversive potential of certain practices is often replaced by the subjects' interaction with or as transnational citizens: Western, or Westernized, gays. While the local is inherently located amid transnational networks, it is also a terrain constituted by different social, historical, and political processes which merit an analysis of their own. Theorists refuse to conceptualize sexual relations in terms of regulatory practices in order to stress the freedom of sexual expression (Glick 2000; Rubin 1992). They argue that 'to operate within the matrix of power is not the same as to replicate relations of domination,' providing the logical framework to understand 'destabilizing practices' (Butler 1990: 30–1). Nevertheless, I argue for an understanding of subversion that accounts for markers of difference as they are produced, stabilized, or destabilized at the local level. Rather than rearticulating repression from a different vantage point, this kind of insight throws light on the different modalities of power in a non-Western cultural terrain.

Reform movements in colonial and post-colonial Keralam involved conspicuous attempts to reform the indigenous culture from its supposedly 'degenerated' conditions. Several authors have analyzed the formation of a new gender order and sexual moralities during the colonial reform period in the region (Devika 2002, 2005; Kodoth 2002; Arunima 2003; Kumaramkandath 2011), as well as in the rest of India and other Third World situations (Jayawardena 1986; Chatterjee 1989; Bacchetta 1999). Likewise, in Keralam, the early nineteenth-century colonial depictions were borrowed as the hegemonic language of post-colonial reform discourse to prescribe changes deemed essential to inaugurate an era of progress. These prescriptions, phrased in the language of Victorian morality, primarily addressed the pragmatic task of subjecting individual bodies to new moral conditions (Kumaramkandath

2011). From this discursive space emerged the husband–wife model of conjugality, befitting 'progressive modern' society.[6] This socio-moral reconfiguration simultaneously branded gender practices and sexual conduct outside the modern conjugal model as deviant behavior influenced by Western lifestyles.

In their post-colonial archeology of sexuality, John and Nair (1998) suggest three sources which operated to consolidate the field of knowledge about sex and the body in nineteenth- and twentieth-century India: demography, social reform discourse, and the anthropology of family and kinship. In contrast to the metropolitan counterpart, in modern India:

> It was not ... the confessional couch or the hystericised women that generated knowledge and anxieties about sexuality ... so much as, on the one hand, the administrative urgency of the colonial power to make sense of and thereby govern a baffling array of 'types and classes' and their family systems, and on the other, the nationalist need to define the dutiful place of the citizen/subjects of the incipient nation. (Ibid.: 8–9)

I maintain that this past has a paramount role in the constitution of contemporary values and perceptions. It is in the context of that proliferation of knowledge that the meanings of both – complying and dissident – bodily practices, gender socialization, and localized sexual sociabilities become significant in relation to a hegemonic sex/gender order.

### The *flute*: an aberrant subjectivity

> It is easy to identify them. They will always keep a distance from the crowd. Or they will often imagine the crowd as a wild animal that can turn violent at any moment. Inside their mind they always have to swing a whip for self protection. From their face they would appear as reclusive.
>
> But full of love deep inside.(*Swavargam* [Same sex], a short story by V. Dileep, Kottayam: D C Books, 2008)

These notes are based on field observation and informal interviews at cruising spots between 2006 and 2009 in three districts of the Keralam region: Thiruvananthapuram, the capital city, in the southern part of the region; Thrissur, in the central part; and Kozhikode, in the northern part. I was raised in the region and speak Malayalam, the local vernacular. In all three districts my initial contacts were established through outreach field workers for local NGOs conducting HIV/AIDS prevention activities, although many of the men I interviewed, owing to their care in keeping their endeavors secret, had never interacted with those NGOs. I conducted on-site formal and informal, mostly in-depth, interviews, seldom taped, owing to the discomfort a tape recorder would cause in those situations. On all occasions, I remained open to my interviewees about the purposes of my interaction and the nature of my research. My interview guide generally addressed: (i) narratives of same-sex experiences; (ii) social hostility and acts of violence; (iii) responses to public and insiders' narratives and tropes in reference to same-sex desires and dissident sexual subjects; (iv) understandings of emerging gay politics; (v) social control; (vi) home, family, and the workplace; (vii) modus operandi and interactions while transgressing sexual norms. Reminiscences of previous confrontations, stories of invitations with and without success, descriptions of sexual acts, and stories of violence were part and parcel of our conversations.

As in other parts of the world where homosexual desire is lived as a personal secret, in Keralam homoerotically inclined men regularly go in search of male sexual partners under the anonymity of the crowds in larger urban centres.[7] Most of these places are not secluded, alien to other public uses, or beyond the reach of state surveillance, but are rather the most available, performing public functions during busy hours. Cruising takes place in markets, bus stations, public parks, public toilets, town squares, and maidans, areas adjacent to campuses, crowded temples and churches, large-scale parking places, and the staircases of large and crowded buildings, as well as dark corners under bridges. Crowds provide ample opportunity for these men to remain unnoticed while looking for a suitable partner, while they secretly share inside knowledge about the cruising map of the city. However, this is hardly a secret, and cruising as an 'anti-social' activity has fallen squarely under instruments of social control. Also, public transportation, empty cinema halls when the films are in progress, dark corners inside porn movie theaters – all are potential spaces in which to express same-sex desires. Despite a repressive regime and the moral separation of same-sex desire as a shameful secret, individuals manage to find spaces where they can express it and build intimate, sometimes long-lasting relations.

Cruising adds complexity to spatial categorizations. The appropriation of public spaces for the purpose of homoerotic encounters transforms the meaning of a public utility to serve an utmost private activity. 'The excitement of breaking the law converges with a myriad of techniques of social control,' investing a 'leaky vulnerable place where exclusion of the unwanted voyeur, the violent gay basher, the security guard and the policemen is almost impossible' with emotional intensity (Plummer 2002: 300). In Keralam, where a commercial sex market is almost non-existent,[8] male individuals search for, and collectively transform, spaces so that they can serve this purpose. When this involves homoerotic desires, they have to do so with great care, as they may be repressed brutally.[9] In order to seize the opportunity afforded by the anonymity of impersonal crowds in urban spaces, they spend a great amount of time loitering around these places in the evening hours, looking for sex partners. The number of lone men in parks and city squares increases around sunset as older and younger couples and families start leaving. While loitering is necessary, they have to take special care to look detached, since that helps to avoid being noticed by policemen, security guards, and those not in the know. The men who cruise come from various backgrounds, cutting across caste, class, and rural/urban differences. This includes migrant laborers from neighboring districts, employees at local shops, factories, and government offices, and passing visitors, as well as students at the local colleges. However, sexual preference is the main social marker organizing cruising dynamics.

Dileep's depiction of same-sex-inclined men (epigraph above) suggests that their sexual desires always cast doubt on their masculinity, making their identification easy. Their physical presence, especially in places that are public, can invite reactions from a hostile (homophobic) public. Markers of male effeminacy, as they deviate from standard models of virile heterosexual reproductive masculinity, are read as signs of transgression. Male homosexuals in Keralam are frequently called *flutes*. This derogative term refers to same-sex-oriented male-bodied persons. This use of *flute* performs a metonymical operation, where oral sex stands for a particular sexual subject: the feminized, hierarchically subordinate, partner. Metaphorically, it also refers to abstract desires, pursuits for pleasure, and deviance. *Flute* is the male homosexual who indulges in oral sex, taking the 'passive' role. The figure of a *flute* refers to an abstract collective imaginary, whose functions are performed by or attributed to specific individuals at defined temporal and physical locations, communicating a variety of pragmatic contents related to same-sex orientation. Given its stigma (Goffman 1963), someone's identification as a *flute* makes sense only in the specific pragmatic communicative contexts where it serves the purpose of expressing interest, solidarity, or rejection. In other everyday contexts such identification is systematically avoided as an attribute of the self. Same-sex-oriented males strategically pass in and out of homosexual social corridors. They avoid unnecessary hazards by manipulating their social – particularly gender – attributes.

> People have a definite image of a *flute*. I can survive without carrying that label until I demonstrate those featured behavior patterns or until my sexual act is seen by any of my friends or neighbors. I have to fix a searching look on my face once I am inside this space, and that is the first signal to convey an impression about me to someone crossing my path here. Then, together with tarrying footsteps, a typical way of walking, a momentary eye contact made in a split second, and turning back to see the other's response (a positive response would be that the other also turns back to see me), the initial round of making a contact takes place. This has to be repeated two or three times before we exchange smiles and start talking with each other. Outside this space I consciously regulate my habits and I don't give any chance to anyone to have a doubt about me. Even then there were several occasions when I got partners outside this space. This is especially so while traveling on crowded buses. Suppose my hands accidentally touched someone's body and he did not move away, as he was supposed to do, then I take it as a positive response to an accidental invitation on my part and make my initial moves. But then it requires only soft and mild touches on the other's body that would seem both accidental and intentional.
> (Sunil, 4 September 2007)

Sunil's account highlights how nuanced the relationship between behavior, identity, and subjectivity is, and the reflexive agency of individuals who craft strategies to find peers and elaborate an insider's knowledge and collective memory. Such ways of expressing, acknowledging, and responding to same-sex desires challenges dominant male scripts and make gender nonconformity a familiar event.

In a variety of cultural contexts, the stigma of homosexuality is exclusively attached to the so-called 'passive' partner in male same-sex intercourse. In Fox's (1995) typology of bisexuality, male individuals who only take the 'active' role regard themselves as heterosexuals. This classification on the basis of sex roles is well documented and for a while became an area within sexuality studies. Taylor (1978) and Carrier (1995) describe '*maricones*' – effeminate men who are said to take the passive role – as a heavily stigmatized identity in Mexican society, whereas '*mayates*' – males who may engage in same-sex intercourse, but only taking the 'active' role – are not stigmatized. De Moya and

Garcia (1996) identify a similar relationship between masculinity and bisexuality in the Dominican Republic. They conclude that among Dominican males bi-eroticism, bisexual behavior, and bisexuality are associated with the social constructions of masculinity and gender roles. As long as he is the one penetrating (either women or feminized men), a man is still a man.

In this sex role-based folk classification, the term *flute* applies exclusively to males who take the 'passive' role. 'I come here to *give* [*kodukkan*], not to *take* [*edukkan*]' (or vice versa), men often say or gesture, to establish the moral pragmatic grounds of their interaction when they make contact and come clean to each other about their mutual erotic interest. It is hard to say when it began to be used with this meaning in local light talk, mocking feminizing mannerisms and speech, and flirting with a voyeuristic flavor. The metaphor captures the meaning of *flute* as passive male homosexual, and the feminizing resonances of that role attribution, also attached to what is constructed as an 'unnatural' sexual desire. The *flute* becomes publicly imaginable only when represented with exaggerated affectation, incessant wandering, obscene gestures, and abject sexuality; a social character dispossessed of a role in the modern gender order and its disciplined forms of life.

However, traditional gender-role-based interpretations of sexual identities miss local cultural dynamics and topographies of same-sex desire. In present-day Keralam, while sex roles are indeed organized by the giver/receiver, active/passive dichotomy, both the *flute and* his partner, called *kodukkunnavan* (giver), share the homosexual stigma. Modernity has brought new specific meanings to such dichotomies. Today in Keralam public culture, same-sex desire is stigmatized irrespective of practice or sex role. *Flute* is not a traditional category like *maricón* in Spanish-speaking countries. Unlike hijra,[10] a traditional, institutionalized transgender category in India, *flute* does not signify a way of life. Its use representing homosexuals is absent from visual records and print literature.

According to Krippendorff (2006), metonyms provide the basis for a human-centered theory of signs. Thus 'the part that is chosen to be a metonym of its whole is not arbitrary,' but 'must be in some sense outstanding, easily recognizable, and play a unique role in the whole' (ibid.: 43). In Keralam the word *flute* carries a more familiar ring than its Malayalam equivalent *Odakkuzhal.* Playing the flute in Malayalam is 'flute *vayikkal.'* *Vayikkal* (literally, 'reading') is a mouth function. Oral sex, regarded as an abhorrent act in the local popular imagination of body and sex, becomes the identifying feature of the deviant persona. The term *vayikkal* has a special connotation in this context. Although largely absent from older visual and print media, it has now become a common reference in audiovisual media, particularly in comedy. In Keralam, the expression of sexual desire – both homo and hetero – is now frequent in film, TV, and stage comedy, where the term *vayikkal* is invoked to suggest – often vulgar – references to male effeminacy and homosexuality. Although the term *flute* is not as frequent, it is hinted, sometimes by association with *vayikkal*, or the mimicking of flute-playing. The deviant sexual act becomes the synonym of a sexual subject.

Nevertheless, the semantic field that arose around the term *flute*, including its capacity to generate humor, can also be read as an interrogation of the pervasive influence of gender norms on sexual orientation and desire. In his study on homosexuality in modern Japan, McLelland (2000) concludes that its visibility in Japanese media such as comic books, women's magazines, TV dramas and talk shows, movies, and popular fiction has not created the space for individuals to express lesbian or gay identities or to come out in actual life. Such a reading, on the one hand, imagines explicit minority identity categories as essentially subversive. On the other hand, it discounts subterranean practices as necessarily tied to the status quo. Despite the simultaneous reinforcement of stereotypes, audiences have become familiar with sexual and gender dissidence, breaking the links between 'biologically determined categories and socially constructed conceptions of sex' (Scott 2005: 74–5). The social imagery around the *flute* not only makes gender nonconformity part and parcel of a local common sense, but also generates its own space by challenging the rigidity of heteronormative regulatory settings.

In his analysis of pre-modern texts in ancient and medieval Greece, Halperin makes a significant distinction between deviant morphology and subjectivity by exploring the difference between anatomy and the narrativization of experience. Whereas the masculine male who indulges in homosexual behavior develops a subjective experience, an anatomical description of the *kinaedo* (effeminate male), diverging from dominant versions of masculine behavior, represents a deviant morphology (2002: 41–3). Deviant sexual acts may be performed in a society by subjects who do not come within the purview of such deviant morphologies. However, the *flute* combines both morphological and physiognomic characteristics to construct a deviant subjectivity. The figure of the *flute*, embedded in familiar stereotypes, cuts across both parameters of deviance, incited by, and reproducing, popularized notions about gender roles and sexual dissidence. This morphology emerges from gendered understandings of the body, desire, and personal ethics. Its descriptions remit to stereotypical constructions of male domination and female subordination. The *flute*'s transgressive desire fits a feckless male, an inept persona, unfit for family life.

## Family, reproduction, and national progress

The spatial organization of homoerotic sociability, configured as a secret milieu largely invisible to outsiders, also reflects and is reflected upon individual subjective trajectories regarding same-sex desire. A large majority of the men searching for a same-sex partner do not identify as homosexual. Many are married to women, and have children, or plan to marry. Few of them resist the social imperative for heterosexual marriage. Still, they transit regularly between their hetero and homo relationships and desires. Their daily lives involve negotiations of different kinds with changing environments. Rather than choosing between one desire and the other, or identifying them with different 'stages' in life, they refer to that transit as a strategy to avoid social surveillance mechanisms. Subjective trajectories between acts of conformity, transgression, and resistance are imagined and narrated as a dual topology of the self and social space, a constant transit marked by entrances and exits between different worlds, and the management of an inner nature and desires, and an outer social persona. These shifting locations are powerful signifiers of the inside 'mechanisms of meaning production' and the 'exterior or outside that defines the subject's own interior boundaries and corporeal surfaces' (Fuss 1991: 3).

The men I interviewed routinely dodged expressions of same-sex desire. Being married and heading one's own family is a primary condition for one's homoerotic inclinations to remain unnoticed. On several occasions the interviewees said that marriage provided them the veil behind which they could pursue their same-sex desire.[11] They all strove to head a family and acquire that dominant symbol of manhood as the first step to entering the corridors of normalcy and proving one's worth in life.[12] The capacity to engage in 'hetero' relations and practices and to participate in the cycle of reproduction is a prime determinant of one's material and symbolic situation within the political, economic, and religious order. But this need brings out the complexities involved in articulating a dissident desire, as happened to Aneesh, whose wife divorced him after he was found having sex with other males.

215

They [his wife's relatives] found me having sex with other males on two or three occasions and they told my wife although she never discussed this with me. On the third occasion she left the house and only after two or three weeks when I visited her at my in-laws' house did she tell me what her problem was. I never knew that my wife had information about this as she never told me before she left. She was quite adamant about her decision although she never revealed the actual reason to my parents or other relatives. (18 January 2008)

The politics of family and reproduction function differently for subjects from different class backgrounds. Sajju is aged thirty-two, married, with one child. He works as a construction laborer for a daily wage of 200 rupees. He is a regular visitor to the Thekkinkadu maidan, a famous cruising site in downtown Thrissur.

I am not quite happy with this, which is more like an addiction, and I have always felt, and still feel, like I am violating all basic moral principles. But I am helpless. I was caught on three occasions by the police. I was brutally tortured and they kept me inside the lockup for whole nights. Once I was also caught by the temple guards who man this place. They chased me to the main road outside the maidan. They caught me there and then dragged me amid the public, who thought that local youngsters had caught a pickpocket in action. They too joined the authorities and I was cruelly beaten. Fortunately for me there was no one who identified me and my face was saved. Back at home I felt ashamed to face my wife and child and I decided to abandon my deviant thoughts and not to come to this place again. But I couldn't resist my temptations and I consulted a psychiatrist. But all his efforts to straighten me produced no result and at last he advised me not to think too much about what I do not wish to be a part of me (that is, my homosexual fantasies), since that can even harm my mental balance. Now I think only about my family.

Sajju still comes to the maidan, has partners, or finds one in the crowd, and they leave searching for dark places in or outside the city. He claims that he is no longer concerned about his desires.

I have to take enough precautions so my family and friends in my locality [a remote village] do not come to know about this. In my village we have regular jokes about *flutes* and I indeed participate in such exchanges. While I know I myself am one, such participation helps me keep my identity underground ... I know I am not fully normal although I appear to be so and that is precisely what is needed. (25 August 2008)

**216**

Most men cruising in public areas belong to the lower and lower middle classes. With the emergence of modern technologies such as computers and the Internet, educated men belonging to the middle or upper classes can avoid the hassle of exposing themselves in public places. Joseph is a medical representative working in Cochin. A constant presence in the Yahoo! messenger chat rooms under a pseudonym, he searches for partners mainly in virtual spaces. He calls himself a bisexual, although that is a secret that he cannot let his family, friends, and colleagues know about.

> I know I have to marry and in fact my marriage is fixed with a girl with whom I have been in love for the last three years. I can't disclose 'this' to her either, and as long as I am not indulging in sex with another woman I am faithful to her. Having sex with a man is not something she needs to be bothered about, although I know I can't reveal these things to her for that could harm our relationship and I indeed love her very much ... [W]hen I have sex with another man that gives me the utmost pleasure. But pleasure is not life and there are other more serious considerations that we need to account for. (27 August 2008)

If, for Sajju, homosexuality is the hallmark of abnormality, for Joseph it stands as a symbol of pleasure. Nevertheless, both feel bound by the duties imposed by the heteronormative order. Sajju and Joseph are not exceptional in this regard. Throughout my interviews and conversations, this oscillation between pleasure and duty, faith and dissidence, the normal and the abnormal, were quite apparent. It applied to men from all classes. Such a wavering between conflicting values is part of a common parlance whenever the topic is discussed. Shaji, a teacher in a local engineering college in Kozhikkode – a district in the northern part of Keralam – who regularly visits cruising sites, puts it thus:

> Our society needs to be developed a lot before it can accept homo-sexuality or bisexuality as just another choice that is open to anyone. In the West it is possible because they are fully developed and there is no need for them to bother about such issues. On the scale of progress they have reached the other end whereas we are not even halfway through it. (22 December 2009)

Thus for Shaji, sexual freedom and material progress are closely linked. In this imagery, there is a persistent negative connection between competing ideas of national progress and moral decay, where the local situation is defined by its singular position in a global national development scale, and the West is invariably adopted as a point of reference, either for its supposed liberal attitudes toward sex, or as the epitome of moral decadence.

Popular ideas about homosexuality in Keralam relate it to medical disorders, unnatural relations, and cultural influences. In a book presented as a pioneering attempt to investigate the rising trend of lesbian suicides in Keralam, K. C. Sebastian claims to have interviewed people from different walks of life, including feminist leaders, writers, physicians, and activists, who, according to the author, shared the view that homosexuality is abnormal, unnatural, and immoral (Sebastian n.d.).[13] A recurrent topic in the book is the identification of local society and culture as a site of moral purity, distinct from the West, where homosexual relations are possible as a result of cultural decadence. The presence of homosexuality 'in western culture indicates the problem with those ... who do not identify sex as divine as we do.'[14]

The role-based, gender nonconformist model is also attributed to cases of female homosexuality in local pop-scientific literature. Another local author writes:

Close observation of a lesbian team [couple] ... will definitely tell you that one always assumes an active role and the other a passive role during sexual intercourse ... [T]he one who plays the dominant role, that is the one who is more masculine than feminine, definitely has physical problems and is helpless by nature under whose constant pressure the other person agrees to a relationship. Once it starts, then this other person will find no escape from it for the 'man' in this lesbian relationship will often threaten to commit suicide or may respond aggressively to any suggestion of separation. (Koottummal 2005: 58–60)

The 'woman' in the relationship is not classified as an 'actual homosexual,' owing to her predominantly feminine qualities (ibid.: 63). The intrusion of femininity into a masculine body and vice versa is considered harmful in the view of this author, who locates them in mutually exclusive realms. He argues that 'the basic concerns of these movements (including lesbianism and rights for homosexuals) are ... pleasure and pleasure alone' (ibid.: 61). These unlimited material pleasures have been made possible by globalization, the author maintains. In its wake, bodily pleasures and experiences are extolled (ibid.: 69).

Apart from a subtext of social concerns about the danger of undermining class and caste differences, the author is more unsettled with the unlimited opportunities for sexual pleasure unleashed by increasingly legitimate homosexual behavior envisaged in globalized discourse. He states: 'AIDS is actually a creation of unlimited sexual desire and lust. The only way to save oneself from it is to sustain a healthy sexual morality in one's life. That is, monogamy, which has evolved out of the history of sexual transactions, should be recognized as a social reality and as the only cultural and sexual backdrop for avoiding this disease' (ibid.: 62–3).

In a recently published volume, homosexuality and emerging queer voices in Keralam are interpreted as part of an emerging neoliberal-global paradigm where the economic realm has gained full control over the social and the moral (K.E.N. 2005).[15] Homosexuality is represented as yet another effect of a materialist perspective that privileges the flesh over moral values. Alternative sexual desires are equated to trafficking, pederasty, and molestation; all premised upon the endorsement of flesh and (animal) instincts over and above social obligations. The pursuit of sexual pleasure outside the means provided and accepted by society amounts to transgressing the conditional relationship between freedom and progress at the cost of the welfare of the whole society (ibid.: 5–10). 'Progress' becomes a cultural container of heteronormative concerns with national and regional moral purity. As Devika observes, the 'desire for development ... has been intimately linked to the construction [of the Malayalee people] as a distinct socio-cultural entity in the post-independent history' (2007: 4).

In this literature, homosexuality brings into sight freewheeling sexual desires, and the pursuit of 'unnatural intimacies,' exposing individual bodies to carnal pleasure. The authors' positions are marked by a conflict between humanitarian consideration and a critique of current moral conditions. These texts are replete with descriptions of body, sex, pleasure, and relations presented through the lens of a natural/unnatural dichotomy. Homosexuality occupies a pivotal place both as a presager of eroding local value structures, and an instance of hedonism. What emerges out of these works is not a common theme but a plurality of concerns related to a conflict between the modern market economy and the realm of moral values, which are seen as diametrically opposed to each other. These texts are part of a wider debate among local intellectuals on questions involving sex, body, and culture, as well as modern and postmodern society and economics. Based on common understandings about the local and its place within global cultural and economic transactions, their emphasis lies on local cultural specificities. The body, as structural base of family and gender relations, emerges as the prime site of immediate reflection on these anxieties. Its control is perceived as a symbol of local values and social order. As Ajith, an interviewee who works in a local automobile shop in Thiruvananthapuram, said:

> I have to confess that for me these things [marriage, masculine behavior, etc.] are just superficial, although this superficiality not only protects my whole life but provides me with necessary emotional support. This [having sex with a male partner] gives me temporary pleasure. Although I can't help being attracted to it almost every day, I can't live with a man, I just want to have sex with one and that's it.

## Conclusion

The transit between the family realm and sites of sexual dissidence is embedded within a larger politics of modernity, challenging the dominant gender regime by alternating between the 'normal' and the 'abnormal' in daily social life. According to Zarilli, embodied practices are:

> intersections where personal, social and cosmological experiences and realities are negotiated. To examine a practice is to examine these multiple sets of relationships and experiences ... Practices always exist within and simultaneously create histories. Likewise, a practice is not a discourse, but implicit in any practice are one or more discourses and perhaps paradigms through which the experience of practice might be reflected upon and possibly explained. (Zarilli 1998: 5–6)

The textuality of same-sex desires rearticulates the commonsense binary between tradition and modernity. The daily experiences of men who engage in homoerotic interests develop specific insights regarding that common sense. The narrators in this research exercise their agency by simultaneously resisting local hegemonic values and transnational ideas, especially those of an emerging gay identity politics. The subjects' unwillingness to admit to same-sex practices as part of their lives emerges from their subterranean life. They are a form of agency, rather than an expression of 'powerlessness' (Seabrook 1999: 126). The problematic and elusive location of these subjects segregates their experiences and bodies from the local frameworks of self and subjectivity. Such frameworks are rooted within culturally idealized life trajectories, common perceptions of femininity and masculinity, and the monogamous heteronormative family.

The *flute* and his anonymous male partners articulate a complex cultural site, intersected by meta-narratives of family, reproduction, and progress. They simultaneously enact and violate hegemonic narratives of body, space, desire, and subjectivity. The acts of transgression operate a decoding of symbols and the regulatory power of these discursive spaces. The male subject with a same-sex desire assembles in his body the predominant markers of gender, while simultaneously subverting their social and spatial boundaries. The iterative shift between the subversive and the 'normal' makes gender an imitating process – imitating the masculine through duties and obligations; as well as the feminine when enacting a 'passive' sex role. Rather than cloning gender archetypes, such practices collapse the gender regimes in which each gender moves, loosening their rigid boundaries and exploring the possibilities of body and desire. Their location reflects the ambivalence of being – alternatively and simultaneously – in and out of local regulatory apparatuses. By conforming to local gender norms and moral expectations, these dissident sexualities constitute at the same time a parallel and ulterior world, embedded in the local trajectories of modernity.

## Notes

1 *Flute* and *kuntan* are common derogatory terms for male homosexuals in Keralam.

2 All names in this chapter are pseudonyms.

3 Critical and reflexive ethnography engages with meanings, social practices, and material relations, while accounting for the researcher's positionality (Naples 2003; Madison 2005; Harvey 1990). Critical ethnography disrupts the tendency to objectify and silence, and allows the less visible subjects to become more apparent (Behar 1993).

4 Reddy's description of the male homosocial universe in Hyderabad focuses mainly on *kothis* – men who assume passive/receptive roles in same-sex encounters – and a range of sub-categories, of which hijras are but one. The *kothi/panthi* model's inclusion in the classificatory grid – *panthis* being the active partners – as gay alongside other modern gay identities obscures the fluid nature of these categories (2004: 156).

However, all these categories signify particular lifestyles – traditional and modern – in a changing world, identified through their self-assertions and their opposition to 'hetero' desires and practices.

5 See also Jackson (1997), Hindley (2001).

6 In Keralam this normative model was put into practice at the expense of a variety of traditional institutions, such as *marumak-kathayam* (matriliny), polyandry, and *sambandham* (conjugal relationships between male youngsters from upper-caste Brahmin families and lower-caste women without marital bonds) (Kodoth 2002; Arunima 2003; Saradamoni 1999). See also Aiyappan 1932, Gough 1952 for earlier surveys.

7 For an elaborate description of cruising venues in India, see Kuku-Siemons (2008) and Seabrook (1999).

8 This is true for both heterosexual and homosexual sociability. Various TV forums (Asianet, *Nammal Tammil*, 1 August 2009; Kairali TV,

*Cross Fire*, 17 July 2009) and Malayalam magazines have addressed a
rising trend of incidents of sexual
violence and harassment against
women in public places, connecting
it to the absence of red-light areas.
With regard to same-sex desire, such
debates take a different turn, examining its legitimacy in moral, ethical,
political, and scientific terms.

9 Violence against homosexuals
in Keralam goes beyond the regime
of law, being more informal than
formal in nature. See Deepa (2005)
on unorganized and invisible forms
of violence against persons with
same-sex desires, particularly in
lesbian relations, in Keralam.

10 Hijras are found in most parts
of India, but are almost completely
absent from public spaces in Keralam. For an account of the ritual
status and traditional significance of
hijras in Indian society, see Nanda
(1990).

11 Some of the men I interviewed
were public activists. Despite this
they kept a 'low profile' to remain
unnoticed as homosexuals.

12 For a thorough examination of
idealized male life cycles in Keralam,
see Osella and Osella (1999).

13 The book is a collection of
articles published by the same
author in *Sameeksha*, a local weekly,
in 1998.

14 Interview with Professor
Sarojini Devi, cited in Sebastian
(n.d.: 29–30).

15 The volume opens with the
translated version of a chapter about
'healthy sexual morality' from Ber-
trand Russell's 1929 book *Marriage
and Morals*. It includes articles by
well-known, respected local intellectuals, Sara Joseph, Ramanunni,
and Dr Pocker, apart from the editor,
K.E.N.

## References

Aiyappan, A. (1932) 'Nayar polyandry,'
*Man*, 32, March.

Altman, D. (1996) 'Rupture or continuity? The internationalization of
gay identities,' *Social Text*, 14(3).

Arunima, G. (2003) *There Comes
Papa: Colonialism and the Trans-
formation of Matriliny in Kerala,
Malabar c. 1850–1940*, New Delhi:
Orient Longman.

Bacchetta, P. (1999) 'When the
(Hindu) nation exiles its queers,'
*Social Text*, 17(4).

Behar, R. (1993) *Translated Woman:
Crossing the border with Esper-
anza's story*, Boston, MA: Beacon.

Butler, J. (1990) *Gender Trouble:
Feminism and the Subversion of
Identity*, New York: Routledge.

Carrier, J. (1995) *De los Otros:
Intimacy and Homosexuality
among Mexican Men*, New York:
Columbia University Press.

Chatterjee, P. (1989) 'Colonialism,
nationalism, and colonialized
women: the contest in India,'
*American Ethnologist*, 16(4).

Collins, D. (2005) 'Identity, mobility,
and urban place-making: exploring gay life in Manila,' *Gender and
Society*, 19(2).

De Moya, A. and A. Garcia (1996)
'AIDS and the enigma of bisexual-
ity in Dominican Republic,' in
P. Aggleton (ed.), *Bisexualities and
AIDS: International Perspectives*,
Bristol: Taylor and Francis.

Deepa, V. N. (2005) 'Queering Kerala:
reflections on Sahayatrika,' in
N. Arvind and G. Bhan (eds),
*Because I Have a Voice: Queer
Politics in India*, New Delhi: Yoda
Press.

Devika, J. (2002) 'Imagining women's
social space in early modern
Keralam,' Working Chapter
series (WPS) no. 329, Centre for

Development Studies (CDS), Thiruvananthapuram.

— (2005) 'The Malayalee sexual revolution: sex, liberation and family planning in Kerala,' *Contributions to Indian Sociology*, 39(3).

— (2007) '"A people united in development": developmentalism in modern Malayalee identity,' WPS no. 386, CDS, Thiruvananthapuram.

Fox, R. (1995) 'Bisexual identities,' in A. R. D. Augelli and C. J. Petterson (eds), *Lesbian, Gay and Bisexual Identities over Lifespan*, New York: OUP.

Fuss, D. (1991) 'Inside/out,' in D. Fuss (ed.), *Inside/out: Lesbian Theories, Gay Theories*, London: Routledge.

Glick, E. (2000) 'Sex positive: feminism, queer theory, and the politics of transgression,' *Feminist Review*, 64.

Goffman, E. (1963) *Stigma: Notes on the Management of Spoiled Identity*, Harmondsworth: Penguin.

Gough, K. (1952) 'Changing kinship usages in the setting of political and economic change among the Nayars of Malabar,' *Journal of the Royal Anthropological Institute of Great Britain and Ireland*, 82(1).

Halperin, D. M. (2002) *How to Do the History of Homosexuality*, Chicago, IL: University of Chicago Press.

Harvey, L. (1990) *Critical Social Research*, London: Macmillan.

Hindley, J. (2001) 'Beyond the stereotypes: transgressive desires and male homosexualities in Latin America,' *Sexualities*, 4.

Jackson, P. A. (1997) 'Thai research on male homosexuality and transgenderism and the cultural limits of Foucaultian analysis,' *Journal of the History of Sexuality*, 8(1).

Jayawardena, K. (1986) *Feminism and Nationalism in the Third World*, London: Zed Books.

John, M. E. and J. Nair (1998) *A Question of Silence? The sexual economies of modern India*, New Delhi: Kali for Women.

Johnson, R. (1986) 'What is cultural studies anyway?' *Social Text*, 16.

K. E. N. (2005) *Lyngika Udareekaranam: Parisaravum Rashtreeyavum* [Liberation of sex: context and politics], Kozhikkode: Progress Publications.

Kodoth, P. (2002) 'Framing custom, directing practices: authority, property and matriliny under colonial law in nineteenth century Malabar,' WPS no. 338, CDS, Thiruvananthapuram.

Koottummal, J. (2005) *Lyngikatha: Nilapadukalude Rashtreeyam* [Sexuality: the politics of standpoints], Thrissur: Kerala Sasthra Sahithya Parishath.

Krippendorff, K. (2006) *The Semantic Turn: A New Foundation for Design*, New York: CRC/Taylor and Francis.

Kuku-Siemons, D. S. (2008) 'Queerspace: sexualized spaces revisited,' Inter Alia, interalia.org. pl, accessed 12 January 2009.

Kumaramkandath, R. (2011) 'Body and desire in the Malayali public sphere: sexual morality in early Malayalam magazines,' *Kerala Sociologist*, 39(2).

Madison, S. D. (2005) *Critical Ethnography: Method, ethics, and performance*, New York: Sage.

McLelland, M. J. (2000) *Male Homosexuality in Modern Japan: Cultural Myths and Social Realities*, London: Routledge.

Nair, V. V. (2006) *Rathiyude Sykathabhoovil* [On the sandbank of sexual pleasure], Kottayam: Mathrubhoomi Books.

Nanda, S. (1990) *Neither Man nor Woman: The Hijras of India*, Belmont: Wadsworth.

Naples, N. (2003) *Feminism and Method: Ethnography, discourse, and activist research*, New York: Routledge.

Osella, F. and C. Osella (1999) *Social Mobility in Kerala: Modernity and Identity in Conflict*, London: Pluto Press.

Plummer, K. (2002) *Sexualities*, London: Taylor and Francis.

Reddy, G. (2004) 'Crossing lines of subjectivity: the negotiation of sexual identity in Hyderabad, India,' in S. Srivasthava (ed.), *Sexual Sites, Seminal Attitudes: Sexualities, Masculinities and Culture in South Asia*, New Delhi: Sage.

Rubin, G. (1992) 'Thinking sex: notes for a radical theory of the politics of sexuality,' in C. Vance (ed.), *Pleasure and Danger: Exploring Female Sexuality*, London: Pandora, pp. 267–319.

Saradamoni, K . (1999) *Matriliny Transformed: Family, Law and Ideology in Twentieth Century Travancore*, New Delhi: Sage.

Scott, A. (2005) *Comedy*, New York: Routledge.

Seabrook, J. (1999) *Love in a Different Climate: Men Who Have Sex with Men in India*, London: Verso.

Sebastian, K. C. (n.d.) *Parasparam Pranayikkunna Sthreekal* [Women who love each other], Kochi: Pranatha Books.

Taylor, C. (1978) 'El ambiente: male homosexual social life in Mexico City,' PhD thesis, University of California, Berkeley.

Zarilli, P. B. (1998) *When the Body Becomes All Eyes: Paradigms, Discourses and Practices of Power in Kalarippayattu, a South Indian Martial Art*, New Delhi: OUP.

# 12 | Female criminality in Brazil: a study on gender and sexuality in a women's prison

FABÍOLA CORDEIRO

## Introduction

In this chapter I address the social and institutional 'management' of sexuality at Talavera Bruce Penitentiary (known as TB), in Rio de Janeiro, Brazil. TB was the first women's prison to be created in the state of Rio de Janeiro, and the second in the country. It was founded in 1942. In the 1980s, it drew public attention as cases of torture were reported, and on different occasions inmates threatened to stage a rebellion. At present, it is regularly chosen for interventions by NGOs and religious groups (especially Pentecostal), and boasts an intense social agenda of events. The national media portrays TB as a model institution, an exception in the degrading scenario of the country's prisons. This discourse is contested by social movements and NGO representatives who denounce violent practices against the inmates.

At different moments in the institutional history of TB, wider social and political changes in Brazilian society converged to draw up rehabilitation projects that involve the management of inmates' sexualities. This 'management' involves two dimensions. The first is the subjection of inmates' sexuality to institutional monitoring and intervention by the deployment of disciplinary mechanisms. The second dimension concerns the exercise of sexuality and inmates' sexual and emotional relations while in jail. Drawing on my research at the Talavera Bruce facility I aim to understand how these disciplinary practices operate within the web of social relations and everyday life in prison, as well as their effects on the ways sexuality is exercised by the inmates.

Studies on jailed women in Brazil have mainly addressed social representations of female criminality, the socio-demographic profile of female convicts, and the circumstances most commonly related to their entering the prison system (Soares 2002; Soares and Ilgenfritz 2002; Souza 2006). There is also an increasing amount of research being carried out on maternity and religiosity in prisons (Lopes 2004; Rodrigues 2005; Santa Rita 2006; Ordónez n.d.). These investigations underscore the prevalence of young women from the poorer segments of the population among prisoners, their biographies being stamped with victimization and violence. However, gender and sexuality have been neglected. A small number of studies address individual and collective development among imprisoned women, homoeroticism, and 'intimate visits,'[1] and the sexual and reproductive health of women in jail (Giordani and Bueno 2002; Giordani et al. 2002; Miranda et al. 2004), focusing on violence/oppression and 'risk behavior.'

In this chapter I introduce some reflections on the discourses, representations, and institutional practices at TB today, focusing on how the grammar of gender and conventions about sexuality compose a normative framework that guides a resocializing ideal for female prisoners. Data was collected in the initial phase of the research project ('Imprisoned sexualities: a study on gender and discipline in women's prisons') currently under way. From May to October 2009, I interviewed seven prisoners discharged from the prison system and two in 'open regime.'[2] At the time of the interview, five interviewees who were on parole had been released from TB less than two months before (one of them less than twenty-four hours).

## Narratives about deviance and normality

Historically, the emergence of prisons for women in Brazil occurred in the context of major social and political changes, and of the penetration in the country of modern discourses on humanization and individualization of the penal system (Lima 1983). Penal reform discourse in the 1940s regarded the woman criminal not only as an ambiguous figure and a specific type of delinquent, but also as a potential motivation to crime. These discourses articulated public representations about gender, sexuality, family, and honor. Female sexual physiology was understood by prevailing medical theories as inherently problematic, easily prone to pathologies and capable of provoking deviations in behavior (Rohden 2001). Criminologists saw this as one of the main explanatory factors of women's engagement in criminality.

In recent decades, the association of women criminals with social and moral degradation remained popular. Some authors suggest that these women are more stigmatized than men criminals; as if committing a crime meant almost a betrayal of the feminine, whose 'nature' should be closely linked to domesticity and maternity (Caridade 1991; Lopes 2004; Rodrigues 2005). The entry of women into the world of crime is also often assumed to be initiated by male loving partners. Thus, women criminals are depicted as creatures of perversity, the victims of female 'nature,' or of male domination (Souza 2006).

Interviewees in this research were not immune to the stereotypes about women who commit crimes. Their narratives produce discursive strategies in an attempt to neutralize the stigma of the female criminal. Their involvement with criminality is often described as a mistake, an error of judgment, or a consequence of drug addiction; therefore something that 'could happen to anyone.' The only interviewee who claimed not to have repented or felt shame for her crimes was Renata, who was arrested for the murder of the man she lived with. For months, he had submitted her and her children to physical and emotional abuse, torture, and private incarceration. In her narrative, the murder is described as a *crime passionel* carried out in a moment of despair. Her victim was the leader of a paramilitary police death squad. To her, the crime was interpreted as a prefigured tragedy brought about by her partner. His cruelty and the degree of vulnerability in which she and her children found themselves made assassination something justifiable and inevitable; as a mother, she had to protect her children.

> He drank and was really bad at home. [One day] he spanked my children. I said, 'It's over. You just signed your death sentence.' He didn't believe me and that was it. It had to happen and here I am [in jail]. ... He thought he had the right to spank my children, to leave marks all over me, and I said: 'No!' ... I went to the DEAM [police unit for women victims of violence]. So they [the officers in charge] would tell him: 'Hey, your wife is here and she is snitching on you.' So he'd come and drag me out, spank me, pull my hair, kick me, call me a slut ... (Renata)

Interviewees raised a number of moralizing/normalizing discourse topics: family,[3] religion, work, and heterosexuality. They all emphasized the exception of their deviation in their family's history and their submission to the family order after being released. Most interviewees mentioned that religious services in prison – or the 'faith in Jesus' – gave them strength to face the horrors of prison and not surrender to its perversions. Having a job in the penitentiary guaranteed differentiated status at TB – a individual cell and better treatment by prison guards. Furthermore, dedication to labor was a morally edifying value.

> The last time I was arrested the deputy told me he had investigated three generations in my family, that he wanted to understand how I ended up involved [in crime]. Because my family is SO decent, is SO straight, is SO ... You know? I have two brothers who are pastors, correct people, faithful to their wives. ... It was the addiction to drugs that led me to this entire situation. (Camila)

Now I want to work and improve my life, just that. ... I'll stay with my mother. We [she, her mother and her brothers] want to live all together. ... My mother was angry, but now she is speaking to me. We talk, she knows everything [about the interviewee]. ... She only tells me not to hang out with anyone. I don't go to *bailes* [balls often sponsored by organized crime], I only go to church. When I get out of here [skills training course for released detainees], I just go home ... My brother set up a room for me, because I still have to work to build my own house. It's in the same backyard. (Karla)

I've got it [a job] for [my] discipline, right? I was quiet, never got into trouble ... I was asking too, right? 'Let me! Let me! Let me!' [work] I worked, reduced my sentence by studying, then reduced my sentence by typing up the [inmates'] newspaper. Just that! That's the way it goes inside the system, right? ... They want quiet people [for the jobs], because they put them in contact with people from the outside world, right? Because some people really freak out! Everything is a reason for beating people up, things get lost ... (Patrícia)

Heterosexuality was mentioned by eight interviewees as a moralizing/normalizing instance. *Lesbianas* (feminine women who partner other feminine women) and, mostly, *sapatões* (masculine women) and their girlfriends were clearly pictured as the *other* in relation to whom the interviewees constructed their image as regenerated persons.[4] Thus, lesbians and *sapatões* and their girlfriends are characterized as the deviants among deviants. Although there was a recognition that what occurs sexually between two people in private concerns them only, sexual involvement between people of the same biological sex was seen as a mark of moral degradation. Two interviewees suggested that this type of behavior should be more directly addressed by institutional controls. Lurdes was emphatic:

They are there [in prison]; they have to pay for their mistake. So they must take to heart what they did wrong. Less freedom, more work! School ... that's taking it to heart. 'Do this; do that!' This is your place; get it? ... I didn't like [seeing women together] ... I found it disgusting. ... If there was no time, if there was only the time to get in, work, sleep, they wouldn't have the time to do that [dating other inmates]. (Lurdes)

*Sapatões* were the main target of moral accusation and disqualification. They were often defined as irredeemable criminals, figures of domination, perversity, and violence, classified as shameless and cowards. Much more than *lesbianas* and other women who had sex with *sapatões*, they were identified as *animals*, those that 'not even the family wants.' The idea that they fitted perfectly in prison to the point of being able to build a life for themselves in there; their rebellious attitudes toward institutional agents; their family abandonment; and their domination of other inmates were all considered signs of their criminal nature.[5]

> An old convict, you know? One that goes out and then comes back in. The street is their vacation, and jail their home. They take a street vacation for fifteen days ... some do ten days. He gets freedom but doesn't keep it ... Then comes back ... Because in the street he turns into a beggar ... Soon he's in again. Not even the family wants him! So then he has to live in jail. ... Geez, some [female] convicts cry when they have to get out. When her release comes, she cries, begs to stay. ... Because the family doesn't want them and they are not up for work. (Renata)

## Sexualities in prison

The permanence of the articulation of beliefs, values, and representations of gender, sexuality, and deviance in the making of the woman criminal, as highlighted by the interviewees, leads to the question to what extent this complex of references continues to guide state prison policy toward women, as well as daily practices and relationships at the penitentiary. Historically, the 'sexual issue' was a 'problem' for criminologists and the state from the inception of the Brazilian penitentiary system. If in the case of male prisons sex was always tolerated as a necessary evil, in women's prisons sexuality and, especially, homoeroticism were repressed until recently.[6] Yet ethnographic studies of Talavera Bruce Penitentiary (Lemgruber 1983; Heilborn 1980) suggested that, at least until the 1980s, sexuality and homoerotic alliances played a very significant role in the social organization, status, and solidarity networks within the prison. Despite extensive changes in the social sphere and in the prison system since then, evidence indicates this is still the case.

Over the past decade demonstrations of affection between inmates have become more tolerated. Persecution of homosexual couples seems to no longer play the same role in the pedagogies of prison. Couples can walk together, embracing one another and holding hands in public, without punishment by the wardens or other inmates. Asked about the main changes in TB between her first stay in the penitentiary (in the late 1980s) and today, Camila responded:

> Times have changed, and so have people's minds: the prisoners, in

**229**

short, criminality. In my days [her first confinement was in the early 1980s], pederasty was a deal very well hidden. Today you get a visit from your daughter and you see some *sapatão* kissing her girl in the mouth, you see? There is no respect any more, you see?

Nevertheless, this reduced rejection of same-sex couples does not mean that the stigma attached to 'homosexuals' does not persevere in other ways. Our interviewees' narratives and informal conversations with prison agents and NGO representatives who work in TB suggest that gender and sexuality are still important factors in the evaluation of and treatment given to the inmates.

Inmates with a masculine demeanour (*sapatões*), their girlfriends, and the so-called *lesbianas* tended to raise greater suspicion of involvement with illicit activities, and were expected to cause disruption, especially because of misunderstandings provoked by jealousy or drug-related debts. Jobs were assigned predominantly to inmates of feminine appearance. *Sapatões* were not recruited for functions that did not involve heavy work, such as janitorial tasks or as *faxinas* (cleaners).[7] Added to this is the fact that even though conjugal unions between prisoners of the same sex were quite common, they were not granted legitimacy. The reallocation of inmates inside TB did not generally take into account maintaining this form of conjugality.

This situation contrasts significantly with the legitimacy granted to heterosexual relationships, evident in the extension of *parlatório* rights to prisoners with male partners. Although, according to official norms, this privilege is conditional upon maintaining conjugal relations prior to imprisonment, in practice inmates who demonstrate good behavior can quite easily manage to obtain permission for intimate visits with male partners they met after entering prison. There are two ways to meet a boyfriend or future conjugal mate in prison: through telephone calls and letters to men suggested by relatives or friends – whether prisoners or not – and, less frequently, through personal contacts with men who show up at the penitentiary to visit relatives or provide some service to the institution. Three of the five interviewees who had received the benefit of intimate visits reported that their partners were men whom they had met in prison. However, one of them ended the relationship before the first sexual encounter.

### The masculine as a value

Heterosexual flirting and courting follow a particular dynamic in prison. If the suitor is himself a prison inmate (the most common situation), the first telephone call or letter is usually followed by the female inmate's attempt to check with the social workers whether there is a photograph of her suitor in the files of the men's prison units. If this strategy is unsuccessful, the would-be partner is asked to send a photograph as soon as possible. If his physical appearance is not compatible with the woman's expectations, his next attempted contact may be frustrated. When flirting continues, the woman also sends her suitor a photograph of herself. Preparing for the portrait involves carefully selecting the clothes to be worn (appealing, but not revealing), having makeup applied and hair and nails done at the TB beauty parlor. Once the woman's picture has been dispatched, it is the man's turn to signal whether he likes the appearance of the potential girlfriend/spouse. If the appreciation is mutual, then it is up to the man to start procedures for permission for intimate visits, after which the couple exchange telephone calls and letters on an almost daily basis.

It should be stressed that physical qualities may become a factor of little importance for the female inmates when the suitor is a free man not involved in criminality or when he is seen as a way of guaranteeing physical and material protection. Carolina's report is typical:

> I saw his picture but I didn't like it: 'Oh, no! What an ugly man ... Oh, no, no, I don't want it. He is too ugly!' I even told Ari [a friend who introduced them by phone] – 'Oh, Ari, you are so cute, you have so many cute friends, and you set me up with the ugliest one?' He said – 'Right, but he is the smartest one, he's got a good financial situation, he will provide for you. He studied law.'

The process of granting permission for intimate visits with male partners (whether inmates or not) was reported to take six months on average, during which tests are made to detect STDs/AIDS and tuberculosis. This process can be brought to a close at any moment if one of the parties changes his or her mind. So in this period there is an intense sexual negotiation between the couple, which is not restricted to the terms of their future sexual interactions.

Telephone calls and letters take the form of an 'exchange' of ideas, revealing their experiences and ways of life inside and outside prison. These contacts are important to create closeness and a feeling of intimacy for the couple. During that period, the woman also assesses her suitor's personality and the degree of possible compatibility between them. It is also fundamental for these women to feel confident about the possibility of a 'future together.' Thus, just as important as the telephone calls and letters is some sort of material proof of the partner's commitment and good intentions. He must play the role of provider for the inmate, which in fact means taking her as his spouse.

> We used to talk by letter. He used to tell me about his life, his family, all that ... So, I told him about myself ... Even before we met, he used to talk to me, treated me like his wife ... When I went to Nelson Hungria [another prison facility for women], his prison was next to the backyard where we sunbathed ... We set a date by letter; he said: 'I got a medical appointment so that I can walk through the backyard and see you.' ... He told the guards I was his wife and they let him stop for a second to see me. He was in the prison for POs [former police officers] and had more benefits. ... A guard at his prison had dealings with the warden at Nelson Hungria and asked permission for him to fetch me a TV; an excuse to see me! ... In May [four months later], I was transferred to Talavera and he started to visit. (Carolina)

In the interactions between the future lovers, romantic discourse and demonstrations of anxiety with regard to the physical encounter are generally appreciated. Nonetheless, any erotic discourse is rejected by the women, in order to appear respectable before the partner. Once permission is granted for intimate visits (which occur every two weeks), the female inmate is expected to stipulate a number of encounters without sexual intercourse – another demonstration of respectability. This period tends to last no longer than one or two encounters, in order not to diminish the partner's interest. Following months of investing in the relationship, to deny the man the reward of the sexual encounter for a very long period is understood as destabilizing for the relationship.

> The first time we didn't do anything, you see? We talked a lot, just that. ... We already had an agreement. It was pretty clear that it wouldn't happen then ... that time ... we would only talk, you see? – to get to know each other better first, before ... Then, it was only the second time we really got to it. ... If it depended on me ... I would have waited a little longer. Yes, I would, you see? But he had already waited for soooo long. He stayed there for all those months insisting, visiting, never failing to provide whatever I needed ... (Patrícia)

Sex is a type of counter-gift (Mauss 1968) in the relational game; the balance between obligation and pleasure is presented as vital for maintaining reciprocity between the partners. It is this equilibrium which guarantees the chance of a conjugal/familiar future. In the interviewees' narratives about interactions with their partners there tends to predominate what could be characterized as a traditional dynamic of gender relations associated with the lower classes of Brazilian society. These dynamics are organized around the value granted to the family, which demands that pleasure be subsumed to social reproduction (constructing a family nucleus) and biological reproduction (having children), which is ensured by the way that women conduct their relationships, based on demanding that the man comply with his obligations (Salem 1982; Heilborn 1993). The women must manage to engage their man in such a project.

The role of provider attributed to men in traditional relationships bears a strong moral dimension in constituting and actualizing their gender identity, besides affecting their capacity to arouse the interest of the opposite sex. Women's work is not given the same value as work carried out by men and is treated as a way to complement the income of the couple or family and a form of moral edification. Men are ascribed the main responsibility for social reproduction and their engagement in this function is what ensures their commitment to their wives and families.

In prison, to have a male partner is a way to guarantee better conditions of subsistence. Poor-quality food (sometimes served past its expiry date) is the only basic need provided by the state. Necessary personal hygiene items (such as soap, tampons, toilet paper, toothpaste, and so on) must be bought by the inmates or brought in by their relatives and/or boyfriends/husbands on visiting days. Furthermore, for inmates whose relationship with the family is disturbed, for those who have nowhere to go when they get out of jail, and for those whose families live in very precarious economic conditions, engaging in a conjugal/familiar relationship seems to help in attenuating uncertainties about their future out of jail.

The advantages of having a 'husband,' however, are not limited to material benefits. In addition to attenuating the 'solitude' of jail and their 'emotional need,' having a man 'by their side' confers social status on female inmates. They win the 'right' to better accommodation, to receive visits from their partner and more respectful treatment from the other inmates, and even from the prison guards. Having a relationship with a man can even serve as a strategy to get rid of persistent sexual harassment. Patrícia's story is a good illustration. A year after she was arrested for international drug-dealing, she began to correspond with one of her brother's workmates (a twenty-three-year-old *motoboy*).[8] Although the young man did not attract her physically ('He was sooooo ugly!'), she decided to go on with the flirting. The man managed to get permission to visit her as her spouse, and then he insisted that they should also try to get permission for *parlatório*. Patrícia said that after three months of trying to get round this situation, she had to give in to her boyfriend's desire. She liked having someone to get dressed up for, someone to support and comfort her, and specially to make her less susceptible to the intense sexual harassment she underwent in prison.

> In there women get a lot of harassment ... So when he started to write I thought – 'Yeah, I gotta answer this!' ... I got into trouble a few times. ... Many people end up being oppressed, you see? They [the *sapatões*] push until they get what they want, and some people give up. When someone doesn't give up, then there's an argument, and it can end up in a fight, you see? ... And when this guy showed up he spared me all that. (Patrícia)

Another three interviewees also admitted having been the target of sexual harassment in Talavera Bruce through passes made at them as well as insinuating and obscene notes, looks, and gestures. They emphasized that this type of situation causes constant fear. To draw the interest of a *sapatão*, even unintentionally, often means having to face the anger of her girlfriend. This type of confrontation can involve the use of knives, razors, and other types of cutting instruments. In this context, being a woman without a 'masculine' partner implies constant insecurity. Andressa's narration is enlightening:

> When we get there, when you are beautiful ... There are a lot of *sapatões* in the prison. Their girlfriends don't want to know if you do *sapatão* or not. If you walk by, you look girly and a *sapatão* looks at you, that's enough to get you into trouble ... I got into a lot of fights because of *sapatões*. I never got involved with a *sapatão*. ... Sometimes, we were playing cards and the boys, the *sapatões*, sat down close to us. ... You turn around and the woman [someone's girlfriend] is coming after you. And there it is just like that: either you beat, or you are beaten. Either you stab, or you are stabbed. I had a pretty rough time, because I had to fight. Sometimes, I had fights in the morning, in the afternoon and at night ... until the girls started to catch my drift. They saw that a *sapatão* for me is like a woman, just the same, there is no difference. (Andressa)

The masculine thus seems to gain an even greater value in the female penitentiary than in Brazilian society at large. One might wonder whether this is one of the outcomes of the quasi-absence of men in the prison environment – with the exception of guards and a few religious and NGO representatives. Men occupy the top position in the social and moral hierarchy within the prison, with *sapatões* second. Like men, *sapatões* provide a form of protection within the prision system; they are expected to play an 'active' sexual role, and are held as a complementary and necessary opposite to the feminine.[9] The wives of *sapatões* are not classified as lesbians or same-sex lovers. By their own classification, they are 'normal' heterosexual women. They do not believe they are having sex with other 'women'; they only have sex with *sapatões* and pay reverence to the virile attributes of their same-sex male partners.

Considering this scenario, I felt it remarkable that three among the eight heterosexual women interviewed claimed to have never wanted any kind of affective-sexual involvements in prison. Two of these women (Renata and Maria) had a history of bad relationships, one of them being arrested for the murder of her husband (Renata). Both attributed the choice of staying alone to the restrictions and 'headaches' that a conjugal union might create. Inmates who had love experiences in prison also complained about men trying to control them. The third inmate who claimed never to have had a boyfriend/ husband in jail (Andressa) attributed her lack of interest to the long period she was 'doped' by intense consumption of drugs: 'I just wanted to sleep, smoke and sniff ...' She and Maria also mentioned the difficulty of meeting, while in jail, a partner who was not involved in crime. Getting involved with a criminal would make the project of abandoning crime and beginning a new life outside prison impossible.

### The dynamics of intimate visits

If, in the reports of the self-declared heterosexual interviewees, a special value was attributed to the masculine, this does not hold true for sex in their narratives of *parlatório* experiences. Although sex (as vaginal intercourse) is taken for granted as a moral obligation on these occasions, emotional aspects such as solitude and the need for affection and self-esteem were often referred to as being the main motivation behind the decision to use this benefit. Added to this is the fact that all interviewees claimed that they did not miss sex at all during their time in jail. Among women who at several moments in the interview resorted to a discourse that could be characterized as traditional/conservative, it is not surprising that when asked about sex and sexuality issues, their answers often deemed this as an aspect of little importance in their lives and relationships.

*Did you miss having sexual contact ... sex, when you were in prison?*
No, not a lot. I missed it, but I've never been much into it, right?
[Patrícia]

*And did you miss being able to have sexual intercourse with your husband wherever you wanted?*
No, no ... I didn't, because I already had something else to do. Work, you know? I worked a lot and it was exhausting. So I didn't have the time. I worked a lot and didn't have the time to think about it. (Lurdes)

In Brazil, a tradition of analyzing social relations – including the sphere of gender and sexuality – from the angle of social class marked studies of the urban lower and middle classes between the late 1970s and the first half of the 1990s. Inspired by the ideas of Dumont (1983), individualism and holism in Brazilian society were discussed as cosmologies that represented the modern and the traditional, suggesting a dichotomy between these two social strata (Velho 1981; Duarte 1987). The middle classes were identified with individualism, the principle of equality, and the notion of the individual as a value which supposedly led to less asymmetrical relations between genders, and the view that sexuality was a relatively autonomous sphere of social life. The lower classes were associated with a holistic ideology based on hierarchy as the core value, leading to more clearly asymmetrical relations between generations and genders and the conception of gender differences as a value.

I am anxious not to fit the narratives of the interviewees and their social practices into this interpretative model. Traditional and modern representations, discourses, and practices coexist, blend together, and are reinvented in different social spaces. Values and moralities are not entities imposed upon people, but rather something dynamic and negotiated in daily social interactions, modulated by specific circumstances and situations. Nonetheless, despite the heterogeneous nature of class insertions and relations, recent studies on heterosexualities in Brazilian society (Leal 2003; Salem 2006; Cordeiro 2008) have advanced the idea that in the context of the lower classes – especially for the heterosexual women of this social stratum – sexuality tends not to feature as a domain of isolated significance, constituting not a specific discourse but rather one embedded in other discursive instances. Sex, desire, pleasure, and sexuality are subsumed under a broader-ranging morality and complex social interactions. As a result, interview questions addressing sexuality issues do not usually elicit answers necessarily focused on or restricted to that topic.

This is not to claim that sexuality is not important for social actors in these contexts, but rather that it tends to make sense only when articulated with other constituent dimensions of personhood. For the interviewees in this project, this clearly appears in the discursive valuation of the incorporation of sexuality in the affective-relational domain, as well as in the valuation of modesty in speaking about sex in public. Nevertheless, sexual intercourse plays a fundamental role in relational dynamics. The consolidation and actualization of the amorous bond, as pointed out above, depends on intensive negotiation, and sex means much more than just sexual intercourse itself. The *parlatório* features as a strategy for maintaining the connection between the couple. When asked about the intimate visits that she had from her husband during her first time in jail, Camila, for instance, pointed out:

> You use that [the intimate visit] ... Like, that is a visit and what you feel needy for is affection, not sex. I didn't miss sex. ... He liked me and I liked him too. I did *parlatório* with him because I didn't want to lose that, right?

I wonder whether the impossibility of properly experiencing conjugality would not result in using these sexual encounters as a space for constituting and legitimizing the couple. However, when it comes to a relationship that began after entering prison, the explicitly sexual nature of the *parlatório* and the presupposed 'obligation' to have sex during these encounters sometimes led to insecurity and discomfort. Even if the boyfriend/spouse offered 'material proof' of his commitment and satisfied the woman's expectations with regard to demonstrations of affection and romanticism, the absence of instruments to formalize the relationship and ensure its continuation in time and outside the prison walls (marriage, starting a household, etc.) implied a feeling of uncertainty concerning the partner's intentions.

The 'ghost' of the *whore* is present insofar as there is the possibility that the *parlatório* is seen by the man only as a way to obtain sex. Carolina, for example, reported that the first few times she had intimate visits with her 'husband' she felt like a 'prostitute' because at the end of the encounters he would hand her some money.

> I felt like a prostitute, you know? And he claimed he was my husband. And then he started bringing money for me on visiting days. So I told him – 'give it a break, look, I feel bad with you bringing me money. Looks like you came to pay for the date, pay for the sex.' ... I think that on the third or fourth date I talked to him about that, really put all the cards on the table. That's how I managed to deal better with this in my head.

Any role other than that of the legitimate spouse is refused. In the case of Karla, her only attempt at having an amorous relationship while in prison met with failure. Before the suitor – a bricklayer she met when he was working in TB – could pay her the first intimate visit, she refused to receive him. She found out that he was married and had a family. Karla would be just 'the other woman.'

> He applied for permission but I didn't want that. I found out that ... a girl that also did *parlatório*, who knew him from the streets, told me he was married. So I called it off. He lied to me! He told me he wasn't married! So I realized he only wanted to take advantage of me. I'm not like that! I canceled the *parlatório*.

In turn, the two interviewees who had the right to a *parlatório* with men with whom they lived in conjugal union and had children before prison (Lourdes and Camila) did not experience any uncertainty about the intentions of their partners regarding *parlatório*. On the contrary, they saw the fact that they were not abandoned as indisputable evidence of the strength of their link with them, since, in general, when a woman is arrested and the boyfriend/husband remains free, it is expected that he will end the relationship.

> I used to tell him – 'Look, if you don't think it's better to stay, then go. Because I already know how I'm going to serve my time in prison. I know I will survive. So you can go and live your life. You don't need to come no more. ... When I get out, I will go to my mother's house and I'm gonna live my life. No hurt feelings, no anger or anything.' But he kept insisting on staying with me. It was he who kept on visiting. (Lurdes)

There is a great contrast between the way the arrest of a male and a female criminal impact their family relations. The literature indicates that most women convicts do not receive any visits at all; and when they do, it is predominantly by female relatives (Frinhani and Souza 2005; Lima 2006; Brito 2007). In male prison units, in turn, long lines of women form on visitation days, carrying all kinds of food and personal hygiene products, many of them accompanied by children. When a wife abandons the husband because he has been arrested, this raises moral objections and disqualifications. But when the wives are arrested, not only is it expected that their partners will abandon them; the women themselves consider it understandable that they move on with their lives.

The wife must accept the role of organizing and managing domestic life and ensuring the union of the family in the face of any adversity. The absence of the husband causes a disruption to family order, especially in terms of material means of subsistence. However, it is not possible to maintain a family core without the central figure of the wife/mother; it is around her that a family is structured. A man needs someone to take care of him, of his house, of his children. The absence of the wife in a home also implies the absence of anyone capable of regulating the nature of the man (who is assumed not to be able to control his lust) and to protect the family from the external threat that other women represent. When that absence is combined with the man's conjugal infidelity, the link uniting the couple becomes fragile and conflict is unavoidable.

> In there [prison], you couldn't even know if your husband was yours, you know? And I knew a lot of things about him from the streets. ... Because in the street you don't care what people say for gossip. Your husband is yours and that's what you believe. But there [in prison] ...

## Conclusion

The narratives analyzed indicate that the establishment of amorous relationships in prison involves a wider process of adaptation to life in prison – a possibility of social insertion in that universe – and a means of acquiring status and of trying to alleviate uncertainty regarding the future. The reports on *parlatório* by the heterosexual interviewees reveal the value of a model of gender relations that can be characterized as traditional, in which the asymmetry between male and female operates as a powerful organizer of the way sexuality is experienced. Together with family, religion, and a disposition for work, heterosexuality becomes a moral condition, one of several normalizing/ moralizing forces deployed in an attempt by women to distinguish themselves from innate criminals.

Nevertheless, it must be remembered that these women refused the domesticity, fragility, and submission that was traditionally expected of them. At some point in their life trajectories, they broke with their families out of dissatisfaction with family rules to live the lives they chose. In some cases, they had deviant careers and committed crimes, even while in prison. They are, then, far from traditional models of femininity. This leads one to wonder to what extent such commitment to a traditional vision of the world came from an attempt to deconstruct, in front of the researcher, the stigma imposed on them as convicts or former prison inmates; to present themselves as someone who wants to be reconciled with that domesticity that they earlier denied.

The interviewees were reached through contacts with officials from the Department of Penitentiary Administration of the State of Rio de Janeiro (SEAP-RJ) and an NGO. During the process of evaluation of their application for parole or for going to a more open regime, the interviewees were selected to take part in an NGO-sponsored training course to enable them to set up and manage their own small businesses. Selection was very competitive, involving an analysis of the applicants' criminal record, classification reports, and letters of recommendation by the director of the penitentiary, as well as interviews with the NGO's social workers and psychologists. Those approved in this process were considered reformed criminals looking for another chance. This introduced a bias in the selection of the interviewees, since it presupposed, in their self-presentation, a commitment to a certain normative discourse. This fact, however, does not make the investigation results less relevant to our research purposes. The representations, values, and categories in their narratives and the ways they construct their social personae inside and outside prison raise important elements for reflection on the pedagogies of women's prisons and on the production of the 'woman criminal' today.

The fact that nearly all interviewees were self-declared heterosexuals was another limitation. As discussed, the conventions and representations about gender and sexuality continue to inform the establishment of structures of status in the prison context. This affects the evaluation of the inmates as more or less 'recoverable' and capable of being successful at 'getting a second chance.' In this sense, it can be asserted that the means by which contact with these women was established make this predominance of heterosexuality among them a significant piece of data.

Finally, the absence of an analysis of the amorous relationships of the single self-declared homosexual interviewee is due to the little material available regarding the dynamics of her relationships. Fabiana spoke very little about her partners and expressed great embarrassment in relation to questions about her sex life and her relationships in TB. It became clear only that all her relationships in prison were very brief and, according to her, 'not serious.'

**Notes**

1 Authorized visits with steady partners – husbands or boyfriends – within prison facilities. In Brazil, this practice is also known as *parlatório*.

2 The decision to include former inmates was due to difficulties in obtaining authorization from the Department of Penitentiary Administration of the State of Rio

de Janeiro (SEAP-RJ) for fieldwork at the penitentiary. Contact with interviewees was facilitated by SEAP-RJ officials and an NGO.

3 The perspective of reinsertion in the family as the most fundamental element in prisoners' resocialization is also omnipresent in state discourse on criminal rehabilitation.

4 Interviewees' use of *'lesbiana'* (lesbian) should not be confused with other public uses of this category in Brazilian society. *Sapatão* ('big shoe') is a pejorative term used in Brazil to refer to same-sex-oriented women; especially those with a masculine demeanor.

5 The self-presentation of the only *sapatão* interviewed contrasts greatly with the way *sapatões* were described by heterosexual interviewees.

6 Heilborn (1980) points out that, until the end of the 1970s, the institutional discourse about the intimate visits varied between the idea that allowing the practice would be 'shameless' and the conception that it favors the preservation of conjugal and family ties.

7 *Faxina* ('cleaner') is the prison term for inmates that have formal jobs in the penitentiary. Their functions include cooking, cleaning services, administrative work, and 'liaisons' between the different sectors of the prison. Since it is a special appointment that allows access to all sectors of the penitentiary, it is the most prestigious occupation that an inmate can hold in prison; except for janitorial occupations.

8 Motorcycle riders who perform delivery services.

9 In spite of their masculine demeanor and the fact that they do not self-identify or are identified by their partners as women, *sapatões* generally do not engage in the discourse of transsexuality. That is, they do not see themselves as people in the wrong bodies (a man inside a female body), but rather as not confined to conventional standards of heteronormativity.

# References

Almeida, R. O. (2001) *Mulheres que Matam*, Rio de Janeiro: Relume Dumará.

Brito, M. A. (2007) 'O Caldo na Panela de Pressão: um olhar etnográfico sobre o presídio para mulheres de Florianópolis,' Unpublished master's dissertation, Universidade Federal de Santa Catarina (UFSC), Brazil.

Caridade, M. A. (1991) 'Sexo, Mulher e Punição – a sexualidade feminina em uma instituição penal,' *Revista Brasileira de Sexualidade Humana*, II(1), January.

Cordeiro, F. (2008) 'Negociando Significados: gênero e coerção sexual em narrativas de jovens brasileiros,' Unpublished master's dissertation, Universidade do Estado do Rio de Janeiro, Brazil.

Duarte, L. F. D. (1987) 'Pouca Vergonha, Muita Vergonha: sexo e moralidade entre as classes trabalhadoras urbanas,' in J. S. Leite Lopes (ed.), *Cultura e Identidade Operária*, São Paulo: UFRJ/Marco Zero/Proed.

Dumont, L. (1983) *Essais sur l'individualisme: une perspective anthropologique sur l'idéologie moderne*, Paris: Le Seuil.

Foucault, M. (1995 [1977]) *Discipline and Punish: The Birth of the Prison*, New York: Vintage.

Frinhani, F. M. D. and L. Souza (2005) 'Mulheres encarceradas e espaço prisional: uma análise de representações sociais,' *Psicologia – Teoria e Prática*, VII(1), June.

Giordani, A. T. and S. M. V. Bueno (2002) 'Direitos humanos de mulheres detentas em situação de vulnerabilidade às DST-Aids,' *DST – Jornal Brasileiro de Doenças Sexualmente Transmissíveis*, XIV(2).

Giordani, A. T., S. M. V. Bueno and L. P. Kantorski (2002) 'Normas, punições castigos e a vulnerabilidade – as DST-Aids no cotidiano de mulheres detentas,' *DST – Jornal Brasileiro de Doenças Sexualmente Transmissíveis*, XIV(2).

Heilborn, M. L. (1980) 'Grades do Parestesco', Unpublished paper, Museu Nacional, Rio de Janeiro, Brazil.

— (1993) 'Gênero e Hierarquia – a costela de Adão revisitada', *Estudos Feministas*, I(1).

Leal, A. F. (2003) 'Uma Antropologia da Experiência Amorosa: Estudo de representações sociais sobre sexualidade,' Unpublished master's dissertation, Universidade Federal do Rio Grande do Sul, Brazil.

Lemgruber, J. (1983) *Cemitério dos vivos: uma análise sociológica de uma prisão de mulheres*, Rio de Janeiro: Achiamé.

Lima, E. M. (1983) *Origens da prisão feminina no Rio de Janeiro: o período das freiras*, Rio de Janeiro: OAB.

Lima, M. (2006) 'Da visita íntima à intimidade da visita: a mulher no sistema prisional,' Unpublished master's dissertation, Universidade de São Paulo, Brazil.

Lopes, R. (2004) 'Prisioneiras de uma Mesma História: o amor materno atrás das grades,' Unpublished

PhD thesis, Universidade de São Paulo, Brazil.

Mauss, M. (1968) *Essai sur le don. Forme et raison de l'échange dans les sociétés archaïques*, Sociologie et anthropologie, Paris: Presses Universitaires de France.

Miranda, A. E., P. R. Merçon-de-Vargas and M. C. Viana (2004) 'Saúde sexual e reprodutiva em penitenciária feminina, Espírito Santo, Brasil,' *Revista de Saúde Pública*, XXXVIII(2), April.

Ordóñez, L. (n.d.) 'Religiosidade: mecanismo de sobrevivência na Penitenciária Feminina do Distrito Federal,' *Comunicações ISER*, LXI.

Rodrigues, G. E. (2005) 'Transgressão, Controle e Religião: um estudo antropológico sobre práticas religiosas na penitenciária feminina do Estado do Rio Grande do Sul,' *Debates do NER*, VI(8).

Rohden, F. (2001) *Uma ciência da diferença: sexo e gênero na medicina da mulher*, Rio de Janeiro: Fiocruz.

Salem, T. (1982) 'Mulheres Faveladas: com a venda nos olhos,' in *Perspectivas Antropológicas da Mulher*, vol. I, Rio de Janeiro: Zahar.

— (2006) 'Tensões entre os Gêneros na Classe Popular: uma discussão com o paradigma holista,' *Mana*, XII(2), October.

Santa Rita, R. P. (2006) 'Mães e Crianças atrás das Grades: em questão o princípio de dignidade da pessoa humana,' Unpublished master's dissertation, Universidade de Brasília, Brazil.

Soares, B. M. (2002) 'Retrato das mulheres presas no Estado do Rio de Janeiro – 1999/2000,' *Boletim CESEC*, I(1).

Soares, B. M. and I. Ilgenfritz (2002)

*Prisioneiras: vida e violência atrás das grades*, Rio de Janeiro: Garamond Universitária.

Souza, S. B. (2006) 'Criminalidade Feminina: trajetórias e confluências na fala das presas do Talavera Bruce,' *Democracia Viva*, XXXIII, October.

Velho, G. (1981) *Individualismo e cultura: notas para uma antropologia da sociedade contemporânea*, Rio de Janeiro: Jorge Zahar.

# 13 | Sexual pleasure and the premarital sexual adventures of young women in Zimbabwe

TSITSI B. MASVAWURE

It is not as if girls don't enjoy sex. From what I have seen here on campus, they do! (Mutsa, first-year female student)

## Introduction

It is not often that one reads about young, heterosexual African women's positive and pleasurable premarital sexual experiences. Often, the literature on female sexuality in Africa portrays women in one of two ways: as sexually passive and unwilling participants in the sexual act, or as sexually 'immoral' and 'loose' if they show any interest in sex at all. Both portrayals are problematic in that, as with all dichotomies, one can only ever be one or the other – never both and certainly never something else entirely. This chapter challenges this stereotypical portrayal of female African sexuality and seeks, in-stead, to foreground young African women's experiences of sexual pleasure and positive sexuality. I argue that, in particular contexts and circumstances, African women can, and do, embody an active sexuality which has sexual pleasure at its core. I especially argue that sex is not always something that is 'done' to women and that women are neither passive nor indifferent participants in the sexual act.

My discussion focuses on the specific experiences of a group of young women based at a university campus in Zimbabwe in order to a) illustrate the various ways in which young women in Zimbabwe experience their sexuality in very positive (not problematic) ways, and b) examine the particular circumstances that make it possible for these young women to actively pursue pleasurable sexual encounters. In the last part of the discussion, I will draw on historical data to illustrate that female sexual pleasure and a positive female sexuality are not necessarily antithetical to 'African traditions and customs.' I argue that the 'demure, reluctantly sexual African woman' is a creation and effect of the colonial encounter, particularly of the missionary project.

244

## African female sexuality as problematic

Vance's observation that female desire is viewed with '[suspicion] from its first tingle' (1984: 4) captures the complexity of writing about African women's positive experiences of sex and sexuality. This is because there are many feminist scholars who insist that sex is nothing more than an enactment of relations of domination between men and women and that, consequently, female (hetero)sexual pleasure is simply an 'eroticisation of subordination' (McKinnon 1989; Kitzinger 1994). Other scholars portray women purely as victims and attribute this to intractable cultural practices and traditional beliefs, which place control of women's sexuality in male hands (see Dunkle et al. 2004; Jewkes 2002; Kaler 1981). However we attribute this 'mistrust of the [heterosexual] pleasures,' as Foucault (1978: 39) termed it – be it to the prudishness of the Victorians or to African 'traditions and customs' or even to the colonial encounter (especially to Christianity) – the key point is that this continues to be the dominant view in much of the literature on African women's sexuality.

An obvious reason for the dominance of these particular scripts is that they do, in fact, capture what is the everyday reality for many women in Africa. Understandably, therefore, writing about women's sexual pleasure seems rather trivial and misguided in the face of these grim realities. The second reason that writing about African women's positive sexual experiences is so difficult arises from the fact that there is a real danger of reinforcing (or appearing to reinforce) racist stereotypes of the 'sexually out of control' and the hypersexual African subject. The controversy surrounding Caldwell et al.'s (1989) paper on 'African sexuality' is a case in point. In it, the authors argue that the 'African' model of sexuality is based on very different ideologies from the 'Eurasian' model and that this must therefore be taken into account by HIV prevention practitioners. African societies, they state, acknowledge that sex is a natural instinct, hence men and women's pre- and extramarital sexual relations are not frowned upon as is the case in the 'Eurasian' model. The authors have subsequently been accused of advancing a racist (see Heald 1995) and sexist theory (see Ahlberg 1994) and for associating female sexual freedom with the spread of disease (HIV in this case).

This chapter addresses the issue of African women's positive and pleasurable premarital sexual experiences and is experimental in two critical respects. First, I capture only heterosexual women's narratives and experiences of pleasure and positive sexuality. I am aware of the limitations of taking such a one-sided approach, given the fact that 'danger and pleasure are ever present realities in many women's lives' (Vance 1984). However, adopting this approach will allow me to explore, in detail, the repertoire of practices and actions that constitute sexual pleasure for the Zimbabwean female students I focus on in this study. The second way that this chapter is experimental is that I present a 'thick description' of female sexuality. As Geertz (1973: 9) defined it, thick description is about 'sorting out the structures of significance ... [and] determining their import' rather than just describing a phenomenon. To do this satisfactorily, a researcher needs to pay particular attention to the meanings that people impute to their actions. In this study this involves sorting through the following questions: what does sexual pleasure mean for the female students in the study and does it hold the same meanings when they pursue it within the context of a university campus and in relation to their 'university student' identities? In answering the various questions that animate this chapter, I shall draw heavily on Turner's (1967) concept of liminality.

**Methodology**

This chapter is part of a larger ethnographic research project, which examined the influence of 'campus cultures' on the sexual practices and HIV-risk behaviors of female and male university students. The campus in question is the University of Zimbabwe, situated in the capital city, Harare, and which has an enrollment of approximately fourteen thousand students. The University of Zimbabwe – or 'UZ' as it is commonly referred to – is the oldest university in Zimbabwe, having been established in 1955 (Gelfand 1978). Up until the early nineties, it was the only university in the whole country and was arguably one of the best in the continent.

Having graduated from the UZ myself, and having subsequently spent four years implementing an HIV prevention program at the same institution, the UZ was a natural choice for my intended ethnography. I began my fieldwork in August 2006, on the very first day of the new academic year. For the next fifteen months, I immersed myself in the world of students as best I could, and employed the ethnographic approach of participant observation. Lunchtimes and evenings yielded the best data, as this was typically when most student-initiated and student-led activities took place. As with most universities in the country, the UZ is a residential campus; it accommodates between three and four thousand students in eleven residence halls. Each residence has at least one area that is designated as a 'common' space, and which can be hired out for private functions. I often attended meetings organized by various student associations in these common rooms. Relationships, dating, and sex were common topics of discussion at these meetings, which were attended by both female and male students. The former, however, were always fewer numerically.

Although I studied a total of twenty female and twenty male students in great detail, this chapter draws on formal and informal conversations I had with six female students between August 2006 and December 2007. The narratives of sexual pleasure presented in this paper all occurred spontaneously. It was only after a student introduced the topic that I would systematically probe for further details. I believe that this particular approach, of allowing issues to emerge naturally during the course of an interaction, and not pre-empting them, greatly minimized the threat of social desirability bias.[1] The latter has been shown to be a major challenge when investigating the sexual practices of unmarried women in Africa (see Cleland et al. 2004). In addition to my conversations with the six female students, I also draw on observations I made during various student-initiated discussion forums I attended, most of which focused specifically on issues of dating, sex, and sexuality. Finally, I conducted extensive archival research at the National Archives of Zimbabwe and spoke with a number of individuals, particularly historians and older women, in an attempt to situate female sexual pleasure in Zimbabwe within a broader historical context.

## Female students' experiences of sexual pleasure

This first week here [pointing to a calendar that had been drawn during the interview] I am on him like mad. And the last days before my period. So, like I just visited here [points out on the calendar again]. This was my last period. I did him here again. We did here, up to here [points to the calendar]. Yah, these first five days. As soon as my period finished, I went to his house. We stayed up to day ten.

There are also these muscle-tightening exercises that you can do. You release the urine, then stop, then release, then stop. It works. It's like so tightened, it's like being a virgin, you know. But you don't have to overdo it. If you tighten when he's inside, you could hurt him. It could crack. [TM: Really?] Yah. It's hard to learn the trick. And there is stuff like when you are indoors and you are a woman ... sometimes it [the vagina] gets too watery, so, if you don't want it to be too watery, you stay indoors without a panty [on]. [TM: And it actually works?] It does. I have tried it. I will be dry most of the day. I won't be producing any stuff. [It's much better] than those [drying agents] that cause cancers and stuff like that.

Mutsa,[2] quoted above, was in her first year of a social science degree program when I first interviewed her. I initially met her at a group discussion that another first-year female student, Rejo, had organized at my request. It was just two months into the academic year and most of my fieldwork in this period focused on new students and their views of 'campus life.' I therefore started off most discussions with the very open question: 'How are you finding campus life, so far?' There were five female students present at the discussion and the room we were in belonged to one of them.

The answers I got to my question were what I had come to expect: ambivalence about campus life. On the one hand, it was 'boring.' 'There is nothing to do here,' 'campus life is dead,' 'it's OK.' Erratic classes, caused by a lecturers' strike, were largely to blame for this lack of enthusiasm, as was the general economic crisis in the country, which could be felt at the campus. Having discussed these general issues at some length, I then explained, as best I could, that I was a doctoral student interested in 'students' views of campus life, love, romance, dating and HIV.' The 'love, romance, dating' part elicited smiles and sideways glances in this group. I then proceeded to explain issues of confidentiality and anonymity and to formally request permission to audio-record the discussion.

The female students' views concerning love and romance initially followed the usual script: abstinence is best and premarital sex is bad. 'Are you saying, then, that you will abstain for the duration of your stay on campus?' I asked. Nods and murmurs of assent. 'Are any of you in relationships at the moment?' I continued. More nods and murmurs. 'All of you?' This time the reaction comprised giggles and some verbal confirmation. 'Supposing, then, that your boyfriend starts pressuring you to have sex with him. What will you do?' Two of the students explained that they belonged to the Seventh Day Adventist church, whose position on premarital sex is clear. Their boyfriends were members of the same church and would therefore never pressure them into having sex. 'But you guys are young and full of hormones,' I insisted, 'what do you do when you feel [sexually] aroused?' One girl stressed that any form of physical intimacy was out of the question: 'I have never had sex and I have never been kissed,' she declared. Another stated that she too was a virgin but that she allowed some physical contact, such as kissing and hugging. Rejo, who was also a member of the same church, explained: 'Me and my boyfriend do everything ... kiss [and] touch. We just don't go all the way.' I turned to Mutsa and her friend: 'How do you guys stop your relationships from becoming sexual?' Mutsa's response was both surprising and refreshing in its frankness:

It's not as if girls don't enjoy sex. From what I have seen here on campus, girls enjoy it more than guys do. This idea that you should wait a while [before having sex] is bull ... I don't see why you should wait, really. Why? Why? Why? What are you waiting for? What do you want to know? I slept with my guy within a month [of dating him]. I couldn't wait!

Saru pitched in:

If you want sex, get a steady boyfriend. Let's not hide behind the saying 'we are not doing it' because we are.

At this point, the conversation was interrupted by a knock on the door, and three well-dressed female students entered. They turned out to be Rejo's friends. They were noncommittal about participating in the research although they did opt to sit in and listen. The group discussion continued for another twenty minutes after that, but I noticed that Mutsa was no longer as vocal. After the discussion I asked her privately about her silence and she explained:

I don't want to be judged. You know, the problem with girls is that they lie a lot. They want to present themselves as something that they are not. But with you, I know that you want this information for your school[work], so I can tell you these things and know that you will not judge me.

Mutsa and Saru were happy to meet with me for further discussions the following day, and it was from this follow-up meeting that the excerpt at the start of this section is derived. A number of things stand out for me in Mutsa's accounts: her willingness to openly admit that she is sexually active – 'why should you wait?'; that she finds sex pleasurable – 'I couldn't wait'; and that she initiates and creates the conditions for pleasurable sex to occur – 'After my period, I go to his place' and 'there are those muscle-tightening exercises ... it works!' It is also significant that she portrays herself as an active and willing participant in the sexual act – 'I did him' and 'We did it' – and never once does she refer to herself as having been done (e.g. 'he did me'). The kegel exercises aimed at 'tightening' her vagina were about her pleasure as much as they were about her boyfriend's pleasure.[3] She denied being under any pressure from her boyfriend to tighten and dry out her vagina: 'He tells me that he doesn't care about such things. But you know how guys are, he probably wouldn't tell me if he [did].'

It is only by resisting the temptation to always see women as 'victims' or 'whores,' and when, as Machera (2004: 165) argues, 'women's sexual desire is depicted as an autonomous gesture [and] as an independent longing for sexual expression, satisfaction and fulfilment,' that the 'structures of significance' (Geertz 1973) in Mutsa's experiences can be sorted out in any meaningful way. For instance, if one draws from Bolton's (1995) fascinating list of the twenty-six different ways that sex is a positive experience – which he aptly termed the 'joys of sex' – Mutsa's account above captures sixteen different ways that sex is a positive experience for her. Sex is play, adventure, transcendence, fun, fantasy, interaction, connectedness, pleasure, liminality, growth, giving, sharing, ecstasy, experience, an expression of emotions, and a source of meaning. Mutsa consciously prepared for her pleasurable sexual encounters in very specific ways – for instance, by tightening and drying out her vagina and by planning visits to her boyfriend's place to coincide with the end of her menstrual cycle so that sex could occur. Play, adventure, and experience were very strong themes in Mutsa's narrative.

In contrast to Mutsa, whose sexual experiences were exclusively reserved for her boyfriend, Chipo, a final-year student, engaged in what I will refer to here as 'lust sex' with multiple and concurrent partners. I had known Chipo for at least a year when I decided to interview her 'formally' about her university experiences. The interview occurred on a Friday afternoon in the offices of the HIV prevention organization that was hosting me. Chipo was one of the organization's volunteers. 'I am free for the rest of the day,' she had declared when I had reminded her that I wanted to interview her. 'We can do it now.'

Two hours later, I knew about every guy that Chipo reported having dated since enrolling at the university two years earlier. There were ten of them. She explained that her enrollment at an all-girls boarding school for her secondary education had made her rather studious and uninterested in dating. 'I had no time for boys!' she reported. That was until she had taken her Advanced Level examinations; it was while awaiting her results that she met her first boyfriend, a much older man who was also a politician. As it turned out during the interview, Chipo preferred dating older and/or politically connected men. As a result, with the exception of two or three, all her boyfriends were much older than she was. Her boyfriend then had political connections and was in his late fifties. A company director that she was involved in an on-off relationship with was in his forties. Her last boyfriend, another politician, was in his late forties. At the time of the interview, she was in concurrent relationships with four men.

In one account, Chipo narrated an incident involving an ex-boyfriend she had bumped into during her second year. It had been many months since the relationship had 'simply fizzled out,' as she described it. 'When we met that day, we could both feel the chemistry between us still. So we arranged to meet later that evening on campus,' she continued. Chipo expected the meeting to culminate in a sexual encounter, so she collected the keys to the room of a friend, who was spending that particular weekend off campus. At that time Chipo did not have on-campus accommodation and was commuting from home. When he visited later that day they had sex, even though her menstrual flow had started that afternoon. 'My period had started earlier that day, but he didn't mind!'

Chipo also described her relationship with a company director, whom I shall refer to here as 'Eddie.' 'I had heard a lot about Eddie, but I had never met him in person. So when I eventually met him I was like "Wow!"' By the end of that first meeting, Chipo and Eddie had been sexually intimate. 'It was the fastest it's ever taken me to be sexual with anyone!' She had laughed long at the recollection then continued, 'But he was very good.' This was in reference to his sexual prowess. This relationship lasted two months before Eddie terminated it. 'We are now just very good friends and we look out for each other.' In later conversations with Chipo, I figured out that 'taking care of each other' meant being available for 'no-strings attached' sexual hook-ups. Months later, I attended a discussion forum in which this particular phenomenon was given a name: 'kissing friends,' or 'friends with benefits.' I realized that it was a common practice among friends of the opposite sex as well as among classmates.

Lust is the dominant theme in the incidents that Chipo chose to share with me that afternoon, and it was her own lust, in particular, which was implicated in her narratives. Furthermore, Chipo did not downplay the fact that she was sexually adventurous and sexually un-inhibited; if anything, she played it up and seemed to thrive on it. Even in her physical appearance, Chipo was deliberately sexual and she wore her feminine sexuality conspicuously, and almost like a badge of honor. Chipo was fair skinned and curvaceous – both characteristics that Zimbabwean men find particularly attractive. Her wide hips and small waist were what one immediately noticed in a first encounter, in large part because she typically dressed in clothes that further exaggerated her curves. Chipo preferred short skirts and form-fitting denims and blouses and she was very much aware of the effect that she had on most men. When I asked how she met her politician boyfriends, for instance, Chipo had pointed to her curves and remarked that men 'couldn't resist all this.'

A third narrative was provided by Justine, a second-year student, who had fallen pregnant in her first year but had since broken up with the father of her child, a fellow student. He had made another girl pregnant, and that was how Justine discovered that he had been cheating on her the whole time that they had been together. Justine was particularly unimpressed by his most recent attempts to get back with her. It was in this context that she started to reminisce about the sexual aspects of the relationship. 'We used to skip class and go to his room to have sex!' she recounted. 'We did this most afternoons. We would have lunch together at the dining hall and then go at it afterwards. One day he paid the janitor to allow me to spend the night in his room. We did it up to ten times that night! We were crazy!' In hindsight, Justine attributed her interest in sex to two things: first, her excitement at having made it to university, and secondly, to her naivety as a first-year female student coming from an all-girls boarding school. By drawing on her university student identity to explain her sexual behavior, Justine situated her experiences in the realm of the liminal. I explore this issue in detail in the discussion that follows.

## Active female sexuality as a liminal experience

Given that female sexuality in contemporary Zimbabwe continues to be more heavily policed than male sexuality (Cheater and Gaidzanwa 1996; Bourdillon 1989), how then is it possible for these female students to enjoy so much sexual freedom? How, too, should this sexual freedom be interpreted? Are the female students making a political statement about gender roles, or are they merely taking advantage of the opportunities offered by the university and by the 'university student experience'? Here, Turner's concept of liminality provides a useful analytical tool. According to Turner (1967: 95), 'liminal entities are neither here nor there; they are betwixt and between the positions arrayed by law, custom, convention ...' Turner uses the concept to explain rites of passage or processes of transformation, which he argues entail three stages: the separation of the individual from the wider society; the transformation itself, which takes place in a space of marginality (the limen); and the reincorporation of the transformed individual back into society. These three states represent the pre-liminal, the liminal and the post-liminal, respectively. Although Turner focused largely on ritual processes, particularly initiation and puberty rites, the term has been applied to diverse phenomena, such as, for instance, therapeutic communities (e.g. St John 2001) and recreational behavior (e.g. Selanniemi 2003). I argue in this chapter that the UZ is experienced in liminal ways by many students and that it is this liminal character which makes it possible for some female students to embody an active and pleasure-pursuing female sexuality.

The UZ has many of the characteristics typical of liminal states. First, it is simultaneously both a part of the wider society and apart from it, and hence 'neither here nor there,' to borrow Turner's own words. Historically, for instance, the UZ was 'exempt from the segregation laws that governed and proscribed mixed residential and other contact across colour lines' (Gaidzanwa 2007: 66). As such, it was the only place in the whole country where blacks and whites could reside together and form meaningful friendships if they so desired. Geographically, the university is located in the fairly affluent, upper-middle-class neighborhood of Mount Pleasant and is within walking distance of various embassies and high commissions. By the time students make the journey to the UZ, mostly from rural areas and working-class neighborhoods, many will have already entered this liminal space. Ideologically, at least.

The second key characteristic of liminal states is their permissiveness (Turner 1967), which allows for the temporary suspension of the everyday. At the UZ, this permissiveness reveals itself in the 'total freedom' that students enjoy at the institution. As one student pointed out to me, 'There is no headmaster here, neither are there any prefects. So what[ever] you do in your room is your own business.' With the exception of the lecture rooms, which are controlled by lecturers, there is very little adult control over students' behavior at the institution. Even janitors who operate in each residence hall function very minimally, focusing mostly on maintaining 'peace and quiet' in the residences. As Justine's experiences show, janitors can be paid to 'look the other way.' The 'total freedom' that characterizes life at the UZ is further cemented by the fact that, in contrast to high school and indeed some tertiary institutions, here (and indeed in most state universities in the country) one cannot be penalized for being in a relationship with a member of the opposite sex or for falling pregnant. As Epstein et al. (2001: 156) argue, it is typically at university that 'sex ceases to be taboo and enters the realm of the expected.'

Each resident student, for instance, is given keys to her or his room and has full control over who they let in or keep out. Furthermore, students are allowed to entertain guests of the opposite sex in their rooms between noon and 10.30 every day; guests do not sign in when they visit the university or when they enter students' residences. Furthermore, the university provides a range of reproductive health services, via the Student Health Services, which include free condoms, other contraceptives, treatment for sexually transmitted infections, and antenatal care services for pregnant students. It is these characteristics which make the UZ a haven for young women's premarital sexual exploration and sexual pleasure-seeking behavior.

That students view university as a sexual marketplace is evident at a discursive level at UZ. All female students at the institution, for instance, are referred to as USAs (pronounced 'you-sar'), which is an acronym for University Spinsters Association, while all male students are referred to as UBAs (pronounced 'you-bar'), which is an acronym for University Bachelors Association. It is telling that these monikers are not exclusively based on gender – the organizations are not called, for example, university females' or women's association and university males' or men's association. Instead, they refer to marital status, and 'singleness' or 'unmarriedness' in particular. If one further considers that even married students are referred to as UBAs and USAs, it is clear that sexual availability (denoted by spinsterhood and bachelorhood) is viewed as an integral aspect of the university student identity. The stereotypes of the 'typical' USA or UBA, which are held by both students and the general public, also tend to be sexual. The 'typical USA,' for instance, is seen as being sexually liberal as well as sexually aggressive. To convince me of the corrupting influence of the UZ on female students, two male students gave the following incidents as illustrations:

> I was shocked to see my home-girl [i.e. girl from his home area] wearing trousers the other day. Down there, where I come from, we are taught to frown on such types of dressing ... (First-year male student)

> Anything happens here on campus. Even what you don't expect. USAs watch 'tutorials' [i.e. soft porn movies] in their residences! Just the other day I found the common room at New Complex Four [a female residence] packed with female students. They were watching a tutorial [i.e. soft porn] on ETV [a South African TV station] and they were enjoying it so much they did not notice me come in! I am telling you [the truth]. Just visit any of the girls' hostels on Friday or Saturday night and you will see what I mean! (Final-year male student)

Interestingly, it is precisely because the female student identity at the UZ is constructed in these ways (as 'out of control' and hypersexual), coupled with the permissive nature of the UZ campus, that the female students discussed in this chapter take advantage of opportunities. Being at the institution, as opposed to being outside of it, makes it easier for them to experience their sexuality in pleasurable ways without having to fear too much for their reputations in society. The 'USA' interpellation is therefore a classic instance of Butlerian performativity: it discursively produces the sexually adventurous and pleasure-seeking female student. By no means, however, should this detract from the agency of the female students concerned, because far from dutifully conforming to a stereotype, as Butler's theory of performativity implies, in practice female students actively co-opt the USA interpellation and use it to achieve their own ends. Therefore, although female sexual agency continues to be tinged with 'moral undertones of condemnation' (Arnfred 2004: 7) at the institution, it is simultaneously and intricately woven into what is considered a 'normal' aspect of the USA interpellation. It is this 'normalization' which ultimately makes it possible for interested female students to embody an active sexuality without incurring tremendous social penalties as they would otherwise.

The last relevant characteristic of liminal states is the latter's association with the 'special' and 'extraordinary.' This is closely related to the fact that liminal states are temporary and never permanent. As such, they represent what Sheilds (1991: 85) referred to as 'moment[s] of discontinuity in the social fabric and a temporary loss of social coordinates.' Turner (1967) argued that new identities almost always entail, and usher in, new and different experiences. In my interactions with the female students, for instance, I observed that they all narrated their on-campus experiences with great excitement, almost as if they were adventures, or games (Masvawure 2010).

A fourth female student, Saru, for instance, was seeing four men at the time I interviewed her. Three were 'outside' men (i.e. non-UZ students or employees), while one was a fellow UZ student. In response to my enquiries, she insisted that none of the outside men was her 'boyfriend' – 'I'm sure that they probably consider me their girlfriend, but I am not' – and she proceeded to detail how she 'managed' these relationships. In the event that all four men wanted to see her on the same day, she would have one visit her between 5 and 7 p.m.; the second man would visit between 7 and 9 p.m. – during which time they would typically go off campus for a meal. Upon being dropped back on campus, she would spend the next hour and a half with her on-campus boyfriend and leave his room at 10.30 when visiting hours ended. She would then spend the night at a fancy bar with the last man and get back to the university only early the following morning. Saru's actions were far from unusual. In fact, female students were well known for their ability to successfully maintain relationships with multiple partners. As Saru's case shows, she used these relationships to experience the 'good life' (e.g. eating out, clubbing) and to access various consumer goods. The female students I spoke to felt justified in their actions, and they argued that they were merely playing the same game as the men that they were involved with. One particular female student had the extraordinary experience of having access to her boyfriend's new BMW all weekend. 'Imagine,' she explained in an interview, 'he left it [the BMW] with me for the whole weekend! He didn't even call to check up on it! We [i.e. she and her friends] even bought new pairs of blue jeans and blue tops to match the blue of the car. And everyone on campus was watching us drive around!' It is clear from the above that the female students also considered their sexuality to be a resource that they could draw upon to acquire desired consumer goods that are typically associated with 'modernity' and middle-class ideas of 'success' (see Masvawure 2010).

All the female students in my study, however, were aware that they could act in these particular ways only during their time at the university and in the specific context of being resident on campus. Only Chipo indicated that her mother knew, and had come to accept, her relationships with older men. The rest simply did not talk about boyfriends with their parents and indicated that their parents would most likely disapprove. Mutsa and Saru, though, were of the opinion that many parents did not want to acknowledge what their daughters were up to on campus, even though they knew: 'How else do they think we survive on campus when they only send us sick money [and then only] once in a while?' they both queried. There was consensus, though, among all the students I spoke to, that their families would be devastated if they fell pregnant before completion of their studies. They also noted that they would definitely be evicted from home as a result. All six female students looked forward to getting married and having children, preferably within a year or two of graduation. The students in question thus considered their time at the UZ as the only time they would ever have to be truly 'free' – that is, when they could be relatively autonomous and enjoy some reprieve from adult and parental surveillance, especially with regard to their sexuality.

## Female university students, 'modernity' and 'anti-structure'

Many Zimbabweans would argue that the kind of premarital pleasure-seeking and positive sexuality exhibited by the female students is characteristic of the 'born free' generation – that is, those born after Zimbabwe's independence in 1980 and who represent the 'new' and 'modern' Zimbabwe. Many would also attribute this type of behavior to the country's ongoing economic crisis, on the one hand, and to the destructive effects of recent forms of 'modernization,' in particular television, the Internet, American hip-hop culture, and the fact that women were granted equal rights to their male counterparts in 1982 through the Legal Age of Majority Act (LAMA) on the other. I maintain that these explanations merely reflect a local discourse and ideology of 'modernity' rather than actual reality on the ground. In essence they represent a commonly held myth about urban female sexuality in the country.

A key symptom of this mythography is the conflation of liminal forms of spatiality – embodied by students and 'youth' more generally – with a temporal movement away from 'tradition.' As a result, anything not confined to ideologically 'traditional' spaces is immediately constructed as 'new' or 'modern' and therefore bad and undesirable (Weiss 1986; Wieringa 2002, 2009). Interesting parallels can be drawn in this regard between public perceptions of female students and public perceptions of so-called 'town women' during the colonial era. Both have always been constructed as dangerous and out-of-control, primarily because of their presence in the city. The latter is not only an urban and modern space, but is also seen as existing outside of traditional systems of control and regulation (Jeater 1993; Scarnecchia 1999). As Schmidt (1996: 157) points out, 'it was assumed that any African female in the urban areas would be "ruined" by some man.' Furthermore, a 'moral panic' (Herdt 2009) gripped colonial Zimbabwe in the fifties and the sexuality of African men and women was dubbed 'the black peril' (Pape 1990), thereby pathologizing it. While the term applied to both sexes, African women found it extremely difficult to secure jobs as 'domestic servants,' because white women feared that they would ruin their marriages (Schmidt 1992).

In an attempt to understand why discussions of active female sexuality in Zimbabwe are framed in terms of the 'modernity versus tradition' discourse, I examined letters that were submitted to popular magazines by African men and women during the colonial era – that is, pre-1980. This approach has been used extensively in the study of sexuality (e.g. Thomas and Cole 2009; Parikh 2005). In my case, I focused on letters that were printed in the *African Parade* between 1953 (when the magazine started) and 1980, when the country attained its independence. The *African Parade* marketed itself as 'the only magazine in Southern Africa that is edited and printed by Africans.'[4] It covered many social issues and catered for urban-based African men and women. I went through all the letters submitted to the 'Answers to your Questions by Jenny,' which was the equivalent of 'agony aunt' columns and was introduced in 1954, specifically to address social concerns faced by African women. I was immediately struck by the similarities in the romantic experiences of young Zimbabwean women then and the female students discussed in this chapter.

First, I did not see much evidence of the 'demure and sexually uninterested' young African woman who dominates much public discourse in the country. As far back as the 1950s (possibly even earlier), young, unmarried Zimbabwean women actively established relationships with the opposite sex and initiated various forms of physical intimacy with men. The following letter by a sixteen-year-old male is illustrative: 'Dear Jenny, whenever I am friendly with a girl, she makes love to me [i.e. asks him out for a date]. Is it wrong for a boy my age to let a girl kiss me if I do not love her?'[5] Jenny's response sheds light about the forms of intimacy that were permissible for young unmarried women and men in those days. Not surprisingly, she questioned the 'respectability' of a young woman who proposed love to a young man so directly. 'African girls,' she opined, 'are prevented by custom and convention to make love to a boy [i.e. ask a boy out] no matter how deeply she loves him.' 'Jenny' proceeded to point out that, traditionally, African girls 'have a way of attracting those that they love, but it is always indirect.' Unexpectedly, she approved of kissing: 'I personally do not think that there is anything very wrong with kissing in itself, except that often it starts a fire which may burn you up ...'[6]

Although none of the letters submitted between 1954 and 1979 made any direct references to premarital sex, many letters were about premarital pregnancies, which indicates that some young women were in fact having sex outside of marriage. In fact, a number of scholars (e.g. Bourdillon 1989; Jeater 1993) have argued that physical intimacy between unmarried young women and men was permitted as long as it did not entail actual penetration (and hence the loss of virginity). In many cases too, pregnancy was often a condition for marriage and penetrative sexual intercourse was allowed for those couples who had made some public gesture of their commitment to get married, such as meeting either party's family.

Secondly, it was not unusual for young women to be involved in relationships with multiple men, as the letter below shows.

> Dear Jenny, I am a young girl who is in love with two boys. One is a driver and the other is a labourer. There is another who is making love to me [i.e. asking her for a date] and [he] is a clerk. Both love me and have promised to marry me. Both are good looking. Who should I marry?[7]

Having multiple partners appears to have been a normal aspect of courtship for both young men and women. Among young women, in particular, multiple partners provided them with an effective strategy for safeguarding against the disappointment of failed engagements. Jenny's response to the young woman in question acknowledged that failed engagements had become a major challenge for young women, and she attributed this to the corrupting influence of 'education' and 'modernity':

> [T]his is the price we pay for our so-called modern civilisation. In the olden days, a promise was worth something, but today it means very little, especially to superficially educated boys and girls you find in towns. Two wrongs don't make a right ... don't degrade yourself ... if you decide to do what he did you have become a fallen woman ...[8]

The last historical point I would like to highlight here is the fact that women, back then, seemed to begin dating (or courting) at very young ages. Many of the women writing to Jenny were between the ages of fifteen and twenty-five, and most were in long-term heterosexual relationships, which had typically started when they were about fourteen years old. Although the historical sources that I examined were silent about female sexual pleasure in pre-colonial and colonial Zimbabwe, they did point to a long history of an active sexuality among young unmarried women in the country.

### Conclusion

This chapter started out with two main aims: a) to document young African women's premarital experiences of sexual pleasure from their point of view, and b) to demonstrate that a pleasure-seeking female sexuality is not necessarily antithetical to so-called African 'traditions' and 'customs.' My discussion has illustrated the different forms that sexual pleasure-seeking behavior takes on a university campus, particularly among female students. Furthermore, I have also shown that, although it is extremely difficult (if not impossible) to determine precisely what the dominant sexual system was in pre-colonial Zimbabwe, there is ample historical evidence of sexual agency among young, unmarried women in the country, which dates back to the colonial era. Additionally, there is enough historical data that demonstrates that the approaches used to manage young unmarried women's sexuality in pre-colonial Zimbabwe were not nearly as prudish as the Victorian-era approaches, which informed most of the colonial government's policies. Current anxieties around active female sexuality thus merely reflect what Wieringa (2009: 208) refers to as 'postcolonial amnesia' – that is, 'the process of selectively memorizing certain aspects of a past while ignoring such aspects as are politically inconvenient ...' Feminist scholar Carole Vance poignantly observed two decades ago that 'women's actual sexual experiences are complicated and unsettling.' Advancing the scholarship on African women's sexualities will therefore require gender and sexuality researchers to acknowledge and embrace the multifaceted and complex realities of women's sexual experiences, however unsettling these may be.

## Notes

1 Women are said to under-report the number of sexual partners and their sexual experiences while men over-report.

2 All names in this chapter are pseudonyms.

3 Kegel is the name of a pelvic floor exercise, named after Dr Arnold Kegel, who devised it.

4 This was the magazine's motto.

5 *African Parade*, September 1954. p. 37.

6 Ibid.

7 Ibid.

8 Ibid.

## References

Ahlberg, B. M. (1994) 'Is there a distinct "African sexuality"? A critical response to the Caldwells,' *Africa*, 64(2).

Arnfred, S. (ed.) (2004) *Re-thinking Sexualities in Africa*, The Netherlands: Nordiska Afrikainstitutet.

Bolton, R. (1995) 'Re-thinking anthropology: the study of AIDS,' in H. Brummelhuis and G. Herdt (eds), *Culture and Sexual Risk: Anthropological Perspectives on HIV and AIDS*, The Netherlands: Gordon and Breach, pp. 285–315.

Bourdillon, M. F. C. (1989) *The Shona Peoples*, Gweru: Mambo Press.

Butler, J. (1993) *Bodies that Matter: On the Discursive Limits of 'Sex,'* New York: Routledge.

Caldwell, J., P. Caldwell and P. Quiggin (1989) 'The social context of AIDS in sub-Saharan Africa,' *Population and Development Review*, 15(2): 185–234.

Cheater, A. and R. B. Gaidzanwa (1996) 'Citizenship in neo-patrilineal states: gender and mobility in southern Africa,' *Journal of Southern African Studies*, 22(2): 189–213.

Cleland, J. et al. (2004) 'Monitoring sexual behaviour in general populations: a synthesis of lessons of the past decade,' *Sexually Transmitted Infections*, 80(ii): 1–7.

Dunkle, K. et al. (2004) 'Gender-based violence, relationship power, and risk of HIV infection in women attending antenatal clinics in South Africa,' *The Lancet*, 363(9419): 1415–21.

Epstein, D., S. O'Flynn and D. Telford (2001) '"Othering" education: sexualities, silences and schooling,' *Review of Research in Education*, 25: 127–79.

Foucault, M. (1978) *The History of Sexuality: An Introduction*, trans. R. Hurley, New York: Vintage.

— (2007) 'Alienation, gender and institutional culture at the University of Zimbabwe,' *Feminist Africa*, 8: 60–82.

Gaidzanwa, R. B. (2007) 'Alienation, Gender and Institutional Culture at the University of Zimbabwe,' in *Feminist Africa* 8: Rethinking Universities I, pp. 60–82.

Geertz, C. (1973) *The Interpretation of Cultures: Selected Essays*, New York: Basic Books.

Gelfand, M. (1978) *A Non-Racial Island of Learning: A History of the University College of Rhodesia from Its Inception to 1966*, Gweru: Mambo Press.

Heald, S. (1995) 'The power of sex: some reflections on Caldwell's "African sexuality" thesis,' *Africa*, 65(4): 489–505.

Heise, L. L. and C. Elias (1995) 'Transforming AIDS prevention to meet women's needs: a focus on developing countries,' *Social Science and Medicine*, 40(7): 931–43.

Herdt, G. (ed.) (2009) *Moral Panics, Sex Panics: Fear and Fight over Sexual Rights*, New York: New York University Press.

Jeater, D. (1993) *Marriage, Power and Perversion: The Construction of Moral Discourse in Southern Rhodesia 1894–1930*, Oxford: Clarendon Press.

Jewkes, R. (2002) 'Intimate partner violence: causes and prevention,' *The Lancet*, 359: 1423–9.

Kaler, A. (1981) 'A threat to the nation and a threat to the men: the banning of Depo-Provera in Zimbabwe,' *Journal of Southern African Studies*, 24(2): 347–76.

Kitzinger, C. (1994) 'Problematising pleasure: radical feminist deconstructions of sexuality and power,' in H. L. Radtke and H. J. Stam (eds), *Power/Gender: Social Relations Theory and Practice*, London: Sage.

Machera, M. (2004) 'Opening a can of worms: a debate on female sexuality in the lecture theatre,' in S. Arnfred (ed.), *Re-thinking Sexualities in Africa*, The Netherlands: Nordiska Afrikainstitutet.

Masvawure, T. B. (2010) '"I just need to be flashy on campus": female students and transactional sex at a university in Zimbabwe,' *Culture, Health and Sexuality*, 12(8): 857–70.

McFadden, P. (2003) 'Sexual pleasure as a feminist choice,' *Feminist Africa*, 2.

McKinnon, C. (1989) 'Sexuality, pornography, and method: "pleasure under patriarchy,"' *Ethics*, 99(2): 314–46.

Pape, J. (1990) 'Black and white: the "perils of sex" in colonial Zimbabwe,' *Journal of Southern African Studies*, 16(4): 699–720.

Parikh, S. (2005) 'From auntie to disco: the bifurcation of risk and pleasure in sex education in Uganda,' in V. Adams and S. L. Pigg (eds), *Sex in Development: Science, Sexuality, and Morality in Global Perspective*, Durham, NC: Duke University Press, pp. 125–58.

Scarnecchia, T. (1999) 'The mapping of respectability and the transformation of African residential space,' in B. Raftopoulos and T. Yoshikuni (eds), *Sites of Struggle: Essays in Zimbabwe's Urban History*, Harare: Weaver Press, pp. 151–62.

Schmidt, E. (1992) 'Race, sex and domestic labour: the question of African female servants in southern Rhodesia 1900–1939,' in K. T. Hansen (ed.), *African Encounters with Domesticity*, New Jersey: Rutgers University Press, pp. 221–41.

— (1996) *Peasants, Traders and Wives: Shona Women in the History of Zimbabwe 1870–1939*, Harare: Baobab Books.

Selanniemi, T. (2003) 'On holiday in the liminoid playground: place, time and self in tourism,' in T. G. Bauer and B. McKercher (eds), *Sex and Tourism: Journeys of Romance, Love and Lust*, New York: Haworth Hospitality Press, pp. 19–34.

Sheilds, R. (1991) *Places on the Margin: Alternative Geographies of Modernity*, New York: Routledge.

St John, G. (2001) 'Alternative cultural heteretopia and the liminoid body: beyond Turner at ConFest,' *Australian Journal of Anthropology*, 12(1): 47–66.

Thomas, L. M. and J. Cole (eds) (2009) *Thinking through Love in Africa*, Chicago, IL: University of Chicago Press.

Turner, V. (1967) *The Forest of Symbols: Aspects of Ndembu ritual*, New York: Cornell University Press.

Vance, C. (1984) *Pleasure and Danger: Exploring Female Sexuality*, London: Routledge.

Weiss, R. (1986) *The Women of Zimbabwe*, London: Kesho Publishers.

Wieringa, S. E. (2002) 'Gender, tradition, sexual diversity and AIDS in postcolonial southern Africa: some suggestions for research,' in D. Lebeau and R. J. Gordon (eds), *Challenges for Anthropology in the 'African Renaissance': A Southern African Contribution*, Windhoek: University of Namibia Press, pp. 124–37.

— (2009) 'Postcolonial amnesia: sexual moral panics, memory and imperial power,' in G. Herdt (ed.), *Moral Panics, Sex Panics: Fear and Fight over Sexual Rights*, New York: New York University Press, pp. 205–34.

# About the contributors

*Iman Al-Ghafari* is an independent researcher and literary translator. She received her PhD with first-class honors from the English Department at Cairo University on 'The quest for identity in the poetry of Sylvia Plath: a feminist approach' (1999). Since 1999 she has lectured widely on women's poetry, and gender issues in literature. She has written extensively on same-sex relations, Arab lesbians, and 'queer' in Arab culture. She received an Erasmus Mundus grant as visiting scholar at the Gender Department at Utrecht University (2010). Her short story 'Behind doors' won an award from the forum Femmes Méditerranées in France (2011). She is post-doctoral research fellow at the Amsterdam Center for Gender and Sexuality

*Hardik Brata Biswas* received his initial training in Comparative Literature at the Jadavpur University, Kolkata, and switched to Women's Studies at the same university, where he completed an MPhil on relations between photography and gender in Bengal and worked towards creating a digital archive of middle-class women's photographs. He is currently writing his PhD dissertation on 'Women and visuality in Bengal from the 1880s to the 1970s' at the School of Women's Studies, Jadavpur University. He has written on *Transgression, Pornography and the Middle-Class Bengali Family* (2011) and edited a collection of nineteenth- and early twentieth-century popular farces in Bengali: *Prohoshoney Kalikaler Bangamahila 1860–1908*. He is also developing a website for resources and debates on sexualities: www.oursexualities. org (under construction).

*Fabíola Cordeiro* holds a master's degree in Collective Health from the State University of Rio de Janeiro, with research experience on sexuality, gender, youth, and violence. She is a researcher at the Latin American Center on Sexuality and Human Rights and a PhD student in sociology at the Federal University of Rio de Janeiro. She has taught social science and trained schoolteachers on sexual and racial diversity issues.

*Huang Yingying* is an associate professor in the Department of Sociology, and deputy director of the Institute of Sexuality and Gender, Renmin University of China. She has conducted research on female sex workers in China since 1999, and her PhD research was about young women's bodies and sexuality in urban China. She promotes an affirmative understanding of sexuality in Chinese society, and social science research on HIV/AIDS in China.

*Rajeev Kumaramkandath* is a PhD scholar of cultural studies at the Center for the Study of Culture and Society, Bangalore, India. His work traces the genealogy of contemporary sexual morality in Keralam, south India. By exploring the trajectories of normativization and cultural formation in the modern history of the region, his work attempts to bring out the nuances and situatedness of homosexuality. He has also been a participant of the GEXcel fellowship program, funded by the Swedish Research Foundation, jointly organized by the University of Orebro and the University of Linkoping.

*Tsitsi B. Masvawure* holds a DPhil in anthropology from the University of Pretoria (South Africa), an MSc in Reproductive and Sexual Health Research from the London School of Hygiene and Tropical Medicine (UK), and an MSc in Sociology and Social Anthropology from the University of Zimbabwe. She is a postdoctoral research fellow at the HIV Center for Clinical and Behavioral Studies at the New York State Psychiatric Institute and Columbia University, New York. She is Alumna and Research Associate at the Center for the Study of AIDS, University of Pretoria in South Africa. Her research interests are in the area of gender, and reproductive and sexual health in low-income countries, with a special focus on gender, HIV, and 'sexual cultures.'

*Basile Ndjio* teaches cultural and political anthropology at the University of Douala (Cameroon), and has been a visiting lecturer or fellow in several universities in Europe and the United States. His most recent works include 'You are where you build: migration, architecture and the transformation of the landscape in the Bamileke Grassfields of West Cameroon,' in *Africa Diaspora* (vol. 2, 2009); 'Shanghai beauties and African desires: migration, trade and Chinese prostitution in Cameroon,' in the *European Journal of Development Research* (vol. 21, 2009); 'Naming the evil: sorcery and democracy in contemporary Cameroon and South Africa,' in *Sorcery in the Black Atlantic*, edited by Luis Nicolau Pares and Roger Sansi (University of Chicago Press, 2011).

*Musa Sadock* is an assistant lecturer in history and a PhD candidate at the University of Dar es Salaam, Tanzania, working on the history of sexually transmitted diseases in Mbozi District, Tanzania, 1905–2005. He was granted a Sephis African Doctoral Dissertation Research Fellowship, offered by the African Population and Health Research Center, in partnership with the International Development Research Center and the Ford Foundation; and American Council of Learned Societies African Humanities Program awards.

*Diego Sempol* is an Artigas Institute of Teachers graduate in history, with a graduate degree in contemporary history from CLAEH University Institute (Uruguay), and is currently a doctoral candidate in social sciences at the National University General Sarmiento/IDES (Argentina). He is an assistant professor and researcher at the Institute of Political Science and the School of Social Sciences at the University of the Republic and a member of the Uruguayan National Researchers System. He chairs the Queer Academic Area Montevideo and is board member of 'Sexualities,' a working paper series issued by CLAGS/CUNY's International Resource Network.

*Abel Sierra Madero* holds a PhD in history from the University of Havana (2009). His research focuses on gender, sexuality, and nationalism. He has lectured in universities in the USA, Spain, the UK, Italy, and Israel. He has been awarded a Casa de las Américas award for his book *Del otro lado del espejo. La sexualidad en la construcción de la nación Cubana* (2006). This book was also awarded the Catauro award (2007) by the Cuban Book Institute for its contribution to the social sciences. He is a member of the Cuban Union of Writers and Artists.

*Alberto Teutle López* holds a degree in social anthropology from the Benemérita Universidad Autónoma de Puebla and is a graduate student in history and ethnohistory in the Escuela Nacional de Antropología e Historia, Mexico. He teaches undergraduate ethnohistory and social anthropology. He co-edited *Florilegio de deseos: nuevos enfoques, estudios y escenarios de la diversidad sexual* (Eón-BUAP, 2010). His work focuses on male homoeroticism, the history of AIDS, neoconservatism and the cultural history of the body.

*Nitya Vasudevan* is currently finishing her PhD dissertation at the Center for the Study of Culture and Society, Bangalore. The thesis deals with the relationship between publicness and the female body, and is entitled 'Turning towards the bodily subject: theorizing the field of visibility in contemporary India.' She is also part of the Researchers-at-Work program on Histories of the Internet at the Center for Internet and Society, and has co-authored a monograph on queerness and the Internet. In the extra-academic realm, she is on the curatorial team of the Bangalore Queer Film Festival.

# Index

www.ingramcontent.com/pod-product-compliance
Lightning Source LLC
Chambersburg PA
CBHW070609270326
41926CB00013B/2479